9780760201679

ST THOMAS AQUINAS
SUMMA THEOLOGIÆ

ST THOMAS AQUINAS

SUMMA THEOLOGIÆ

Latin text and English translation,
Introductions, Notes, Appendices
and Glossaries

NON NISI TE

BLACKFRIARS

IN CONJUNCTION WITH

McGRAW-HILL BOOK COMPANY, NEW YORK, AND
EYRE & SPOTTISWOODE, LONDON

PIÆ MEMORIÆ
JOANNIS
PP. XXIII
DICATUM

IN AN AUDIENCE, 13 December 1963, to a group representing the Dominican Editors and the combined Publishers of the New English *Summa*, His Holiness Pope Paul VI warmly welcomed and encouraged their undertaking. A letter from His Eminence Cardinal Cicognani, Cardinal Secretary of State, 6 February 1968, expresses the continued interest of the Holy Father in the progress of the work, 'which does honour to the Dominican Order, and the Publishers, and is to be considered without doubt as greatly contributing to the growth and spread of a genuinely Catholic culture', and communicates his particular Apostolic Blessing.

To
Fr Thomas Gilby O.P.

ST THOMAS AQUINAS

SUMMA THEOLOGIÆ
VOLUME 41

VIRTUES OF JUSTICE IN THE HUMAN COMMUNITY
(2a2æ. 101–22)

Latin text, English translation, Introduction,
Notes, Appendices & Glossary

T. C. O'BRIEN
Hartford Seminary Foundation, Hartford, Conn.

NIHIL OBSTAT
JOHN M. T. BARTON, S.T.D., L.S.S.
Censor Deputatus

IMPRIMI POTEST
✠ VICTOR GUAZZELLI
Vic. Gen.
Westminster, 19 October 1971

© BLACKFRIARS 1972
[EXCEPTING LATIN TEXT OF 'DE PARTIBUS POTENTIALIBUS JUSTITIÆ']
LIBRARY OF CONGRESS CATALOG CARD NUMBER: 63-11128
07-002016-7
PRINTED IN GREAT BRITAIN BY EYRE AND SPOTTISWOODE LIMITED

CONTENTS

xiii   Editorial Notes
xv   Introduction

QUESTION 101. THE VIRTUE OF PIETY
3   Article 1.   whether piety is directed towards certain people
7   Article 2.   whether it includes supporting parents
9   Article 3.   whether it is a special virtue
13   Article 4.   whether the service of God supersedes duties of piety

QUESTION 102. THE VIRTUE OF RESPECT
21   Article 1.   whether it is a specific virtue distinct from others
25   Article 2.   in what does its service consist?
27   Article 3.   respect and piety compared

QUESTION 103. DULIA, THE VIRTUE OF RESPECTFUL SERVICE
33   Article 1.   whether honour is something purely mental or also external
37   Article 2.   whether only those who are superior to us are to be honoured
39   Article 3.   whether *dulia* is a specific virtue distinct from *latria*
43   Article 4.   whether there are many forms of *dulia*

QUESTION 104. OBEDIENCE
47   Article 1.   whether one man is bound to obey another
51   Article 2.   whether obedience is a specific virtue
57   Article 3.   whether it is the greatest of all virtues
63   Article 4.   whether God is to be obeyed in all matters
67   Article 5.   whether subjects are bound to obey their superiors in all points
71   Article 6.   whether Christians have to obey civil authority

QUESTION 105. DISOBEDIENCE
75   Article 1.   whether disobedience is a mortal sin
77   Article 2.   whether it is the worst sin of all

QUESTION 106. THANKS OR GRATITUDE
83   Article 1.   whether gratitude is a specific virtue distinct from others

85	Article 2.	whether the duty to thank God is more pressing for one without sin than for a penitent
89	Article 3.	whether a person must thank everyone who does him a kindness
93	Article 4.	whether a person need return a kindness without delay
95	Article 5.	whether repayment of a favour should be matched to the sentiment or to the deed of the benefactor
99	Article 6.	whether anyone in repaying should give something more than he received

QUESTION 107. INGRATITUDE

103	Article 1.	whether ingratitude is always sinful
105	Article 2.	whether it is a special kind of sin
109	Article 3.	whether the sin of ingratitude is always mortal
111	Article 4.	whether favours should be denied to the ungrateful

QUESTION 108. VENGEANCE

115	Article 1.	whether vengeance is permissible
121	Article 2.	whether it is one specific virtue
123	Article 3.	whether it should be carried out by means of the conventional forms of punishment
125	Article 4.	whether it is to be taken upon those whose offence is involuntary

QUESTION 109. TRUTH

133	Article 1.	whether truth is a virtue
135	Article 2.	whether it is a special virtue
139	Article 3.	whether it is a part of justice
143	Article 4.	whether the virtue of truth leans more to understatement

QUESTION 110. LYING

147	Article 1.	whether to lie is always against truth
151	Article 2.	whether the division of the lie into those that are useful, humorous or malicious is broad enough
155	Article 3.	whether every lie is sinful
163	Article 4.	whether every lie is a mortal sin

QUESTION 111. DECEPTION AND HYPOCRISY

169	Article 1.	whether in every case deception is sinful
173	Article 2.	whether hypocrisy is the same as deception

175	Article 3.	whether hypocrisy is against the virtue of truth
179	Article 4.	whether it is always a mortal sin

QUESTION 112. BOASTING
185	Article 1.	whether boasting is against truthfulness
189	Article 2.	whether it is a mortal sin

QUESTION 113. FALSE MODESTY
193	Article 1.	whether mock modesty is sinful
195	Article 2.	whether it is less sinful than boasting

QUESTION 114. FRIENDLINESS
199	Article 1.	whether friendliness is a specific virtue
203	Article 2.	whether it is a part of justice

QUESTION 115. FLATTERY
207	Article 1.	whether flattery is a sin
209	Article 2.	whether it is a mortal sin

QUESTION 116. QUARRELLING
215	Article 1.	whether quarrelling is against friendliness or affability
217	Article 2.	whether it is a sin more serious than flattery

QUESTION 117. LIBERALITY
221	Article 1.	whether liberality is a virtue
225	Article 2.	whether it is concerned with money
227	Article 3.	whether the act of liberality is the use of money
229	Article 4.	whether giving is above all characteristic of the generous man
233	Article 5.	whether liberality is a part of justice
235	Article 6.	whether it is the highest virtue of all

QUESTION 118. AVARICE
241	Article 1.	whether avarice is sinful
245	Article 2.	whether it is a specific sin
247	Article 3.	whether it is against liberality
249	Article 4.	whether it is always a mortal sin
253	Article 5.	whether it is the worst sin
257	Article 6.	whether it is a spiritual sin
259	Article 7.	whether it is a capital vice
261	Article 8.	whether those usually listed are the daughters of avarice

CONTENTS

QUESTION 119. PRODIGALITY
- 267   Article 1. whether prodigality is the opposite of avarice
- 269   Article 2. whether it is sinful
- 273   Article 3. whether it is a sin more serious than avarice

QUESTION 120. EPIEIKEIA OR EQUITY
- 277   Article 1. whether epieikeia is a virtue
- 279   Article 2. whether it is a part of justice

QUESTION 121. THE GIFT OF PIETY
- 285   Article 1. whether Piety is one of the Gifts
- 287   Article 2. whether the second Beatitude, *Blessed are the meek*, corresponds to the Gift of Piety

QUESTION 122. PRECEPTS ABOUT JUSTICE
- 291   Article 1. whether the Ten Commandments are precepts of justice
- 293   Article 2. whether the first of the Ten Commandments is well put
- 297   Article 3. and the second precept of the Decalogue
- 301   Article 4. and the third
- 309   Article 5. and the fourth
- 313   Article 6. and are the remaining six commandments

Appendices
- 316   1. Legal Debt, Moral Debt
- 321   2. Epieikeia
- 324   Glossary
- 331   Index

EDITORIAL NOTES

THE TEXT AND TRANSLATION

THE LATIN TEXT mainly reflects that of the 'Leonine' edition, commissioned by Leo XIII at the end of the last century. Variant readings from the Piana edition of 1570–71 published under the auspices of Pius V (modern edition, Ottawa, 1941), are noted throughout and, where they seem more in keeping with the sense, substituted in the text. Paragraphing and punctuation of the Latin text are those of the editor. The English has been prepared to be read independently of the Latin text, but reference to this is, of course, made easy in the present edition. Experience with students who have neither a knowledge of Latin nor prior acquaintance with St Thomas's thought has influenced the revisions of the translation on the side of greater literalness. The Latin itself is not imaginative, the vocabulary neither rich nor varied. One suspects that even the medieval student had to become initiated into the sparseness of Scholastic style, the burden that basic technical terms were made to bear. Explanatory notes are meant to assist the modern reader with technical terms; the plainness and economy of language, the editor believes, were meant in order to keep rhetoric from obscuring clarity and consistency of thought.

FOOTNOTES

Those signified by a superior number are usually the references given by St Thomas and tracked down by the Leonine Commission, with the exception of no. 1 to each article which refers to parallel texts in his writings. Those signified alphabetically are editorial references and explanatory remarks.

REFERENCES

Biblical references are to the Vulgate; Patristic references to Migne (PG, Greek Fathers; PL, Latin Fathers). When the English titles are well known, references to the works of St Thomas and Aristotle are in English. Titles of St Thomas's works are abbreviated as follows:

Summa Theologiæ, without title. Part, question, article, reply; e.g. 1a. 70, 1 ad 2. 2a2æ. 25, 4.

Summa Contra Gentiles, *CG*. Book, chapter; e.g. *CG* II, 14.

Scriptum in IV Libros Sententiarum, *Sent*. Book, distinction, question, article, solution or *quæstiuncula*, reply; e.g. II *Sent*. 15, 1, 1, ii ad 3.

EDITORIAL NOTES

Compendium Theologiæ, Compend. theol.
Scriptural commentaries (*lecturæ, expositiones reportata*): Job, *In Job*; Psalms, *In Psal.*; Isaiah, *In Isa.*; Jeremiah, *In Jerem.*; St Matthew, *In Matt.*; St John, *In Joann.*; Epistles of St Paul, e.g. *In 1 Cor.* Chapter, verse, *lectio* as required.
Philosophical commentaries: On the *Liber de Causis, In De causis*. Aristotle: *Peri Hermeneias, In Periherm.*; Posterior Analytics, *In Poster.*; Physics, *In Physic.*; *De Cælo et Mundo, In De cæl.*; *De Generatione et Corruptuone, In De gen.*; Metereologica, *In De metereor.*; *De anima, In De anima*; *De sensu et sensato, In De sensu*; *De memoria et reminiscentia, In De memor.*; Metaphysics, *In Meta.*; Nicomachean Ethics, *In Ethic.*; Politics, *In Pol.*, Book, chapter, *lectio* as required, also for Expositions in Boethius, *Liber de Hebdomadibus* and *Liber de Trinitate, In de hebd.* and *In De Trin.*, and on Dionysius *De divinis nominibus, In De div. nom.*
References to Aristotle give the Bekker numeration.
Quæstiones quodlibetales, Quodl.
Complete titles are given for other works, including the 10 series of *Quæstiones Disputatæ*.
Denz. refers to Denzinger-Schönmetzer, Freiburg, 1093.

ACKNOWLEDGMENT

The editor is grateful for the opportunity he had to consult a first draft of the translation of the Questions in this volume prepared by Fr Finbar Synnott, then of the English and now of the South African Dominicans. His careful work was an invaluable point of reference in the deliberation and choice regarding the translation of many technical and stylized terms in the treatise.

T. C. O'B.

INTRODUCTION

THE PROLOGUE of the Second Part of the Second Part of the *Summa* states that the aim of this more particular consideration of the moral life is to leave out nothing relevant to it. The methodological principle with regard to topics that apply to all men[1] is this: 'The whole subject of morals being reduced to a consideration of the virtues, these are further reducible to seven: three theological and four cardinal virtues.' Of chief interest to the contents of this volume is a further reduction, by which, namely, all moral virtues are aligned with one of the cardinal or principal virtues. With regard to those considered as annexed to justice, the contents of the present volume, an indispensable preliminary is 2a2æ. 80.

The device by which the reduction is worked out is the concept of 'potential parts' of a virtue:[2] i.e. virtues that are allied to a cardinal virtue as potential parts have some affinity with the principal virtue but in some sense fall short of its complete meaning. Question 80 shows that religion, piety, respect, gratitude, vengeance, truth, friendliness and liberality have an affinity with justice in that they also regard another person. They do not exhibit the strict meaning of justice, either because the indebtedness they discharge cannot be rendered exactly (*secundum æqualitatem*), which is the case with religion, piety, respect; or because the debt they fulfil is not a legal, but a moral debt,[3] which is the case with the other virtues mentioned.

The *Secunda Pars* of the *Summa Theologiæ* has been rightly recognized as the first coherent systematization of Christian moral theology. Yet to appreciate the work in depth it is imperative to recognize that its author was not out to contrive an *a priori* schema in a vacuum. Thus the organization of the treatise on justice must be seen as first of all a work of literary classification. This is to say that it was fashioned within the medieval intellectual ambience where the work of dialectic and synthesis operated along with, and in a sense was regulated by, the 'method or technique of

---

[1]Questions 1–170, as distinguished against topics related to special states and offices, Questions 171–89.
[2]See 2a2æ. 80, also 2a2æ. 48: 'Potential parts of any virtue are those adjunct virtues that have reference to some secondary act or objective, and so in a sense lack the full power (*potentia*) of the principal virtue.' See 2a2æ. 128 and 143. Note that the cardinal virtues are called principal, the potential parts secondary, but not necessarily in the sense that the cardinal virtues are more perfect; rather they deal with more urgent and frequently occurring aspects of the moral life, and the right dispositions towards such matters are a kind of foundation for other like yet distinctive virtues; see *De virtutibus cardinalibus* 1 ad 12.
[3]See Appendix 1.

INTRODUCTION

authorities'. This phrase of M.-D. Chenu[4] means that the work of the medieval theologian directly involved privileged texts, the writings, possessed often only in relatively brief excerpts, of Church Fathers and other writers, Christian and non-Christian, that by long usage had come to be regarded as authoritative statements on theological topics. By academic custom the theologian was obliged to deal with these; this literature was presumed to form part of the data of theology.[5]

Only from about 1250, i.e. after the possession in the West, through Robert Grosseteste's Latin translation (*c.* 1245) of Aristotle's *Nicomachean Ethics*, was there any attempt at organizing a treatise on justice. But theologians, of course, had discussed and written about the virtues, and with regard to justice the capital text, the 'authority', was a quotation from Cicero. The text is from *Rhetorici libri duo qui vocantur De Inventione* (invention, i.e. a determination of topic, being the first phase in the art of rhetoric), a work of his youth that Cicero himself later scorned, in *De oratore* I, 5. The context is a discussion of virtue, the parts of which are prudence, justice, courage, temperance; because of their moral beauty (*honestas*) these recommend themselves as themes for forensic oratory. Religion, piety, respect, gratitude, vengeance and truth are related to justice because they are included in the law of nature.[6] That the prob-

---

[4]See *Towards Understanding St Thomas* (tr. A. M. Landry & D. Hughes; Chicago, 1964) pp. 126-49.

[5]The method of Scholastic theology developed through the interplay of dialectics and authorities: the aim was to achieve concordance, consistency, coherence.

[6]Because of its prominence in Questions 101-18, it is useful to have the whole text at hand: 'Justice is a habit of mind which gives every man his desert while preserving the common advantage . . . The law of nature is that which is not born of opinion, but implanted in us by a kind of innate instinct: it includes religion, duty, gratitude, revenge, reverence and truth. Religion is that which brings men to serve and worship a higher order of nature which they call divine. Duty is the feeling which renders kind offices and loving service to one's kind and country. Gratitude embraces the memory of friendships and of services rendered by another, and the desire to requite these benefits. Revenge is the act of defending or avenging ourselves and so warding off violence, injury or anything which is likely to be prejudicial. Reverence is the feeling by which men of distinguished position are held worthy of respect and honour. Truth is the quality by which events in the past, present or future are referred to without alteration of material fact.'

'Justitia est habitus animi communi utilitate conservata suam cuique tribuens dignitatem . . . Naturæ jus est quod non opinio genuit, sed quædam in natura vis insevit, ut religionem, pietatem, gratiam, vindicationem, observantiam, veritatem. Religio est, quæ superioris cujusdam naturæ quam divinam vocant, curam cærimoniamque affert; pietas, per quam sanguine conjunctis patriæque benivolum officium et diligens tribuitur cultus; gratia, in qua amicitiarum et officiorum alterius memoria et remunerandi voluntas continetur; vindicatio, per quam vis aut injuria et omnino omne, quod obfuturum est, defendendo aut ulciscendo propulsatur;

INTRODUCTION

lematic in Question 80 is primarily one of accounting for literature on the virtue of justice is clear from the formulation, *whether the virtues allied to justice are appropriately (convenienter) assigned*.[7] The variation in the structure of the article reinforces the point; there is no argument 'on the other hand' (*sed contra*), but just the one set of arguments from differing authorities, followed by the Reply.[8] Clearly Cicero's list, given in obj. 1, is the point of reference throughout. The burden of the Reply is to assign a plausible reason for annexing the virtues in this list to the virtue of justice; the responses seek to bring into concordance with Cicero the list of Macrobius (ad 2), of William of Paris (ad 3), and of Andronicus of Rhodes (ad 4).[9] Obviously, St Thomas's approach to this literature is not historico-critical;[10] he is content in Scholastic fashion to advance a dialectical principle that will deal adequately with the authorities in question, and will account for this part of the theological data concerning the sphere of justice. That this kind of literary classification is involved is of significance for the interpretation of the contents of this volume.

The operation of the technique of authority, not only in the present treatise but throughout the *Summa*, often determines the language, the phrasing of problems, the argumentation. And frequently, while allowing the privileged texts to define the discussion, the understanding and interpretation that St Thomas intends is quite removed from that of the author he quotes, even if this be Aristotle or Augustine.[11] The language adopted from sources that dominates so much of the present treatise presents problems. We do not readily think of respect for parents and loyalty to

---

observantia, per quam homines aliqua dignitate antecedentes cultu quodam et honore dignantur; veritas, per quam immutata ea quæ sunt aut ante fuerunt aut futura sunt dicuntur.' Text and translation, in Loeb Classical Library edition, H. M. Hubbell (London, Cambridge, Mass., 1949), pp. 328–9.

[7]The usual form in similar articles; see 1a2æ. 68, 4; 69, 3; 70, 3; 84, 4; 2a2æ. 48; 122; 128; 143, etc.

[8]The same structure is followed in parallel articles on the other cardinal virtues: prudence, 2a2æ. 48; courage, 128; temperance, 143; like Question 80 they have a single article.

[9]Note that Aristotle's epieikeia (see Question 120) is allied to legal justice (ad 5). The implication is that it is the meaning of particular justice that is the criterion for evaluating the other virtues. Legal justice regards the public good of a community; particular justice is between individuals. See 2a2æ. 58, 5–8.

[10]All references to Cicero's *Rhetoric* are from the same brief excerpt, Book I, ch. 53; see 101, 1, sed contra; 2 ad 3; 3, sed contra; 102, 1, obj. 1 & sed contra; 2, sed contra; 103, 4; 106, 1, sed contra; 108, sed contra & Reply; 109, 1, obj. 3; 3, sed contra.

[11]See R. A. Gauthier, *Magnanimité* (Paris, 1951); idem, *L'Éthique à Nicomaque* (2d ed. Louvain, 1970) II, pp. 125–31; 241–99; Vol. 26 of this series, ed. T. C. O'Brien Appendix 6.

country as contained in the one concept and expressed in the one term; yet this is the connotation of *pietas* here. Vengeance does not sound like a virtue. *Dulia*, its meaning derived from Augustine's *City of God*, has its primary reference to what to-day is regarded as a moral monstrosity, slavery. One might conjecture that St Thomas himself experienced the constriction arising from the language of accepted texts; certainly one must be prepared to look through the formulae and discover meanings intended beyond the words.

A further point: one phalanx of 'Thomists' has marched under the banner of a Thomas of flawless consistency; he is to be read like the Bible, any apparent discrepancies being evaporated by conciliatory exegesis. In the present instance this would require explaining away the fact that some virtues (liberality, friendliness, truth) allied to justice in Question 80 are sharply separated from justice in 1a2æ. 60, 5 because they are concerned with inner emotions, not outward actions.[12] This view of the *Summa* as a logical monolith would also require some doctrinal reason why the order of virtues given in Question 80 (religion, piety, respect, truth, gratitude, vengeance, liberality, friendliness) is not followed in Questions 101-18. Nor is the distinction between legal and moral debt as applied in Question 80 thereafter interpreted in the same way.[13] The explanation in point of fact for these 'inconsistencies' is the functioning of literature, of texts, as theological data. Aristotle's *Ethics* is the reason why in 1a2æ. 60, 5 the number of all the moral virtues is determined to be eleven; the various authorities in Question 80 are the reason why the list of possible parts of justice alone numbers twenty-two. The first level of inquiry is one of literary classification; no ironclad, exhaustive or apodictic schema of the moral life itself is intended.[14] The meaning of virtue is the criterion by which St Thomas judges the complexities of living the moral life; to understand that judgment means first of all to know the difference between what is purely formal, organizational, methodological and what is of content, real, substantial. He would not propose that a person becomes virtuous by patterning his life on a systematic schema of virtues; that is artificial. The real innerconnection of virtues in the dynamics of the moral life is in the right judgment of prudence and the habitual responsiveness of the appetites to that judgment through the virtues.[15] The virtues become a key to understanding the thought when they are seen above all in their relation to the moral realities to which they respond.

---

[12]See 1a2æ. 60, 2 [13]See Appendix 1
[14]See Question 81, Prologue, where the order of the following treatise is set out, and some of the virtues mentioned in Question 80 freely located elsewhere in the *Summa*.
[15]See 1a2æ. 65, 1-3

INTRODUCTION

To reduce all moral matters to a consideration of the virtues is to fashion a moral theology that is pre-eminently a moral of the good. St Thomas's moral is prescriptive by being descriptive. It is meant to be 'practical knowledge' that is directive of action, but it serves this purpose by pointing to the intrinsic exigencies of ends, of human goods, and by indicating the specific variations in the good in terms of the specific objectives of human actions, in the 'good of reason', which is the good of virtue.[16] That which is descriptive of virtue—and, by opposition, of sin—is the normative and the judgmental in this moral theory. The present volume contains a description and evaluation of a sector of the order of justice, the order of human community and communication. Cicero and others provide the language. But the Questions here are not a 'natural social ethic'; they are rather a theology in which it is presupposed that natural values of justice are present still in the life of grace, and are ultimately transformed through the workings of the Gift of Piety under the Holy Spirit.

The revision of the order of considering the virtues from that outlined in Question 80 is not casual. The treatise is in fact regulated by a principle of diminishing indebtedness, from a debt owed to God and to other superiors, to a debt owed to equals.[17] But always there is an order of true justice, an order where there is some form of real indebtedness, the honouring of which makes the community of man possible, a community in which men can possess and peaceably enjoy the goods of human existence. For the indebtedness is based radically on a metaphysics of divine causality and government. The true human response is a rightful acknowledgment of dependence upon those who make it possible for one to be a participant in the human community. In 1a. 103, 4 & 6 the interpretation of God's governance is shown to include both the primacy of God's own lordship and the sharing in this government by creatures whom God causes to be causes, sources of being and development for others. This notion is constantly present in the discussion of the virtues of veneration (see 101, 1; 102, 1 & 2; 103, 3; 104, 1; 106, 1). The exigency, the indebtedness here is one of a 'necessity of justice' (104, 1 & 2) that requires a human 'conversion of effect to cause' (106, 3), a human response by the reasoned choice to acknowledge dependence upon superiors. These virtues imply a recognition that the community of man is not one of undifferentiated equality; its form is not anarchic, but hierarchic; not orderlessness, but a sacred order. The community of man exists and each individual participates in its resources because physical, moral, spiritual, cultural values are derived from the causality of God, both direct and participated (103, 3). The maintenance of

---

[16]See 1a2æ. 61, 1 ad 1
[17]See also 2a2æ. 122, 6

that community is the work of the virtues allied to justice. Ultimately it is a sacred work, for it looks to a sacred order, one deriving from God. Only in the recognition, not only of God's supreme and absolute lordship, but of the fact of his communicating a share in his dominion that makes others our superiors and so constitutes the human community, can that community be preserved. Only by respect for all their sources can the advantages and values in human life be maintained. In a word, the other virtues of veneration depend upon the virtue of religion. St Thomas adds warmth and illumination to the full significance of the hierarchical order of justice when in 102, 1 he compares those who are sources of our being or betterment in any way to *fathers*; there is a graduated participation in the fatherhood of God that is honoured by all the virtues of veneration. Into this line of thought there is also introduced the meaning of respecting and honouring all men, indispensable to the society of man (103, 2). Ultimately the whole order of justice is transformed by the meaning of the Gift of Piety, for then it is not God's fatherhood simply as lord that suffuses all the acts of the just man, but the fatherhood of God the Father of our Lord Jesus Christ, a fatherhood not only of lordship but of love.

As the virtues honouring superiors are differentiated among themselves according to degree of indebtedness, so also as a group they are differentiated from truth, friendliness and liberality, virtues that regard a diminished form of debt. Yet for these too an objective indebtedness remains: it is the debt owed to the human community as such, a debt based on the social nature of man, that he is created by God to live with others; that he is dependent upon the social structure and must contribute to its humane perdurance. The relations of man to man are not satisfied by the coldly correct calculations of commutative justice itself; there must be humaneness, the reasonableness of candour, civility, even of a degree of generosity. Because God has made man a social being, words, actions, possessions have a necessary reference to others. The exigencies of being part of the community of man require the virtues that contribute to that community's life. To recognize that to maintain honourable, courteous, even beneficent relations towards others is a part of justice, is to recognize that without which the society of man cannot survive (109, 3).

The enumeration and systematization of virtues can seem to be artificial, an undue 'multiplication of entities' in the moral life. Yet looking to justice we realize that the good of virtue, the good of reason, is more eminently present, since more of the judgment and discernment of reason is needed in relationships with others; we should, therefore, expect a further refinement and multiplicity of moral values as human existence has become more complex. Two examples may be suggested. The virtue of piety as it includes respecting and honouring one's country is spoken of by St Thomas

with words that have an Italian ring: piety binds together *compatriotas in natali solo*.[18] He perhaps measured patriotism to one's native soil on the scale of the Kingdom of Sicily; a first footstep on the moon, the menace of nuclear or ecological suicide have made us conscious of the Good Earth, the native soil of which we are all compatriots, and of a debt in piety to respect, to revive, to preserve the planet itself. Or take the use of language in contemporary life. We are pressured to chatter at cocktail parties with strangers as though they were intimates; we are tempted to use 'in' words—
—like 'input', 'finalize', 'package', 'linguistics' (when we mean language)—
lest we appear not to know them; we are assailed by the use of mass media, whether by politicians or peddlers, and expected by our reactions to match the predictions of market research; we are presumed to want to project a self-image in keeping with the patterns of advertising and fashion. There is room for truth, for candour, for simplicity, for appropriate speech and appropriate reticence. There may even be room for St Thomas and his evaluation of justice among men.

---

[18]III *Sent.* 33, 3, 4, sol. 1 ad 2.

DEINDE, POST RELIGIONEM, considerandum est de pietate. Cujus opposita vitia ex ipsius consideratione innotescunt.

Quæstio 101. de pietate

Circa pietatem ergo quæruntur quatuor:

1. ad quos pietas se extendat;
2. quid per pietatem aliquibus exhibeatur;
3. utrum pietas sit specialis virtus;
4. utrum religionis obtentu sit pietatis officium prætermittendum.

articulus 1. utrum pietas se extendat ad determinatas personas aliquorum hominum

AD PRIMUM sic proceditur:[1] 1. Videtur quod pietas non se extendat ad determinatas personas aliquorum hominum. Dicit enim Augustinus quod *pietas proprie Dei cultus intelligi solet, quam Græci eusebiam vocant.*[2] Sed Dei cultus non dicitur per comparationem ad homines, sed solum ad Deum. Ergo pietas non se extendit determinate ad aliquas hominum personas.

2. Præterea, Gregorius dicit, *Pietas in die suo convivium exhibet, quia cordis viscera misericordiæ operibus replet.*[3] Sed opera misericordiæ sunt omnibus exhibenda, ut patet per Augustinum.[4] Ergo pietas non se extendit determinate ad aliquas speciales personas.

---

[1] cf *In I Tim.* 4, *lect.* 2
[2] *De civ. Dei* x, 1. PL 41, 279
[3] *Moral.* I, 32, PL 75, 547. In matters concerning the spiritual life, this work of St Gregory the Great (*c.* 540–604), Pope and last of the great Latin Fathers, was a primary source in the Middle Ages. The work is an exposition of the Book of Job, with emphasis on the moral sense of the text; the full title, *Moralium Libri, sive Expositio in Librum B. Job, Libri XXXV.*
[4] *De doctr. christ.* I, 30. PL 34, 31
[a] The Latin *pietas*, as this Question shows, designates many different, though allied, moral attitudes; one constant connoted by the term is the 'sacredness' of these attitudes. All attempts at translating *pietas* by one adequate and restrictive English word—e.g. dutifulness, reverence, devotion, loyalty—prove unsatisfactory. Consult the Oxford (1933) and Webster (1959) dictionaries on the choice of 'piety'. Still there remains some dissatisfaction with the term, because we do not ordinarily think of the relationship to parents and to country as the one kind of moral response (perhaps the affinity of filial piety with charity explains why, cf 2a2æ. 26, 7). We have to allow 'piety' to be given the meaning it had for the Romans by letting

NEXT, AFTER RELIGION, we must move on to look at the virtue of piety,[a] an investigation which will also point up the vices against it.[b]

Question 101. piety

Regarding piety there are four points of inquiry:

1. its range;
2. its marks;
3. its distinctness;
4. the problem of precedence between the service of God and duties in piety.

article 1. whether piety is directed towards certain people[c]

THE FIRST POINT:[1] 1. The range of piety does not seem to be a particular class of people. For Augustine observes that *'pietas'*, *in Greek 'eusebeia'*, *is usually taken in its strict sense to mean the worship of God*.[2] The 'worship of God', however, refers to acts offered not to human beings, but to God alone. So the special reference of *'pietas'* is not to human beings at all.

2. Further, Gregory states that *'pietas' has its days of feasting, for it fills the heart's desires with works of mercy*.[3] Works of mercy, as Augustine points out,[4] are to be shown to all. The reach of piety is, therefore, not to be narrowed down to special individuals.

---

this Question explain the term. In Roman use *pietas* connoted the attitude towards intimates, family, *deos parentes*, as contrasted with *fidelitas*, the attitude towards outsiders. Cicero especially extended its meaning to include the cult of fatherland; cf *De Inventione* 22 & 66. Macrobius, *In Somnum Scipionis* 3, exemplifies the Roman usage, *Justitiam cole, et pietatem, quæ cum sit magna in parentibus et propinquis, tum in patria maxima est*. Remember, too, that a whole new meaning is given *pietas* as it is used to designate one of the Gifts of the Holy Ghost; cf 121, 1 ad 1 & 3.
[b]cf 2a2æ. Prologue; part of the doctrinal order is to consider sins and vices by contrast with the virtues they oppose.
[c]One reason for the clumsy *ad determinatas personas aliquorum hominum* is to stress piety as a part of justice. The phrase even may allow for the personification of *patria* clearly involved in piety as patriotism. 1a2æ. 60, 3 states that the meaning and variations of justice are found on the meaning and variations in debt or indebtedness, which is the exact match, the determinate order or commensurate adjustment of certain objects or actions to other persons. Art. 1, then, establishes the existence of a particular interpersonal relationship; art. 2 spells out the form of indebtedness; art. 3 shows consequently that piety is a specific virtue; art. 4 merely deals with a possible moral dilemma.

3. Præterea, multæ sunt aliæ in humanis rebus communicationes præter consanguineorum* et concivium communicationem, ut patet per Philosophum,[5] et super quamlibet earum aliqua amicitia fundatur, quæ videtur esse pietatis virtus, ut dicit glossa[6] *ad Tim.*, super illud, *Habentes ¦quidem speciem pietatis.*[7] Ergo non solum ad consanguineos et concives pietas se extendit.

SED CONTRA est quod Tullius dicit, quod *pietas est per quam sanguine junctis, patriæque benevolis officium et diligens tribuitur cultus.*[8]

RESPONSIO: Dicendum quod homo efficitur diversimode aliis debitor, secundum eorum diversam excellentiam et diversa beneficia ab eis suscepta. In utroque autem Deus summum obtinet locum; qui et excellentissimus est, et est nobis essendi et gubernationis primum principium; secundario vero nostri esse et gubernationis principia sunt parentes et patria, a quibus et in qua nati et nutriti sumus. Et ideo post Deum est homo maxime debitor parentibus et patriæ.

Unde sicut ad religionem pertinet cultum Deo exhibere, ita secundario gradu ad pietatem pertinet exhibere cultum parentibus et patriæ.

In cultu autem parentum includitur cultus omnium consanguineorum, quia etiam consanguinei ex hoc dicuntur, quod ex eisdem parentibus processerunt, ut patet per Philosophum.[9] In cultu autem patriæ intelligitur

---

*We follow the Piana reading here; the Leonine has *consanguinitatem*, consanguinity.
[5]*Ethics* VIII, 11. 1161a10; 12. 1161b11. St Thomas regularly refers to Aristotle as *the* Philosopher. The *Ethics* refers to the *Nicomachean Ethics*; rarely in the *Summa* does St Thomas cite the *Eudemian Ethics* (e.g. 1a2æ. 9, 4).
[6]*Glossa interlinearis*. In this series the *Glossa ordinaria* is referred to as *the Gloss*, others as a gloss. Among the biblical glosses cited by St Thomas, the *Glossa ordinaria* and the *Glossa interlinearis* are both attributed in Migne, *Patrologia Latina* (113) to Walafridus Strabo (+849); but only some elements are traceable to him; in their finished form both are from the school of Anselm of Laon (+1117). Other citations can be traced to the *Glossa Lombardi*, i.e. of Peter Lombard (+1160). See Smalley, B., 'La Glossa ordinaria' in *Recherches de théologie ancienne et médiévale* 9 (1937) 365-400; de Blic, J. 'L'Œuvre exégetique de Valafrid Strabon et La Glossa ordinaria', ibid 16 (1949), 5-28.
[7]II *Timothy* 3, 5
[8]*Rhetorica* (or *De inventione oratoria*) II, 53. Many elements of the Stoic moral philosophy of Cicero (Marcus Tullius Cicero, 106-43 B.C.) were taken over by Christian writers, e.g. the *De officiis* of St Ambrose. The citation here is one of the primary loci on which St Thomas relies in the present treatise (see 2a2æ. 80) both for the enumeration of the virtues and the ideal of upright social living.
[9]*Ethics* VIII, 12. 1161b29
[d]on *amicitia* cf 2a2æ. 114, 1 & ad 1. The term had a much broader application than 'friendship' does in English.
[e]The Vulgate here has *speciem pietatis*; the translation here is the Douay; the

3. Further, as Aristotle notes,[5] in human affairs there are many relationships other than those between blood relatives or fellow countrymen, each of them being the basis of some form of friendship.[d] And a gloss[6] on II *Timothy*—*having an appearance of godliness*[7] (*pietatis*)[e]—seems to identify friendship with piety. The range of piety, therefore, is wider at least than relatives and compatriots.

ON THE OTHER HAND, Cicero maintains, *This is pietas: to fulfil one's duty and conscientious service towards our own flesh and blood and those having the interests of our country at heart*.[8]

REPLY: Indebtedness to others arises in a variety of ways matching their own superiority and the diverse benefits received from them.[f] On both counts God holds first place; he is both absolutely supreme and the first source of our existence and progress through life.[g] Next, on the basis of birth and upbringing, parents and country are the closest sources of our existence and development; as a consequence everyone is indebted first of all under God to his parents and his fatherland.

Therefore, as it is for the virtue of religion to pay homage to God,[h] so on the next level, it is up to piety to render its own kind of homage to parents and country.

Note that in its meaning homage to parents extends to blood relatives as well, i.e. to those so called because, as Aristotle notes,[9] they share our

---

Confraternity, *having a semblance indeed of piety*. The Greek term used by St Paul, *eusebeias*, doubtless has little to do with the virtue being discussed in this Question.

[f]It will be seen that this is a theme running through the Questions on the virtues of reverence: the two bases for this kind of indebtedness are the intrinsic worth of those to whom we are so indebted (cf 106, 1) and their actual benefactions in our regard.

[g]'progress through life' for *gubernatio*; in 102, 2 we read, *Gubernare autem est movere aliquos ad debitum finem*, to govern is to conduct people to an appropriate end. Here *gubernatio* has a passive connotation.

[h]'homage' for *cultus*, a term which, along with *colere*, runs throughout these questions. A minimal sense of the term as 'taking care' is given in 81, 1 ad 4 (cf also *CG* III, 119), but in progressive use *cultus* stands for the form of indebtedness arising from the superiority of others over us and their benefactions towards us. The term is nuanced accordingly; there is a *cultus* owed to God, one of supreme reverence (*latria*) and absolute subjection (*servitus*) (cf 81, 3 ad 2); to parents we owe a *cultus* of reverence and service (*obsequium*), which includes obedience (cf 101, 2); to those who have any distinctive excellence we owe the *cultus* of giving them honour; when they are authorities having power to command, the *cultus* also includes obedience (cf 102, 2). Gratefulness is a special case; its *cultus* does not have the strict sense of indebtedness, but is the response appropriate to graciousness. Cf art. 2; 102, 2. *De Trin.* I, 1, 2. *CG* III, 119.

cultus omnium concivium, et omnium patriæ amicorum. Et ideo ad hoc pietas principaliter se extendit.

1. Ad primum ergo dicendum quod in majori includitur minus. Et ideo cultus qui Deo debetur, includit in se, sicut aliquid particulare, cultum qui debetur parentibus: unde dicitur *Malach.*,[10] *Si ego pater, ubi est honor meus?* Et ideo nomen pietatis etiam ad divinum cultum refertur.

2. Ad secundum dicendum quod, sicut Augustinus dicit, *more vulgi nomen pietatis etiam in operibus misericordiæ frequentatur: quod ideo arbitror evenisse, quia hæc fieri præcipue mandat Deus quæ sibi præ sacrificiis placere testatur; ex qua consuetudine factum est ut Deus ipse pius dicatur.*[11]

3. Ad tertium dicendum quod communicationes consanguineorum et concivium magis referuntur ad principia nostri esse quam aliæ communicationes; et ideo ad has nomen pietatis magis extenditur.

articulus 2. utrum pietas exhibeat parentibus sustentationem

AD SECUNDUM sic proceditur:[1] 1. Videtur quod pietas non exhibeat parentibus sustentationem. Ad pietatem enim videtur pertinere illud præceptum Decalogi, *Honora patrem tuum et matrem tuam.*[2] Sed ibi non præcipitur nisi honoris exhibitio. Ergo ad pietatem non pertinet sustentationem parentibus exhibere.

2. Præterea, illis homo debet thesaurizare quos tenetur sustentare. Sed secundum Apostolum, ut habetur II *ad Cor.*, *filii non debent thesaurizare parentibus.*[3] Ergo non tenentur eos per pietatem sustentare.

3. Præterea, pietas non solum extendit se ad parentes, sed etiam ad alios consanguineos et concives, ut dictum est.[4] Sed non tenetur aliquis omnes consanguineos et concives sustentare. Ergo nec etiam tenetur ad sustentationem parentum.

SED CONTRA est quod Dominus *Matt.* redarguit Pharisæos quod impediebant filios ne parentibus sustentationem exhiberent.[5]

[10]*Malachy* 1, 6   [11]*De civ. Dei* X, 1. PL 41, 279
[1]*In II Cor.* 12, lect. 5. *In Ethic.* IX, lect. 2. *De duobus præceptis caritatis*
[2]*Exodus* 20, 12   [3]II *Corinthians* 12, 14   [4]art 1   [5]*Matthew* 15, 3
[1]The basis for the special indebtedness, the *cultus*, here is given, namely that we are born and exist in dependence on certain paternal or parental sources of our whole being. These rank after God, participants in his own divine causality over us (cf 1a. 103, 4 & 6). In 102, 1 & 103, 3 St Thomas will indicate that the hierarchy of virtues of homage matches the hierarchy of beneficent causes over us, from God on down; all of them attend to a duty that is thereby sacred. Here the conclusion shows that the full scope of piety is parents, kin, country and fellow-citizens 122, 5 ad 2 indicates that homage towards parents comes first, because it is by being born of these parents that we share in the benefits of homeland. Indebtedness to relatives is based on blood; it is honouring 'family' as the source of what we are;

lineage; and homage towards country includes what we should show to all fellow citizens and well-wishers. This is the full range of piety.[1]

Hence: 1. The greater takes in the less; thus the kind of homage owed to God already embraces as but a partial form of itself the kind owed to parents—thus *Malachi, If then I be a father where is my honour?*[10] This is the explanation of the use of *pietas* to refer to homage towards God.[j]

2. Augustine observes, *In ordinary speech you hear the term 'pietas' in connection with acts of mercy. This, I feel, happens because God has stressed the obligation to perform them, and even given utterance to a preference for them over sacrifice. Even the usage of calling God himself 'pious' has this practical origin.*[11]

3. Ties of blood and native origin have a more direct bearing upon the sources of our existence and development than do other human relationships; this is why the term 'piety' has a more apposite application here.

article 2. whether piety entails supporting parents

THE SECOND POINT:[1] 1. Apparently piety does not include the support of parents. One of the Ten Commandments—*Honour thy father and thy mother*[2]—has reference to piety and simply enjoins showing them honour. Therefore this virtue has nothing to do with supporting parents.

2. Further, a duty to support someone includes the duty to put aside savings for them. Yet *neither ought the children to lay up for the parents.*[3] Nor, then, does piety entail an obligation to support them.

3. Further, piety extends not only to parents, but to relatives and countrymen as well,[4] and surely no one has to support all of these. Neither, then, must parents be supported.

ON THE OTHER HAND our Lord rebuked the Pharisees for preventing children from providing for their parents.[5]

---

the degree of indebtedness is gradated with the degree of consanguinity (cf *In Ethic.* VIII, *lect.* 12). Similarly what we owe our fellow-citizens is based on their sharing with us one soil, one cultural heritage. Piety, both as filial and as patriotic, is a virtue based on blood, bone, soil, but also upon all the benefits, spiritual, material, cultural, moral, that go to make up the kind of human existence we have by being born into this family, this native land; cf art. 3 the expression *principium connaturale*. Hence patriotism is not 'political'; nor is it the same as legal justice, this being a concern for the public good, the actual order in civil society; cf art. 3 ad 3. The article suggests further that wherever we are dependent for a whole side of our life, piety has place. Thus for the Christian, towards the Church, wherein he receives existence as a new creature in grace; for a religious, towards his Order and its founder, sources of a special kind of existence within the Church (cf 2a2æ. 183, 2).
[j]cf 2a2æ. 81, 1 ad 2.

RESPONSIO: Dicendum quod parentibus et concivibus aliquid debetur dupliciter: uno modo per se; alio modo per accidens. Per se quidem debetur eis id quod decet patrem, inquantum pater est: qui cum sit superior, quasi principium filii existens, debetur ei a filio reverentia et obsequium. Per accidens autem aliquid debetur patri, quod decet eum accipere secundum aliquid quod ei accidit; puta si sit infirmus, quod visitetur et ejus curationi intendatur; si sit pauper, quod sustentetur, et sic de aliis hujusmodi, quæ omnia sub debito obsequio continentur. Et ideo Tullius dicit quod pietas exhibet et officium et cultum ut officium referatur ad obsequium, cultus vero ad reverentiam sive honorem.[6] Quia, ut dicit Augustinus, *dicimur colere homines, quos honorifica vel recordatione vel præsentia frequentamus*.[7]

1. Ad primum ergo dicendum, quod in honoratione parentum intelligitur omnis subventio quæ debet parentibus exhiberi, ut Dominus interpretatur, *Matt*.,[8] et hoc ideo quia subventio fit patri ex debito, tanquam majori.

2. Ad secundum dicendum quod quia pater habet rationem principii, filius autem habet rationem a principio existentis, ideo per se patri convenit ut subveniat filio; et propter hoc non solum ad horam debet ei subvenire sed ad totam suam vitam, quod est thesaurizare. Sed quod filius aliquid conferat patri, hoc est per accidens ratione alicujus necessitatis instantis, in qua tenetur ei subvenire, non autem thesaurizare quasi in longinquum, quia naturaliter non parentes filiorum, sed filii parentum sunt successores.

3. Ad tertium dicendum quod cultus et officium, ut Tullius dicit, *debetur omnibus sanguine junctis et patriæ benevolis*,[9] non tamen æqualiter omnibus, sed præcipue parentibus, aliis autem secundum propriam facultatem et decentiam personarum.

articulus 3. utrum pietas sit specialis virtus ab aliis distincta

AD TERTIUM sic proceditur: 1. Videtur quod pietas non sit specialis virtus ab aliis distincta. Exhibere enim obsequium et cultum aliquibus ex amore

---

[6]*Rhetorica* II, 53
[8]*Matthew* 15, 3
[7]*De civ. Dei* X, 1. PL 41, 278
[9]*Rhetorica* II, 53

[a]*per se* and *per accidens* have varying meanings (cf *In Poster*. I, *lect*. 10); it is helpful to try to vary the translation to express the proper meaning. The ad 2 makes explicit what *per se* means in the present instance.
[b]Throughout where the text has simply *pater* we translate 'parents', because what is said of the father applies to both parents. Fatherhood was, of course, for St Thomas the nobler causal influence; cf 2a2æ. 26, 10.
[c]The homage (*cultus*) owed in piety to parents as such includes in higher form all the expressions of deference shown to any particular superior or benefactor, because the beneficence of parents touches the whole of human existence. Thus their

REPLY: The grounds for obligation towards parents are two, those arising from the very nature of the case, and those from special circumstances.[a] Because they are who they are, parents[b] have a right to everything that goes with the status of parenthood, namely the respect and deference owed by a son to those who, as sources of life, are above him.[c]

In special contingencies parents also have a right to whatever plain decency shows to be suited to their situation—in sickness to be visited, in poverty to be helped out, etc.[d] In truth all such acts are implicit in the obligation of being a dutiful son.[e] This is why Cicero declares that piety shows itself in *duty* and *homage*, 'duty' standing for deeds of service and 'homage' for respect or honour.[6] Augustine states that *we are said to pay homage (colere) to those whom we cherish by doing honour either to their memory or their company*.[7]

Hence: 1. Take honouring parents as our Lord interprets it,[8] i.e. for every sort of assistance that is their due. The reason is that rendering assistance towards parents is a debt owed to those over us.

2. To be a parent means to be a source of life; to be a child, to be the recipient of life. Normally, then, it is for parents to make provision for the child, and not only for immediate needs, but also for setting him up in life; hence St Paul speaks of them *laying up*. When a child does give aid to parents, it is an exceptional case, brought on by some besetting need. Even so, the obligation is to support, not to provide a nest-egg; nature indicates not that parents are heirs of the children, but children of the parents.

3. As Cicero states, respect and dutifulness are due to all *related to us by blood or common allegiance*;[9] but this does not apply to all in equal measure. Rather parents come first, then others, depending on our own resources and the claims of their ties to us.

article 3. whether piety is a specific virtue, distinct from the rest

THE THIRD POINT: 1. It seems that there is no special virtue of piety, distinct from other virtues. It is love that prompts us to offer service and

---

due is a unique respect (*reverentia*), surpassing that of the virtue of respectfulness (*observantia*; cf 102); the deference (*obsequium*) owed them includes obedience (cf 102, 2).

[d]Understand this contingent indebtedness as applying also to the spiritual indigence of parents, when namely they are in a condition of moral deterioration. To make 'exact' rules about the obligation to support parents (or even blood relatives—cf ad 3) we can apply those given in 2a2æ. 32, 5, but with greater strictness, i.e. at greater cost to the donor, because of the blood-ties. In the United States, many states have civil, not however criminal, laws urging the obligation of children to indigent parents.

[e]And also of a loyal citizen: i.e. apply these points to the duties of patriotism, in the case, e.g., of the native son in a developing country.

procedit. Sed hoc pertinet ad pietatem. Ergo pietas non est virtus a caritate distincta.

2. Præterea, cultum Deo exhibere est proprium religionis. Sed etiam pietas exhibet cultum Deo, ut dicit Augustinus.[1] Ergo pietas non distinguitur a religione.

3. Præterea, pietas quæ exhibet cultum et officium patriæ, videtur esse idem cum justitia legali, quæ respicit bonum commune. Sed justitia legalis est virtus generalis, ut patet per Philosophum.[2] Ergo pietas non est virtus specialis.

SED CONTRA est quod ponitur a Tullio pars justitiæ.[3]

RESPONSIO: Dicendum quod aliqua virtus specialis est ex hoc quod respicit aliquod objectum secundum aliquam specialem rationem. Cum autem ad rationem justitiæ pertineat quod debitum alii reddat, ubi invenitur specialis ratio debiti alicui personæ, ibi est specialis virtus. Debetur autem aliquid alicui specialiter, quia est connaturale principium producens in esse et gubernans. Hoc autem principium respicit pietas, inquantum parentibus et patriæ, et his qui ad hæc ordinantur, officium et cultum impendit. Et ideo pietas est specialis virtus.

1. Ad primum ergo dicendum quod sicut religio est quædam protestatio fidei, spei et caritatis, quibus homo primordialiter ordinatur in Deum, ita etiam pietas est quædam protestatio caritatis, quam quis habet ad parentes et ad patriam.

---

[1]*De civ. Dei* x, 1. PL 41, 279
[2]*Ethics* v, 1, 1129b29; 1130a9; 2, 1130b18   [3]*Rhet.* II, 53
[a]'Legal' also called 'general' justice is explained in 1a2æ. 60, 3 ad 2 & 2a2æ. 58, 5–7.
[b]'public good' for *bonum commune*. The Latin phrase is employed in many senses: 1. in the abstract for goodness in general—the objective of the will—as a substitute for *communis ratio boni* or *bonum in communi*, cf. 1a. 82, 4. 1a2æ. 1, 6; 9, 1; 10, 1; 2. for the collective good of a group, e.g. as here of a civil society, cf loc. cit. note *a*; 3. for the divine good as source and goal of all good, cf 1a. 60, 5; 103, 2; 1a2æ. 109, 3. Cf also 1a. 8, 2. *In Meta.* XII, *lect.* 12. *CG* III, 17.
[c]2a2æ. 58, 5 & 6 should be read here for the meaning of 'general virtue'; cf also 1a2æ. 61, 3. Briefly, a 'general virtue', while specific in the way described here in the Reply, has as objective a broader end for human activity and so the virtue directs (commands, *imperat*) other virtues towards this broader end, e.g. charity towards the love of God; religion, towards God's service; legal justice, towards the welfare of the community; cf 2a2æ. 23, 4 ad 2 & 3; 81, 4 ad 1; 127, 4.
[d]'objective' for *objectum*. Here a basic point in St Thomas's teaching on acts, powers and habits is reiterated. These are all 'specified', i.e. receive their determinate nature, through the causal influence of their objective, i.e. that to which they respond. An act, and through it a power or habit, terminates in a certain reality,

homage to others, both works of piety. Piety is not therefore a virtue differing from charity.

2. Further, homage to God is the concern of the virtue of religion, and since, as Augustine asserts,[1] piety offers homage to God, it does not differ from religion.

3. Further, piety understood as patriotism seems identical with legal justice,[a] the bearing of which is towards the public good.[b] Aristotle has shown that this type of justice is a general virtue.[2] Piety, then, cannot be a specific one.[c]

ON THE OTHER HAND Cicero classifies piety as a part of justice.[3]

REPLY: What makes any virtue to be specific is that its relationship to its objective is based on some specific moral value in the objective.[d] Since honouring a debt towards someone else is a function of justice generally, a specific kind of justice arises wherever there is a specific basis for indebtedness to any person.[e] This is the case in regard to anyone who, in the natural course of things, is a source of our life and its development. In rendering its service and homage piety is the response towards those sources—parents, homeland and those related to either one. Consequently, it is a special virtue.

Hence: 1. Just as religion bears witness as it were to faith, hope and charity, which are fundamental in a person's relationship to God, so also piety gives expression to the love we have for parents and country.[f]

---

called the *objectum materiale* because of some special value or interest, the *formalis ratio objecti*, in the thing; it is this that specifies the act, power or habit. When the *formalis ratio objecti* is a psychological value, i.e. cognitional or appetitive, it differentiates the knowing or appetitive acts, powers or habits. In the objectives of a human act, there is also a moral value—*ratio boni humani*—i.e. some feature that calls for a specific kind of human response from the will, the appetites or the moral habits modifying these. All this obviously implies an 'objective' morality, so often rejected currently. In St Thomas's complete view, however, the actual living of the moral life is highly 'subjective', in the sense, namely, that it is by a personal, concrete moral perception, decision and intention that each man assesses and confronts objective moral values. (See 1a2æ. 63, 4; Vol. 18 of this series, Appendixes 11–15.) A person's acts, powers, virtues, vices 'get specified' because with all his individual energies he becomes involved, and therefore morally involved, with the people and things of his experience.

[e] cf 1a2æ. 60, 3

[f] 2a2æ. 19, 2 ad 3 points out that charity is a union of love between children and parents; we may add also here, among fellow-citizens (fatherland cannot be personalized to the extent that we can have charity towards it). In both cases the natural ties mark a preference of intensity in charity (cf 2a2æ. 26, 7–11, especially 8;

(*footnote f continued on page 12.*)

2. Ad secundum dicendum quod Deus longe excellentiori modo est principium essendi et gubernationis quam pater vel patria. Et ideo alia virtus est religio, quæ cultum Deo exhibet, a pietate, quæ exhibet cultum parentibus et patriæ. Sed ea quæ sunt creaturarum, per quamdam superexcellentiam et causalitatem transferuntur in Deum, ut Dionysius dicit.[4] Unde per excellentiam pietas cultus Dei nominatur, sicut et Deus excellenter dicitur Pater noster.

3. Ad tertium dicendum quod pietas se extendit ad patriam secundum quod est nobis quoddam essendi principium; sed justitia legalis respicit bonum patriæ secundum quod est bonum commune. Et ideo justitia legalis magis habet quod sit virtus generalis quam pietas.

articulus 4. *utrum occasione religionis sint prætermittenda pietatis officia in parentes*

AD QUARTUM sic proceditur.[1] 1. Videtur quod occasione religionis sint prætermittenda pietatis officia in parentes. Dicit enim Dominus *Luc.*, *Si quis venit ad me, et non odit patrem suum, et matrem, et uxorem, et filios, et fratres, et sorores adhuc autem et animam suam, non potest meus esse discipulus.*[2] Unde et in laudem Jacobi et Joannis dicitur, quod *relictis retibus et patre, secuti sunt Christum;*[3] et in laudem Levitarum dicitur, *Qui dixerit patri suo et matri suæ: Nescio vos; et fratribus suis: Ignoro vos, et nescierunt filios suos, hi custodierunt eloquium tuum.*[4] Sed ignorando parentes et alios consanguineos, vel etiam odiendo eos, necesse est quod prætermittantur pietatis officia. Ergo propter religionem officia pietatis sunt prætermittenda.

2. Præterea, *Matt.* et *Luc.* dicitur quod Dominus dicenti sibi, *Permitte*

---

[4]*De divinis nominibus* 1. PG 3, 593. The Pseudo-Dionysius or Denis is an anonymous Neo-Platonic writer of *c.* A.D. 500, probably from Syria, identified throughout the Middle Ages with the Areopagite of *Acts* 17, 34. His work thus was credited with quasi-apostolic authority, and determined the theology of mysticism.
[1]Opusc. *Contra pestiferam doctrinam retrahentium homines a religionis ingressu.*
[2]*Luke* 14, 26   [3]*Matthew* 15, 22   [4]*Deuteronomy* 33, 9

(*footnote f continued from on page 11.*)
n.b. the remark in ant. 7 that charity assimilates to itself all natural ties of noble affection). Whether towards God or towards man, the love of charity is primary, most intimate, personal and warm—the shared experience of loving another self. But for St Thomas the love of charity is for the other as he is; for God as Father and Lord; for parents as sources of life, etc. So it does not obliterate reverence, duty, service, homage, obedience, but rather fosters them (see 1a2æ. 65, 3). Hence the virtues of veneration attend to the indebtedness towards superiors whom we love. The distinction of objectives and virtues is not a word game, but a recognition of the identity and true relationships of the parties sharing in charity's love. Charity, then, is immediately an affective union with the beloved; piety responds to the one loved as one to whom we also owe due homage, because the beloved is father or mother or countryman.

2. God is the source of our existence and progress in life in a way far surpassing parents or fatherland. The virtue of religion with its homage to God is different, then, from the piety which pays homage to parents and country. Still, as Dionysius says,[4] in a transferred sense, we attribute to God, on the basis of the divine causality and eminence,[g] whatever we find in creatures. Even as God, therefore, is called our father par excellence, in the same way homage to him is termed piety.

3. Piety is the response towards country as it stands as a source of our own existence; legal justice is directed towards the welfare of our country as this is a good which is collective. We thus should expect legal justice rather than piety to be a general virtue.[h]

article 4. whether duties of piety towards parents should give way in favour of the service of God

THE FOURTH POINT:[1] 1. In case of conflict it would seem that duties in piety are to be set aside in favour of those of religion. Our Lord declares, *If any man comes to me and hate not his father and mother and wife and children and brethren and sisters, yea and his own life also, he cannot be my disciple.*[2] In this sense the words, *And they forthwith left their nets and father and followed him*[3] are spoken as a tribute to James and John. As also, *Who hath said to his father and to his mother, I do not know you, And to his brethren, I know you not; and their own children they have not known, these have kept thy word,*[4] in praise of the Levites. Now to turn one's back on parents and other relatives, and much more to hate them, inevitably means putting aside the duties of piety. Such a course, then, is dictated for reasons of religion.

2. Further, in both *Matthew* and *Luke* to the words, *Suffer me first to go and bury my father,* there is our Lord's rejoinder, *Let the dead bury their*

---

[g] cf 1a. 13, 1, 2, 3 & 5.
[h] For the distinction here (it is in fact between *bonum privatum* and *bonum commune* —cf 1a2æ. 60, 3 ad 2; and refer to note *b* above).

Recall that legal justice is justice in its strict form, concerned with an exact indebtedness; piety, a potential part, concerned with an unacquittable debt (see Introduction). Further, patriotism pays homage to fatherland as it is for each person a given source of physical existence and human heritage. Legal justice is bent upon creating the well-being of the nation, an end to be accomplished by observance of its laws, etc. And this community soundness is intended so that all citizens will receive the benefits meant to be derived from the civil community. Legal justice is general, then, as it directs all virtuous activity to bring about this communal goal, the welfare of the nation. In a word, piety is an attitude towards my country for what it has done for me; legal justice, for what I must do towards my country as a political community or state.

me primum ire et sepelire patrem meum, respondit, *Sine ut mortui sepeliant mortuos suos. Tu autem vade, et annuntia regnum Dei*,[5] quod pertinet ad religionem, sepultura autem patris pertinet ad pietatis officium. Ergo pietatis officium est prætermittendum propter religionem.

3. Præterea, Deus per excellentiam dicitur Pater noster. Sed sicut per pietatis obsequia colimus parentes, ita per religionem colimus Deum. Ergo prætermittenda sunt pietatis obsequia propter religionis cultum.

4. Præterea, religiosi tenentur ex voto, quod transgredi non licet, suæ religionis observantias implere, secundum quas suis parentibus subvenire impediuntur, tum propter paupertatem, quia proprio carent, tum etiam propter obedientiam,* quia sine licentia suorum prælatorum eis claustrum exire non licet. Ergo propter religionem prætermittenda sunt pietatis officia in parentes.

SED CONTRA est quod Dominus, redarguit Pharisæos qui, intuitu religionis, honorem parentibus debitum subtrahere docebant.[6]

RESPONSIO: Dicendum quod religio et pietas sunt duæ virtutes. Nulla autem virtus alii virtuti contrariatur aut repugnat, quia, secundum Philosophum, bonum non est bono contrarium.[7] Unde non potest esse quod pietas et religio se mutuo impediant, ut propter actum unius actus alterius excludatur.

Cujuslibet autem virtutis actus, ut ex supra dictis patet,[8] debitis circumstantiis limitatur; quas si prætereat, jam non erit virtutis actus sed vitii. Unde ad pietatem pertinet officium et cultum parentibus exhibere secundum debitum modum. Non est autem debitus modus ut plus homo tendat ad colendum patrem quam ad colendum Deum; sed, sicut Ambrosius dicit *necessitudini generis divinæ religionis pietas antefertur*.[9]

Si ergo cultus parentum abstrahat nos a cultu Dei, jam non esset pietatis

---

*Leonine: *inobedientiam*, disobedience
[5]*Matthew* 8, 22; *Luke* 9, 58   [6]*Matthew* 15, 3
[7]*Categories* 8. 13b36   [8]1a2æ. 18, 3
[9]On *Luke* (12, 52) I. PL 15, 1827. St Ambrose (c. 339–97), Archbishop of Milan, one of the four great Latin Fathers of the Church; friend of Augustine; his moral writings were esteemed in the Middle Ages.
aOn circumstances, cf 1a2æ. 7, 18 and Vol. 18 of this series, Appendix 12; on the particular point about virtue, 1a2æ. 64, 1 ad 2; 4

Circumstances are compared to a moral objective as accidents to a substance; they are the moral surroundings conditioning an objective. The significance of the point summarized in the Reply is that the act of virtue is not a mere response to a moral 'type', to an abstraction; as a moral act, an act of virtue does not just happen. If moral objectives are 'given' in a theory of objective morality, they are also 'created' by the individual acting here and now, i.e. by the process of formulating his own singular moral judgment, he presents to himself the integral moral good

dead, but go thou and preach the kingdom of God.[5] This is an act of the service of God; the burial of one's father, a work of piety. Such works, therefore, are to give way to those of religion.

3. Further, God is called our father par excellence. While through the works of piety we honour parents, it is God we honour through those of religion. The service of religion, then, takes precedence over that of piety.

4. Further, members of religious orders are bound by inviolable vow to keep the rules of their community. According to rule they are prevented from supporting their parents; because of poverty they are without means of their own; because of obedience they have no right to go out of their cloister without leave of their superior. Here is a case, then, where duties towards parents are set aside for the sake of religion.

ON THE OTHER HAND we have our Lord's reproof to the Pharisees' teaching that the honour owed parents was to be dispensed with for religious motives.[6]

REPLY: Both religion and piety are virtues. No virtue is incompatible with or set against another one; Aristotle states that one good does not conflict with another.[7] It is therefore impossible for piety and religion so to oppose each other that the act of one is thwarted by the act of the other.

The reason is that the act of every virtue is circumscribed, as already noted,[8] by the observance of due circumstances, so that if one should fail to attend to any of these the act will no longer be virtuous but sinful.[a] Consequently attendance to the duties and homage owed to parents is marked by the measure called for. This measure does not press a person to be more intent upon concern for parents than upon honouring God; rather, following the words of Ambrose, *piety in serving God takes precedence over the demands of our own flesh and blood.*[9] It follows that if homage towards our parents should draw us away from the service of God,

---

he is to choose. By that judgment he regulates and measures his own act and the good he proposes to himself is a measured good. To pursue a 'pure moral objective' would be to isolate this and so the conflict envisaged here could arise. In fact there is no moral objective, God apart, that is not measurable by relation to the person acting, to other persons, to other moral objectives. These relationships are the circumstances; it is by reference to them that the good of virtue is said to be a measured good, a 'mean'. To act virtuously the individual must appraise and place before himself the whole moral good, the integral issue in this concrete situation; by his judgment he thus 'creates' the moral good he is to choose. To propose a 'pure objective' in isolation is not to propose a moral *good*, and so not the true objective of a virtuous act, at all. This is the meaning of circumstances, with their implication of the personal, subjective, responsible role of conscience and the processes of prudence.

parentum insistere cultui contra Deum. Unde Hieronymus dicit, *Per calcatum perge patrem, per calcatam perge matrem, siccis oculis ad vexillum crucis evola. Summum genus pietatis est in hac re fuisse crudelem.*[10] Et ideo in tali casu dimittenda sunt officia pietatis in parentes propter divinum religionis cultum.

Si vero exhibendo debita obsequia parentibus, non abstrahamur a divino cultu, hoc jam pertinebit ad pietatem, et sic non oportebit propter religionem pietatem deserere.

1. Ad primum ergo dicendum quod Gregorius, exponens illud verbum Domini, dicit quod *parentes, quos adversarios in via Dei patimur, odiendo et fugiendo nescire debemus.*[11] Si enim parentes nostri nos provocent ad peccandum, et abstrahant nos a cultu divino, debemus quantum ad hoc eos deserere et odire. Et hoc modo dicuntur Levitæ suos consanguineos ignorasse, quia idolatris secundum mandatum Domini non pepercerunt, ut habetur *Exod.*[12] Jacobus autem et Joannes laudantur ex hoc quod sunt secuti Dominum, dimisso parente, non quia eorum pater eos provocaret ad malum, sed quia aliter æstimabant ipsum posse vitam transigere, eis Christum sequentibus.

2. Ad secundum dicendum quod Dominus ideo prohibuit discipulum a sepultura patris, quia, sicut Chrysostomus dicit, *per hoc eum Dominus a multis malis eripuit, puta luctibus, et mæroribus, et aliis quæ hinc expectantur; post sepulturam enim erat necesse et testamenta scrutari, et hæreditatis divisionem, et alia hujusmodi; et præcipue quia alii erant qui complere poterant hujus funeris sepulturam.*[13]

Vel, sicut Cyrillus exponit *Super Luc., discipulus ille non petit quod patrem jam defunctum sepeliret, sed adhuc viventem in senectute sustentaret, usquequo sepeliretur: quod Dominus non concessit, quia erant alii qui ejus curam habere poterant, linea parentelæ adstricti.*[14]

3. Ad tertium dicendum quod hoc ipsum quod parentibus carnalibus ex pietate exhibemus in Deum referimus ; sicut et alia misericordiæ opera, quæ quibuscumque proximis impendimus, Deo exhibita videntur, secundum illud *Matt.,Quod uni ex minimis meis fecistis, mihi fecistis.*[15] Et ideo si carnalibus parentibus nostra obsequia sint necessaria, ut sine his sustentari non possint, nec nos ad aliquid contra Deum inducant, non debemus intuitu religionis eos deserere. Si autem sine peccato eorum obsequiis vacare non possumus, vel etiam si absque nostro obsequio possunt sus-

---

[10] Epistola 14 (*Ad Heliodorum*). PL 22, 348. St Jerome (*c.* 342–420), biblical scholar; one of the four great Latin Fathers.
[11] *Homil. in Evang.* 27. PL 76, 1275
[12] *Exodus* 32, 26
[13] *Comm. in Matth. Evang.* 27. PG 57, 348. St John Chrysostom (*c.* 347–407) bishop of Constantinople, one of the great Greek Fathers, preacher of great acclaim,

to persist would not be an act of piety at all. Hence Jerome's words, *Rally to the banner of the cross and step over even a prostrate father or mother. Cruelty of this sort is the highest form of filial piety.*[10] In such circumstances, then, obligations in piety towards parents are to be set aside for the sake of the duties of religion.

Whenever, on the other hand, we are not held back from homage to God by attending to the filial duties owed to parents, these remain an act of the virtue of piety. The conclusion is that to forsake piety for religion will never be required.

Hence: 1. Gregory's explanation of our Lord's statement is that, *rejecting them and leaving them, we must refuse to recognize as parents those we find to be obstacles in our path to God.*[11] He means that if our parents urge us to sin and lead us away from honouring God, then on that point we should abandon and detest them. This is the sense in which the Levites are spoken of as having refused to recognize their own flesh and blood, for, observing the Lord's commandment, they were merciless to idolaters.[12] James and John, in turn, are commended for following our Lord, leaving their father behind, not because he was prompting them to evil, but because they judged that while they were following Christ, he could make another life for himself.

2. Our Lord forbade the disciple to bury his father because, as Chrysostom writes, *In this way our Lord drew him away from much harm, for example the bickering and grief attendant upon such an occasion. For after the burial there would have been the task of going into the father's will, parcelling out the inheritance, etc. But above all, in this case there were others on hand able to take care of the burial.*[13]

Or if you prefer, take Cyril's explanation—*the disciple was not asking to bury a dead father, but to support one still living, until he did die; this our Lord refused, there being others of the same parentage able to take on the care of the father.*[14]

3. *As long as you did it to one of these my least brethren, you did it to me,*[15] so that what piety renders to our earthly parents is itself an offering to God, just like other works of mercy on behalf of any of our fellows. If our parents are so in need of help that our support is indispensable and they are not occasions of sin for us, it follows that we ought not abandon them for reasons of religion. Should we, however, be unable to look after

---

moral expositor of the Gospels; his homilies on *Matthew* were particularly prized by St Thomas.
[14]*Explanatio in Lucae Evang.* on 9, 59. St Cyril of Alexandria (d. 444), Greek Father, opponent of Nestorianism. St Thomas has these fragments in his *Catena Aurea.*
[15]*Matthew* 25, 40

tentari, licitum est eorum obsequia præstermittere, ad hoc quod amplius religioni vacemus.

4. Ad quartum dicendum quod aliud dicendum est de eo qui est adhuc in sæculo constitutus et aliud de eo qui jam est in religione professus. Ille enim qui est in sæculo constitutus, si habet parentes, qui sine ipso sustentari non possunt, non debet, eis relicitis, religionem intrare, quia transgrederetur præceptum de honoratione parentum. Quamvis quidam dicant, quod etiam in hoc casu licite posset eos deserere, eorum curam Deo committens. Sed si quis recte consideret, hoc esset tentare Deum; cum habens ex humano consilio quid ageret, periculo parentes exponeret sub spe divini auxilii. Si vero sine eo parentes vitam transigere possent, licitum esset ei desertis parentibus religionem intrare, quia filii non tenentur ad sustentationem parentum nisi causa necessitatis, ut dictum est.[16]

Ille vero qui jam est in religione professus, reputatur jam quasi mortuus mundo: unde non debet occasione sustentationis parentum exire claustrum, in quo Christo consepelitur, et se iterum sæcularibus negotiis implicare. Tenetur tamen, salva sui prælati obedientia, et suæ religionis statu, pium studium adhibere, qualiter ejus parentibus subveniatur.

---

[16] In the Reply
[b] *professus* means one who has bound himself to the religious life by vow.
[c] Alexander of Hales, *Summa Theologica*, Quaracchi, III, 822, refers to opinions about this point and the edition cited gives as sources, William of Auxerre, and John of la Rochelle. *Quidam* in the usage of the medievals ordinarily referred to

them without sinning and their maintenance be possible without our aid, it is right to let care of them give way to a fuller dedication to religion.

4. Different judgments apply to one still living the life of a layman and one already professed[b] in the religious life. If the first has parents unable to maintain themselves without him, he must not abandon them in order to enter a religious order; that would be breaking the commandment on honouring parents. It is true that some theologians[c] maintain that it would be permissible even in this case to leave parents, entrusting their care to God.[d] But in common sense this would be tempting God, namely to have a course of action clear to human prudence and yet to expose parents to peril under the presumption that God will take care of everything. If parents can manage without him, however, it is right for such a person to leave them and enter religious life; children are obliged to the support of their parents only in case of existing need.[16]

Because he is counted as dead to the world, one already professed in religious life should not for the sake of his parents' support leave the cloister where he is buried together with Christ and become involved again in secular affairs. Still, within the limits of obedience to superiors, he is bound to expend every effort towards improving his parents' state.

---

magistri, professors who taught at the University of Paris at some time since its foundation 1207. The anonymous citation has the implication that they were not *auctores* like the Fathers of the Church. The 'method of authorities is a core element in medieval Scholasticism; cf M.-D. Chenu, *Towards Understanding St. Thomas*, tr. A. M. Landry & D. Hughes, Chicago, 1964, 126-55.
[d]cf 2a2æ. 189, 6.

DEINDE CONSIDERANDUM EST de observantia et partibus ejus per quæ de oppositis vitiis erit manifestum.

Quæstio 102. de observantia

Circa observantia autem quæruntur tria:

1. utrum observantia sit specialis virtus ab aliis distincta;
2. quid observantia exhibeat;
3. de comparatione ejus ad pietatem.

articulus 1. *utrum observantia sit specialis virtus ab aliis distincta*

AD PRIMUM sic proceditur: 1. Videtur quod observantia non sit specialis virtus ab aliis distincta. Virtutes enim distinguuntur secundum objecta. Sed objectum observantiæ non distinguitur ab objecto pietatis; dicit enim Tullius in sua *Rhet.* quod *observantia est per quam homines aliqua dignitate antecedentes quodam cultu et honore dignantur.*[1] Sed cultum et honorem etiam pietas exhibet parentibus, qui dignitate antecedunt. Ergo observantia non est virtus distincta a pietate.

2. Præterea, sicut hominibus in dignitate constitutis debetur honor et cultus, ita etiam eis qui excellunt scientia et virtute. Sed non est aliqua specialis virtus per quam honorem et cultum exhibeamus hominibus qui scientiæ vel virtutis excellentiam habent. Ergo etiam observantia, per quam cultum et honorem exhibemus his qui nos in dignitate antecedunt, non est specialis virtus ab aliis distincta.

---

[1]*Rhet.* II, 53

[a]'Observance' for *observantia* is listed as archaic by both Oxford and Webster. 'Respectfulness' is awkward. 'Respect' seems to satisfy; it connotes a mental attitude (the note of attentive recognition, from *observare*, should not be forgotten); it is a cool word and broad enough to fit the variations in the attitudes of *observantia* towards different people (see note *b*). 'Reverence', even though used to describe the response of *observantia* in art. 1, seems too strong a translation. Cicero again is the source (see obj. 1 below) of whatever recognition this virtue was given in Christian writings; St Augustine simply repeats him in *De quæst. lxxxiii.* PL 40, 2-21, cf Isidore, PL 83, 51 & 1250; Peter Abelard, PL 178, 1654.

[b]The sense of 'parts' here needs explanation. Superiority and beneficence are the basis for the virtues of veneration (cf 101,1, note *f*). The higher forms, religion and piety, regard those who are sources of our whole being; the homage they pay contains in a simple, unified way, whatever lesser virtues show (102, 1 ad 1). Respect is a response to more particularized influences (102, 1); this is why it has 'parts'. The indebtedness it honours is divisible, first, in the sense that superiority and beneficence are separable, i.e. there are those who have some superiority in virtue, learning, skill, etc., but are not sources of betterment to us. Hence respect can have

NEXT, THE VIRTUE OF RESPECT[a] (102) along with its parts[b] (103-104). What the opposed vices are will thereby be clear.

Question 102. respect

There are three points of inquiry:

1. whether respect is a special virtue, distinct from others;
2. marks of respect;
3. respect compared to piety.

article 1. whether respect is a specific kind of virtue, different from others

THE FIRST POINT: 1. Respect gives no evidence of being a virtue differing specifically from others. Virtues differ where their objectives differ and there is no such distinction between respect and piety. Cicero says, *It is the virtue of respect by which persons eminent in any position of dignity receive the deference of a certain service and honour*;[1] and it is also the place of piety to offer service and honour to those superior in dignity, namely parents. The two, then, are not different virtues.

2. Further, even as honour and homage are the just due of those in authority,[c] so also of those pre-eminent in learning or virtue. Yet there is no special virtue to deal with the second sort of people. Neither, then, is respect, with its concern for showing homage and honour to authority, a virtue specifically distinct from others.

---

a strict sense and a diminished sense (art. 1 ad 2); its tribute is varied accordingly (art. 2). Secondly, the indebtedness is divisible into various kinds so that respect has as many species, called subjective parts, as there are specific forms of human guidance exercised over us; cf 103, 4. One such species is *dulia*, the attitude of slave towards master, which undoubtedly is considered because St Augustine mentions it in *De civ. Dei* X, PL 41, 278. Finally, there is a unique sort of indebtedness in this area, based on that peculiar influence one person has over another by way of *command* (cf III *Sent*. 9, 2, 2 ad 3). This creates a special moral value and a special difficulty, so that there is a special virtue, namely obedience, contained under respect; cf 104, 3 ad 1. Obedience can be classified as a potential part of respect in the way such parts are assigned to the virtue of prudence in 2a2æ. 48.

c'*hominibus in aliqua dignitate constitutis*' and other similar phrases are translated 'those in authority' in accord with the Reply. The context, that such persons are sources of our betterment, must be kept in mind. The expression derives from Cicero, *Dignitas, alicujus honesta et cultu et honore et verecundia digna auctoritas*, dignity, someone's rightful authority, which is worthy of homage and honour and deference, *Inv. Rhetor*. I, 2, 55; cf Augustine, *De quæst. lxxxv*. PL 40, 22. St Thomas explains a richer sense of *dignitas* in 2a2æ. 63, 2.

3. Præterea, hominibus in dignitate constitutis multa debentur, ad quæ solvenda lex cogit, secundum illud ad *Rom.*, *Reddite omnibus debita, cui tributum, tributum*, etc.[2] Ea vero ad quæ per legem compellimur, pertinent ad justitiam legalem, seu etiam ad justitiam specialem. Ergo observantia non est per se specialis virtus ab aliis distincta.

SED CONTRA est quod Tullius condividit* observantiam aliis justitiæ partibus, quæ sunt speciales virtutes.[3]

RESPONSIO: Dicendum quod, sicut ex dictis patet,[4] necesse est ut eo modo per quemdam ordinatum descensum distinguantur virtutes, sicut excellentia personarum quibus est aliquid reddendum. Sicut autem carnalis pater particulariter participat rationem principii, quæ universaliter invenitur in Deo, ita etiam persona quæ quantum ad aliquid providentiam circa nos gerit, particulariter participat proprietatem patris, quia pater est principium et generationis, et educationis, et disciplinæ, et omnium quæ ad perfectionem humanæ vitæ pertinent. Persona autem in dignitate constituta est sicut principium gubernationis respectu aliquarum rerum—sicut princeps civitatis in rebus civilibus, dux autem exercitus in rebus bellicis, magister autem in disciplinis, et simile est in aliis. Et inde est quod omnes tales personæ patres appellantur, propter similitudinem curæ; sicut servi Naaman dixerunt ad eum, *Pater, etsi rem grandem dixisset tibi propheta*, etc.[5] Et ideo sicut sub religione, per quam cultus tribuitur Deo, quodammodo invenitur pietas, per quam coluntur parentes, ita sub pietate invenitur observantia, per quam cultus et honor exhibetur personis in dignitate constitutis.

1. Ad primum ergo dicendum quod, sicut dictum est supra,[6] religio per quamdam supereminentiam pietas dicitur, et tamen pietas proprie dicta a religione distinguitur; ita etiam pietas per quamdam excellentiam potest dici observantia, et tamen observantia proprie dicta a pietate distinguitur.

2. Ad secundum dicendum quod aliquis ex hoc quod est in aliqua dignitate constitutus, non solum quamdam status excellentiam habet, sed etiam quamdam potestatem gubernandi subditos. Unde competit ei ratio principii, prout est aliorum gubernator. Ex hoc autem quod aliquis habet

---

*Piana: *condividendo*, in the course of dividing
[2]*Romans* 13, 7 [3]*Rhet.* II, 53
[4]101, 1 [5]IV *Kings* 5, 13
[6]101, 3 ad 2
[d]On the distinction of general and particular justice, cf 2a2æ. 58, 5, 7, 8. The denominations come from their objectives—the public good in the one case, the rights of individuals in the other.
[e]Compare this article with 101, 1 and 106, 1, to perceive the exalted meaning of

3. Further, as the text, *Render therefore to all men their dues; tribute to whom tribute is due*,[2] etc. indicates, law binds us to fulfil our many obligations towards persons in authority. A specific form of justice, i.e. legal justice,[d] has as its concern all duties under law. Thus respect does not have anything about it to make it a specific virtue distinct from others.

ON THE OTHER HAND Cicero divides respect against other parts of justice, themselves all specific virtues.[3]

REPLY: I have already made it clear[4] that there is need to trace a hierarchy of virtues to correspond to the hierarchy of persons to whom we are indebted. In the gradation of such persons, parents share the status of being a particular source of life as God is its universal source; so also anyone who exercises care over us in any line, to that extent shares the character of a parent, i.e. one who is the source of birth, upbringing, education and all that contributes to progress in life. Now a person who has some authority stands as a source of guidance in regard to some special endeavour—in civil matters, the head of the state, in warfare, the army commander, in education, the teacher, etc. And—as in the text where the servants of Naaman say to him, *Father, if the prophet had bid thee do some great thing*,[5] etc—all such people can be called fathers because of a resemblance in the way they care for us. Therefore as piety with its homage to parents is derived in a way from the virtue of religion with its homage to God, so also the virtue of respect through which homage and honour are shown to those in authority stands in similar relation to piety.[e]

Hence: 1. As has been said,[6] religion is given the name *pietas* in an eminent sense; but in its strict sense piety differs from religion. In turn piety could be called respect par excellence, but strictly speaking the two are different virtues.

2. When a person is in a position of authority, he has not only eminence of rank but also some particular power to rule over those subject to him. It is as one who governs others, then, that he stands as a giver of life. Endowments of learning or virtue on the other hand do not give a person

---

these virtues. This article most explicitly expresses the high sense of their foundation: namely the way God's own fatherhood is communicated to others. St Thomas does not speak of a cold order of duties, but sees in the hierarchy of causes the warmth of God's paternal care and providence. This is why these virtues have a sacred character, why there is a religious aspect to their response to the divinely arranged, fatherly sources of our life and betterment. Whatever meaning these virtues had in the Roman mind, they receive new significance, new warmth, new 'sanctity' by reason of the Christian concept of God's Fatherhood. This is why, too, their functions are taken up and enhanced by the working of the Gift of Piety; cf 121, 1.

perfectionem scientiæ vel virtutis, non sortitur rationem principii quantum ad alios, sed solum quamdam excellentiam in seipso. Et ideo specialiter quædam virtus determinatur ad exhibendum honorem et cultum his qui sunt in dignitate constituti. Verum, quia per scientiam et virtutem et omnia alia hujusmodi aliquis idoneus redditur ad dignitatis statum, reverentia quæ propter quamcumque excellentiam aliquibus exhibetur, ad eamdem virtutem pertinet.

3. Ad tertium dicendum quod ad justitiam specialem proprie sumptam pertinet reddere æquale ei cui aliquid debetur. Quod quidem non potest fieri ad virtuosos et ad eos qui bene statu dignitatis utuntur, sicut nec ad Deum, nec ad parentes. Et ideo ad quamdam virtutem adjunctam hoc pertinet, non autem ad justitiam specialem, quæ est principalis virtus. Justitia vero legalis se extendit ad actus omnium virtutum, ut supra dictum est.[7]

articulus 2. utrum ad observantiam pertineat exhibere cultum et honorem his qui sunt in dignitate constituti

AD SECUNDUM sic proceditur:[1] 1. Videtur quod ad observantiam non pertineat exhibere cultum et honorem his qui sunt in dignitate constituti, quia, ut Augustinus dicit,[2] colere dicimur illas personas quas in quodam honore habemus; et sic idem esse videtur cultus et honor. Inconvenienter ergo determinatur quod observantia exhibet in dignitate constitutis cultum et honorem.

2. Præterea, ad justitiam pertinet reddere debitum; unde et ad observantiam, quæ ponitur justitiæ pars, pertinet. Sed cultum et honorem non debemus omnibus in dignitate constitutis, sed solum his qui super nos prælationem habent. Ergo inconvenienter determinatur quod eis observantia exhibet cultum et honorem.

3. Præterea, superioribus nostris in dignitate constitutis non solum debemus honorem, sed etiam timorem et aliquam munerum largitionem, secundum illud ad *Rom., Reddite omnibus debita: cui tributum, tributum; cui vectigal, vectigal; cui timorem, timorem; cui honorem, honorem.*[3] Debemus etiam eis reverentiam et subjectionem, secundum illud *Hebr. Obedite præpositis vestris, et subjacete eis.*[4] Non ergo convenienter determinatur quod observantia exhibet cultum et honorem.

SED CONTRA est quod Tullius dicit, quod *observantia est per quam homines aliqua dignitate antecedentes quodam cultu et honore dignantur.*[5]

---

[7]2a2æ. 58, 5 & 6
[1]*De duobus præceptis caritatis*

this distinction but simply go to make up personal worth. This is why there is a special virtue bent upon offering honour and homage only to those in authority. Still it is true that one becomes fit for a position of rank through learning, virtue and the like; so the deference which is shown to others because of superiority of any sort engages this same virtue.

3. The function of particular justice in its strict sense is the exact acquittal of a debt. There is no such possibility with regard to the virtuous, to those who exercise authority for our welfare, nor to God or parents. In each of these cases there is no place for particular justice, a principal virtue, but for one of the allied virtues. General justice, as has been said,[7] ranges over the acts of all virtues.

article 2. whether it is the part of respect to offer homage and honour to those in authority

THE SECOND POINT:[1] 1. It does not appear to be the business of respect to pay homage and honour to authority. As Augustine says,[2] we are said to pay homage to the people we hold in honour, so that homage and honour seem the same. Therefore there is no point to maintaining that homage and honour are the tributes of respect to those in authority.

2. In another way, since satisfying obligations is a work of justice, it is also the concern of respect, a part of justice. There is no obligation, however, to pay honour and homage to all who are in positions of authority, but only to those who have authority over us. Consequently there is no proper basis for asserting without qualification that respect pays its tribute to those in authority.

3. Moreover, we owe to superiors not merely honour, but fear as well, and even the bestowal of gifts—*Render therefore to all men their dues. Tribute, to whom tribute is due; custom, to whom custom; fear to whom fear, honour, to whom honour;*[3] reverence and submission as well—*Obey your prelates and be subject to them.*[4] The restriction of the virtue of respect, then, to offering homage and honour is unfounded.

ON THE OTHER HAND there is Cicero's description that *it is through the virtue of respect that persons eminent in some position of authority receive the deference of a certain homage and honour.*[5]

---

[2]*De civ. Dei* X, 1. PL 41, 278
[3]*Romans* 13, 7
[4]*Hebrews* 13, 17
[5]*Rhet.* II, 53

RESPONSIO: Dicendum quod ad eos qui sunt in dignitate constituti pertinet gubernare subditos. Gubernare autem est movere aliquos in debitum finem, sicut nauta gubernat navem, ducendo eam ad portum. Omne autem movens habet excellentiam quamdam et virtutem supra id quod movetur. Unde oportet quod in eo qui est in dignitate constitutus, primo consideretur excellentia status cum quadam potestate in subditos; secundo ipsum gubernationis officium.

Ratione igitur excellentiæ debetur ei honor, qui est quædam recognitio excellentiæ alicujus. Ratione autem officii gubernationis, debetur ei cultus, qui in quodam obsequio consistit, dum scilicet aliquis obedit eorum imperio, et vicem beneficiis eorum pro suo modo rependit.

1. Ad primum ergo dicendum quod in cultu non solum intelligitur honor, sed etiam quæcumque alia quæ pertinent ad decentes actus quibus homo ad alium ordinatur.

2. Ad secundum dicendum quod, sicut supra dictum est,[6] duplex est debitum: unum quidem legale, ad quod reddendum homo lege compellitur; et sic debet homo honorem et cultum his qui sunt in dignitate constituti, prælationem super ipsum habentes. Aliud autem est debitum morale, quod ex quadam honestate debetur; et hoc modo debemus cultum et honorem his qui sunt in dignitate constituti, etiamsi non simus eis subjecti.

3. Ad tertium dicendum quod excellentiæ eorum qui sunt in dignitate constituti debetur honor ratione sublimioris gradus; timor autem ratione potestatis, quam habent ad coercendum; officio vero gubernationis ipsorum debetur obedientia, per quam subditi moventur ad imperium præsidentium; et tributa, quæ sunt quædam stipienda laboris ipsorum.

articulus 3. utrum observantia sit potior virtus quam pietas

AD TERTIUM sic proceditur: 1. Videtur quod observantia sit potior virtus quam pietas. Princeps enim, cui cultus per observantiam exhibetur, comparatur ad patrem, qui pietate colitur, sicut universalis gubernator ad particularem; nam familia, quam pater gubernat, est pars civitatis, quæ

---

[6]2a2æ. 80
[a]*excellentia* throughout means any sort of eminence or superiority. A more exact use is given in 2a2æ. 162, 4.
[b]St Thomas frequently applies such notions from the philosophy of nature (cf 104, 1). Literally the comparison is between an active cause that imparts movement and the passive subject receiving it. 'Influence' is used here to allow for the particular application, which is not to a physical causality but to human relationships—guidance, direction, command.
[c]*excellentia status* recalls the same point in art. 1 ad 2, i.e. that the persons to whom respect is owed receive it not primarily on the basis of their personal worth, but of their position. *Status* can mean any established office or position—civic, military, academic.

REPLY: It is the charge of those placed in a position of authority to govern their subjects. And 'to govern' means to guide others to an appointed goal, somewhat as the sailor 'governs' his ship in steering it to harbour. Now everything exercising influence upon another has an eminence[a] and a form of power higher than that of the recipient.[b] In the instance of one holding authority we should take into consideration, first, his superior status[c] with power over subjects, and secondly, the actual duty of governing them.

On grounds of superiority, he has a right to honour, which means in fact the acknowledgment of another's eminence. On grounds of the task of governing he has a right to homage, which consists in a definite service,[d] namely that his commands be obeyed and his good offices be recompensed in due measure.

Hence: 1. 'Homage' embraces not only honour but also anything else implied in those actions appropriate to one person's subordination to another.

2. As previously made clear,[6] there are two kinds of debt. The first is termed 'legal', in the sense that a person is held by positive law to pay it; and it is in this way that a person is indebted as to honour and homage to those authorities who have actual power over him. The other kind of debt is called 'moral', in the sense that it is owed on the grounds of plain decency.[e] This is the sort of indebtedness obliging us to pay homage and honour to all in authority, even when we are not actually their subjects.

3. Honour is owed to the eminence of those in authority, on the grounds of their superior rank; fear, on the basis of their power of sanctions. Their task of governing gives them a claim to obedience—the response of subjects to the command of those over them—and to tribute, as a kind of remuneration for their labours.

article 3. whether respect has higher standing as a virtue than piety

THE THIRD POINT: 1. Respect seems a more important virtue than piety. The ruler, honoured by the virtue of respect, in comparison to parents, honoured by piety, stands as a universal to a particular governor. For the family, which the parents rule, is but a part of the state, which the ruler

---

[d]Note that in 101, 2 *officium* is made synonyomous with *obsequium*, *cultus* with *honor*. The verbal inconsistency points to the neutrality of the terms themselves. The particular meanings are made clear enough in each context. As noted already, 101, 1, note *h*, *cultus* seems to be the broadest term, expressing what is rendered variously by all the virtues of veneration (cf ad 1); even so in a stricter use it is separable from honour, as this and the following Question indicate.
[e]See Appendix 1.

gubernatur a principe. Sed universalis virtus potior est, et magis ei inferiora subduntur. Ergo observantia est potior virtus quam pietas.

2. Præterea, illi qui sunt in dignitate constituti curam gerunt boni communis. Consanguinei autem pertinent ad bonum privatum, quod est propter bonum commune contemnendum; unde laudabiliter aliqui pro bono communi periculis mortis seipsos exponunt. Ergo observantia, per quam exhibetur cultus his qui sunt in dignitate constituti, est potior virtus quam pietas, quæ exhibet cultum personis sanguine junctis.

3. Præterea, honor et reverentia maxime debetur virtuosis post Deum. Sed virtuosis exhibetur honor et reverentia per observantiæ virtutem, ut dictum est.[1] Ergo observantia est præcipua post religionem.

SED CONTRA est quod præcepta legis dantur de actibus virtutum. Immediate autem post præcepta religionis, quæ pertinent ad primam tabulam, subditur præceptum de honoratione parentum, quod pertinet ad pietatem. Ergo pietas immediate sequitur religionem ordine dignitatis.

RESPONSIO: Dicendum quod personis in dignitate constitutis potest aliquid exhiberi dupliciter. Uno modo in ordine ad bonum commune, puta cum aliquis eis servit in administratione reipublicæ; et hoc jam non pertinet ad observantiam, sed ad pietatem, quæ cultum exhibet non solum patri, sed etiam patriæ.

Alio modo exhibetur aliquid personis in dignitate constitutis pertinens specialiter ad personalem eorum utilitatem vel gloriam; et hoc proprie pertinet ad observantiam, secundum quod a pietate distinguitur.

Et ideo comparatio observantiæ ad pietatem necesse est quod attendatur secundum diversas habitudines diversarum personarum ad nos, quas respicit utraque virtus. Manifestum est autem quod personæ parentum, et eorum qui sunt nobis sanguine conjuncti, substantialius nobis conjunguntur quam personæ quæ sunt in dignitate constitutæ. Magis enim ad substantiam pertinet generatio et educatio, cujus principium est pater, quam exterior gubernatio, cujus principium sunt illi qui in dignitate constituuntur. Et per hoc pietas observantiæ præeminet, inquantum cultum reddit personis magis conjunctis, quibus magis obligamur.

1. Ad primum ergo dicendum quod princeps comparatur ad patrem, sicut universalis virtus ad particularem, quantum ad exteriorem gubernationem, non autem quantum ad hoc quod pater est principium generationis;

---

[1] art. 1 ad 2
[a] The allusion is to the two tables of stone given to Moses, cf *Exodus* 31, 18; *Deuteronomy* 5, 22. The medievals thought that the first table contained the first three commandments, about duties towards God; the second, the other seven, about duties to neighbour; cf 1a2æ. 100, 8.

governs. A virtue with a universal scope is the more important and has other virtues under its control. Respect, then, is the higher of the two.

2. Further, while people in authority are engaged upon the public welfare, relatives form part of our personal well-being. This is to be set aside in favour of the public good; so much so that some men laudably endanger their own lives for it. Respect, with its concern for serving those in authority, is, consequently, a more important virtue than piety, with its concern for relatives.

3. Moreover, under God the virtuous have chief claim to honour and reverence. Since, as noted above,[1] the virtue of respect looks to this, it is, after religion, the chief virtue.

ON THE OTHER HAND acts of the virtues are laid down in the commandments of the Law, and right after the precepts regarding religion, which form the first tablet,[a] comes that of honouring parents, the concern of piety. In order of rank, then, piety comes right after religion.

REPLY: There are two possible ways to render service to those in authority First with a view to the public good; an example is assistance given to their civil administration. When this is the case, it is not respect that is engaged but rather piety itself, the bearing of which is not solely towards parents but towards country as well.[b]

In another way those in authority can be the recipients of a particular homage towards their personal well-being and glory. Here respect as distinct from piety comes into play.

Consequently any comparison between respect and piety has necessarily to look to the various relationships which the different people encompassed by each virtue have to us. Clearly the bond uniting us to parents and relatives is more deeply rooted than the one relating us to people in authority; birth and upbringing, which have their source in our parents, form more of a part of our very being than does the direction of our life in the community, of which those in authority are the source. Herein is the reason why piety has precedence over respect—it pays homage to those closer to us, who by that fact have a more pressing claim on us.[c]

Hence: 1. The comparison of ruler to parents as of a universal to a particular source of power applies as far as directing our life in the

---

[b] An echo of Cicero and of all who have shared a lofty sense of public service. Compare this point also with 101, 3 ad 3; perhaps some inconsistency is involved.
[c] A new dimension is given here (and in ad 3) to the principles regulating indebtedness; the closeness to the debtor is added to superiority and beneficence (cf 101, 1). A similar point is made in connection with love of neighbour in 2a2æ. 26, 7.

sic enim comparatur ad ipsum virtus divina, quæ est omnium productiva in esse.

2. Ad secundum dicendum quod ex ea parte qua personæ in dignitate constitutæ ordinantur ad bonum commune, non pertinet earum cultus ad observantiam, sed ad pietatem, ut dictum est.[2]

3. Ad tertium dicendum quod exhibitio honoris vel cultus non solum est proportionanda personæ cui exhibetur secundum se consideratæ, sed etiam secundum quod ad exhibentes comparatur. Quamvis ergo virtuosi secundum se considerati sint magis digni honore quam personæ parentum, tamen filii magis obligantur propter beneficia suscepta ab ipsis parentibus et conjunctionem naturalem ad exhibendum cultum et honorem parentibus quam extraneis virtuosis.

community is concerned, but not as to parents being a source of life. Here the only apt term of comparison is the divine power, the source of all existence.

2. In so far as those in authority are involved with the public good, homage to them, as has been pointed out,[2] is the province, not of respect, but of patriotism.

3. Honour and homage ought to be measured not only to the personal worth of the recipient, but also to his relationship to those offering them. While, then, the virtuous may be personally more worthy of honour than our parents, still children are more obliged to pay homage and honour to parents than to the virtuous stranger, on the basis of benefits received and of ties of flesh and blood.

---

[2] In the Reply

DEINDE CONSIDERANDUM EST de partibus observantiæ:
et primo de dulia quæ exhibet honorem et cætera ad hoc pertinentia;
secundo, de obedientia, per quam earum obeditur imperio.

Quæstio 103. de dulia

Circa primum quæruntur quatuor:
1. utrum honor sit aliquid spirituale, vel corporale;
2. utrum honor debeatur solis superioribus;
3. utrum dulia, cujus est exhibere honorem et cultum superioribus, sit specialis virtus a latria distincta;
4. utrum per species distinguatur.

articulus 1. utrum honor importet aliquid corporale

AD PRIMUM sic proceditur:[1] 1. Videtur quod honor non importet aliquid corporale. Honor enim est exhibitio reverentiæ in testimonium virtutis, ut potest accipi a Philosopho in *Ethic*.[2] Sed exhibitio reverentiæ est aliquid spirituale; revereri enim est actus timoris, ut supra habitum est.[3] Ergo honor est aliquid spirituale.

2. Præterea, secundum Philosophum in *Ethic.*, *honor est præmium virtutis*.[4] Virtutis autem, quæ principaliter in spiritualibus consistit, præmium non est aliquid corporale, cum præmium sit potius merito. Ergo honor non consistit in corporalibus.

3. Præterea, honor a laude distinguitur, et etiam a gloria. Sed laus, et gloria in exterioribus consistunt. Ergo honor consistit in interioribus et* spiritualibus.

SED CONTRA est quod Hieronymus, exponens illud 1 *Ad Tim.* 5, *Viduas*

---

*Piana omits *et*
[1] cf *In Ethic.* I, lect. 18
[3] 2a2æ. 81, 2 ad 1
[a] See above, 102, 1, note *b*.
[2] *Ethics* I, 5. 1095b26; cf VIII, 8. 1159a22
[4] *Ethics* IV, 3. 1123b35

[b] The reason for considering *dulia* at all is that it forms part of a traditional terminology deriving from St Augustine's *City of God* as cited in art. 3 obj. 1 and *sed contra*. In its original sense (cf art. 3 & 4) as the right attitude of slaves or servants, *dulia* would now simply be a curiosity. The Question does, however, make precise the idea of honour—as honouring—and is a commentary on the varying ways of honouring superiors, especially as the appropriate virtues include an externalizing of an inner attitude (cf the parallel consideration in 81, 7). Here too St Thomas

NEXT, THE PARTS of the virtue of respect:[a]

> first, *dulia*, the virtue of respectful service,[b] which shows honour and similar signs to persons over us (103);
> second, obedience, through which their precepts are observed (104).

Question 103. *dulia*, the virtue of respectful service

Here there are four points of inquiry:

1. whether honour is something purely mental or also external;
2. whether only those above us have a right to honour;
3. whether *dulia*, with its concern to pay honour and homage to superiors, is a specific virtue, differing from *latria*;
4. whether it has its own specific types.

article 1. whether honour includes some tangible sign

THE FIRST POINT:[1] 1. Honour, it would seem, does not include any outward element. We gather from Aristotle's *Ethics*[2] that it means showing reverence as an acknowledgment of virtue.[c] Since, as we hold,[3] to revere is to fear, to offer reverence is a mental attitude. So, therefore, is honouring.

2. Further, another remark of Aristotle shows that *honour is the reward of virtue*.[4] Virtue itself being chiefly something interior, its reward is nothing material, since a reward should always surpass the title to it. Honour, then, is not made up of externals.

3. Further, honour is something different from either praise or glory. Both of these being outward, honour is inward, something of the soul.

ON THE OTHER HAND commenting on the verse, *Let the priests that rule*

---

explains the use of the terms *dulia, hyperdulia* and *latria* to distinguish the kinds of veneration shown to the saints, the Mother of God, and God himself respectively.
[c]Honour is closely connected with virtue in Aristotle's *Ethics*. The happiness of man consists in virtuous activity; the moral ideal he considers is not related to a transcendent end, God, but consists in the moral beauty and nobility (*honestas*) of virtue itself. Honour by others is the sign that a person has attained a state of moral well-being and harmony. St Thomas uses Aristotelean notions, but they are fitted into a theological view of virtue and moral life that Aristotle's *Ethics* does not share. See also 2a2æ. 129 on magnanimity. A. A. Gauthier, *Aristote, L'Éthique à Nicomaque* (2d ed., 2 vol. in 4, Louvain, 1970) I, 128-31; 241-4; idem, *Magnanimité* (Paris, 1951).

honora quæ vere viduæ sunt, et qui bene præsunt presbyteri, duplici honore digni habeantur,[5] etc., dicit. *Honor in præsentiarum vel pro͟ͅeleemosyna, vel pro*† *munere accipitur.*[6] Utrumque autem houm ad corporalia pertinet. Ergo honor in corporalibus consistit.

RESPONSIO: Dicendum quod honor testificationem quamdam importat de excellentia alicujus. Unde homines qui volunt honorari, testimonium suæ excellentiæ quærunt, ut per Philosophum patet in *Ethic.*[7] Testimonium autem redditur vel coram Deo, vel coram hominibus. Coram Deo quidem, qui inspector est cordium, testimonium conscientiæ sufficit. Et ideo honor quoad Deum potest consistere in solo interiori motu cordis, dum scilicet aliquis recogitat vel Dei excellentiam, vel etiam alterius hominis coram Deo.

Sed quoad homines aliquis non potest testimonium ferre nisi per aliqua signa exteriora vel verbis, puta cum aliquis ore pronuntiat excellentiam alicujus; vel factis, sicut inclinationibus, obviationibus, et aliis hujusmodi, vel etiam exterioribus rebus, puta in munerum oblatione, aut imaginum institutione, vel aliis hujusmodi. Et secundum hoc honor in signis exterioribus et corporalibus consistit.

1. Ad primum ergo dicendum quod reverentia non est idem quod honor. Sed ex una parte est primum motivum ad honorandum, inquantum scilicet aliquis ex reverentia quam habet ad aliquem, eum honorat; ex alia vero parte est honoris finis, inquantum scilicet aliquis ad hoc honoratur ut in reverentia habeatur ab aliis.

2. Ad secundum dicendum quod, sicut Philosophus ibidem dicit,[8] honor non est sufficiens virtutis præmium; sed nihil potest esse in humanis rebus et corporalibus majus honore, inquantum scilicet ipsæ corporales res sunt signa demonstrativa excellentis virtutis. Est autem debitum bono et pulchro, ut manifestetur, secundum illud *Matt.*, *Neque accendunt lucernam el ponunt eam sub modio, sed super candelabrum, ut luceat omnibus qui in domo sunt.*[9] Et pro tanto præmium virtutis dicitur honor.

3. Ad tertium dicendum quod laus distinguitur ab honore dupliciter. Uno modo, quia laus consistit in solis signis verborum, honor autem in quibuscumque exterioribus signis, et secundum hoc laus in honore includitur. Alio modo, quia per exhibitionem honoris testimonium reddimus de excellentia bonitatis alicujus absolute; sed per laudem testificamur de bonitate alicujus in ordine ad finem, sicut laudamus bene operantem propter finem. Honor autem est etiam optimorum, quæ non ordinantur ad finem, sed jam sunt in fine, ut patet per Philosophum in 1 *Ethic.*[10] Gloria autem est effectus honoris et laudis, quia ex hoc quod testificamur de bonitate alicujus, clarescit bonitas ejus in notitia plurimorum,

---

†Piana omits *pro*

well be esteemed worthy of double honour,[5] etc., Jerome states, *Honour here stands either for alms or for repayment.*[6] Since both involve outward actions, so does honour.

REPLY: To honour means to attest to someone's superiority. Thus, as Aristotle shows,[7] people seeking honour are looking for a testimony te their personal worth. Now there is one kind of witness to truth before God and another before men. Since God is *the searcher of hearts*, it is possible to honour God simply interiorly, for example by meditating on his eminence or even on the godliness of another person.

Where, however, it is a question of giving testimony before men, there has to be some outward token—words, when we praise the merits of another; actions, such as bows, salutations, etc.; even objects, as when presentations are made, medals struck, etc. This is the sense in which honour consists in externals.

Hence: 1. Reverence is not identical with honour. On the one side it is a primary motive for doing honour to someone, namely because we hold him in reverence; on the other, it is one of the purposes for doing honour, namely in that we honour a person in order that others will reverence him.

2. In the same work[8] Aristotle also makes the point that honour is not an adequate reward for virtue; there is just no better action or object than honour at our disposal, and its outward marks stand as tokens attesting to superior virtue. Indeed goodness and beauty should be made manifest—*Neither do men light a candle and put it under a bushel, but upon a candlestick that it may shine to all that are in the house.*[9] This is the sense in which honour is called the reward of virtue.

3. Praise and honour differ in two ways.[d] The first is that signs of praise consist in words alone; of honour, in any sort of outward mark. On this basis 'honour' includes 'praise'. The second difference is that in honouring someone we offer unqualified testimony to his outstanding worth; by praise, we attest his worth in relation to some goal, praising him for his effectiveness. As Aristotle notes,[10] honour is given for the loftiest deeds, not because they are useful but just because of their own worth.

Glory is rather a result of both honour and praise, in the sense that from our testimonial to someone's good qualities these become clearly

---

[5] *1 Timothy* 5, 17
[6] Ep. 123. PL 22, 1049
[7] *Ethics* VIII, 8. 1159a22
[8] *Ethics* IV, 3. 1124a7
[9] *Matthew* 5, 15
[10] *Ethics* I, 20, 1102a1
[d] cf 1a2æ. 2, 2 & 3.

et hoc importat nomen gloriæ. Nam gloria dicitur, quasi claria, unde *Ad Rom.*[11] dicit quædam glossa Ambrosii quod *gloria est clara cum laude notitia.*[12]

articulus 2. utrum honor proprie debeatur superioribus

AD SECUNDUM sic proceditur:[1] 1. Videtur quod honor non proprie debeatur superioribus. Angelus enim est superior quolibet homine viatore, secundum illud *Matt.*, *Qui minor est in regno cœlorum, major est Joanne Baptista.*[2] Sed angelus prohibuit Joannem volentem se honorare, ut patet *Apoc.*[3] Ergo honor non debetur superioribus.

2. Præterea, honor debetur alicui in testimonium virtutis, ut dictum est.[4] Sed quandoque contingit quod superiores non sunt virtuosi. Ergo eis non debetur honor, sicut nec dæmonibus, qui tamen superiores nobis sunt ordine naturæ.

3. Præterea, Apostolus dicit *ad Rom.*, *Honore invicem prævenientes;*[5] et 1 *Petr.*, *Omnes honorate.*[6] Sed hoc non esset servandum, si solis superioribus honor deberetur. Ergo honor non debetur proprie superioribus.

4. Præterea, 1 dicitur quod Tobias habebat *decem talenta ex his quibus erat honoratus a rege;*[7] legitur etiam *Esther* quod Assuerus honoravit Mardochæum, et coram eo fecit clamari, *Hoc honore dignus est quem rex honorare voluerit.*[8] Ergo honor etiam exhibetur inferioribus; et ita videtur quod honor non debetur proprie superioribus.

SED CONTRA est quod Philosophus dicit in *Ethic.* quod *honor debetur optimis.*[9]

RESPONSIO: Dicendum quod, sicut supra dictum est,[10] honor nihil aliud est quam quædam protestatio de excellentia bonitatis alicujus. Potest autem alicujus excellentia considerari, non solum per comparationem ad honorantem, ut scilicet sit excellentior eo qui honorat,* sed etiam secundum se, vel per comparationem ad aliquos alios. Et secundum hoc honor semper debetur alicui propter aliquam excellentiam vel superioritatem. Non enim oportet quod ille qui honoratur sit excellentior honorante, sed forte quibusdam aliis vel etiam ipso honorante quantum ad aliquid, et non simpliciter.

---

*Leonine: *honoratur*
[11]*Romans* 16, 27 is the verse that has this gloss
[1]cf 2a2æ. 63, 3. III *Sent.* 9, 2, 3. *In Ethic.* IV, lect. 9
[3]*Apocalypse* 22, 8. Cf. art. 1, obj. 1   [5]*Romans* 12, 10
[7]*Tobias* 1, 16   [8]*Esther* 6, 11
[9]*Ethics* I, 12. 1101b22   [10]art. 1

[12]*Glossa ordinaria*
[2]*Matthew* 11, 11
[6]1 Peter 2, 17

known to many. This is what 'glory' suggests, namely 'clarity', as the *Gloss*, from Ambrose on *Romans*,[11] states, *glory is renown, brilliant and acclaimed.*[12]

article 2. whether, strictly speaking, we should honour only those who are superior to us

THE SECOND POINT:[1] 1. It seems that honour is not the due of superiors exclusively. From *Matthew—He that is lesser in the kingdom of heaven is greater than John the Baptist*[2]—we have it that an angel is above any human wayfarer.[a] Yet when John attempted to honour him, the angel forbade it.[3] Honour, then, is not owed to those above us.

2. Further, while honour, as we have mentioned,[4] is owed to anyone as a tribute to virtue, it at times happens that superiors are not virtuous. Honour is no more due to them than to the devils for their superiority in nature to us.

3. Further, the precept contained in St Paul—*With honour preventing one another*[5]—and in St Peter—*Honour all men*[6]—would not be observed were honour due only to those above us. Therefore it is not theirs exclusively.

4. Further, there are clear cases of those of lower station receiving honour. Tobias, who *had ten talents of silver of that with which he had been honoured by the king*;[7] and Mordecai, honoured by Ashuerus, who ordered proclaimed in his presence, *This honour is he worthy of whom the king hath a mind to honour.*[8] Apparently, then, it is not owed to superiors alone.

ON THE OTHER HAND there is Aristotle's statement, *honour belongs by right to the best of men.*[9]

REPLY: As we have stated,[10] the exact meaning of honour is an acknowledgment of someone's outstanding worth. Now someone's good qualities can be counted outstanding not only in comparison to the one doing honour—as though the one honoured must always excel the one doing honour—but also in their own right or by comparison to others. From this point of view excellence or superiority in any line gives a person a claim to honour. There is nothing to say that the one honoured must be better than the one doing him honour; it is enough that he be superior either to others or to the one doing him honour in some respect, even if not altogether.

---

[a]*viator* (from *via*, way) is one still on life's journey; the *comprehensor* (cf 3a. 15, 10) is one who has reached the goal of life, the vision of God (cf *Philippians*, 3, 11–13).

1. Ad primum ergo dicendum quod angelus prohibuit Joannem non a quacumque honoratione, sed ab honoratione adorationis latriæ, quæ debetur Deo; vel etiam ab honoratione duliæ, ut ostenderet ipsius Joannis dignitatem, qua per Christum erat angelis adæquatus *secundum spem gloriæ filiorum Dei*.[11] Et ideo nolebat ab eo honorari tanquam superior.

2. Ad secundum dicendum quod si prælati sunt mali, non honorantur propter excellentiam propriæ virtutis sed propter excellentiam dignitatis, secundum quam sunt Dei ministri. Et etiam in eis honoratur tota communitas cui præsunt. Dæmones autem sunt irrevocabiliter mali, et pro inimicis habendi magis quam honorandi.

3. Ad tertium dicendum quod in quolibet invenitur aliquid ex quo potest aliquis eum superiorem reputare, secundum illud *Ad Philip. In humilitate superiores invicem arbitrantes*.[12] Et secundum hoc etiam omnes se invicem debent honore prævenire.

4. Ad quartum dicendum quod privatæ personæ interdum honorantur a regibus, non quia sint eis superiores secundum ordinem dignitatis, sed propter aliquam excellentiam virtutis ipsarum. Et secundum hoc honorati sunt Tobias et Mardochæus a regibus.

articulus 3. *utrum dulia sit specialis virtus a latria distincta*

AD TERTIUM sic proceditur:[1] 1. Videtur quod dulia non sit specialis virtus a latria distincta. Quia super illud Psalm., *Domine Deus meus, in te speravi*, dicit glossa,[2] *Domine omnium per potentiam, cui debetur dulia; Deus per creationem, cui debetur latria*.[3] Sed non est distincta virtus quæ ordinatur in Deum, secundum quod est Dominus, et secundum quod est Deus. Ergo dulia non est virtus distincta a latria.

2. Præterea, secundum Philosophum, in *Ethic.*, *amari simile est ei quod est honorari*.[4] Sed eadem est virtus caritatis qua amatur Deus et qua amatur proximus. Ergo dulia, qua honoratur proximus, non est alia virtus a latria, qua honoratur Deus.

3. Præterea, idem est motus quo aliquis movetur in imaginem et in rem cujus est imago. Sed per duliam honoratur homo, inquantum est ad Dei

---

[11] *Romans* 5, 2   [12] *Philippians* 2, 3
[1] III *Sent.* 9, 2, 1; *In Psalm.* 40
[2] *Psalm* 7, 1
[3] *Interlinearis; Lombardi.* PL 191, 111
[4] *Ethics* VIII, 8. 1159a16
[b] For the theological connotations of *irrevocabiliter*, see 1a. 63, 4; 64, 2.
[c] This is not a pious exhortation to invent reasons for respecting others. Indebtedness, the basis for the virtues of respect, is universal among men. Those who are in some obviously superior station are themselves indebted to their inferiors, at least to the extent of acknowledging that the same divine beneficence that has given them

Hence: 1. The angel did not forbid outright that John do him honour, but that he offer the adoration due to God alone. Then again he may have forestalled John from showing honour like a slave, in order to point up John's own dignity by which through Christ John was put on a par with the angels in *the likeness of the hope of glory of the children of God*.[10] Wherefore the angel refused to be venerated as John's superior.

2. Where those in authority are wicked, they are not honoured for their own superior virtue, but for their superior rank as representatives of God. In their person, as well, honour is shown to the whole community over which they rule. The devils, on the other hand, are irreversibly[b] wicked and are to be treated with enmity, not honour.

3. In every man there is some basis why another can look on him as superior; *In humility, let each esteem others better than themselves*.[11] In this sense we all are bound to outdo each other in showing honour.[c]

4. Private individuals are sometimes honoured by royalty, not as being superior in rank, but because of high virtue. This was the case with Tobias and Mordecai.

article 3. whether dulia is a specific virtue distinct from latria

THE THIRD POINT:[1] 1. *Dulia*, the virtue of respectful service, is apparently not a virtue specifically distinct from *latria* or adoration. A gloss on the Psalm, *O Lord, my God, in thee have I put my trust*,[2] adds, *Oh Lord over all by power, to whom dulia is due; Oh God of all by creation, to whom adoration is due*.[3] Even as there are not distinct virtues relating us to God as Lord and as God, neither are *dulia* and *latria* distinct.

2. Further, Aristotle notes that *receiving honour is like receiving love*.[4] Since, then, the charity by which God and neighbour receive our love is the one virtue, so the virtue by which each receives our honour is one.

3. Further, the response to an image and to the one it reflects is one. Now *dulia* pays honour to a person as the image of God, since *Wisdom*

---

superiority has also given to others another sort of excellence. It is clear that in the complexity of modern life no man can claim to maintain his station alone; he needs the perhaps less conspicuous gifts of others; their services, their trades, their labours are necessary to maintain the economic, cultural, or social setting of his superiority. A further implication is that the virtues of respect are not only the virtues of inferiors. Parents must respect their children; those who rule, their subjects. All are debtors to each other, because all are indebted to the same divine beneficence. As superiors give due recognition to this, they will show respect for those who are below them, and who manifest, continue or further those very qualities by which one man is another's superior. The love of charity does not efface the order of rank traced into human life; the virtues of respect implement charity by honouring the debts of mutual respect incumbent on all.

imaginem factus; dicitur enim *Sap.* de impiis, quod *non judicaverunt honorem animarum sanctarum, quoniam Deus creavit hominem inexterminabilem, et ad imaginem suæ similitudinis fecit illum.*[5] Ergo dulia non est alia virtus a latria, qua honoratur Deus.

SED CONTRA est quod Augustinus dicit quod *alia est servitus quæ debetur hominibus, secundum quam præcipit Apostolus servos dominis suis subditos esse, quæ scilicet græce dulia dicitur, alia vero latria quæ dicitur servitus pertinens ad colendum Deum.*[6]

RESPONSIO: Dicendum quod secundum ea quæ supra dicta sunt,[7] ubi est alia ratio debiti, ibi necesse est quod sit alia virtus, quæ debitum reddat. Alia autem ratione debetur servitus Deo et homini sicut et alia ratione dominium competit Deo et homini. Nam Deus plenarium et principale dominium habet respectu totius et cujuslibet creaturæ, quæ totaliter ejus subjicitur potestati; homo autem participat quamdam similitudinem divini dominii secundum quod habet particularem potestatem super aliquem hominem vel super aliquam creaturam. Et ideo dulia, quæ debitam servitutem exhibet homini dominanti, alia virtus est a latria, quæ exhibet debitam servitutem divino dominio.

Et est quædam observantiæ species, quia per observantiam honoramus quascumque personas dignitate præcellentes; per duliam autem proprie sumptam servi dominos suos venerantur, dulia enim græce servitus dicitur.

1. Ad primum ergo dicendum quod sicut religio per excellentiam dicitur pietas inquantum Deus est per excellentiam pater, ita etiam latria per excellentiam dicitur dulia inquantum Deus excellenter est dominus. Non autem creatura participat potentiam creandi, ratione cujus Deo debetur latria. Et ideo glossa illa distinxit attribuens latriam Deo secundum creationem, quæ creaturæ non communicatur; duliam vero secundum dominium, quod creaturæ communicatur.

2. Ad secundum dicendum quod ratio diligendi proximum Deus est; non enim per caritatem diligimus in proximo nisi Deum. Et ideo eadem caritas est qua diligitur Deus et proximus. Sunt tamen aliæ amicitiæ

---

[5]*Wisdom* 2, 22   [6]*De civ. Dei* x, 1. PL 41, 278   [7]101, 3
[a]See above 102, 1, note *b.*
[b]cf 1a. 45, 1 & 5; 103, 3, 4 & 6.
[c]cf 23, 5; 25, 1; 26, 2. The meaning of the love of charity is not that the human person is regarded as an object, the occasion for loving God. Rather, by the communication of his life to others, God has made it to be a primary quality of the person that he is 'of God'. The divine love has created the circle that makes charity one; in loving God we love him in himself and in others; and in loving others we love God because they are his.
[d]cf 23, 1, where charity is described as a kind of friendship; this is why the term

says of the wicked, *They esteemed not the honour of holy souls, for God created man incorruptible, and to the image of his own likeness he made him.*[5] Therefore *dulia* is not a virtue distinct from *latria* which honours God.

ON THE OTHER HAND Augustine writes, *The service due to men and the reason for St Paul's precept that slaves be subject to their masters is called* dulia *in Greek, and is different from* latria, *the service belonging to the worship of God.*[6]

REPLY: As we have already established,[7] wherever there is a different basis of indebtedness, the virtue respecting the debt is different. Service is owed to God and to man for reasons that differ even as dominion belongs to God and to man in different ways. God's dominion is absolute and primary over all creation and every creature in it, since everything is completely subordinated to his power. A man shares a limited likeness to God's control, inasmuch as he holds some particular power either over another person or over some creature. Therefore *dulia*, which pays the service due a man because he is master, is a virtue different from *latria* with its offering of the service due to God's lordship over all.

Dulia is one of the species of the virtue of respect, this being the virtue by which we show honour to all persons of superior rank, and in its strict sense *dulia* is the virtue by which slaves show respect to their masters; 'slavery' in Greek is *dulia*.[a]

Hence: 1. Religion is termed piety par excellence because of God's pre-eminence as a father; similarly *latria* is *dulia* par excellence because God is lord of lords. No creature takes part in God's creative power, the reason why adoration is his due. That is the point of the distinction in the gloss, assigning adoration to God on the basis of his uncommunicated creative act; *dulia*, to the creature on the basis of a dominion in which he receives a share.[b]

2. There is one virtue of charity towards God and neighbour because God is the reason for loving our neighbour; by charity we are really loving God in our neighbour.[c] Apart from charity, however, there are also other forms of friendship, differing from charity and based on the various motives for loving our fellows.[d] In a way somewhat similar the bases for

---

amicitia is introduced here. *Amicitia* in the vocabulary of St Thomas has a broader meaning than the word 'friendship'; it is applied to any form of upright relationship between human beings (cf 26, 7 and above 101, 3, note *f*); it is also the name of the virtue of friendliness (see below, Question 114). Note also that in St Thomas's theology charity does not obliterate the meaning or value of other human relationships (26, 7) nor do away with the place of human virtues regulating these relationships (cf 1a2æ. 65, 2 & 3).

differentes a caritate secundum alias rationes quibus homines amantur. Et similiter cum sit alia ratio serviendi Deo et homini, aut honorandi utrumque, non est eadem virtus latria et dulia.

3. Ad tertium dicendum quod motus qui est in imaginem inquantum est imago refertur in rem cujus est imago; non tamen omnis motus qui est in imaginem refertur in eam inquantum est imago; et ideo quandoque est alius motus specie in imaginem et motus in rem. Sic ergo dicendum est quod honor vel subjectio duliæ respicit absolute quamdam hominis dignitatem; licet enim secundum illam dignitatem sit homo ad imaginem vel similitudinem Dei, non tamen semper homo, quando reverentiam alteri exhibet, refert hoc actu in Deum.

Vel dicendum quod motus qui est in imaginem quodammodo est in rem, non tamen motus qui est in rem oportet quod sit in imaginem. Et ideo reverentia quæ exhibetur alicui, inquantum est imago Dei, redundat quodammodo in Deum. Alia tamen est reverentia quæ ipsi Deo exhibetur, quæ nullo modo pertinet ad ejus imaginem.

articulus 4. utrum dulia habeat diversas species

AD QUARTUM sic proceditur:[1] 1. Videtur quod dulia habet diversas species. Per duliam enim exhibetur honor proximo. Diversa autem ratione honorantur diversi proximi, sicut rex, pater et magister, ut patet per Philosophum.[2] Cum ergo diversa ratio objecti diversificet speciem virtutis, videtur quod dulia dividatur in virtutes specie differentes.

2. Præterea, medium differt specie ab extremis, sicut pallidum ab albo et nigro. Sed hyperdulia videtur esse medium inter latriam et duliam; exhibetur enim creaturis quæ habent specialem affinitatem ad Deum, sicut beatæ Virgini inquantum est mater Dei. Ergo videtur quod duliæ sint species differentes, una quidem dulia simpliciter, alia vero hyperdulia.

3. Præterea, sicut in creatura rationali invenitur imago Dei ratione cujus honoratur, ita etiam in creatura irrationali invenitur vestigium Dei. Sed alia ratio similitudinis importatur in nomine imaginis et in nomine vestigii. Ergo etiam oportet secundum hoc diversas species duliæ attendi, præsertim cum quibusdam irrationabilibus creaturis honor exhibeatur, sicut ligno sanctæ crucis et aliis hujusmodi.

SED CONTRA est quod dulia contra latriam dividitur. Latria autem non dividitur per diversas species. Ergo nec dulia.

---

[1] cf III *Sent.* 9, 2, 2   [2] *Ethics* IX, 2. 1165a14
[e] See 1a. 93 on the theology of the image of God.

serving or paying homage to God and to another human being are different; so then are the virtues of *latria* and *dulia*.

3. True enough, regard for an image as image is really regard for what it reflects; but since not every reaction to an image is one to it as image, there are times when the response to an image and to its exemplar are specifically different. Thus honour or the subjection of *dulia* are attitudes towards a particular dignity in a person taken on his own merits, and even though that eminent quality in him is in fact a reflection of God, still the one who reveres the person does not always avert to God at all.

Even granted that in some way the response to an image is also one to its exemplar, still not every response to an exemplar *ipso facto* extends to its image. Accordingly, reverence shown to another as God's image is somehow also reverence for God; but there is a separate reverence towards God himself without reference to his image.[e]

article 4. whether there are many types of dulia

THE FOURTH POINT:[1] 1. Apparently there are differing types of *dulia*. Through it honour is offered to our fellow man and, as Aristotle points out,[2] there are different grounds for honouring different people—the king, for instance, parents, teachers, etc. Since a different value in the objective makes for a different species of virtue,[a] it would seem that *dulia* should be divided into specifically distinct virtues.

2. Further, a mean differs in kind from its extremes; grey, for example, from white and black. Midway between *latria* and *dulia* we apparently have *hyperdulia*, since this is offered to creatures having some exceptional closeness to God, for example, to the Blessed Virgin, his mother. Does this, then, not indicate distinct species of *dulia*, namely the ordinary and the exceptional?

3. Further, something like the image of God which is in creatures of intelligence and is the reason for showing them honour, there is in subrational creatures a trace of God.[b] Since honour is indeed shown to such beings—to the wood of the Cross for instance—it seems there should be different types of *dulia* corresponding to the difference in likeness to God connoted by the terms 'image' and 'trace.'

ON THE OTHER HAND since its counterpart, *latria*, is not broken down into species, neither should *dulia* be.

---

[a]This principle, applied in the second half of the Reply, is constantly used in the *Secunda Pars*. For explanation, see 1a. 77, 3; 1a2æ. 18, 2; 54, 2; 72, 1; above 101, 3 note *d*; also Vol. 18 of this series, Appendix 11.
[b]For the distinction between 'image' and 'trace', cf 1a. 93, 2 & 6. Vol. 13, ed. E. Hill.

RESPONSIO: Dicendum quod dulia potest accipi dupliciter. Uno modo communiter, secundum quod exhibet reverentiam cuicumque homini ratione cujuscumque excellentiæ et sic continet sub se pietatem et observantiam, et quamcumque hujusmodi virtutem quæ homini reverentiam exhibet. Et secundum hoc habebit partes specie diversas.

Alio modo potest sumi stricte, prout secundum eam reverentiam exhibet servus domino, nam dulia servitus dicitur, ut dictum est.[3] Et secundum hoc non dividitur in diversas species, sed est una specierum observantiæ, quam Tullius ponit,[4] eo quod alia ratione servus revereatur dominum, miles ducem, discipulus magistrum, et sic de aliis hujusmodi.

1. Ad primum ergo dicendum quod ratio illa procedit de dulia communiter sumpta.

2. Ad secundum dicendum quod hyperdulia est potissima species duliæ communiter sumptæ; maxima enim reverentia debetur homini ex affinitate quam habet ad Deum.

3. Ad tertium dicendum quod creaturæ irrationali in se consideratæ non debetur ab homine aliqua subjectio vel honor quin potius omnis talis creatura est naturaliter homini subjecta. Quod autem crux Christi honoretur, hoc fit eodem honore quo Christus honoratur; sicut purpura regis honoratur eodem honore quo rex, ut Damascenus dicit.[5]

---

[3]art. 3
[4]*Rhet.* II, 53
[5]*De fide orthodoxa* IV, 3. PG 94, 1105. St John Damascene (d. 749), the last Greek Father; regarded by some as the first systematic theologian. This work was discovered by the medievals in the 13th century and had marked influence, e.g. on the analysis of the human act in 1a2æ. 8–17 and in the *Tertia Pars*.

RESPECTFUL SERVICE

REPLY: The term *dulia* admits of two senses. One is generic and applies to showing reverence towards all sorts of people, whatever their particular superiority. So taken its meaning includes piety, respect and all the virtues concerned with reverential attitudes towards humans. In this sense *dulia* clearly has specifically distinct parts.[c]
Or it can have a restricted sense, corresponding to its literal meaning, 'slavery',[3] and signifying the submissive attitude of slave for master. So taken, rather than containing species under it, *dulia* is itself one of the species of *respect* in Cicero's list:[4] and justifiably, since the slave reveres his master, the soldier his commander, the pupil his teacher, etc., all for different reasons.

Hence: 1. This argument takes *dulia* in its generic sense.

2. It is quite true that *hyperdulia* is the supreme species of *dulia* taken in a broad sense. Nearness to God gives a person a claim to the highest sort of reverence.[d]

3. Neither honour nor submission is owed by any human being to a non-rational creature as such; instead it is natural for every such creature to be subject to man. When the Cross is venerated, it is with a veneration given to Christ himself,[e] even as it is the king who is honoured in the salute to his colours; this John Damascene points out.[5]

---

[c] cf above 102, 1, note *b*. If *dulia* be taken as a general virtue, i.e. as a term designating all the virtues of respect and veneration, then the virtues mentioned would be its subjective parts. This is the way prudence is understood in 2a2æ. 47, when its species or subjective parts are set forth.
[d] cf 3a. 25, 5.
[e] cf 3a. 25, 4.

Quæstio 104. de obedientia

DEINDE CONSIDERANDUM EST de obedientia. Et circa hoc quæruntur sex:

1. utrum homo debeat obedire homini;
2. utrum obedientia sit specialis virtus;
3. de comparatione ejus ad alteras virtutes;
4. utrum Deo sit in omnibus obediendum;
5. utrum subditi suis prælatis teneantur in omnibus obedire;
6. utrum fideles teneantur sæcularibus potestatibus obedire.

articulus 1. *utrum unus homo teneatur alteri obedire*

AD PRIMUM sic proceditur:[1] 1. Videtur quod unus homo non teneatur alteri obedire. Non est enim aliquid faciendum contra institutionem divinam. Sed hoc habet divina institutio ut homo suo consilio regatur, secundum illud *Eccli.*, *Deus ab initio constituit hominem, et reliquit illum in manu consilii sui.*[2] Ergo non tenetur unus homo alteri obedire.

2. Præterea, si aliquis alicui teneretur obedire oporteret quod haberet voluntatem præcipientis tanquam regulam suæ actionis. Sed sola divina voluntas quæ semper est recta est regula humanæ actionis. Ergo non tenetur homo obedire nisi Deo.

3. Præterea servitia quanto sunt magis gratuita tanto sunt magis accepta. Sed id quod homo ex debito facit, non est gratuitum. Si ergo homo tenetur ex debito aliis obedire in bonis operibus faciendis, ex hoc ipso redderetur minus acceptabile opus bonum quod ex obedientia fieret. Non ergo tenetur homo alteri obedire.

SED CONTRA est quod præcipitur *Ad Heb.*, *Obedite præpositis vestris, et subjacete eis.*[3]

RESPONSIO: Dicendum quod sicut actiones rerum naturalium procedunt ex potentiis naturalibus, ita etiam operationes humanæ procedunt ex humana voluntate. Oportuit autem in rebus naturalibus ut superiora moverent inferiora ad suas actiones per excellentiam naturalis virtutis collatæ divinitus. Unde etiam oportet in rebus humanis quod superiores moveant inferiores per suam voluntatem ex vi auctoritatis divinitus ordinatæ.

---

[1] cf *In Tit.* 3, lect. 1. 2a2æ. 186, 5 & 8
[2] *Ecclesiasticus* 15, 14   [3] *Hebrews* 13, 17
[a] See above 102, 1, note *b*.
[b] There is a parallel in that both kinds of activity proceed from inner sources. But

Question 104. obedience

NEXT, IS OBEDIENCE, and there are six points of inquiry:[a]
1. whether one man should obey another;
2. whether obedience is a specific virtue;
3. obedience compared with other virtues;
4. whether God is to be obeyed in all matters;
5. whether subjects are bound to obey their superiors on all points;
6. whether the faithful have to obey civil authority.

article 1. whether one man need obey another

THE FIRST POINT:[1] 1. No one, it seems, is bound to obey anyone else. Nothing should ever be done against God's disposition of things. The text, *God made man from the beginning and left him in the hand of his own counsel*,[2] shows that God has arranged for every man to be guided by his own judgment. No one, then, has any obligation to obey anyone else.

2. Further, to be bound to obey another would amount to having the will of the one commanding as the rule of one's actions. Since for every man the divine will alone in its unfailing rectitude is the norm of action, each is held to obey God alone.

3. Further, the more a service is done out of good-will, the more pleasing it is. What a person does from indebtedness, however, is not done with complete spontaneity. The very fact of doing good works under pressure of obedience, then, would make such works less acceptable. So no obedience is owed to anyone.

ON THE OTHER HAND we have a precept, *Obey your prelates and be subject to them.*[3]

REPLY: As activities of nature issue from natural powers, so human activities flow from the human will.[b] Now in the first case there is a necessary natural pattern whereby the higher beings, through a superiority in power bestowed by God, influence the activities of the lower. Similarly

---

as ad 1 indicates, the parallel is an analogy and the diversity between physical actions and willed actions determines the meaning and force of the whole Reply. A pattern of subordination, which is a given fact in human affairs, is shown to be reasonable; but ad 1 makes clear that the subordination is of a specifically human kind, and that obedience is the response of a human being, an act of free choice. Sheer compliance with authority is not obedience.

Movere autem per rationem et voluntatem est præcipere. Et ideo sicut ex ipso ordine naturali divinitus instituto inferiora in rebus naturalibus necesse habent subjici motioni superiorum, ita etiam in rebus humanis ex ordine juris naturalis et divini tenentur inferiores suis superioribus obedire.

1. Ad primum ergo dicendum quod Deus reliquit hominem in manu consilii sui, non quia liceat ei facere omne quod velit, sed quia ad id quod faciendum est non cogitur necessitate naturæ, sicut creaturæ irrationales, sed libera electione ex proprio consilio procedente. Et sicut ad alia facienda debet procedere proprio consilio, ita etiam ad hoc quod obediat suis superioribus, dicit enim Gregorius quod *dum alienæ voci humiliter subdimur, nosmetipsos in corde superamus.*[4]

2. Ad secundum dicendum quod divina voluntas est prima regula qua regulantur omnes rationales voluntates, cui una magis appropinquat quam alia, secundum ordinem divinitus institutum. Et ideo voluntas unius hominis præcipientis potest esse quasi secunda regula voluntatis alterius obedientis.

3. Ad tertium dicendum quod aliquid potest judicari gratuitum dupliciter: uno modo ex parte ipsius operis, quia scilicet homo ad id non obligatur; alio modo ex parte operantis, quia scilicet libera voluntate hoc facit. Opus autem redditur virtuosum et laudabile et meritorium præcipue secundum quod ex voluntate procedit. Et ideo quamvis obedire sit debitum, si prompta* voluntate aliquis obediat, non propter hoc minuitur ejus meritum, maxime apud Deum, qui non solum exteriora opera verum etiam interiorem voluntatem videt.

---

*Piana: *propria*, his own
[4]*Moral.* xxxv, 14. PL 76, 765
[c]See 1a2æ. 17, 1.
[d]The word 'necessity' for the translation is used to bring out the parallel argumentation, and also to avoid using the term 'obliged' or 'bound' for *tenentur*. In St Thomas's view the moral order has its origins not in arbitrarily imposed duties or obligations, but in the specifically human and inner finality of man's actions. The necessity under which man operates is not that of executing imperatives, but of directing his actions towards goals that he perceives to require certain types of human responses. 'Obligation' is first of all the inner finality or end-wardness of a human action; one instance of this finality is the response to those who rightly impose commands, but the response is a *choice* to obey because in this instance obeying is the good to be achieved by acting. See Vol. 18 of this series, Appendix 1, n. 5; Appendix 4; Stevens, G., 'Moral Obligation in St. Thomas', *Modern Schoolman* XL (1962) 1–21.
[e]On *electio* and *consilium* see 1a2æ. 13 & 14. By these allusions to the dynamics of all moral, free acts, the freedom in obedience is stressed. To be virtuous, i.e. to be really obedient, obeying must be free; every act of obedience is above all the choice *to obey*; the choice to do *what* is commanded is secondary.

it is altogether right that in the affairs of men superiors have influence over inferiors through the power of will in virtue of an authority determined by God.

Now to influence another by the power of will and reason is to command.[c] Consequently there is a parallel between the natural necessity with which the lower in nature are subject to the higher by reason of the natural pattern established by God, and the necessity arising out of natural and divine law that in the course of human affairs subordinates be obedient to their superiors.[d]

Hence: 1. God left man in the hand of his own counsel, not in the sense that he could do whatever he pleases, but that he approach every act, not under the stricture of a natural necessity, in the way non-rational creatures do, but out of free choice issuing from his own counsel. Just as he should undertake everything else from this personal decision, so should he face obeying superiors.[e] On this point Gregory notes, *When we submit humbly to another's will, in our heart we are rising above ourselves.*[4]

2. The divine will is, of course, the first norm regulating all rational wills, but according to the way God has arranged things one of those may be closer to his will than another. This is the reason why the will of one person giving a command can stand as a secondary norm for the will of the one obeying.[f]

3. There are two ways whereby something can be viewed as an act of good will: first of all, looking to the deed itself, which may be something not obligatory; secondly, looking to the person acting, who may act with complete willingness. Now the main reason why any deed is virtuous, honourable and meritorious is that it issues from the will. For this reason, even though to obey is an obligatory act, this still does not diminish its merit if the person obeying does so willingly, and above all in God's eyes, who does not just see externals but the inner willingness itself.[g]

---

[f]cf 1a2æ. 19, 9. The choice to obey presupposes an assent that there is a given human relationship, that of superior-subject, i.e. given as part of the hierarchical structure through which God has determined to govern the world. That there is the superior-subject relationship is implicitly accepted in the choice to obey; it is the basis for making the will of another human being a secondary norm of action; it is the reason why obedience is a virtue. St Thomas maintains that the conscience of the one who obeys remains decisive, i.e. it is the one who obeys who makes the choice to obey, and so the soundness and the justification of such a choice is here stressed; cf also 1a2æ. 19, 10. St Thomas would not approve a facile use of the phrase 'the will of God' as comfort either to superiors or subjects; within the limits of their relationship (art. 4–5) both are assured that it is God's will that the one command and the other obey; there is no such guarantee that the content of the command is God's will.

[g]cf 1a2æ. 114, 4 ad 2; 2a2æ. 186, 5 ad 5.

articulus 2. *utrum obedientia sit specialis virtus*

AD SECUNDUM sic proceditur:[1] 1. Videtur quod obedientia non sit specialis virtus. Obedientiæ enim inobedientia opponitur. Sed inobedientia est generale peccatum; dicit enim Ambrosius quod *peccatum est inobedientia legis divinæ*.[2] Ergo obedientia non est specialis virtus, sed generalis.

2. Præterea, omnis virtus specialis aut est theologica aut moralis. Sed obedientia non est virtus theologica, quia neque continetur sub fide, neque sub spe, neque sub caritate. Similiter etiam non est virtus moralis, quia non est in medio superflui et diminuti; quanto enim aliquis est magis obediens tanto magis laudatur. Ergo obedientia non est specialis virtus.

3. Præterea, Gregorius dicit quod *obedientia tanto magis est meritoria et laudabilis, quanto minus habet de suo*.[3] Sed quælibet specialis virtus tanto magis laudatur, quanto magis habet de suo, eo quod ad virtutem requiritur ut sit volens et eligens, sicut dicitur in *Ethic*.[4] Ergo obedientia non est virtus specialis.

4. Præterea, virtutes differunt specie secundum objecta. Objectum autem obedientiæ esse videtur superioris præceptum, quod multipliciter diversificari videtur, secundum diversos superioritatis gradus. Ergo obedientia est virtus generalis, sub se multas virtutes speciales comprehendens.

SED CONTRA est quod obedientia a quibusdam ponitur pars justitiæ, ut supra dictum est.[5]

RESPONSIO: Dicendum quod ad omnia opera bona quæ specialem habent laudis rationem, specialis virtus determinatur; hoc enim proprie competit virtuti ut opus bonum reddat. Obedire autem superiori debitum est secundum divinum ordinem rebus inditum, ut ostensum est,[6] et per consequens est bonum, cum bonum consistat in modo, specie et ordine, ut Augustinus dicit.[7]

Habet autem hic actus specialem rationem laudis ex speciali objecto. Cum enim inferiores suis superioribus multa debeant exhibere, inter cætera hoc est unum speciale quod tenentur eorum præceptis obedire.

---

[1] cf II *Sent*. 35, 2 ad 5; 44, 2, 1; III, 33, 3, 4, iii ad 1
[2] *De paradiso* 8. PL 14, 309
[3] *Moral*. xxxv, 14. PL 76, 766
[4] *Ethics* II, 4. 1105a31   [5] 2a2æ. 80
[6] art. 1   [7] *De nat. boni* 3. PL 42, 553
[a] On 'general virtue' see above 101, 3, note *c*. The meaning here is that of a characteristic common to all virtuous actions; cf 1a2æ. 61, 1–4.
[b] On the term 'theological virtue' see 1a2æ. 62, 1.
[c] Here 'general virtue' has the sense of 'generic' as in the case of prudence in 2a2æ. 47.

article 2. whether obedience is a special virtue

THE SECOND POINT:[1] 1. Obedience does not seem to be a specific virtue. Its opposite is disobedience, which is a general sin, since Ambrose remarks that all sin is *disobedience to the law of God*.[2] So too obedience is not a special but a general virtue.[a]

2. Further, every specific virtue is either theological or moral. Obedience is not theological[b] because it is not included under faith, hope or charity; nor is it moral, because it does not hold to a mean between excess and defect—the more a person obeys the more he is praised. In no sense, then, is obedience a specific virtue.

3. Further, on Gregory's authority, *The less of self there is in it, the more meritorious and laudable is the obedience*.[3] By contrast, each specific virtue is the more praised, the more there is of oneself in it, since a requisite of virtue is willingness and freedom, as Aristotle says.[4] Obedience then, is not a special virtue.

4. Further, objectives determine specific differences in virtues. As its objective, obedience apparently has the precept of a superior and there are many kinds of precept corresponding to the many levels of authority. On this score obedience is a general virtue[c] with many sub-species.

ON THE OTHER HAND, as we have mentioned,[5] some authors make obedience a part of justice.

REPLY: There is a specific virtue to match every sort of good deed having some specially commendable quality.[d] For this is what is distinctive of virtue, that it makes an action good. As we have shown,[6] to obey superiors is something required of us in keeping with the order which God has established, and so it is a good action—the good, in Augustine's words, consisting in *proportion, species and order*.[7]

The specifically commendable quality of this act derives from its specific objective. Of the many distinct duties inferiors owe to superiors, one is obedience to their commands. Consequently, obedience is a specific virtue, its special objective being a precept, tacit or expressed.

---

[d]For the term 'commendable' or 'praiseworthy' in moral discussion, see Aristotle, *Ethics* III 5. 1114a23. Any human action has the quality of being praiseworthy or blameworthy according as it lies within the responsibility of the will (1a2æ. 21, 4; see also Vol. 18 of this series, p. 111, note c). Goodness, praiseworthiness and rightness are all attributed to a human action because of different values that it has, but these all derive primarily from the objective of the act. Possibly St Thomas chooses here to argue from the praiseworthiness of obedience because of the text of St Gregory cited in obj. 3.

Unde obedientia est specialis virtus, et ejus speciale objectum est præceptum tacitum vel expressum. Voluntas enim superioris quocumque modo innotescat, est quoddam tacitum præceptum, et tanto videtur obedientia promptior quanto expressum præceptum obediendo prævenit, voluntate superioris intellecta.

1. Ad primum ergo dicendum quod nihil prohibet duas speciales rationes ad quas duæ speciales virtutes respiciunt in uno et eodem materiali objecto concurrere; sicut miles defendendo castrum regis et implet opus fortitudinis, non refugiens mortis pericula propter bonum, et opus justitiæ, debitum servitium domino suo reddens.

Sic igitur ratio præcepti quam attendit obedientia concurrit cum actibus omnium virtutum, non tamen cum omnibus virtutum actibus, quia non omnes actus virtutum sunt in præcepto, ut supra habitum est.[8] Similiter etiam quædam quandoque sub præcepto cadunt quæ ad nullam aliam virtutem pertinent, ut patet in his quæ non sunt mala nisi quia prohibita. Sic ergo si obedientia proprie accipiatur, secundum quod respicit per intentionem formalem rationem præcepti, erit specialis virtus et inobedientia peccatum speciale. Secundum hoc enim ad obedientiam requiritur quod impleat aliquis actum justitiæ vel alterius virtutis intendens implere præceptum; et ad inobedientiam requiritur quod actualiter comtemnat præceptum. Si vero obedientia large accipiatur pro executione cujuscumque quod potest cadere sub præcepto, et inobedientia pro omissione ejusdem ex quacumque intentione, sic obedientia erit generalis virtus et inobedientia generale peccatum.

2. Ad secundum dicendum quod obedientia non est virtus theologica; non enim per se objectum ejus est Deus, sed præceptum superioris cujuscumque, vel expressum vel interpretativum, scilicet simplex verbum prælati ejus indicans voluntatem, cui obedit promptus obediens, secundum illud *ad Tit., dicto obedire*, etc.[9] Est autem virtus moralis, cum sit pars justitiæ; et est medium inter superfluum et diminutum.

Attenditur autem ejus superfluum, non quidem secundum quantum, sed secundum alias circumstantias, inquantum scilicet aliquis obedit vel cui non debet, vel in quibus non debet, sicut etiam supra de religione

---

[8] 1a2æ. 96, 3; 100, 2   [9] *Titus* 3, 1
[e] This proviso preserves the point that obedience is specifically directed towards commands; the sign of willingness suggested does not advocate subservience to a superior's purely personal whims or wishes.
[f] On objective see above 101, 3, note *d*.
[g] cf 1a2æ. 71, 6 ad 4. *CG* III, 129.
[h] Sometimes obedience and disobedience are designated 'material', when taken in their general sense; 'formal', when taken in their specific sense; cf 105, 1 ad 1. The explanation here again emphasizes that obedience properly means a choice to obey, a choice of some particular act because it is commanded. On the way in

(Note that no matter how it becomes known, the will of a superior amounts to a silent precept, and obedience looks to be the more willing, when its action does not wait for a spoken command, provided the superior's will is really known.)[e]

Hence: 1. There is nothing against two specific moral values, the concern of two specific virtues, being simultaneously present in the same material objective.[f] The soldier, for example, defending his king's stronghold, is at once exercising a work of courage—standing fast in the face of danger for the sake of the right, and a work of justice—performing a service owed to his lord.

Applying this: the moral value which is *precept*, the specific interest of obedience, is found present in acts of all the virtues (though it does not apply to every virtuous act, since, as already determined,[8] not all come under precept). In addition, some matters become the content of a precept which are not the concern of any virtue, as is clear in the case of acts which are evil solely because they are forbidden.[g] Accordingly, obedience is a specific virtue and disobedience a specific sin when obedience is taken in its strict sense, namely the intentional concern for a precept as a moral value.[h] For an act of obedience in this sense it will be required that one perform an act of justice or some other virtue with the intention of observing a precept; and disobedience will entail actual contempt for the precept. Obedience is a general virtue and disobedience a general sin when they are taken in a broad sense, as simply the performance, or the omission, for any reason, of some act which might happen also to be a matter of precept.

2. It is true that obedience is not a theological virtue, since its direct objective is not God, but the precept of some superior. This precept may be expressed or inferred from a simple statement of the superior indicating his will;[i] one eager to obey carries even this out, in keeping with the text, *Obey at a word*.[9] Since it is a part of justice, however, and stands as a mean between excess and defect, obedience is a moral virtue.

Excess here is not a question of amount, but of other circumstances, namely of obeying either a person *whom* or in matters *wherein* we should not obey;[j] something similar has been said above about the virtue of

---

which one moral act can attend to and contain many moral values, cf 1a2æ. 18, 7 and Vol. 18 of this series, ed. T. Gilby, Appendix 14.

[i]*interpretativum* simply means that even when a superior does not give an outright command, but says, e.g., 'Would you mind . . .?' his expression can be taken as an occasion for virtuous obedience.

[j]On moral circumstances, see above 101, 4 note *a*; Vol. 18 of this series, on 1a2æ. 18, 3, note *a*, pp. 12-13. The point on excess and defect is raised in order to show that obedience is a moral virtue, having the property or attribute of striking a mean between extremes; cf 1a2æ. 64, 1 & 2.

dictum est.[10] Potest etiam dici, quod sicut in justitia superfluum est in eo qui retinet alienum, diminutum autem in eo cui non redditur quod debetur, ut Philosophus dicit in v *Ethic.*,[11] ita etiam obedientia medium est inter superfluum, quod attenditur ex parte ejus qui subtrahit superiori obedientiæ debitum, quia superabundat in implendo propriam voluntatem; et diminutum, quod attenditur ex parte superioris cui non obeditur. Unde secundum hoc obedientia non erit medium duarum malitiarum sicut supra de justitia dictum est.[12]

3. Ad tertium dicendum quod obedientia sicut et quælibet virtus debet habere promptam voluntatem in suum proprium objectum, non autem in quod repugnans est ei. Proprium autem objectum obedientiæ est præceptum, quod quidem ex alterius voluntate procedit. Unde obedientia reddit promptam hominis voluntatem ad implendum voluntatem alterius, scilicet præcipientis. Si autem id quod ei præcipitur sit propter se ei volitum etiam absque ratione præcepti, sicut accidit in prosperis, jam ex propria voluntate tendit in illud, et non videtur illud implere propter præceptum sed propter voluntatem propriam. Sed quando illud quod præcipitur nullo modo est secundum se volitum, sed est secundum se consideratum propriæ voluntati repugnans, sicut accidit in asperis, tunc omnino manifestum est quod non impletur nisi propter præceptum. Et ideo Gregorius dicit quod *obedientia quæ habet aliquid de suo in prosperis, est vel nulla, vel minor,* quia scilicet voluntas propria non videtur principaliter tendere ad implendum præceptum, sed ad assequendum proprium volitum; *in adversis autem, vel difficilibus est major,*[13] quia voluntas propria in nihil aliud tendit quam in præceptum.

Sed hoc intelligendum est secundum id quod exterius apparet. Secundum tamen Dei judicium, qui corda rimatur, potest contingere quod etiam in prosperis obedientia aliquid de suo habens non propter hoc sit minus laudabilis, si scilicet propria voluntas obedientis non minus devote tendat ad impletionem præcepti.

4. Ad quartum dicendum quod reverentia directe respicit personam excellentem; et ideo secundum diversam rationem excellentiæ diversas species habet. Obedientia vero respicit præceptum personæ excellentis; et ideo non est nisi unius rationis. Sed quia propter reverentiam personæ

---

[10]2a2æ. 81, 5 ad 3; cf 92, 2
[11]*Ethics* v, 4. 1132a10
[12]2a2æ. 58, 10 ad 2
[13]*Moral.* xxxv, 14. PL 76, 766
[k]The one act avoids the moral imbalance of a subject having his own way when he has no right to it, and the superior not having his way when he does have a right to it. The parallel with justice, from 2a2æ. 58, 10, seems to imply that the command of the superior is similar to the real, objective, mean to which justice attends. Each

religion.[10] Another way of putting it is that, as Aristotle says,[11] in cases of justice there is excess where one retains another's possessions; defect, where one fails to pay a debt. Similarly, an act of obedience is also a mean, namely between excess—measured with reference to the person holding back what is owed in obedience to a superior by overdoing his own will, and defect—measured with reference to the superior from whom obedience is held back. Accordingly, obedience does not stand as a mean between two kinds of vice, even as justice does not,[k] a point already determined.[12]

3. Obedience, like any other virtue, necessarily includes the will being prompt with respect to the objective of the virtue, not with regard to what runs counter to the will.[1] But what is peculiar about the objective of obedience is that it is a precept issuing from the will of someone else, so that obedience makes a person's will ready to carry out the will of another, i.e. of a superior. If, then, as in the case of the agreeable, a task commanded is itself desirable, apart from having the quality of being commanded, a person would want to do it anyway and to all appearances carries it out not because he is commanded but because he wants to. On the other hand, as in the case of the disagreeable, the task commanded has nothing to recommend it and is of such a nature as to go counter to personal preference, clearly it is carried out solely because of the command. This is what Gregory has in mind, saying, *Obedience which contains anything of self in congenial matters is non-existent or minimal*—i.e. because the person's will would seem bent mainly not on carrying out the command but on seeking self-satisfaction; *in trying or difficult matters it is greater*[13] —i.e. personal will is concerned wholly with the command.

All that has been said, however, is to be understood as to what meets the eye. In God's judgment, who searches hearts, it may well happen that even in agreeable matters an obedience which is accompanied by an element of personal preference is just as praiseworthy, when, namely, the personal will of the one obeying is equally bent upon fulfilling the command.[m]

4. Reverence has to do directly with the person who has some sort of eminence, so that there are as many kinds of reverence as there are forms of eminence. Obedience rather has to do with the precept of the person of rank, and is therefore always one in kind. Still, inasmuch as it is out of reverence for the person that obedience to his precept is owed, it follows

---

virtue attends to a virtuous mean, not as between two vices, but in a response to an objective that stands as a mean between too much and too little.

[1]The statement is meant to emphasize the proper objective of obedience, the command that it obeys; it makes the will want to obey the command, not necessarily to like *what* is commanded.

[m]cf 2a2æ. 27, 8 ad 3.

obedientia debetur ejus præcepto, consequens est quod obedientia omnis*
hominis sit eadem specie, ex diversis tamen specie causis procedens.

articulus 3. *utrum obedientia sit maxima virtutum*

AD TERTIUM sic proceditur:[1] 1. Videtur quod obedientia sit maxima virtutum. Dicitur enim 1 *Reg.*, *Melior est obedientia quam victimæ*.[2] Sed oblatio victimarum pertinet ad religionem, quæ est potissima inter omnes virtutes morales, ut ex supra dictis patet.[3] Ergo obedientia est potissima inter omnes virtutes.

2. Præterea, Gregorius dicit quod *obedientia sola virtus est quæ virtutes cæteras menti inserit, insertasque custodit*.[4] Sed causa potior est effectu. Ergo obedientia est potior omnibus virtutibus.

3. Præterea, Gregorius dicit, quod *nunquam per obedientiam malum debet fieri; aliquando autem per obedientiam bonum, quod agimus, intermitti debet*.[5] Sed non prætermittitur aliquid nisi pro meliori. Ergo obedientia, pro qua prætermittuntur bona aliarum virtutum, est virtutibus aliis melior.

SED CONTRA est quod obedientia habet laudem ex eo quod ex caritate procedit; dicit enim Gregorius quod *obedientia non servili metu, sed caritatis affectu servanda est, non timore pœnæ, sed amore justitiæ*.[6] Ergo caritas est potior virtus quam obedientia.

RESPONSIO: Dicendum quod sicut peccatum consistit in hoc quod homo, contempto Deo, commutabilibus bonis inhæret, ita meritum virtuosi actus consistit in hoc quod homo, contemptis bonis creatis, Deo inhæret sicut fini. Finis autem potior est his quæ sunt ad finem. Si ergo bona creata propter hoc contemnantur ut Deo inhæreatur, major est laus virtutis ex hoc quod Deo inhæret quam ex hoc quod bona terrena contemnit. Et ideo illæ† virtutes quibus Deo secundum se inhæretur, scilicet theologicæ,

---

*Piana: omits *omnis*
†Piana: omits *illæ*

[1]cf 2a2æ. 186, 8 *In Philipp.* 2, *lect.* 3   [2]1 *Kings* 15, 22   [3]2a2æ. 81, 6
[4]*Moral.* xxxv, 14. PL 76, 766   [5]ibid   [6]ibid
[m]See above 101, 1, and notes *b* & *e*. *Causis* is here translated 'motives' because obedience serves the ends of all the virtues of respect; they imperate or command obedience because fulfilling the precept of one who has the right to issue it is part of showing him due reverence. The objection is thus answered: obedience does have one objective, but it also has a relationship to all the virtues of respect (cf art. 3 ad 1). The way in which obedience itself has a kind of direction over other virtues is considered in art. 3.
[a]cf 1a2æ. 71–89 for a discussion of sin (Vol. 25–7 in this series); the references there to *bonum commutabile* are many. In a moral evaluation, all creaturely goods are

that all obedience is one specific virtue, but originates in specifically different motives.

article 3. whether obedience is the greatest of all virtues

THE THIRD POINT:[1] 1. Obedience appears to be the highest of all virtues. Since *Obedience is better than sacrifice*,[2] and sacrifice is part of religion, the supreme moral virtue,[3] obedience must be the most important virtue.

2. Further, Gregory claims that *only obedience introduces other virtues into the soul and safeguards their presence*.[4] Since a cause is always superior to its effect, obedience must be the supreme virtue.

3. Further, while we should never refrain from doing a good except to do something better, Gregory asserts that *although evil must never be done out of obedience, obedience should at times make us defer some good we are doing*.[5] Obedience, then, is better than other virtues, since their good acts are postponed on its account.

ON THE OTHER HAND, obedience is praiseworthy because charity is its source; *Hold to obedience not out of craven fear but out of a spirit of love, not out of dread of punishment but out of love for the right*.[6] Charity is therefore superior.

REPLY: Somewhat in the way that sin consists in setting one's heart on creaturely goods, God being ignored, the merit of a virtuous act consists in the opposite, i.e. putting aside the attraction of creatures and holding fast to God.[a] Since an end is of greater importance than subordinate objectives,[b] and since creaturely goods are set aside for the sake of holding fast to God, a virtue ranks higher if it is a way of cleaving to God rather than a way of restraint from earthly goods. This is why the theological virtues, through which we are united to God as he is in himself,[c] excel the

---

qualified as 'changeable', i.e. in comparison to God, the final unchanging good and measure of every moral choice. There is not a perfect equation between the virtuous act and the sinful act, but an analogy. The virtuous act is always a positive choice of the full moral value of its objective, including the relationship of that objective to God; the sinful act is sinful not because there is a positive choice to reject God, but because there is a failure to make a choice in which the relationship of the objective to God is included. The sin is thus the choice of a changing good as though it were an absolute; see 1a2æ. 73, 1.

[b]*ea quæ sunt ad finem* as used by St Thomas connotes both the intrinsic moral significance and the further, consequent relation to end of things we ordinarily call 'means'.

[c]See 1a2æ. 62, 1; 2a2æ. 1, 2; 17, 1, 2, 6; 23. 1-4. St Thomas's teaching is that faith, hope and charity in their acts are ways of union with God himself.

sunt potiores virtutibus moralibus, quibus aliquid terrenum contemnitur ut Deo inhæreatur.

Inter virtutes autem morales tanto aliqua potior est quanto aliquis majus* aliquid contemnit ut Deo inhæreat. Sunt autem tria genera bonorum humanorum quæ homo potest contemnere propter Deum: quorum infimum sunt exteriora bona; medium autem sunt bona corporis; supremum autem sunt bona animæ inter quæ quodammodo præcipuum est voluntas, inquantum scilicet per voluntatem homo omnibus aliis bonis utitur. Et ideo per se loquendo laudabilior est obedientiæ virtus, quæ propter Deum contemnit propriam voluntatem, quam aliæ virtutes morales, quæ propter Deum aliqua alia bona contemnunt. Unde Gregorius dicit quod *obedientia victimis jure præponitur, quia per victimas aliena caro, per obedientiam vero voluntas propria mactatur.*[7]

Unde etiam quæcumque alia virtutum opera ex hoc meritoria sunt apud Deum quod fiunt ut obediatur voluntati divinæ. Nam si quis etiam martyrium sustineret vel omnia sua pauperibus erogaret, nisi hæc ordinaret ad impletionem divinæ voluntatis, quod directe ad obedientiam pertinet, meritoria esse non possent; sicut nec si fierent sine caritate, quæ sine obedientia esse non potest. Dicitur enim 1 *Joan.* quod *qui dicit se nosse Deum, et mandata ejus non custodit, mendax est, qui autem servat verba ejus, vere in hoc caritas Dei perfecta est.*[8] Et hoc ideo est, quia amicitia facit idem velle et nolle.

1. Ad primum ergo dicendum quod obedientia procedit ex reverentia, quæ exhibet cultum et honorem superiori. Et quantum ad hoc sub diversis virtutibus continetur, licet secundum se considerata prout respicit rationem præcepti sit una specialis virtus. Inquantum ergo procedit ex reverentia prælatorum, continetur quodammodo sub observantia; inquantum vero procedit ex reverentia parentum, sub pietate; inquantum vero procedit ex reverentia Dei, sub religione, et pertinet ad devotionem, quæ est

---

*Piana: *magis*; the sense is the same
[7]*Moral.* xxxv, 14. PL 76, 766
[8]1 *John* 2, 4
[d]Moral virtue is not its own reward in any conception of the Christian life as a way of union with God, not a way of right conduct. The restraint of moral virtue is directed towards serving this union.
[e]See 1a. 82, 3, for a discussion of the primacy of intellect over will in St Thomas's teaching.
[f]The worth of obedience is brought out on the basis of moral virtues being ways of restraint; this is a relative superiority. Virtues like justice and religion excel obedience from the more positive aspects of the moral values to which they attend; cf 1a2æ, 66, 3–5; 2a2æ. 81, 6; 123, 12.
[g]These lines must be understood in the light of ad 2 below, and of 1a2æ. 106–8, on the New Law, and |3a. 47, 2 & ad 3. St Thomas here implies the connection between charity and obedience in the Christian life. Obedience need not here be

moral virtues, through which some temporal advantage is given up for the sake of union with God.[d]

The gradation of moral virtues is this: the nobler the good it forgoes for the sake of God, the higher is the virtue. The classes of human goods a person can forgo in his quest for God are three. The least important is the good in external possessions; next is that of physical well-being; above all others is that of endowments of soul. Among such endowments, the will, in one sense, holds first place,[e] since by his will a person deals with all else that is desirable. In these terms, the virtue of obedience is more praiseworthy than other moral virtues, seeing that by obedience a person gives up his own will for God's sake, and by other moral virtues something less.[f] Gregory therefore says, *Obedience rightly is rated above sacrifice, for in sacrifice the flesh of another being is offered; in obedience, one's own will.*[7]

For this reason, as well, any of the acts of other virtues stand before God as meritorious because they are done out of obedience to his will. Even suffering martyrdom or distributing one's goods to the poor would no more be meritorious if not done in fulfilment of God's will, i.e. as acts of obedience, than if they were done without charity, which in turn cannot exist without obedience.[g] The *First Letter of John* states, *He who saith that he knoweth him and keepeth not his commands is a liar . . . But he that keepeth his word in him in very deed the charity of God is perfected.*[8] This is so because friendship makes friends one in what they will and in what they reject.[h]

Hence: 1. Obedience originates in reverence, which is intent upon offering homage and honour to a superior. From this standpoint it is included under many virtues, even though it is in itself one specific virtue, having precept as its objective. Accordingly, as prompted by reverence for those in authority obedience is included under respect; by reverence towards parents, under piety; and towards God, under religion.[i] In regard to religion, obedience is part of devotion,[j] the chief act of religion, and for this reason obedience to God is more praiseworthy than offering him

---

understood as 'formal' (cf art. 2); neither should charity be reduced to mere obedience to precepts. It is not obedience, but charity that unites us to God; the charity given to us by the Holy Spirit makes obedience and all other works meritorious. But charity is a union of wills with God's will and it has pleased God to command as a Father; n.b. 1a2æ. 106, 2; 108, 1 & 2. The author knows quite well the gratuitousness of grace and charity, and the relationship between Law and Gospel. What has often passed for Roman Catholic moral teaching has not always evidenced the same sensitivity.

[h]From Sallust, *Catalin* 20.
[i]cf 103, 1 ad 1; above, art. 2, note *m*.
[j]cf 2a2æ. 82, 1 & 2 on devotion; Vol. 39, ed. K. O. O'Rourke, Appendix 2.

principalis actus religionis. Unde secundum hoc laudabilius est obedire Deo quam sacrificium offerre: et etiam quia *in sacrificio immolatur aliena caro, per obedientiam autem propria voluntas*, ut Gregorius dicit.[9]

Specialiter tamen in casu in quo loquebatur Samuel, melius fuisset Sauli obedire Deo, quam animalia pinguia Amalecitarum in sacrificium offerre contra Dei mandatum.

2. Ad secundum dicendum quod ad obedientiam pertinent omnes actus virtutum prout sunt in præcepto. Inquantum ergo actus virtutum operantur causaliter vel dispositive ad earum generationem et conservationem intantum dicitur quod obedientia omnes virtutes menti inserit et custodit. Nec tamen sequitur quod obedientia sit simpliciter omnibus virtutibus prior, propter duo. Primo, quia licet actus virtutis cadat sub præcepto, potest tamen aliquis implere actum virtutis non attendens ad rationem præcepti. Unde si aliqua virtus sit, cujus objectum sit naturaliter prius quam præceptum, illa virtus dicitur naturaliter prior quam obedientia, ut patet de fide, per quam nobis divinæ auctoritatis sublimitas innotescit, ex qua competit ei potestas præcipiendi. Secundo, quia infusio gratiæ et virtutum potest præcedere etiam tempore omnem actum virtuosum. Et secundum hoc neque tempore, neque natura est obedientia omnibus aliis virtutibus prior.

3. Ad tertium dicendum quod duplex est bonum. Quoddam, ad quod faciendum homo ex necessitate tenetur, sicut amare Deum, vel aliquid hujusmodi. Et tale bonum nullo modo debet propter obedientiam prætermitti. Est autem aliud bonum, ad quod homo non tenetur ex necessitate.

---

[9]*Moral.* xxxv, 14. PL 76, 765
[k]The allusion is to 1 *Kings* 15, 9–15, see objection 1.
[l]cf 1a2æ. 94, 3; 96, 3.
[m]cf 1a2æ. 51, 2–4; 52, 3; 63, 2 & 3; 114, 8; 2a2æ. 24, 2–6. *Causaliter* here refers to an efficient cause, one which by its own activity produces an effect; *dispositive* refers to a cause, the action of which produces a condition preparatory to the effect of an efficient cause. The preparation is called a 'disposition'; thus the marble cut by a quarry-man (the dispositive cause) with regard to the statue carved by the sculptor. The texts cited above will make clear the reason for introducing the distinction here. The so-called natural or acquired virtues would have the person exercising their acts as the efficient cause. The virtues given with grace (the supernatural or 'infused' virtues) can have God alone as their efficient cause. The acts of a person under grace are considered by St Thomas to be preparations or dispositions for the reception of God's action bestowing or increasing these grace-given qualities; cf also 1a2æ. 109, 6; 112, 2; 112 *passim*.
[n]St Thomas frequently uses the comparison of things according to a sequence or priority of nature and a sequence or priority of time. The temporal sequence is clear. A sequence or priority of nature is one in meaning, in causality, or in the nature of what the compared elements are, namely where the presence or existence of one is presupposed to the presence or existence of the other; cf 2a2æ. 17, 8.

sacrifice. We may also add Gregory's words, *In sacrifice it is the flesh of another being that is immolated; in obedience, one's own will.*⁹

Note that in the case to which Samuel referred, it would have been a better thing for Saul to have obeyed God rather than to have offered the fat of the animals of the Amalekites in sacrifice, contrary to God's command.ᵏ

2. Obedience becomes involved in all acts of virtue to the extent that they are matters of precept.ˡ The basis for saying, therefore, that obedience introduces all virtues into the soul and safeguards their presence, is the degree to which acts of virtue function as causes or dispositions for the origin and preservation of the virtuous habits.ᵐ

From this, however, no outright precedence of obedience over other virtues can be inferred; and for two reasons. First, even though an act of virtue might be a matter of precept, it is still possible for someone to perform this act without being motivated by the precept. Thus, should there be a virtue with an objective which by its very nature is presupposed to any precept, this virtue itself has precedence over obedience.ⁿ Such is true with regard to faith, which makes known to us the majesty of God's authority, the reason for his power to lay down precepts. Secondly, the infusion of grace and the virtues may precede in time any actual exercise of virtue.º Accordingly, obedience has priority neither of time nor of meaning over all other virtues.

3. There are two kinds of good works.ᵖ To one sort we are bound strictly, e.g. to love God.ᑫ Such works must under no consideration be set aside out of obedience. There are, however, other good works to which we are not strictly bound. These a person must sometimes forgo for the sake of obedience, since obedience does bind strictly, and we must not do good at the cost of incurring blame.ʳ Gregory does point out, however,

---

º*infusio*, cf 1a2æ. 63, 3; God's bestowal of grace and virtue is pictured as a 'pouring into' the soul. The main case in point here is the baptism of an infant, who, although incapable of personal response, is held in Roman Catholic teaching to be the recipient of grace and the virtues. Of the adult receiving grace for the first time or recovering grace after sin, St Thomas teaches that the infusion of grace does not temporally precede the exercise of certain virtuous acts; cf 1a2æ. 113, 2, 3, 7 & 8.

ᵖThe distinction here is between works of precept and works of counsel, e.g. between the contents of the Ten Commandments and the life of voluntary poverty; cf 1a2æ. 108, 4; 2a2æ. 184, 3.

ᑫ1a2æ. 108, 4 explains: . . . *in the New Law precepts are laid down with regard to those matters which are necessary for reaching the end that is eternal happiness. Counsels should rather concern those matters that enable a person better and more securely to reach this end.*

ʳOn 'blame' for *culpa*, cf 1a2æ. 21, 2 and Vol. 18 of this series, p. 110, note e. The idea here is the equivalent of saying, of course, that we cannot do any good act that would involve sinful neglect of a higher good.

Et tale bonum debet homo quandoque propter obedientiam prætermittere, ad quam ex necessitate homo tenetur, quia non debet homo aliquod bonum facere culpam incurrendo. Et tamen, sicut ibidem Gregorius dicit, *qui ab uno quolibet bono subjectos vetat, necesse est ut multa concedat, ne obedientis mens funditus intereat, si a bonis omnibus repulsa penitus jejunet.*[10] Et sic per obedientiam et alia bona, potest damnum unius boni recompensari.

articulus 4. *utrum in omnibus sit Deo obediendum*

AD QUARTUM sic proceditur.[1] 1. Videtur quod non in omnibus sit Deo obediendum. Dicitur enim *Matt.* quod Dominus duobus cæcis curatis præcepit dicens, *Videte ne quis sciat. Illi autem exeuntes diffamaverunt eum per totam terram illam.*[2] Nec tamen ex hoc culpantur. Ergo videtur quod non teneamur in omnibus obedire Deo.

2. Præterea, nullus tenetur aliquid facere contra virtutem. Sed inveniuntur quædam præcepta Dei contra virtutem; sicut quod* præcepit Abrahæ ut occideret filium innocentem, ut habetur *Gen.*,[3] et Judæis, ut furarentur res Ægyptiorum, ut habetur *Exod.*,[4] quæ sunt contra justitiam; et Oseæ, quod acciperet mulierem adulteram, quod est contra castitatem.[5] Ergo non in omnibus est obediendum Deo.

3. Præterea, quicumque obedit Deo, conformat voluntatem suam voluntati divinæ etiam in volito. Sed non quantum ad omnia tenemur conformare voluntatem nostram voluntati divinæ in volito, ut supra habitum est.[6] Ergo non in omnibus tenetur homo Deo obedire.

SED CONTRA est quod dicitur *Exod., Omnia, quæcumque locutus est Dominus, faciemus, et erimus obedientes.*[7]

RESPONSIO: Dicendum quod, sicut supra dictum est,[8] ille qui obedit movetur per imperium ejus cui obedit, sicut res naturales moventur per suos motores. Sicut autem Deus est primus motor omnium quæ naturaliter moventur, ita etiam est primus motor omnium voluntatum, ut ex supra dictis patet.[9] Et ideo sicut naturali necessitate omnia naturalia subduntur

---

*Piana: omits *quod*
[10]*Moral.* xxxv, 14. PL 76, 766
[1]2a2æ. 154, 2 ad 2. *In Joann.* 2, *lect.* 1
[2]*Matthew* 9, 30
[3]*Genesis* 22, 2
[4]*Exodus* 11, 2
[5]*Osee* 1, 2
[6]1a2æ. 19, 10

that *whoever forbids his subjects to do some good, must create other opportunities for them, lest the souls of those who obey perish from starvation, by being kept from all good works.*[10] Thus the loss of one good work can be compensated through obedience plus other good works.

article 4. whether God should be obeyed in all things

THE FOURTH POINT:[1] 1. God should not, it seems, be obeyed in every case.[a] Our Lord commanded the two blind men he had cured, *See that no man know this. But they going out spread his fame abroad in all that country.*[2] They were not censured for this, and so it seems that we are not in every instance bound to obey God.

2. Further, no one is held to an act contrary to virtue. Yet there are instances where God's commands are against virtue: against justice, for Abraham to slay his innocent son,[3] and for the Hebrews to rob the Egyptians;[4] against chastity, for Osee to take a wife of fornication.[5] Therefore, God is not to be obeyed in all things.

3. Further, anyone who obeys God matches his will to God's even in regard to the matter willed. We are not bound in all cases, however, to conform to the divine will as to what we will,[b] as I have already pointed out.[6] We do not have to give obedience to God, therefore, in every case.

ON THE OTHER HAND *All things that the Lord hath spoken we will do. We will be obedient.*[7]

REPLY: Anyone who obeys is prompted by the command of the one obeyed, even as inanimate nature is under the influence of its moving forces.[8] Just as God is the primary mover over all beings that are subject to the forces of nature, so he is over all wills.[9] This parallel, therefore, is established: as all the elements in nature are by the exigencies of nature

---

[7]*Exodus* 24, 7
[8]art. 1
[9]1a2æ. 9, 6
[a]Art. 4–6 deal with the limits of obedience to various superiors; the first two articles touch on the essential issues; art. 6 discusses a problem recurrent throughout Christian history.
[b]This alludes to a technical distinction made in the place cited here. Part of the goodness of any act of will must be in willing an objective in accord with its relationship to God; since, however, we cannot know God's designs in particular, we cannot always be sure that the content of our choice is what God actually wills.

divinæ motioni, ita etiam quadam necessitate justitiæ omnes voluntates tenentur obedire divino imperio.

1. Ad primum ergo dicendum quod Dominus cæcis dixit ut miraculum occultarent non quasi intendens eos per virtutem divini præcepti obligare, sed, sicut Gregorius dicit, *Servis suis sese sequentibus exemplum dedit, ut ipsi quidem virtutes suas occultari desiderent, et tamen ut alii eorum exemplo proficiant, prodantur inviti.*[10]

2. Ad secundum dicendum quod, sicut Deus nihil operatur contra naturam, quia *hoc est natura uniuscujusque rei quod in ea Deus operatur*, ut habetur in *Glossa* ad *Rom.*,[11] operatur tamen aliquid contra solitum cursum naturæ; ita etiam nihil Deus potest præcipere contra virtutem, quia in hoc principaliter consistit virtus et rectitudo voluntatis humanæ quod Dei voluntati conformetur et ejus sequatur imperium, quamvis sit contra consuetum virtutis modum.

Secundum hoc ergo præceptum Abrahæ factum, quod filium innocentem occideret, non fuit contra justitiam, quia Deus est auctor mortis et vitæ. Similiter nec fuit contra justitiam quod mandavit Judæis, ut res Ægyptiorum acciperent, quia ejus sunt omnia, et cui voluerit dat illa. Similiter etiam non fuit contra castitatem præceptum Osee factum* ut mulierem adulteram acciperet, quia ipse Deus est humanæ generationis ordinator, et ille est debitus modus mulieribus utendi quem Deus instituit. Unde patet quod prædicti nec obediendo Deo nec obedire volendo peccaverunt.

3. Ad tertium dicendum quod etsi non semper teneatur homo velle quod Deus vult, semper tamen tenetur velle quod Deus vult eum velle. Et hoc homini præcipue innotescit per præceptum divinum; et ideo tenetur homo in omnibus divinis præceptis obedire.

---

*Leonine: *and Osee factum.*
[10]*Moral.* XIX, 23. PL 76, 120
[11]*Ordinaria ad Rom.* 11, 24; also Augustine, *Contra Faustum* XXI, 3. PL 42, 390
cThe reasoning here is an extension of the Reply of art. 1, and should be read keeping in mind the analogy there (see notes b & c). On God's universal causality 'moving' all things, cf 1a. 105, especially 4 & 5. This is part of God's governing all beings. The divine causality is suited to the nature of each creature, and affects man through law (cf 1a2æ. 91, 2; 94, 1), a point here suggested by the term *imperio*. The *necessitate justitiæ*, 'demands of moral rightness', means a free response in a chosen obedience to God's rule. The universality of God's right to be obeyed rests on the primacy of his causality.
dcf 1a. 105, 6.
eModern studies of literary forms in the Bible would have other explanations of these 'cases'. The modern understanding of biblical inerrancy also differs from that of the medievals. St Thomas deals with these problems in many places, e.g. 1a2æ. 94, 5 ad 2; 100, 8; 2a2æ. 154, 2 ad 2; *De Potentia* I, 6; *De Malo* VIII, 1 ad 17; 15, 1 ad 8; I *Sent.* 47, 1, 4; III *Sent.* 37, 4 ad 3. These instances seemed to

subject to God moving, so all wills are bound under the demands of moral rightness to obey God ruling.^c

Hence: 1. Our Lord in telling the blind men to keep the miracle quiet had no intention of obliging them by the power of a divine command. Rather, as Gregory sees it, *He gave as an ideal to his followers that they prefer to keep their own virtues hidden, yet allow them, however reluctantly, to be publicized as an example helpful to others.*[10]

2. God does not act against nature, seeing that *it is of the nature of all things to have God working within them.*[11] He does, however, at times act contrary to the usual natural pattern.^d Similarly, God cannot command anything contrary to virtue since the meaning of virtue and the uprightness of man's will consist mainly in being in accord with God's will and in responding to his command, even when this runs counter to the usual way in which virtue works.^e

The precept for Abraham to kill his innocent son was not contrary to justice, since God himself is the author of life and death. Likewise, it was not against justice to order the Jews to take the belongings of the Egyptians, since all things are the possessions of God, who can bestow them upon whom he wills. Nor was it against chastity that Osee receive a command to take an adulteress to himself, since God has set out the conditions of human procreation and the proper way for man to be joined to woman is whatever way God determines. Those mentioned, then, did not sin either in obeying or in being willing to obey God.

3. Granted that a person is not always bound to will the same thing God wills, he is bound to will what God wants him to will.^f Since the knowledge of what this is comes chiefly through the divine commandments, a person is obliged to obey these in all cases.^g

---

trouble him; he is too certain of the intelligible order in God's operations to entertain the voluntarism of later Nominalists, with its recourse to the divine *potentia absoluta* as a kind of arbitrariness that does away with intelligibility. He seeks always to defend the objective validity and consistency of moral values and the truth that they have their foundation in God's law, which is a pattern of wisdom and order; see *CG* III, 129. With regard to the cases at hand he concludes that the essential moral values have been realized in ways that depart from the usual pattern.

^fThis is not tautological; "what God wants him to will" refers to a value or motive in the object chosen, i.e. part of its goodness is the quality of being in accord with God's will in the judgment of the person acting. He can be sure of this as one of his reasons for choosing; he cannot be sure that the concrete thing chosen is willed by God.

^gcf 1a2æ. 108, 1–3. St Thomas rejects antinomianism, the position that grace does away with the law, the commandments. Grace and charity interiorly unite the person to God and put his will in accord with the divine. This is the newness and freedom of the New Law; the commandments towards which the person in grace is attuned become an aid to living in accord with the union of soul and will with God.

articulus 5. *utrum subditi teneantur suis superioribus in omnibus obedire*

AD QUINTUM sic proceditur:[1] 1. Videtur quod subditi teneantur suis superioribus in omnibus obedire. Dicit enim Apostolus *Ad Coloss.*, *Filii, obedite parentibus per omnia;* et postea subdit, *Servi, obedite per omnia dominis carnalibus.*[2] Ergo eadem ratione alii subditi debent prælatis suis in omnibus obedire.

2. Præterea, prælati sunt medii inter Deum et subditos, secundum illud *Deut.*, *Ego sequester et medius fui inter Deum et vos in tempore illo, ut annuntiarem vobis verba ejus.*[3] Sed ab extremo in extremum non pervenitur nisi per medium. Ergo præcepta prælati sunt reputanda tanquam præcepta Dei; unde et Apostolus dicit, *Ad Gal.*, *Sicut angelum Dei excepistis me, sicut Christum Jesum;*[4] et 1 ad *Thess.* II, *Cum accepissetis a nobis verbum auditus Dei, accepistis illud, non ut verbum hominum, sed, sicut vere est, verbum Dei.*[5] Ergo sicut homo debet Deo obedire in omnibus, ita et prælatis.

3. Præterea, sicut religiosi profitendo vovent castitatem et paupertatem, ita et obedientiam. Sed religiosus tenetur quantum ad omnia servare castitatem et paupertatem. Ergo similiter quantum ad omnia tenetur obedire.

SED CONTRA est quod dicitur *Act.*, *Obedire oportet Deo magis quam hominibus.*[6] Sed quandoque præcepta prælatorum sunt contra Deum. Ergo non in omnibus prælatis est obediendum.

RESPONSIO: Dicendum quod, sicut dictum est,[7] obediens movetur ad imperium præcipientis quadam necessitate justitiæ, sicut res naturalis movetur ex virtute sui motoris necessitate naturæ. Quod autem aliqua res naturalis non moveatur a suo motore, potest contingere dupliciter. Uno modo propter impedimentum quod provenit ex fortiori virtute alterius moventis, sicut lignum non comburitur ab igne, si fortior vis aquæ impediat. Alio modo ex defectu ordinis mobilis ad motorem, quia etsi subjiciatur ejus actioni quantum ad aliquid, non tamen quantum ad omnia, sicut humor quandoque subjicitur actioni caloris quantum ad calefieri, non tamen quantum ad exsiccari, sive consumi.

---

[1]cf *In Titum* 3, *lect.* 1. *In Joannem* 2, *lect.* 1. *In Romanos* 13, *lect.* 1
[2]*Colossians* 3, 20 & 22   [3]*Deuteronomy* 5, 5
[4]*Galatians* 4, 14   [5]I *Thessalonians* 2, 13
[6]*Acts* 5, 29   [7]art. 1 & 4
[a]*motor* and *mobile* are correlatives and reflect the technical sense that the verbs *movere* (active) and *moveri* (passive) have in St Thomas's usage. *Movere* means to move in the sense of actively bringing about a change; the source of the activity is the *motor*. *Moveri* means 'to be moved' or 'to be in the process of change'; the

OBEDIENCE

article 5. whether subjects are bound to obey their superiors in all matters

THE FIFTH POINT:[1] 1. It appears that subjects must obey their superiors in all matters. *Children obey your parents in all things*, St Paul says; and later on, *Servants, obey in all things your masters according to the flesh.*[2] Similarly, then, the obedience of other subordinates must be universal.

2. Further, the text, *I was the mediator and stood between the Lord and you at that time to show you his words*[3] indicates that superiors are mediators between God and their subjects. Since to go from one end to another involves passing through the middle, the precepts of a superior are to be counted as commands of God. This point is made by St Paul, *You received me as an angel of God even as Christ Jesus;*[4] and, *When you had received of us the word of the hearing of God, you received it, not as the word of men, but, as it is indeed, the word of God.*[5] Even as God, so also superiors are to be obeyed in all matters.

3. Further, just as religious vow by their profession chastity and poverty, so also obedience. Since they are bound to observe chastity and poverty in all cases, so also obedience.

ON THE OTHER HAND *we ought to obey God rather than men*,[6] and at times the commands of superiors run counter to those of God. Hence an obedience without exception is not to be given to superiors.

REPLY: As has been said,[7] by the demands of moral rightness one who obeys is under the influence of a superior's command in a way similar to the sub-rational creature being by force of nature under the influence of the power of its mover. There are two ways in which it can happen that some sub-rational being is not moved by its mover. The first is interference coming from the stronger power of another moving force; for example, wood is not burned by fire when stronger water-power intervenes. The second comes from a lack of complete subjection in a recipient to its moving force,[a] i.e. there is subjection in some respect but not in all; for example, moisture may receive the action of heat to the point of being warmed, but not of being dried up or evaporated.

---

subject undergoing change is considered to be passive, to be the recipient of the influence of another; this subject is the *mobile*. The terms derive from the view that since a subject undergoing change is in the process of acquiring what it lacks, it cannot confer the process of change upon itself; it cannot move itself, but can only be moved by another. The process of change is called *motus*. The English terms 'mover', 'movement', 'move' do not readily convey the differences here indicated.

SUMMA THEOLOGIÆ, 2a2æ. 104, 5

Similiter ex duobus potest contingere quod subditus suo superiori non teneatur in omnibus obedire. Uno modo propter præceptum majoris potestatis. Ut enim dicitur *Ad Rom.* super illud, *Qui potestati resistunt, ipsi sibi damnationem acquirunt,*[8] dicit glossa, *si quid jusserit curator, numquid est tibi faciendum, si contra proconsulem jubeat? Rursum si quid proconsul jubeat, et aliud imperator, numquid dubitatur, illo contempto, isti esse serviendum? Ergo si aliud imperator, aliud Deus jubeat, contempto illo, obtemperandum est Deo.*[9]

Alio modo non tenetur inferior suo superiori obedire, si ei aliquid præcipiat in quo ei non subdatur. Dicit enim Seneca, *Errat, si quis existimat servitutem in totum hominem descendere; pars enim melior excepta est: corpora obnoxia sunt et adscripta dominis, mens quidem est sui juris.*[10] Et ideo in his quæ pertinent ad interiorem motum voluntatis, homo non tenetur homini obedire, sed solum Deo.

Tenetur autem homo homini obedire in his quæ exterius per corpus sunt agenda; in quibus tamen secundum ea quæ ad naturam corporis pertinent, homo homini obedire non tenetur, sed solum Deo, quia omnes homines natura sunt pares, puta in his quæ pertinent ad corporis sustentationem et prolis generationem. Unde non tenentur nec servi dominis, nec filii parentibus obedire de matrimonio contrahendo vel virginitate servanda aut aliquo alio hujusmodi. Sed in his quæ pertinent ad dispositionem actuum et rerum humanarum tenetur subditus suo superiori obedire secundum rationem superioritatis; sicut miles duci exercitus in his quæ pertinent ad bellum, servus domino in his quæ pertinent ad servilia opera exequenda, filius patri in his quæ pertinent ad disciplinam vitæ et curam domesticam, et sic de aliis.

1. Ad primum ergo dicendum quod hoc quod Apostolus dicit, intelligendum est *per omnia* quantum ad illa quæ pertinent ad jus patriæ, vel dominativæ potestatis.

---

[8]*Romans* 13, 2
[9]*Lombardi*. PL 191, 1505; also in Augustine, *Serm.* LXIII, 8. PL 38, 421
[10]*De beneficiis* III, 20. Lucius Annæus Seneca (*c.* A.D. 4–65), Stoic moral philosopher whose lofty moral theory was much quoted by Christian writers; an apocryphal correspondence with St Paul was taken by some to be proof that he was a Christian.
[b]*motus* is used here not in its proper sense (see note *a*) but in a transferred sense, to mean action or operation; cf 1a. 9, 1 ad 1. As a general principle St Thomas maintains that no human superior has power over the inner life of other human beings; cf 1a2æ. 96, 3 ad 2; 4; 100, 9. Thus strictly speaking a human superior does not command the act of obedience, but the outward fulfilment of his command. The subject's obligation to render virtuous obedience is not to the superior precisely but to his own conscience, to the requirements of virtuous living, and so ultimately to God. In Roman Catholic theology certain qualifications of the ecclesiastical power to command have been developed. The Church is recognized as exercising a vicarious divine power in certain areas, and thus as sharing in the power of God even

Carrying over the parallel: there are two ways it can happen that a subordinate is not bound to obey a superior in everything. The first is because of the precept of a higher superior; a gloss on *Romans, He that resisteth the power, resisteth the ordinance of God,*[8] comments, *Should a commissioner issue an order, are you to comply if it be contrary to the bidding of a proconsul? Again, if the proconsul command one thing and the emperor another, would you hesitate to disregard the first and observe the other? Therefore if the emperor order one thing and God another, it is God who is to be obeyed.*[9]

The second way is for a command to be given in a matter where no subjection to the superior exists. Seneca's remark is to the point, *He is mistaken who supposes that slavery takes in the whole person. It touches not the better part; the body may be subject and consigned to an owner, but thoughts are free.*[10] The force of this is that we are not bound to obey man but God alone in matters which concern the inner life[b] of the will.

Those matters in which one man is bound to obey another are outward actions involving the body. Even so, he is not bound to obey humans but God alone in regard to what belongs to the very nature of physical life, since in these matters all men are equal: for example in what concerns taking food and begetting children. This is why there is no obligation either of slaves towards their master or of children towards their parents to obey with regard to contracting marriage, vowing virginity, or the like.[c] In what relates to the control of human conduct and affairs,[d] a subject is bound to obey his superiors within the limits of the authority in question—a soldier, his commander in military matters; a slave, his master in carrying out the labours of his service; a child, its parents in what concerns upbringing, running the household, etc.

Hence: 1. St Paul's words mean 'all' within the limits of a father's or master's right to command.

---

over mind and will. In areas where the Church governs in a purely human, religio-social way, there are some acts commanded that are not merely exterior, but are mixed, e.g. the faithful are commanded to receive the Eucharist at least annually and so to confess their sins when this is necessary. Interior acts are implied in these precepts. In the case of religious there are acts which a superior can command that also involve interior acts; cf ad 3; 185, 1 ad 2 & 5 ad 1.

[c]The statement must be understood of the essentials of such acts. Clearly parents have the right to control and regulate their children's lives in these matters as long as the children remain minors; the State can pass health laws concerning food and drugs, or law regulating the age required or other civil aspects of marriage. The statement is also of interest to the question of the right of the State to make sterilization a punishment for crime.

[d]cf 1a2æ. 100, 3; civil law is concerned primarily with justice and with other areas of virtue only to the degree that they touch upon justice; cf also 1a2æ. 96, 4, on the power of just laws to bind in conscience, and Vol. 28 of this series, p. 129 note *a* on penal laws.

2. Ad secundum dicendum quod Deo subjicitur homo simpliciter quantum ad omnia et interiora et exteriora; et ideo in omnibus ei obedire tenetur. Subditi autem non subjiciuntur suis superioribus quantum ad omnia, sed quantum ad aliqua determinate, et quantum ad illa medii sunt inter Deum et subditos. Quantum ad alia vero immediate subduntur Deo, a quo instruuntur per legem naturalem vel scriptam.

3. Ad tertium dicendum quod religiosi obedientiam profitentur quantum ad regularem conversationem, secundum quam suis prælatis subduntur. Et ideo quantum ad illa sola obedire tenentur quæ possunt ad regularem conversationem pertinere; et hæc est obedientia sufficiens ad salutem. Si autem etiam in aliis obedire voluerint, hoc pertinebit ad cumulum perfectionis, dum tamen illa non sint contra Deum aut contra professionem regulæ, quia talis obedientia esset illicita.

Sic ergo potest triplex obedientia distingui: una sufficiens ad salutem, quæ scilicet obedit in his ad quæ obligatur; alia perfecta, quæ obedit in omnibus licitis; alia indiscreta, quæ etiam in illicitis obedit.

articulus 6. utrum Christiani teneantur sæcularibus potestatibus obedire

AD SEXTUM sic proceditur:[1] 1. Videtur quod Christiani non teneantur sæcularibus potestatibus obedire, quia, super illud *Matt.*, *Ergo liberi sunt filii*,[2] dicit *Glossa*, *Si in quolibet regno filii illius regis, qui regno illi præfertur, sunt liberi, tunc filii regis illius, cui omnia regna subduntur, in quolibet regno liberi esse debent.*[3] Sed Christiani per fidem Christi facti sunt filii Dei, secundum illud *Joan.*, *Dedit eis potestatem filios Dei fieri, his qui credunt in nomine ejus.*[4] Ergo non tenentur potestatibus sæcularibus obedire.

2. Præterea, *Ad Rom.* dicitur, *Mortificati estis legi per corpus Christi*,[5] et loquitur de lege divina Veteris Testamenti. Sed minor est lex humana, per quam homines sæcularibus potestatibus subduntur, quam lex divina Veteris Testamenti. Ergo multo magis homines per hoc quod sunt facti membra corporis Christi liberantur a lege subjectionis qua sæcularibus principibus obstringebantur.

3. Præterea, latronibus, qui per violentiam opprimunt, homines obedire non tenentur. Sed Augustinus dicit, *Remota justitia, quid sunt regna, nisi magna latrocinia?*[6] Cum ergo dominia principum sæcularium plerumque

---

[1] II *Sent.* 44, 2, 2. *In Romanos* 13, *lect.* 1
[2] *Matthew* 17, 27
[3] *Ordinaria*; also Augustine, *Quæst. Evangel.* I, 23 on *Matt.* 17, 27. PL 35, 1327
[4] *John* 1, 12   [5] *Romans* 7, 4
[6] *De civ. Dei* IV, 4. PL 41, 115
[e] For the distinction between natural law and positive law, cf 1a2æ. 91, 2 & 3; on the divine origin of all just laws, 1a2æ. 93, 3.
[f] cf 2a2æ. 186, 5 ad 1 & ad 4, on the universality of the obedience proper to religious.

2. Man is subject to God utterly and in all matters, internal and external; thus he is bound to a universal obedience. In contrast, subjects are not under their superiors in all regards, but only within fixed limits; here superiors are mediators between God and the subject. In other respects subjects are under the authority of God directly, who manifests his will through law, natural and positive.[e]

3. Religious make profession of obedience with regard to the observances of their community, and on this basis are subject to their superiors. The obedience to which they are bound and which is necessary for their salvation, therefore, bears only upon matters affecting their manner of life.[f] Should they wish to extend their obedience to other matters, this would involve an extra degree of perfection, so long as nothing forbidden by God or by their rule were done, for then obedience would be wrong.

From this we see three kinds of obedience: one sufficient for salvation, extending namely to matters of obligation; a second, perfect obedience, embracing all that is permissible; a third, indiscriminate obedience, going even beyond what is lawful.

article 6. whether Christians must obey civil authority

THE SIXTH POINT:[1] 1. There seems to be no good reason why Christians should be bound to obey civil authority.[a] On *Matthew, Then the children are free,*[2] the *Gloss* comments, *If in any kingdom the sons of the ruling monarch are free, then, wherever they are, the sons of that king whose rule is over all, must be free.*[3] And the text, *He gave them power to be made the sons of God,*[4] shows that by faith in Christ Christians become sons of God. Consequently, they are not bound to obey the secular arm.

2. Further, even with regard to the divine law in the Old Testament *Romans* states that *you are become dead to the law by the body of Christ.*[5] Human laws, the instrument whereby people are subjected to civil authority, are something less than the divine Old Testament law. *A fortiori* by becoming members of the body of Christ, therefore, people are freed from the laws binding them to the secular power.

3. Further, we have no obligation to obey thieves accosting us, and Augustine has it that *where justice is wanting, what is the regime but a band of brigands?*[6] Since, then, the regime of secular rulers is often marked

---

Religious obedience is a special kind, since it is vowed with regard to the whole disposition of one's life.

[a]Ever since St Paul's time antinomianism has been preached in the name of the Christian's freedom from law through grace; cf 1a2æ. 108, 1. The three objections touch on points raised perennially against the Christian's subjection to civil authority, e.g. by the 16th-century Anabaptists and by others seeking a theological reason for passive non-resistance to the State.

cum injustitia exerceantur vel ab aliqua injusta usurpatione principium sumpserint, videtur quod non sit principibus sæcularibus obediendum a Christianis.

SED CONTRA est quod dicitur *Ad Tit.*, *Admone illos, principibus et potestatibus subditos esse;*[7] et 1 *Pet.*, *Subjecti estote omni humanæ creaturæ propter Deum, sive regi, quasi præcellenti, sive ducibus tanquam ab eo missis.*[8]

RESPONSIO: Dicendum quod fides Christi est justitiæ principium et causa, secundum illud *Rom.*, *Justitia Dei per fidem Jesu Christi*,[9] et ideo per fidem Jesu Christi non tollitur ordo justitiæ sed magis firmatur. Ordo autem justitiæ requirit ut inferiores suis superioribus obediant; aliter enim non posset humanarum rerum status conservari. Et ideo per fidem Christi non excusantur fideles quin principibus sæcularibus obedire teneantur.

1. Ad primum ergo dicendum quod, sicut supra dictum est,[10] servitus, qua homo homini subjicitur, ad corpus pertinet non ad animam, quæ libera manet. Nunc autem in statu hujus vitæ per gratiam Christi liberamur a defectibus animæ non autem a defectibus corporis, ut patet per Apostolum *Ad Rom.*, qui dicit de seipso, quod *mente servit legi Dei, carne autem legi peccati*.[11] Et ideo illi qui fiunt filii Dei per gratiam, liberi sunt a spirituali servitute peccati, non autem a servitute corporali, qua temporalibus dominis tenentur adstricti, ut dicit *Glossa*[12] super illud 1 *Ad Tim.*, *Quicumque sunt sub jugo servi*, etc.[13]

2. Ad secundum dicendum quod lex vetus fuit figura Novi Testamenti et ideo debuit cessare, veritate veniente. Non autem est simile de lege humana, per quam homo subjicitur homini. Et tamen etiam ex lege divina homo tenetur homini obedire.

3. Ad tertium dicendum quod principibus sæcularibus intantum homo obedire tenetur inquantum ordo justitiæ requirit. Et ideo si non habeant justum principatum sed usurpatum, vel si injusta præcipiant, non tenentur eis subditi obedire nisi forte per accidens propter vitandum scandalum vel periculum.

---

[7]*Titus* 3, 1
[8]1 *Peter* 2, 13
[9]*Romans* 3, 22
[10]art. 5
[11]*Romans* 7, 25
[12]*Ordinaria; Lombardi.* PL 192, 357
[13]1 *Timothy* 6, 1
[b]The argument calls for use of the Pauline sense of *justitia* here, then the specific sense in the rest of the Reply; cf 1a2æ. 113, 1. For the Christian every aspect of virtuous living is prompted by the grace relationship which he receives through living faith in Christ.

by injustice, or else they have unjustly usurped power, it seems that Christians should not obey them.

ON THE OTHER HAND there are these texts, *Admonish them to be subject to princes and powers;*[7] *Be ye subject to every human creature for God's sake, whether it be to kings as excelling or to governors as sent by him.*[8]

REPLY: Following *Romans, The justice of God by faith of Jesus Christ,*[9] faith in Christ is the source and support of all righteousness.[b] For this reason the order of justice[c] is not abolished but strengthened through the faith of Christ. Now the order of justice calls for inferiors to be subject to their superiors; otherwise it would be impossible to maintain stability in human affairs. Thus, their faith in Christ does not exempt the faithful from the duty to obey civil authority.

Hence: 1. As I have said,[10] the subjection whereby one man is under another's power applies to the body not the soul, which remains free. In our earthly condition we are free through Christ's grace from ills of soul but not from those of the body, as is clear from St Paul saying about himself that *he served the law of God, but in his members the mind of sin.*[11] Hence, those who through grace have been made sons of God are free from the spiritual bondage of sin but not from the outward service wherein they are said to be bound to temporal masters, by the *Gloss*[12] on *whosoever are servants under the yoke,* etc.[13]

2. The Old Law, as the figure of the New Testament, had to pass away with the coming of the reality it prefigured. The same does not hold true with regard to human laws that subject man to the authority of other men. Note also that it is from divine law itself that one man is held to obey another.

3. The obligation to obey civil authority is measured by what the order of justice requires. For this reason when any regime holds its power not by right but by usurpation, or commands what is wrong, subjects have no duty to obey, except for such extraneous reasons as avoidance of scandal or risk.[d]

---

[c]*ordo justitiæ* has the same meaning here as throughout the discussion of the virtues of respect.

[d]*scandalum* here means that the community would suffer more serious harm, whether material or spiritual, than that brought on in the status quo. On the question of civil disobedience or revolution against an unjust regime, cf 2a2æ. 40; 42, 2 ad 3; *In Polit.* III, lect. 6; *In Ethic.* VIII, lect. 10. Where scandal or risk would be involved, subjects are still not held to *obey*, since unjust commands have no moral standing; rather subjects should observe charity, a higher justice or some other virtue in their restraint from outright disobedience.

Quæstio 105. de inobedientia

DEINDE CONSIDERANDUM EST de inobedientia. Et circa hoc quæruntur duo:
1. utrum sit peccatum mortale;
2. utrum sit gravissimum peccatorum.

articulus 1. utrum inobedientia sit peccatum mortale

AD PRIMUM sic proceditur: 1. Videtur quod inobedientia non sit peccatum mortale. Omne enim peccatum est inobedientia, ut patet per definitionem Ambrosii superius positam.[1] Si ergo inobedientia esset peccatum mortale, omne peccatum esset mortale.

2. Præterea, Gregorius dicit *Moral.* quod *inobedientia oritur ex inani gloria*.[2] Sed inanis gloria non est peccatum mortale. Ergo nec inobedientia.

3. Præterea, tunc dicitur aliquis esse inobediens quando superioris præceptum non implet. Sed superiores multoties præcepta multiplicant, quæ vix aut nunquam omnia possunt observari. Si ergo inobedientia esset peccatum mortale, sequeretur quod homo non posset vitare mortale peccatum, quod est inconveniens. Non ergo inobedientia est peccatum mortale.

SED CONTRA est quod *Ad Rom.* et II *Ad Tim.* inter alia peccata mortalia computatur* *parentibus non obedientes*.[3]

RESPONSIO: Dicendum quod, sicut supra dictum est,[4] peccatum mortale est quod contrariatur caritati, per quam est spiritualis vita. Caritate autem diligitur Deus et proximus. Exigit autem caritas Dei ut ejus mandatis obediatur, ut supra dictum est.[5] Et ideo inobedientem esse divinis præceptis est peccatum mortale quasi divinæ dilectioni contrarium.

---

*Piana: *computantur*
[1] cf above, 104, 2, obj. 1
[2] *Moral.* XXXI, 45. PL 76, 621
[3] *Romans* 1, 30; II *Timothy* 3, 2
[4] 1a2æ. 72, 5; 88, 2; 2a2æ. 24, 12; 35, 3
[5] 2a2æ. 24, 12; 104, 3
[a] The direct presupposition of these two articles is 104, 3.
[b] A sin is denominated mortal on the basis of a comparison between the effect of a gravely wrong moral act upon the soul, and the effect of a fatal illness upon the body. That any single moral action can destroy the life of the soul presupposes that this life is grace, and is exercised primarily through charity. Grace and charity are given by God alone; when they are lost, the life that they bestow ceases. Mortal

Question 105. disobedience

NEXT, DISOBEDIENCE, WITH two points of inquiry:[a]
1. whether it is a mortal sin;
2. and the most serious of all sins.

article 1. whether disobedience is a mortal sin

THE FIRST POINT: 1. Disobedience does not seem to be a mortal sin. In Ambrose's definition, given before,[1] every sin is disobedience. If, therefore, disobedience were a mortal sin, every sin would be mortal.

2. Further, Gregory says that *disobedience issues from vainglory*,[2] which is not mortal. Neither, then, is disobedience.

3. Further, someone is said to be disobedient when he does not observe the precept of a superior. Quite often, however, superiors add precept to precept, and the ensemble can rarely if ever be fulfilled. Were disobedience a mortal sin it would follow that mortal sin would be unavoidable, and this is inadmissible. Therefore disobedience is not a mortal sin.

ON THE OTHER HAND, in *Romans* and II *Timothy* among other mortal sins there is listed *disobedient to parents*.[3]

REPLY: As I have pointed out,[4] a mortal sin is one that is in opposition to charity,[b] through which the soul has life. By charity we love God and neighbour. Love for God requires that we keep his commands, as stated earlier.[5] To be disobedient to God's commandments, therefore, is a sin that is mortal, incompatible with loving him.[c] Moreover to obey superiors

---

sin has no meaning in a purely natural ethic; a person could certainly commit seriously wrong moral actions, but by his own powers he could also redirect himself to right moral living; see 1a2æ. 63, 2 ad 2. In the life of grace and charity, however, no such self-rectification is possible; an act opposed to the vital communion of charity with God simply cuts off the grace-life; cf 1a2æ. 88, 1. A sin is said to be mortal by its opposition to charity because the life of grace is lived by actions; the opposition is of an evil act to the act of grace, loving God.

[c]This principle is uniformly applied to the question whether some sort of sin is mortal; cf 2a2æ. 35, 3; 36, 3; 37, 1; 55, 2; 59, 4; 66, 6; 69, 1 ad 1; 76, 3; 98, 3; 110, 4; 111, 4; 112, 2; 118, 4; 125, 3; 132, 3; 148, 2; 150, 3; 154, 2 & 5; 158, 3; 162, 5. Note, however, that the direct opposition of a sinful act is to the act of its contrary virtue; cf 1a2æ. 71, 1 & 4. Only certain sins are opposed in this direct way to charity, e.g. hatred of God or neighbour. The direct opposition of other sins to some specific virtuous act is also an indirect or consequent opposition to love for God or neighbour: the sinful act against a specific virtue excludes the

(*footnote c continued on page 76.*)

In præceptis autem divinis continetur quod etiam superioribus obediatur. Et ideo etiam inobedientia, qua quis inobediens est præceptis superiorum, est peccatum mortale quasi divinæ dilectioni contrarium, secundum illud *Ad Rom.*, *Qui potestati resistit, Dei ordinationi resistit.*[6] Contrariatur insuper dilectioni proximi, inquantum superiori proximo subtrahit obedientiam quam ei debet.

1. Ad primum ergo dicendum quod illa definitio Ambrosii datur de peccato mortali, quod habet perfectam peccati rationem. Peccatum autem veniale non est inobedientia, quia non est contra præceptum, sed præter præceptum. Nec etiam omne peccatum mortale est inobedientia proprie et per se loquendo, sed solum tunc quando aliquis præceptum contemnit, quia ex fine morales actus speciem habent. Cum autem facit aliquid contra præceptum, non propter præcepti contemptum sed propter aliquid aliud, est inobedientia materialiter tantum sed pertinet formaliter ad aliam speciem peccati.

2. Ad secundum dicendum quod inanis gloria appetit manifestationem alicujus excellentiæ. Et quia videtur ad quamdam excellentiam pertinere quod homo præceptis alterius non subdatur, inde est quod inobedientia ex inani gloria oritur. Nihil autem prohibet ex peccato veniali oriri mortale, cum veniale sit dispositio ad mortale.

3. Ad tertium dicendum quod nullus obligatur ad impossibile, et ideo si tot præcepta prælatus aliquis ingerat seu injungat* quod subditus ea implere non possit, excusatur a peccato. Et ideo prælati abstinere debent a multitudine præceptorum.

articulus 2. utrum inobedientia sit gravissimum peccatorum

AD SECUNDUM sic proceditur: 1. Videtur quod inobedientia sit gravissimum peccatum. Dicitur enim 1 *Reg.* 15, *Quasi peccatum ariolandi est repugnare, et quasi scelus idololatriæ nolle acquiescere*[1] Sed idololatria est gravissimum peccatum, ut supra habitum est.[2] Ergo inobedientia est gravissimum peccatum.

---

*Leonine: omits *seu injungat*, or imposes
[6]*Romans* 13, 2   [1]1 *Kings* 15, 23   [2]2a2æ. 94, 3

(*footnote c continued from page 75*)
union of will with God or neighbour (cf 1a2æ. 65, 2 & 3; 2a2æ. 23, 8; QD *De caritate* 3, on charity as the 'form' of all the virtues). Once the principle is accepted, however, there remains the question of which sinful acts are thus incompatible with charity, by their very nature (cf 1a2æ. 88, 2). The history of moral theology has seen a legalistic multiplication of 'objectively mortal sins' on the basis of their being contrary to law, or being heinous or shameful; such legalism neglects the primacy of charity and so the true evil of mortal sin. The exaltation of charity, on the other hand, that obliterates any objective moral order, any moral absolute, becomes easily a practical antinomianism, which surely destroys the effective, measuring influence of charity on each personal moral choice.

is also one of God's commandments, and so disobedience, even to the precepts of superiors, is a mortal sin for being contrary to the love of God,[d] following *Romans, He that resisteth the power, resisteth the ordinance of God*.[6]

Disobedience also runs counter to the love of neighbour in that it keeps back from a neighbour, namely the superior, an obedience owed to him.

Hence: 1. Ambrose's definition is meant for mortal sin, which is sin in the full sense. Venial sin, however, is not really disobedience, not being directly against a precept,[e] but apart from precept. With regard to mortal sin, not every one is a form of disobedience strictly speaking, but only one in which there is contempt for a precept.[f] Since moral actions take their species from their ends[g] when a person acts contrary to a precept not from contempt but from some other motive, there is only a *de facto* disobedience, in his act, but in its specific nature the act is some other kind of sin.[h]

2. Vainglory craves to show off some form of superiority; because to refuse to submit to another's commands gives the impression of adding to one's own superiority, disobedience does arise from vainglory. But there is nothing against a mortal sin having its origin in a venial sin, since venial sin paves the way for mortal sin.[i]

3. Since no one is obliged to the impossible, if any superior lays down or imposes so many precepts that they cannot possibly be kept, the subject is without guilt. Accordingly those in authority should refrain from multiplying precepts.

article 2. whether disobedience is the worst sin of all

THE SECOND POINT: 1. Disobedience seems to be the most serious sin of all.[a] *It is like the sin of witchcraft to rebel, and like the crime of idolatry to refuse to obey*.[1] Since idolatry, as I have stated earlier,[2] is the most serious kind of sin, so is disobedience.

---

[d]cf 104, 3, note *g*; 24, 12.
[e]cf 1a2æ. 88, 2; certain acts are recognized as of their very nature morally wrong, yet not incompatible with the habitual choice of charity to love God above all. They are 'venially' sinful, i.e. they do not destroy charity, the interior source of pardon and rectification.
[f]The statement relies on 104, 2 and ad 1. On contempt, see 186, 9 and 3.
[g]See 1a2æ. 1, 3; 18, 1-7, and Vol. 18, ed. T. Gilby, Appendix 14, pp. 176-9.
[h]Again the use of *materialiter-formaliter*; see 104, 1, note *h*. Here the allusion is that the nature or quality of a moral act is called its 'form;' see 104, 1, note *g*.
[i]See 1a2æ. 98, 3; 2a2æ. 24, 10.
On the gradation of gravity and guilt in sins, see 1a2æ. 73; 2a2æ. 10, 3; 39, 2.

2. Præterea, illud peccatum dicitur esse in Spiritum Sanctum per quod tolluntur impedimenta peccati, ut supra dictum est.³ Sed per inobedientiam contemnit homo præceptum, quod maxime retrahit hominem a peccando. Ergo inobedientia est peccatum in Spiritum Sanctum; et ita est gravissimum peccatum.

3. Præterea, Apostolus dicit *ad Rom.* quod *per unius in obedientiam peccatores multi constituti sunt.*⁴ Sed causa videtur esse potior effectu. Ergo inobedientia videtur esse gravius peccatum quam alia quæ ex ea causantur.

SED CONTRA est quod gravius est contemnere præcipientem quam præceptum. Sed quædam peccata sunt contra ipsam personam præcipientis, sicut patet de blasphemia et homicidio. Ergo inobedientia non est gravissimum peccatum.

RESPONSIO: Dicendum quod non omnis inobedientia est æquale peccatum. Potest enim una inobedientia esse gravior altera dupliciter. Uno modo ex parte præcipientis, quamvis enim omnem curam homo apponere debeat ad hoc quod cuilibet superiori obediat, tamen magis est debitum quod homo obediat superiori quam inferiori potestati. Cujus signum est quod præceptum inferioris prætermittitur, si sit præcepto superioris contrarium. Unde consequens est quod quanto superior est ille qui præcipit, tanto ei inobedientem esse sit gravius. Et sic inobedientem esse Deo est gravius quam inobedientem esse homini.

Secundo ex parte præceptorum, non enim præcipiens æqualiter vult impleri omnia quæ mandat; magis enim unusquisque præcipiens vult finem et id quod est fini propinquius. Et ideo tanto est inobedientia gravior quanto præceptum quod quis præterit magis est de intentione illius qui præcipit. Et in præceptis quidem Dei manifestum est quod quanto præceptum datur de meliori tanto est ejus inobedientia gravior. Quia cum voluntas Dei per se feratur ad bonum, quanto aliquid est melius tanto Deus vult illud magis impleri. Unde qui inobediens est præcepto de dilectione Dei, gravius peccat quam qui inobediens est præcepto de dilectione proximi. Voluntas autem hominis non semper magis fertur in melius. Et ideo ubi obligamur ex solo hominis præcepto, non est gravius peccatum ex eo quod majus bonum præteritur, sed ex eo quod præteritur illud quod est magis de intentione præcipientis.

Sic ergo oportet secundum diversos inobedientiæ gradus diversis peccatorum* gradibus comparare. Nam inobedientia qua contemnitur Dei

---

*The Leonine reading is followed throughout this paragraph. Some 18th-century editions (e.g. Venice, 1756) have *præceptorum* here for *peccatorum*. The Leonine edition gives no variant readings here from the manuscript traditions; the change must have been made on the basis of a theological interpretation. The text does not need such a change.

2. Further, a sin against the Holy Ghost, as already stated,[3] is one that removes the deterrents against sin. Through disobedience, however, a person spurns a precept, which is the strongest restraint against sin. Hence disobedience is a sin against the Holy Spirit and is a most serious sin.

3. Further, St Paul declares, *By the disobedience of one man many were made sinners*.[4] Since a cause seems to be greater than its effect, disobedience would appear to be a sin more serious than others that are caused by it.

ON THE OTHER HAND it is a more serious matter to show contempt for the person of the one issuing the precept than for the precept itself. But some sins, blasphemy for example or murder, are against the very person of the superior. Disobedience is therefore not the gravest of sins.

REPLY: Not every act of disobedience is equally sinful. The basis for one act being worse than another is twofold. First there is question of who the superior is. For while it is true that everyone should be careful about obeying all superiors, still there is a more pressing urgency with regard to obeying a superior who has greater authority than one who has less. A sign of this is that in case of conflict the command of the second is set aside. It follows that disobedience is the more serious the higher the authority commanding; thus to be disobedient to God is worse than to be disobedient to a human being.

Secondly, there are the precepts themselves. The will of the superior that his commands be carried out is not uniform; everyone's interest is above all in the end and in whatever is closely connected with it. On this basis, one act of disobedience will be the more serious in proportion to the priority that the broken precept has in the superior's intention. In particular: as to God's commandments, disobedience will clearly be worse as the good upon which the precept bears is more important. The reason for this is that since the objective of God's will is the good, the higher the good the more God wills its accomplishment. Thus someone disobeying the commandment to love God sins more seriously than one failing to obey the commandment concerning love for neighbour. The will of a human being, however, is not always more intent upon the higher good. Accordingly, in a case where our obligations arise solely because of a human precept, a sin will be worse not because some better good is left undone, but because something more urgently intended by a superior is left undone.

We must thus compare disobedience, on the basis of its gradations, to different gradations of sins. An act of disobedience that is in contempt of a

---

[3] 2a2æ. 14, 2   [4] *Romans* 5, 19

præceptum ex ipsa ratione inobedientiæ gravius est peccatum quam peccatum quo peccatur in hominem si secerneretur inobedientia Dei, (et hoc dico,† quia qui contra proximum peccat, etiam contra Dei præceptum agit). Si tamen in aliquo potiori præceptum Dei contamneret, adhuc peccatum gravius esset. Inobedientia autem qua contemnitur præceptum hominis levior est peccato quo contemnitur ipse præcipiens; quia ex reverentia præcipientis procedere debet reverentia præcepti. Et similiter peccatum quod directe pertinet ad contemptum Dei, sicut blasphemia vel aliquid hujusmodi, gravius est, etiam semota per intellectum inobedientia a peccato, quam esset illud peccatum in quo contemnitur solum Dei præceptum.

1. Ad primum ergo dicendum quod illa comparatio Samuelis non est æqualitatis, sed similitudinis, quia inobedientia redundat in contemptum Dei sicut et idololatria, licet idololatria magis.

2. Ad secundum dicendum quod non omnis inobedientia est peccatum in Spiritum Sanctum sed solum illa cui obstinatio adhibetur. Non enim contemptus cujuscumque quod peccatum impedit constituit peccatum in Spiritum Sanctum; alioquin cujuslibet boni contemptus esset peccatum in Spiritum Sanctum, quia per quodlibet bonum potest homo impediri a peccato. Sed bonorum illorum contemptus facit peccatum in Spiritum Sanctum quæ directe ducunt ad pœnitentiam et remissionem peccatorum.

3. Ad tertium dicendum quod primum peccatum primi parentis, ex quo in omnes peccatum emanavit, non fuit inobedientia secundum quod est speciale peccatum sed superbia, ex qua homo ad inobedientiam processit. Unde Apostolus in verbis illis videtur accipere inobedientiam secundum quod generaliter se habet ad omne peccatum.

---

†Piana: *et hoc ideo dico*, I therefore mention this.
[b]See *Matthew* 12, 31-2; *Mark* 3, 28-30; *Luke* 12, 10. St Thomas discusses this concept, about which St Augustine made a great deal, in 2a2æ. 14, 2-4. For St Thomas the essential mark of a sin against the Holy Spirit is contempt for those things that

divine precept is worse simply as a sin of disobedience than any sin against a human being, apart even from the fact that the second does include disobedience against God. (I mention this because one sinning against his neighbour also acts against a divine commandment.) The sin will be all the more serious if God's commandment is ignored in some more important matter. An act of disobedience which is in contempt of the precept of a human being is less sinful than contempt for the person of a superior, since reverence for a precept should be based on reverence for the superior himself. Similarly, a sin involving direct contempt for God, blasphemy or the like, is more grievous—abstracting even from the disobedience included—than a sin in which it is simply a commandment of God that is spurned.

Hence: 1. Samuel's comparison is not literal but metaphorical, and means that disobedience amounts to some sort of contempt for God, even though idolatry is a worse sort.

2. Not every form of disobedience but only one which is compounded by obstinacy is a sin against the Holy Ghost.[b] What constitutes a sin against the Holy Spirit is not contempt for whatever inhibits sin; otherwise the spurning of any sort of good would be such a sin, since a person can be kept from sinning by any kind of good. What makes for a sin against the Holy Spirit is rather contempt for those goods that are directly conducive to repentance and pardon.

3. The first sin of the first parents, the source of sin for all men, was not disobedience but pride, which prompted the man to disobey.[c] Consequently it seems that this text of St Paul is using the term disobedience in the broad sense in which it is a general characteristic of every sort of sin.

---

would deter a person from sinning. Following Peter Lombard's use of Augustine, the medievals listed such sins as despair, presumption, final impenitence, obstinacy in evil, rejection of known divine truth, envy of the grace in another.

[c]See 2a2æ. 163, 1 & ad 1. On the first sin of the first man, see 1a2æ. 81 and Vol. 26 of this series.

DEINDE CONSIDERANDUM EST de gratia sive gratitudine et ingratitudine.

Quæstio 106. de gratia sive gratitudine

Circa gratiam autem quæruntur sex:
1. utrum gratia sit specialis virtus ab aliis distincta;
2. quis teneatur ad majores gratiarum actiones Deo, utrum innocens vel pœnitens;
3. utrum semper teneatur homo ad gratias pro beneficiis humanis reddendas;
4. utrum retributio gratiarum sit differenda;
5. utrum sit mensuranda secundum acceptum beneficium, vel secundum dantis affectum;
6. utrum oporteat aliquid majus rependere.

articulus 1. utrum gratia sit specialis virtus ab aliis distincta

AD PRIMUM sic proceditur:[1] 1. Videtur quod gratia non sit virtus specialis ab aliis distincta. Maxima enim beneficia a Deo et a parentibus accepimus. Sed honor quem Deo retribuimus pertinet ad virtutem religionis; honor autem quem retribuimus parentibus pertinet ad virtutem pietatis. Ergo gratia sive gratitudo non est virtus ab aliis distincta.

2. Præterea, retributio proportionalis pertinet ad justitiam commutativam, ut patet per Philosophum in *Ethic.*[2] Sed *gratiæ redduntur, ut retributio sit*, ut ibidem dicitur.[3] Ergo redditio gratiarum, quæ pertinet ad gratitudinem, est actus justitiæ. Non ergo gratitudo est specialis virtus ab aliis distincta.

3. Præterea, recompensatio requiritur ad amicitiam conservandam, ut patet per Philosophum in *Ethic.*[4] Sed amicitia se habet ad omnes virtutes, propter quas homo amatur. Ergo gratia sive gratitudo, ad quam pertinet recompensare beneficia, non est specialis virtus.

SED CONTRA ex quod Tullius ponit gratiam specialem justitiæ partem.[5]

RESPONSIO: Dicendum quod, sicut supra dictum est,[6] secundum diversas causas ex quibus aliquid debetur necesse est diversificari debiti reddendi rationem, ita tamen quod semper in majori illud quod minus est contineatur.

---

[1] 1a2æ. 60, 3 [2] *Ethics* v, 5. 1132b31 [3] *Ethics* v, 5. 1133a2
[4] *Ethics* VIII, 13. 1162b2; IX, 1. 1163b32 [5] *Rhet.* II, 53 [6] 1a2æ. 60, 3

NEXT, THANKS[a] OR gratitude (106), and ingratitude (107).

Question 106. gratitude

There are six points of inquiry with regard to gratitude:

1. whether it is a separate virtue, distinct from others;
2. who is bound to be more grateful to God, the sinless or the penitent?
3. whether a person is obliged always to show gratitude for the kindnesses of other people;
4. whether the return of favours is to be put off;
5. whether repayment is to be measured by the favour received or the sentiment behind it;
6. whether the repayment should be something more.

article 1. whether gratitude is a specific virtue distinct from others

THE FIRST POINT:[1] 1. Apparently gratitude is not a special virtue, distinct from others. Of the benefits we receive, those from God and parents are greatest. Now the honour by which we acknowledge what God has given is the act of the virtue of religion; that in regard to parents, of piety. Thanks or gratitude, then, is not a virtue differing from others.

2. Further, Aristotle's *Ethics* makes it clear that suitable repayment is the concern of commutative justice.[2] And, as he says in the same text, *The purpose of thanks is repayment*.[3] Giving thanks, the act of gratitude, is thus an act of justice, and gratitude is not a specific virtue, distinct from others.

3. Further, Aristotle also points[4] out that returning favours is necessary in order to preserve friendship. Friendship, in turn, is related to all the virtues, since all are motives for love. Since the part of gratitude is to repay kindness, it is not a special virtue.

ON THE OTHER HAND Cicero makes gratitude a specific part of justice.[5]

REPLY: As I have already explained,[6] the grounds for satisfying a debt necessarily differ depending on the different causes of indebtedness, but in such a way that a greater indebtedness always includes one that is less.

---

[a] On the Latin term *gratia* used in this sense, cf 1a2æ. 110, 1. *Webster* gives this meaning for 'thanks' *kindly or grateful thought; gratitude; also grace, favor* . . .

In Deo autem primo et principaliter invenitur causa debiti, in eo quod ipse est primum principium omnium bonorum nostrorum; secundario autem in patre, quia* est proximum nostræ generationis et disciplinæ principium; tertio autem in persona quæ dignitate præcellit ex qua communia beneficia procedunt; quarto autem in aliquo benefactore a quo aliqua particularia et privata beneficia percepimus, pro quibus particulariter ei obligamur.

Quia ergo non quidquid debemus Deo vel patri vel personæ dignitate præcellenti debemus alicui benefactorum a quo aliquod particulare beneficium recepimus. Inde est quod post religionem qua debitum cultum Deo impendimus, et pietatem qua colimus parentes, et observantiam qua colimus personas dignitate præcellentes, est gratia sive gratitudo quæ benefactoribus gratiam recompensat. Et distinguitur a præmissis virtutibus sicut quodlibet† posteriorum distinguitur a priori quasi ab eo deficiens.

1. Ad primum ergo dicendum quod sicut religio est quædam superexcellens pietas, ita est quædam excellens gratia sive gratitudo. Unde et gratiarum actio ad Deum supra posita est[7] inter ea quæ ad religionem pertinent.

2. Ad secundum dicendum quod retributio proportionalis pertinet ad justitiam commutativam quando attenditur secundum debitum legale, puta si pacto firmetur ut tantum pro tanto retribuatur. Sed ad virtutem gratiæ sive gratitudinis retributio pertinet quæ fit ex solo debito honestatis quam scilicet aliquis sponte facit. Unde et gratitudo est minus grata, si sit coacta, ut Seneca dicit.[8]

3. Ad tertium dicendum quod cum vera amicitia supra virtutem fundetur, quidquid est virtuti contrarium in amico est amicitiæ impeditivum; et quidquid est virtuosum est amicitiæ provocativum. Et secundum hoc per recompensationem beneficiorum amicitia conservatur; quamvis recompensatio beneficiorum ad virtutem gratitudinis specialiter pertineat.

articulus 2. utrum magis teneatur ad gratias reddendas Deo innocens quam pœnitens

AD SECUNDUM sic proceditur:[1] 1. Videtur quod magis teneatur ad gratias reddendas Deo innocens quam pœnitens. Quanto enim aliquis majus donum a Deo percipit tanto magis ad gratiarum actiones tenetur. Sed majus est donum innocentiæ quam justitiæ restitutæ. Ergo videtur quod magis teneatur ad gratiarum actionem innocens quam pœnitens.

2. Præterea, sicut benefactori debetur gratiarum actio, ita et dilectio.

---

*Leonine: *quod*
†Leonine: *quælibet*

First and foremost the cause for our indebtedness is in God, the primary source of all that we have; next, in parents upon whom we directly depend for our birth and upbringing; thirdly, in civic officials through whose hands we receive the advantages that are ours as citizens; fourthly, in any benefactor from whom we have received some special, personal kindness that puts us under a particular obligation.

We do not, however, offer what we owe to God, parents or civil authority to everyone who does us a personal favour. This is why gratitude, which returns thanks for kindness, ranks after religion, by which we offer worship due to God; after piety, by which we honour parents; and after respect, by which we honour public officials. Gratitude is distinct from these others in the way that anything secondary is distinct from something primary, namely as something less.

Hence: 1. As religion is a pre-eminent form of piety, so also is it a higher form of gratitude. This is why thanking God was included above among the concerns of the virtue of religion.[7]

2. Whenever it is based on legal debt, exact repayment is a matter of commutative justice; for example if fixed terms of exchange are stipulated by contract. What engages gratitude is rather repayment based simply on a debt in honour, one respected out of good will. Accordingly, there is scant thanks in forced gratitude, as Seneca points out.[8]

3. Since virtue is the basis for real friendship, anything between friends that is against virtue in one of the friends is an obstacle to friendship; anything favouring virtue, a help. This is why friendship is safeguarded by the acknowledgment of favour received, even though this act itself is directly the concern of the virtue of gratitude.

article 2. whether the duty to thank God is more pressing for one without sin than for a penitent

THE SECOND POINT:[1] 1. The innocent is apparently more strictly bound than the penitent to give thanks to God. The greater the gift received from God, the greater the obligation to thanks. Since innocence is a more precious gift than the gift of righteousness restored,[a] the obligation to gratitude seems greater for the innocent than for the penitent.

2. Further, love as well as thanks is owed to a benefactor. Now Augustine writes, *Where is there a man who, once reflecting on his own frailty, dares*

---

[7] 2a2æ. 83, 7
[8] *De benef.* III, 7
[1] cf IV *Sent.* 22, 1, 2, ii. 3a. 89
[a] *justitia* is the state of being right before God through grace after sin; the process of regaining righteousness is justification; cf 1a2æ. 113, 1.

Sed Augustinus dicit, *Quis hominum suam cogitans infirmitatem audet viribus suis tribuere castitatem atque innocentiam suam, ut minus amet te, quasi minus fuerit ei necessaria misericordia tua qua condonas* peccata conversis ad te?*[2] Et postea subdit, *Et ideo tantumdem, imo amplius te diligat, quia per quem me videt tantis peccatorum meorum languoribus exui, per eum se videt tantis peccatorum languoribus non implicari.*[3] Ergo etiam magis tenetur ad gratiam reddendam innocens quam pœnitens.

3. Præterea, quanto gratuitum beneficium est magis continuatum, tanto major pro eo debetur gratiarum actio. Sed in innocente magis continuatur divinæ gratiæ beneficium quam in pœnitente; dicit enim Augustinus ibidem, *Gratiæ tuæ deputo et misericordiæ tuæ, quia peccata mea tanquam glaciem solvisti; gratiæ tuæ deputo et quæcumque non feci mala; quid enim facere non potui? Et omnia mihi dimissa esse fateor, et quæ mea sponte feci mala, et quæ te duce non feci.*[4] Ergo magis tenetur ad gratiarum actionem innocens quam pœnitens.

SED CONTRA est quod dicitur *Luc., Cui plus dimittitur, plus diligit.*[5] Ergo eadem ratione plus tenetur ad gratiarum actiones.

RESPONSIO: Dicendum quod actio gratiarum in accipiente respicit gratiam dantis; unde ubi est major gratia ex parte dantis, ibi requiritur major gratiarum actio ex parte recipientis. Gratia autem est quod† gratis datur. Unde dupliciter potest esse ex parte dantis major gratia. Uno modo ex quantitate dati et hoc modo innocens tenetur ad majores gratiarum actiones, quia majus donum ei datur a Deo et magis continuatum, cæteris paribus, absolute loquendo.

Alio modo potest dici major gratia, quia magis datur gratis. Et secundum hoc magis tenetur ad gratiarum actiones pœnitens quam innocens, quia magis gratis datur illud quod ei datur a Deo; cum enim esset dignus pœna, datur ei gratia. Et sic licet illud donum quod datur innocenti, sit absolute consideratum majus, tamen donum quod datur pœnitenti est majus in comparatione ad ipsum; sicut etiam parvum donum pauperi datum est ei majus quam diviti magnum. Et quia actus circa singularia sunt, in his quæ agenda sunt magis consideratur quod est hic vel nunc tale quam quod est simpliciter tale, sicut Philosophus dicit in *Ethic.* de voluntario et involuntario.[6]

---

*Leonine: *donans* for *qua condonas*
†Piana: *quia*, because
[2]*Confessions* II, 7. PL 32, 681   [3]ibid   [4]ibid
[5]*Luke* 7, 42   [6]*Ethics* III, 1. 1110a12
[b]*tale* has the force of indicating the essence or quality of a thing; here it is translated as 'true' in keeping with the purpose of the Reply: to determine a practical

ascribe purity and innocence to his own resources so as to love you less, as though being less in need of the mercy whereby you pardon the sins of those who come back to you?[2] And he continues, *He should, then, love you as much, nay more, because when he sees the one through whom I have cast off the mortal maladies of my sins, he sees the one through whom he has been kept safe from equally grave ills.*[3] The sinless man, then, is bound to be grateful more than the penitent.

3. Further, when a favour has been of long standing, gratitude for it must be all the greater. In the case of one without sin, the favour of God's grace has been more continuous than in the case of one who repents. As Augustine points out, *To your grace and mercy I credit my sins being melted like ice; and to your mercy and grace, whatever of evil I have not done—for what might I not have done! And I confess that both have been forgiven me, the wrongs I did willingly, and those I did not do because you steered me from them.*[4] The innocent, then, are more bound to give thanks than the repentant.

ON THE OTHER HAND, *To whom more is forgiven, he loveth more.*[5] And for the same reason he is expected to be more grateful.

REPLY: The thanks of the one who receives responds to the graciousness of the one who gives, and should therefore be greater where greater favour has been shown. A favour (*gratia*) is something done freely (*gratis*), and there are two ways in which it can be greater on the part of the one who gives. First, by reason of the value of the gift. On this count (other things being equal in this comparison) the sinless are more obliged to give thanks, since God has bestowed on them a greater gift and one of longer standing.

In another way a favour can be termed greater because of being shown more freely. From this standpoint the penitent is more bound to give thanks than the innocent person, because what he receives from God is given more freely; whereas he deserves punishment, instead the penitent receives God's grace. Thus while the gift given to the innocent is objectively greater, that given to the penitent is greater when compared to what he is; for example a trivial gift bestowed on a poor man is more precious than an expensive one given to a rich man. Since human actions are about concrete situations, decision about how to act takes into account what is true here and now rather than absolutely, as Aristotle says[6] concerning the voluntary and the involuntary.[b]

---

judgment about the case raised. Both the innocent and the penitent have a reason to see why they have greater cause for gratitude. Obviously, the second paragraph of the Reply presupposes that equal grace is given to each. In the given situation, the grace and the reason for gratitude are greater for the penitent.

Et per hoc patet responsio ad objecta.

articulus 3. *utrum homo teneatur ad gratiarum actiones omni homini benefacienti*

AD TERTIUM sic proceditur: 1. Videtur quod homo non teneatur ad gratiarum actiones omni homini benefacienti. Potest enim aliquis sibi benefacere, sicut et sibi ipsi nocere, secundum illud *Eccli.*, *Qui sibi nequam est, cui alii bonus erit?*[1] Sed homo sibi ipsi non potest gratias agere, quia gratiarum actio videtur transire ab uno in alterum. Ergo non omni benefactori debetur gratiarum actio.

2. Præterea, gratiarum actio est quædam gratiæ recompensatio. Sed aliqua beneficia non cum gratia dantur, sed magis cum contumelia et tarditate vel tristitia. Ergo non semper benefactori sunt gratiæ reddendæ.

3. Præterea, nulli debetur gratiarum actio ex eo quod suam utilitatem procurat. Sed quandoque aliqui aliqua beneficia dant propter suam utilitatem. Ergo eis non debetur gratiarum actio.

4. Præterea, servo non debetur gratiarum actio, quia hoc ipsum quod est, domini est. Sed quandoque contingit servum in dominum beneficium facere vel* beneficum esse. Ergo non omni benefactori debetur gratiarum actio.

5. Præterea, nullus tenetur ad id quod facere non potest honeste et utiliter. Sed quandoque contingit quod ille qui beneficium tribuit est in statu magnæ felicitatis, cui inutiliter aliquid recompensaretur pro suscepto beneficio. Quandoque etiam contingit quod benefactor mutatur de virtute in vitium, et sic videtur quod ei honeste recompensari non potest. Quandoque etiam ille qui accipit beneficium, pauper est et omnino recompensare non potest. Ergo videtur quod non semper teneatur homo ad gratiarum recompensationem.

6. Præterea, nullus debet pro alio facere quod ei non expedit sed est ei nocivum. Sed quandoque contingit quod recompensatio beneficii est nociva vel inutilis ei cui recompensatur. Ergo non est semper beneficium recompensandum per gratiarum actionem.

SED CONTRA est quod dicitur 1 *ad Thess.*, *In omnibus gratias agite.*[2]

RESPONSIO: Dicendum quod omnis effectus naturaliter ad suam causam convertitur. Unde Dionysius dicit 1 cap. *De div. nom.*, quod *Deus omnia in se convertit, tanquam omnium causa.*[3] Semper enim oportet quod effectus

---

*Leonine: omits *beneficium facere vel*
[1]*Ecclesiasticus* 14, 5
[2]1 *Thessalonians* 5, 18
[3]*De div. nom.* 1. PG 3, 593

From this the reply to the first set of arguments is clear.

article 3. whether a person must thank everyone who does him a kindness

THE THIRD POINT: 1. It seems that no one is obliged to thank every single one who is good to him. According to the text, *He that is evil to himself, to whom will he be good?*[1] good as well as evil can be done to oneself. Yet no one can really be thankful to himself, since thanks seems to pass from one person to another. Not to every benefactor, therefore, is gratitude owed.

2. Further, while thanksgiving is a way of repaying graciousness, not every good turn is done with grace; rather, some are done with contempt, reluctance or regret. Therefore thanks are not always in order.

3. Further, no thanks are due to someone for serving his own interests. At times people do favours for this purpose. To them, no thanks are due.

4. Further, a slave has no claim to gratitude, since in his very person he belongs to the master. And yet there are times when a slave either does a favour for his master, or is disposed to do so. Thus thanks are not due in every case to one doing a favour.

5. Further, no one is held to what he cannot do virtuously and to good purpose. Now it sometimes happens that a benefactor is so well off that it would be pointless to make any return for a favour received from him. Or it happens that a benefactor has fallen from virtue into vice, so that no virtuous way of repaying him seems possible. Sometimes, as well, the recipient is poor and utterly incapable of repaying. Thus it would seem that one is not always held to return favours.

6. Further, no one may do for another what is not advantageous but harmful to him. Occasionally, however, it may be the case that returning a favour is harmful, or at best not to the advantage of the person to be repaid. Not in every case, then, is a favour to be repaid.

ON THE OTHER HAND there are the words of 1 *Thessalonians, In all things give thanks.*[2]

REPLY: In the nature of things every effect turns back to its cause; thus Dionysius states, *As the cause of all, God turns all things to himself,*[3] meaning that an effect necessarily serves the purposes of its agent cause.[a] Clearly,

---

[a] cf 1a2æ. 109, 6 on *convertitur, conversio*. In St Thomas's mind the terms connote the correspondence necessarily existing between agent, effect, and the purpose of the agent. The effect comes to be and exists as it is because the agent acts and acts for a purpose. Since such correspondence is part of the nature of things, the idea serves to show the necessity of virtue requiring the response of beneficiary to benefactor.

ordinetur ad finem agentis. Manifestum est autem quod benefactor inquantum hujusmodi est causa beneficiati. Et ideo naturalis ordo requirit ut ille qui suscepit beneficium, per gratiarum recompensationem convertatur ad benefactorem secundum modum utriusque. Et sicut de patre dictum est supra,[4] et benefactori quidem, inquantum hujusmodi debetur honor et reverentia eo quod habet rationem principii; sed per accidens debetur ei subventio vel sustentatio si indigeat.

1. Ad primum ergo dicendum quod, sicut Seneca dicit, *sicut non est liberalis qui sibi donat, nec clemens qui sibi ignoscit, nec misericors qui malis suis tangitur, sed qui aliis; ita etiam nemo sibi ipsi beneficium dat; sed naturæ suæ paret, quæ movet ad refutanda nociva, et ad appetenda proficua.*[5] Unde in his quæ sunt ad seipsum non habet locum gratitudo et ingratitudo, non enim potest homo sibi aliquid denegare nisi sibi retinendo.

Metaphorice tamen illa quæ ad alterum proprie dicuntur accipiuntur in his quæ sunt ad seipsum, sicut de justitia dicit Philosophus in v *Ethic.*,[6] inquantum scilicet accipiuntur diversæ partes hominis sicut diversæ personæ.

2. Ad secundum dicendum quod boni animi est ut magis attendat* ad bonum quam ad malum. Et ideo si aliquis beneficium dedit non eo modo quo debuit, non omnino† debet recipiens a gratiarum actione cessare. Minus tamen quam si modo debito præstitisset, quia etiam beneficium minus est; quia, ut Seneca dicit, *multum celeritas fecit, multum abstulit mora.*[7]

3. Ad tertium dicendum quod, sicut Seneca dicit, *Multum interest utrum aliquis beneficium nobis det sua causa, an nostra, an sua et nostra. Ille qui totus ad se spectat, et nobis prodest, quia aliter sibi prodesse non potest, eo mihi loco habendus videtur quo qui pecori suo pabulum prospicit. Si modo me in consortium admisit, si duos cogitavit, ingratus sum non solum injustus, nisi gaudeam hoc illi profuisse quod proderat mihi. Summæ malignitatis est non vocare beneficium, nisi quod dantem aliquo incommodo afficit.*[8]

4. Ad quartum dicendum quod, sicut Seneca dicit, *Quamdiu servus præstat quod a servo exigi solet, ministerium est; ubi plus quam quod servo necesse est, beneficium est. Ubi enim in affectum amici transit, si tamen transit, desint vocari ministerium.*[9] Et ideo etiam servis ultra debitum facientibus gratiæ sunt habendæ.

5. Ad quintum dicendum quod etiam pauper ingratus non est, si faciat quod possit. Sicut enim beneficium magis in affectu consistit quam in

---

*Piana: *attendatur*
†Piana: *ideo*, therefore, for *omnino*, altogether
[4]above 101, 2   [5]*De benef.* v, 9   [6]*Ethics* v, 11. 1138b5
[7]*De benef.* 11, 6

a benefactor as such stands as cause in relation to the one whom he helps. As a consequence, the nature of the case requires that a recipient respond to his benefactor in a way that reflects their relationship. As mentioned in the case of parents,[4] this means that the one doing a kindness, as the source of a good, has a claim to honour and reverence, and in exceptional circumstances, also to help or support should he be in need.

Hence: 1. As Seneca has written, *Even as one is generous not by making a gift to self but to others, merciful, not by forgiving self but others, compassionate, not in being touched by his own misfortunes but by those of others, so no one is a benefactor to self, but is rather simply following the dictates of nature to avoid the harmful and seek the beneficial.*[5] Thus in matters of self-concern neither gratitude nor ingratitude has any place; after all it is only possible for a person to deny himself something by keeping it back himself.

As Aristotle says, however, in regard to justice,[6] terms which in their proper sense refer to interpersonal relations are applied metaphorically to attitudes towards self, by conceiving of the various elements in a human being as though each were a distinct person.

2. To be more conscious of good than of evil is a mark of goodness of heart. For this reason, even should someone do a favour for the wrong reasons, the recipient ought not therefore to refrain altogether from thanks. Still the thanks will be less than if things were as they should be, since in fact the favour is diminished; as Seneca notes, *promptness enhances a favour; delay tarnishes it.*[7]

3. Here is how Seneca replies: *It makes a great difference whether someone does a service in his own interest, or at the same time in his own and ours. If it is a case of sheer self-concern, and he helps us only because he cannot otherwise advance his own interests, I regard him as I would someone tending to the fodder for cattle. But if he has joined his interests to mine, if he is thinking of both of us, then should I fail to be glad that what was to my advantage was also to his, I would be ungrateful and unjust. To count as a favour only what makes the giver the loser is the worst sort of maliciousness.*[8]

4. Again Seneca: *As long as a slave is simply doing what he is supposed to do, this is mere service; but where he goes beyond, then a favour is involved. For once friendliness becomes his motive, if it does, then it is no longer a matter of mere service.*[9] Therefore there must be gratitude even towards slaves when they do more than what is required.

5. Even the pauper is not without gratitude so long as he does what is in his power; the chief meaning of a favour is in the heart not the deed, and it is the same with repayment. Hence Seneca says, *To receive a favour*

---

[8]*De benef.* VI, 12 & 13
[9]ibid III, 21

effectu, ita etiam recompensatio magis in affectu consistit. Unde Seneca dicit, *Qui grate beneficium accipit, primam ejus pensionem solvit. Quod grate autem ad nos beneficia pervenerint, indicemus effusis affectibus, quod non ipso tantum audiente, sed ubique testemur*[10].

Et hoc patet quod quantumcumque in felicitate existenti potest recompensatio beneficii fieri per exhibitionem reverentiæ et honoris. Unde Philosophus dicit in *Ethic.* quod *superexcellenti quidem debet fieri honoris retributio, indigenti autem retributio lucri.*[11] Et Seneca dicit, *Multa sunt per quæ quicquid debemus, reddere et felicibus possumus: fidele consilium, assidua conversatio, sermo communis, et sine adulatione jucundus.*[12] Et ideo non oportet ut homo optet indigentiam ejus seu miseriam qui beneficium dedit ad hoc quod beneficium recompensetur quia, ut Seneca dicit, *Si hoc ei optares, cujus nullum beneficium haberes, inhumanum erat votum. Quanto inhumanius ei optas cui beneficium debes?*[13]

Si autem ille qui beneficium dedit in pejus mutatus est, debet tamen ei fieri recompensatio secundum statum ipsius, ut scilicet ad virtutem reducatur si sit possibile. Si autem sit insanabilis propter malitiam, tunc aliter est affectus quam prius erat. Et ideo non debetur ei recompensatio beneficii sicut prius. Et tamen quantum fieri potest salva honestate, memoria debet haberi præstiti beneficii, ut patet per Philosophum.[14]

6. Ad sextum dicendum quod, sicut dictum est,[15] recompensatio beneficii præcipue pendet ex affectu; et ideo eo modo debet recompensatio fieri quo magis sit utilis. Si tamen postea per ejus incuriam in damnum ipsius vertatur, non imputatur recompensanti, ut Seneca dicit, *Reddendum mihi est, non servandum, cum reddidero, ac tuendum.*[16]

articulus 4. utrum homo debeat statim beneficium recompensare

AD QUARTUM sic proceditur: 1. Videtur quod homo debeat statim beneficium recompensare. Illa enim quæ debemus sine certo termino, tenemur restituere statim. Sed non est aliquis terminus præscriptus recompensationi beneficiorum; quæ tamen cadit sub debito, ut dictum est.[1] Ergo tenetur homo statim beneficium recompensare.

2. Præterea, quanto aliquod bonum fit ex majore animi fervore tanto videtur esse laudabilius. Sed ex fervore animi videtur procedere quod homo nullas moras adhibeat in faciendo quod debet. Ergo videtur esse laudabilius quod statim homo beneficium reddat.

---

[10]*De benef.* II, 22
[11]*Ethics* VIII, 14. 1163b2
[12]*De benef.* VI, 29
[13]ibid 26
[14]*Ethics* IX, 3. 1165b13 & 31

gratefully is already to begin repayment. We should show that we are thankful for favours that have come our way by the outpourings of our heart, and attest to it not only for our benefactor to hear, but everywhere.[10]

This also makes clear that no matter how well off someone may be, repayment can still be made to him, namely by showing him respect and honour. Thus Aristotle remarks that *to one of high station repayment should be honour; to one in need, money.*[11] And Seneca, *The means by which we can pay back whatever we owe to the well off are many: loyal counsel, staunch companionship, unaffected and unfawning conversation.*[12] Neither is it right for anyone to half-wish need or suffering on a benefactor so as to have an opportunity to repay him, because, in Seneca's words, *It would be heartless to wish these things on one from whom you have received nothing; how much more so to wish them on one whose kindness has made you his debtor.*[13]

When a benefactor has changed for the worse, repayment should still be made, but suited to his condition, i.e. of a kind that will, if possible, bring him back to a life of virtue. If, however, because of his bad will he cannot be reached, then in a sense he has become a different person and no longer has the right to repayment for his good services. Yet, as Aristotle makes plain,[14] to the degree compatible with what is morally right, the memory of his goodness to us should be kept fresh.

6. As noted,[15] gratefulness depends chiefly on intent; and so repayment should be made in whatever way would be more useful to the benefactor. If later, through his neglect, it should prove detrimental to him, this is not the fault of the one repaying. As Seneca says, *It is up to me to repay; once this is done, it is not for me to watch over and safeguard my repayment.*[16]

article 4. whether a person need return a kindness without delay

THE FOURTH POINT: 1. It seems as though we should pay back a favour immediately. We are bound, unless a time has been fixed, to repay what we owe at once. There is no fixed time limit for the return of a favour, which, as indicated,[1] comes under the heading of a debt. Therefore a person is bound to return a favour immediately.

2. Further, the greater the eagerness with which any good deed is done, the more praiseworthy[a] it seems to be. But eagerness seems to prompt a person to lose no time in fulfilling an obligation. Therefore it seems more praiseworthy to return a kindness without delay.

---

[15] above ad 5
[16] *De benef.* VII, 19
[1] above art. 3
[a] See above, 104, 2, note c.

3. Præterea, Seneca dicit quod *proprium benefactoris est libenter et cito facere*.² Sed recompensatio debet beneficium adæquare. Ergo debet statim recompensare.

SED CONTRA est quod Seneca dicit, *Qui festinat reddere, non animum habet grati hominis, sed debitoris*.³

RESPONSIO: Dicendum quod sicut in beneficio dando duo considerantur, scilicet affectus et donum, ita etiam hæc duo considerantur in recompensatione beneficii. Et quantum quidem ad affectum,* recompensatio statim fieri debet; unde Seneca dicit, *Vis reddere beneficium? accipe benigne*.⁴

Quantum autem ad donum, debet expectari tempus quo recompensatio sit benefactori opportuna. Si autem non convenienti tempore statim velit aliquod munus pro munere reddere, non videtur esse virtuosa recompensatio.† Ut enim Seneca dicit, *si nimis cito cupit solvere, invitus debet; et qui invitus debet, ingratus est*.⁵

1. Ad primum ergo dicendum quod debitum legale est statim solvendum, alioquin non esset conservata justitiæ æqualitas, si unus retineret rem alterius absque ejus voluntate. Sed debitum morale dependet ex honestate debentis, et ideo oportet reddi debito tempore secundum quod exigit rectitudo virtutis.

2. Ad secundum dicendum quod fervor voluntatis non est virtuosus nisi sit ratione ordinatus, et ideo si aliquis ex fervore animi præoccupet debitum tempus non erit laudandus.

3. Ad tertium dicendum quod beneficia etiam sunt opportuno tempore danda, et tunc non est amplius tardandum cum opportunum tempus advenerit. Et idem etiam observari oportet in beneficiorum recompensatione.

articulus 5. utrum gratiarum actio sit attendenda secundum affectum beneficiantis,‡ an secundum effectum

AD QUINTUM sic proceditur:¹ 1. Videtur quod beneficiorum recompensatio non sit attendenda secundum affectum beneficiantis, sed secundum effectum. Recompensatio enim beneficiis debetur. Sed beneficium in effectu consistit, ut ipsum nomen sonat. Ergo recompensatio debet attendi secundum effectum.

---

*Piana: *effectum*, effect
†Piana: adds *sed invita*, but unwilling
‡Leonine and Piana both have *beneficiantis* here and in art. 6, instead of the more usual *benefacientis* (as in art. 3).
²*De benef.* II, 5

3. Further, Seneca notes that *it is the mark of the benefactor to act willingly and promptly;*[2] and repayment should match the kindness received. So it should be quick.

ON THE OTHER HAND, there is Seneca, *One who is in a rush to pay back has the spirit not of the grateful, but of the debtor.*[3]

REPLY: Just as in the bestowal of a kindness so also in its repayment there are two necessary considerations, the sentiment and the deed. As to the first, reciprocation should be immediate; thus Seneca remarks, *Do you wish to acknowledge a kindness? Then accept it with good grace.*[4]

That which is given in return, however, should be timed to the best interests of the benefactor. If in fact someone wishes to give gift for gift, not at an appropriate time but right away, his repayment gives the impression of not being virtuous. As Seneca puts it, *One who is anxious to make speedy repayment is unwilling to be under obligation to another and this is to be ungrateful.*[5]

Hence: 1. A legal debt is to be paid immediately, since the balance of justice would be upset if one man kept what belongs to another against the other's will. A moral debt is determined in reference to the virtuousness of the debtor,[b] and so should be honoured at a time that is appropriate to what the rectitude of virtue calls for.

2. Since eagerness of will is virtuous only when moderated by reason, a deed should not be commended when out of eagerness someone acts prematurely.

4. Kindnesses should also be done at the right moment; when it comes, there should be no delay. Therefore the same course should also be followed in reciprocating.

article 5. whether repayment of a favour should be matched to the sentiment or to the deed of the benefactor

THE FIFTH POINT:[1] 1. The return of favours should be measured, it seems, not by the sentiment of the benefactor, but by what he does. Repayment is owed for good deeds, and as the words themselves indicate, good deeds are something done. Repayment, then, should match the deed.

---

[3]*De benef.* IV, 40
[4]ibid II, 35
[5]ibid IV, 17
[1]*In Ethic.* VIII, *lect.* 13; IX, *lect.* 1
[b]*ex honestate debentis* is a good expression of St Thomas's understanding of the moral debt.

2. Præterea, gratia, quæ recompensat beneficia, est pars justitiæ. Sed justitia respicit æqualitatem dati et accepti. Ergo et in gratiarum recompensatione attendendus est magis effectus quam affectus beneficiantis.

3. Præterea, nullus potest attendere ad id quod ignorat. Sed solus Deus cognoscit interiorem affectum. Ergo non potest fieri gratiæ recompensatio secundum affectum.

SED CONTRA est quod Seneca dicit, *Nonnunquam magis nos obligat qui dedit parva magnifice, et qui exiguum tribuit, sed libenter.*[2]

RESPONSIO: Dicendum quod recompensatio beneficii potest ad tres virtutes pertinere, scilicet ad justitiam, ad gratiam et ad amicitiam. Ad justitiam quidem pertinet, quando recompensatio habet rationem debiti legalis, sicut in mutuo et aliis hujusmodi. Et in tali recompensatio debet attendi secundum quantitatem dati. Ad amicitiam autem pertinet recompensatio beneficii, et similiter ad virtutem gratiæ, secundum quod habet rationem debit moralis; aliter tamen et aliter. Nam in recompensatione amicitiæ oportet respectum haberi ad amicitiæ causam. Unde in amicitia utili debet recompensatio fieri secundum utilitatem quam quis ex beneficio consecutus est. In amicitia autem honesti debet in recompensatione haberi respectus ad electionem sive ad affectum dantis, quia hoc præcipue requiritur ad virtutem, ut dicitur in *Ethic.*[3]

Et similiter quia gratia respicit beneficium secundum quod est gratis impensum, quod quidem pertinet ad affectum, ideo etiam gratiæ recompensatio attendit magis affectum dantis quam effectum.

1. Ad primum ergo dicendum quod omnis actus moralis ex voluntate dependet. Unde beneficium secundum quod est laudabile prout ei gratiæ recompensatio debetur, materialiter quidem consistit in effectu, sed formaliter et principaliter in voluntate. Unde Seneca dicit, *Beneficium non in eo quod fit aut datur consistit, sed in ipso dantis aut facientis animo.*[4]

2. Ad secundum dicendum quod gratia est pars justitiæ, non quidem sicut species generis, sed per quamdam reductionem ad genus justitiæ, ut

---

[2]*De benef.* I, 7
[3]*Ethics* VIII, 13. 1163a21
[4]*De benef.* I, 6
[a]*amicitia*, on the wide sense this term has, see above 103, 3, note *d*; also 114 below.
[b]cf 1a2æ. 26, 4 ad 3, where St Thomas speaks of three senses of friendship, *amicitia utilis*, *delectabilis* and *honesti*; the qualifying words are genitives that indicate the basis or purpose of the friendship. *Amicitia honesti* alone is perfect friendship; the connotation is that mutual regard, love for the other as a person and another self are primary; its basis is the true human qualities of the friends, thus its connection with virtue. The motives of utility or convenience and pleasure are also found in

2. Further, as a form of repayment, gratitude is a part of justice and justice attends to equalizing what is given with what is received. So in returning favours it is the deed rather than the intent of the benefactor that counts.

3. Further, we cannot base our actions on the unknown. God alone knows the heart of a man. The return of favours, then, cannot be gauged by the spirit behind them.

ON THE OTHER HAND there is Seneca's statement, *Often enough we are under a greater obligation to one who has given us a little, but wholeheartedly; a trifle, but generously.*[2]

REPLY: Return for a good received can be the concern of any one of three virtues, justice, gratitude, or friendship.[a] Justice is engaged when the repayment comes under the title of legal debt, for example in the case of a loan or the like. In such an instance the amount given is the measure of the recompense. Friendship comes in and gratitude as well—but each in its own way—when the repayment has the quality of a moral debt. In reciprocation out of friendship, that on which the friendship is based should serve as the norm. For this reason in a friendship of convenience,[b] repayment should correspond to the advantage gained through the favour received. But in the case of a perfect friendship, it is to our friend's preference or love for us that we must look, since, as Aristotle notes,[3] this is the chief requisite for virtue.

Similarly, repayment made out of gratitude regards the sentiment of the giver more than what he has given, since gratefulness is the response to a favour done out of good-will, which is an inner sentiment.

Hence: 1. Every moral act stands in dependence on the will. For this reason where a favour is morally good—and it is as such that it calls for acknowledgment—the matter consists in some deed, but the meaning and main element in the will-act.[c] Seneca writes, *A favour lies not in the deed of the gift, but in the sentiment of the giver.*[4]

2. It is true that gratitude is a part of justice, not, however, in the sense that it is a species under a genus, but that in a way it amounts to the type

---

friendship; *amicitia utilis* and *delectabilis* do not necessarily have a pejorative sense. A relationship in which one's own convenience or pleasure is the sole motive would not be friendship in its full sense; a true friendship, however, also serves the interests or pleasures of each of the friends. The kind of friendship will depend on what is dominant. Here *amicitia utilis* is understood of a relationship in which self-interest is dominant, and it is thus contrasted with *amicitia honesti*.

[c]Again *materialiter-formaliter*. The first refers to the favour simply as a fact or human phenomenon; the second refers to its inner, moral value.

supra dictum est.[5] Unde non oportet quod eadem ratio debiti attendatur in utraque virtute.

3. Ad tertium dicendum quod affectum hominis per se quidem solus Deus videt, sed secundum quod per aliqua signa manifestatur potest etiam ipsum homo cognoscere. Et hoc modo affectus beneficiantis cognoscitur ex ipso modo quo beneficium tribuitur, puta quia gaudenter et prompte aliquis beneficium impendit.

articulus 6. utrum oporteat aliquem plus exhibere in recompensatione quam susceperit in beneficio

AD SEXTUM sic proceditur: 1. Videtur quod non oporteat aliquem plus exhibere in recompensatione quam susceperit in beneficio. Quibusdam enim sicut parentibus nec etiam æqualis recompensatio fieri potest, sicut Philosophus dicit in *Ethic.*[1] Sed virtus non conatur ad impossibile. Non ergo gratiæ recompensatio tendit ad aliquid majus.

2. Præterea, si aliquis plus recompensat quam in beneficio acceperit, ex hoc ipso quasi aliquid de novo dat. Sed ad beneficium de novo datum tenetur homo gratiam recompensare. Ergo ille qui primo beneficium dederat, tenebitur aliquid majus recompensare, et sic procederetur in infinitum. Sed virtus non conatur ad infinitum, quia *infinitum aufert naturam boni*, ut dicitur in *Meta.*[2] Ergo gratiæ recompensatio non debet excedere acceptum beneficium.

3. Præterea, justitia in æqualitate consistit. Sed majus est quidam æqualitatis excessus. Cum ergo in qualibet virtute excessus sit vitiosus, videtur quod recompensare aliquid majus accepto beneficio sit vitiosum et justitiæ oppositum.

SED CONTRA est quod Philosophus dicit in *Ethic.*, *Refamulari oportet ei qui gratiam fecit, et rursum ipsum incipere.*[3] Quod quidem fit dum aliquid majus retribuitur. Ergo recompensatio debet tendere ad hoc quod aliquid majus faciat.

RESPONSIO: Dicendum quod, sicut dictum est,[4] recompensatio gratiæ respicit beneficium secundum voluntatem beneficiantis. In quo quidem præcipue hoc commendabile videtur quod gratis beneficium contulit, ad quod non tenebatur. Et ideo qui beneficium accepit ad hoc obligatur ex debito honestatis ut similiter aliquid gratis impendat. Non autem videtur gratis aliquid impendere nisi excedat quantitatem accepti beneficii. Quia quamdiu recompensat minus vel æquale, non videtur facere gratis sed

---

[5]2a2æ. 80

of virtue justice is, as noted earlier.[5] Thus there is no reason to look for an identical kind of indebtedness in both virtues.

3. It is true that God alone sees the heart as it really is; yet as this is manifested in certain signs, a human being can also know it. Accordingly, we are aware of the benefactor's intent from his manner of doing a favour, e.g. if he does it gladly and readily.

article 6. whether anyone in repaying should give something more than he received

THE SIXTH POINT: 1. No one, it seems, in repaying a favour should give more than he received. As Aristotle remarks,[1] to make even an equivalent return to some people, parents for example, is impossible and virtue does not strive for the impossible. Therefore the repayment of gratitude does not try for something greater.

2. Further, should anyone give back more than he received, then this is more like a completely new gift and the other person incurs a new obligation to gratefulness that is to be acquitted by a still greater repayment, and so on indefinitely. The striving of virtue, however, is not towards the indefinite; *indefiniteness takes away the quality of goodness*, it says in the *Metaphysics*.[2] Therefore the repayment of gratitude must not exceed the favour received.

3. Further, quality is the mark of justice, and what is too much exceeds this equality. Excess being wrong in the sphere of any virtue, it seems that a recompense that surpasses a favour received is wrong and against justice.

ON THE OTHER HAND Aristotle says that *we should do kindness in turn to one who has been kind to us, and take the initiative in doing a kindness at another time.*[3] We do this by reciprocating with something better. Thus repayment should seek expression in something greater.

REPLY: As I have said before,[4] giving thanks is a response to a kindness as this depends on the intent of the benefactor. What is chiefly praiseworthy in his act is that he freely bestowed a favour not demanded of him. Thus the recipient is bound out of a debt of honour to make a return with equal graciousness. He would not seem to be doing this, however, were he not to go beyond the value of the gift received. Something less or equivalent would not look like a grateful acknowledgment, but like mere payment for

---

[1] *Ethics* VIII, 14. 1163b15
[2] *Metaphysics* I, 2. 994b12
[3] *Ethics* V, 5. 1133a4
[4] art. 5

reddere quod accepit. Et ideo gratiæ recompensatio semper tendit ut pro suo posse aliquid majus retribuat.

1. Ad primum ergo dicendum quod, sicut dictum est,[5] in recompensatione beneficii magis est considerandus affectus quam effectus. Si ergo consideremus effectum beneficii quod filius a parentibus accepit, scilicet esset et vivere, nihil æquale filius recompensare potest, ut Philosophus dicit.[6] Si autem attendamus ad ipsam voluntatem dantis et retribuentis, sic potest filius aliquid majus patri retribuere, ut Seneca dicit.[7] Si tamen non posset, sufficeret ad gratitudinem recompensandi voluntas.

2. Ad secundum dicendum quod debitum gratitudinis ex caritate derivatur, quæ quanto plus solvitur tanto magis debetur, secundum illud *ad Rom., Nemini quidquam debeatis, nisi ut invicem diligatis.*[8] Et ideo non est inconveniens, si obligatio gratitudinis interminabilis sit.

3. Ad tertium dicendum quod sicut in justitia quæ est virtus cardinalis attenditur æqualitas rerum ita in gratitudine attenditur æqualitas voluntatum, ut scilicet sicut ex promptitudine voluntatis beneficus aliquid* exhibuit ad quod non tenebatur, ita etiam ille qui suscepit beneficium aliquid supra debitum recompenset.

---

*Piana: beneficium aliquis; sense the same
[5]art. 3 ad 5; art. 5   [6]*Ethics* VIII, 14. 1163b15
[7]*De benef.* III, 29
[8]*Romans* 13, 8

what was received. Therefore the recompense of gratitude should as far as possible make a point of giving back something better.

Hence: 1. As noted already,[5] in giving thanks the heart counts more than the deed. If therefore we consider the benefits received from parents, namely existence and life, then the child can make no equivalent return, as Aristotle is saying.[6] But from the standpoint of willingness to give and repay, it is possible for a child even to surpass parents, as Seneca notes.[7] And even if it were not possible, the very willingness would satisfy the virtue of gratitude.

2. The indebtedness gratitude honours has its origins in charity, and charity is a debt that increases the more it is paid, according to *Romans, Owe no man anything but to love one another*.[8] Consequently, there is nothing unreasonable for the obligation of gratitude to be endless.

3. As in the cardinal virtue of justice equality is reckoned in terms of external objects, so the equality in gratitude is one of wills.[a] This means that on the one side one person with a ready willingness does a favour to which he was not bound, and on the other, the recipient makes recompense that surpasses mere obligation.

---

[a]This is another comment on the distinction between legal and moral debt; it is also an indication that gratitude and the other virtues being discussed have only a similarity to justice; cf. 1a2æ. 64, 2. See Appendix 1.

Quæstio 107. de ingratitudine

DEINDE CONSIDERANDUM EST de ingratitudine. Et circa hoc quæruntur quatuor:

1. utrum ingratitudo semper sit peccatum;
2. utrum ingratitudo sit peccatum speciale;
3. utrum omnis ingratitudo sit peccatum mortale;
4. utrum ingratis sint beneficia subtrahenda.

articulus 1. utrum ingratitudo sit semper peccatum

AD PRIMUM sic proceditur: 1. Videtur quod ingratitudo non semper sit peccatum. Dicit enim Seneca quod *ingratus est qui non reddit beneficium*.[1] Sed quandoque aliquis non posset recompensare beneficium nisi peccando, puta si auxiliatus est homini ad peccandum. Cum ergo abstinere a peccato non sit peccatum, videtur quod ingratitudo non semper sit peccatum.

2. Præterea, omne peccatum est in potestate peccantis, quia secundum Augustinum, *nullus peccat in eo quod vitare non potest*.[2] Sed quandoque non est in potestate peccantis ingratitudinem vitare, puta cum non habet unde reddat. Oblivio etiam non est in potestate nostra, cum tamen Seneca dicat quod *ingratissimus omnium est qui oblitus est*.[3] Ergo ingratitudo non semper est peccatum.

3. Præterea, non videtur peccare* qui non vult aliquid debere, secundum illud Apostoli *Ad Rom.*, *Nemini quidquam debeatis*.[4] Sed *qui invitus debet, ingratus est*, ut Seneca dicit.[5] Ergo non semper ingratitudo est peccatum.

SED CONTRA est quod II *ad Tim.*, ingratitudo connumeratur aliis peccatis cum dicitur, *Parentibus non obedientes, ingrati, scelesti*.[6]

RESPONSIO: Dicendum quod, sicut dictum est,[7] debitum gratitudinis est quoddam debitum honestatis quam virtus requirit. Ex hoc autem aliquid est peccatum quod repugnat virtuti. Unde manifestum est quod omnis ingratitudo est peccatum.

1. Ad primum ergo dicendum quod gratitudo respicit beneficium; ille autem qui alicui auxiliatur ad peccandum non confert beneficium sed magis nocumentum. Et ideo non debetur ei gratiarum actio, nisi forte propter voluntatem bonam, si sit deceptus, dum credidit adjuvare ad bonum et

---

*Leonine: *recompensare*, to pay back, for *peccare*
[1]*De benef.* III, 1

Question 107. ingratitude

NEXT, INGRATITUDE, UNDER four points of inquiry:

1. whether ingratitude is always sinful;
2. a specific kind of sin;
3. and in every case a mortal sin;
4. whether favours must be withheld from ingrates.

article 1. whether ingratitude is always sinful

THE FIRST POINT: 1. Apparently ungratefulness is not always sinful. Seneca states, *One who does not return a favour is ungrateful*.[1] But to return a favour without sinning is sometimes impossible; when, for example, someone has helped a person to sin. Since to refrain from sinning is not sinful, neither does ungratefulness seem to be so.

2. Further, every sin lies within the sinner's control; *No one sins*, says Augustine, *in a matter beyond his control*.[2] Now at times it is not in a person's power to avoid ingratitude, for example, when he lacks means. Then too forgetfulness is beyond our control, yet Seneca says, *The worst of all ingrates is the one who forgets*.[3] Consequently, to be ungrateful is not always sinful.

3. Further, one who, following St Paul's words, *Owe no man anything*,[4] does not wish to be indebted, does not seem to be sinning. Yet Seneca says, *One unwilling to be indebted is ungrateful*.[5] So ingratitude is not always a sin.

ON THE OTHER HAND, in II *Timothy* ingratitude is listed with other sins, *Disobedient to parents, ungrateful, wicked*.[6]

REPLY: As I have remarked already,[7] the debt of gratitude is a debt in the uprightness that virtue requires and anything against virtue is sinful. Therefore it is clear that all ingratitude is sinful.

Hence: 1. Gratitude is a response to a kindness received, and one assisting another to sin does not do a kindness but an injury. No thanks is owed to such a person, then, except perhaps if he had good intentions, being under the erroneous impression that he was helping in something

---

[2] *De lib. arbit.* III, 18. PL 32, 1295. *Retract.* I, 9. PL 32, 596
[3] *De benef.* III, 1
[4] *Romans* 13, 8
[5] *De benef.* IV, 40
[6] II *Timothy* 3, 2
[7] Above 106, 1 ad 2; 4 ad 1; 6

adjuvit ad peccandum. Et tunc non debetur talis recompensatio ut adjuvetur ad peccandum, quia hoc non esset recompensare bonum sed malum, quod contrariatur gratitudini.

2. Ad secundum dicendum quod nullus propter impotentiam reddendi ab ingratitudine excusatur, ex quo ad debitum gratitudinis reddendum sufficet sola voluntas, ut dictum est.[8] Oblivio autem beneficii ad ingratitudinem pertinet, non quidem illa quæ provenit ex naturali defectu, qui non subjacet voluntati, sed illa quæ ex negligentia provenit. Ut enim dicit Seneca, *Apparet illum non sæpe de reddendo cogitasse cui obrepsit oblivio.*[9]

3. Ad tertium dicendum quod debitum gratitudinis ex debito amoris derivatur, a quo nullus debet velle absolvi. Unde quod aliquis invitus hoc debitum debeat videtur provenire ex defectu amoris ad eum qui beneficium dedit.

articulus 2. utrum ingratitudo sit speciale peccatum

AD SECUNDUM sic proceditur:[1] 1. Videtur quod ingratitudo non sit speciale peccatum. Quicumque enim peccat contra Deum agit, qui est summus benefactor. Sed hoc pertinet ad ingratitudinem. Ergo ingratitudo non est speciale peccatum.

2. Præterea, nullum speciale peccatum sub diversis peccatorum generibus continetur. Sed diversis peccatorum generibus potest aliquis esse ingratus; puta si quis benefactori detrahat, si quis furetur vel aliquid aliud hujusmodi contra eum committat. Ergo ingratitudo non est speciale peccatum.

3. Præterea, Seneca dicit, *Ingratus est qui dissimulat, ingratus est qui non reddit, et ingratissimus omnium qui oblitus est.*[2] Sed ista non videntur ad unam peccati speciem pertinere. Ergo ingratitudo non est speciale peccatum.

SED CONTRA est quod ingratitudo opponitur gratitudini sive gratiæ, quæ est specialis virtus. Ergo est speciale peccatum.

---

[8] above 106, 1 ad 1
[9] *De benef.* III, 1
[1] cf 3a. 88, 4. IV *Sent.* 22, 1, 2, i
[2] *De benef.* III, 1
[a] The parallel place in the *Summa*, 3a. 88, 2–4 (especially 4) clarifies the sense of this article. A special sin is contrasted with a general condition that may be present in all or many sins; it is a sin which by its objective is directly opposed to the act of a specific virtue; but see 1a2æ. 73, 1. In his classification of moral acts St Thomas uses the terminology by which logic classifies beings (cf 1a2æ. 1, 3; 18 and Vol. 18,

good, when in fact he was encouraging sin. Even so what is due him in return is not assistance for him to sin, since this would be repaying not with good but with evil and would be contrary to gratitude.

2. No one is excused from the sin of ingratitude by the inability to repay, since, as we have shown,[8] good will alone suffices to acquit the debt of gratitude. Forgetfulness of a favour is a mark of ungratefulness; not, however, the forgetfulness that comes from a natural failing and as such is involuntary, but the forgetfulness deriving from negligence. For in Seneca's words, *One who grows to forget shows that he hardly gave a thought to making any repayment.*[9]

3. A debt in gratitude has its origins in the indebtedness of love, from which no one should want to be freed. Consequently, for someone to be unwilling to owe this debt appears to issue from a lack of love towards the benefactor.

article 2. whether ingratitude is a special kind of sin

THE SECOND POINT:[1] 1. Ingratitude is apparently not a special kind of sin.[a] Everyone who sins acts against God, the supreme benefactor. This involves ingratitude, which, therefore, is not one species of sin.

2. Further, one specific sin is not contained under different species of sin. Yet someone can be ungrateful through sinful acts of different kinds, committing against his benefactor detraction, theft, etc. Therefore ingratitude is not one species of sin.

3. Further, we have Seneca's remark, *One who takes no notice of a favour is ungrateful; one who fails to return it, more so; one who forgets it, the most ungrateful of all.*[2] These do not seem to involve the one sort of sin. Ungratefulness, then, is not one sort of sin.

ON THE OTHER HAND ingratitude is the opposite of one specific virtue, gratitude or thanks, and so is itself a specific sin.

---

ed. T. Gilby, Appendix 10–14, 72, 1 & 9; 88, 2). In this usage he frequently puts the term *genus* as equivalent to *species* (see obj. 2 and ad 2). The usage derives from Peter Lombard's classification of certain acts as *bonum in genere* or *malum in genere*, against the moral indifferentism of Peter Abelard, who made intention the exclusive source of moral good or evil (Peter Lombard, *Sent. IV*, 36). The evolution of the Scholastic interpretation of the phrase is traced by O. Lottin, 'Le problème de la moralité intrinsèque d'Abélard à Saint-Thomas d'Aquin'. *Rev. Thomiste* 1934, pp. 477–515. St Thomas uses the terminology to signify the good or evil an act has from its objective; see 1a2æ. 18, 2, but also ibid 4 for another usage.

RESPONSIO: Dicendum quod omne vitium ex defectu virtutis nominatur, quod* magis virtuti opponitur, sicut illiberalitas magis opponitur liberalitati quam prodigalitas. Potest autem virtuti gratitudinis aliquod vitium opponi per excessum, puta si recompensatio beneficii fiat vel pro quibus non debet, vel citius quam debet, ut ex dictis patet.³ Sed magis opponitur gratitudini vitium quod est per defectum, quia virtus gratitudinis, ut supra habitum est,⁴ in aliquid amplius tendit. Et ideo proprie ingratitudo nominatur ex gratitudinis defectu. Omnis autem defectus seu privatio speciem sortitur secundum habitum oppositum; differunt enim cæcitas et surditas secundum differentiam visus et auditus. Unde sicut gratitudo vel gratia est una specialis virtus, ita etiam ingratitudo est unum speciale peccatum.

Habet tamen diversos gradus secundum ordinem eorum quæ ad gratitudinem requiruntur. In qua primum est quod homo acceptum beneficium recognoscat; secundum est quod laudet et gratias agat; tertium est quod retribuat pro loco et tempore secundum suam facultatem. Sed quia quod est ultimum in generatione est primum in resolutione, ideo primus ingratitudinis gradus est ut homo beneficium non retribuat; secundus est ut dissimulet, quasi non demonstrans se beneficium accepisse; tertius et gravissimus est quod non recognoscat sive per oblivionem sive quocumque alio modo.

Et quia in affirmatione opposita intelligitur negatio, ideo ad primum ingratitudinis gradum pertinet quod aliquis retribuat mala pro bonis; ad secundum, quod beneficium vituperet; ad tertium, quod beneficium quasi maleficium reputet.

1. Ad primum ergo dicendum quod in quolibet peccato est materialis ingratitudo ad Deum, inquantum scilicet facit homo aliquid quod potest ad ingratitudinem pertinere. Formalis† autem ingratitudo est quando actualiter beneficium contemnitur; et hoc est speciale peccatum.

2. Ad secundum dicendum quod nihil prohibet formalem rationem alicujus specialis peccati in pluribus peccatorum generibus materialiter inveniri. Et secundum hoc in multis generibus peccatorum invenitur ingratitudinis ratio.

---

*Piana: *qui* which (i.e. in apposition to *defectu*)
†Piana: *formaliter*, formally
³art. 1 ad 1; 106, 4   ⁴106, 6
ᵇThe statement is a kind of dialectical principle. The presupposition is that moral virtue, being concerned with achieving the mean between excess and defect, has opposed to it a vice by way of defect and one by way of excess. Whether or not they have received distinctive names, one may be named by opposition to virtue (e.g. intemperance). As appears in Aristotle's *Ethics* and St Thomas's commentary, the basis is that the vice so named more directly attacks the human inclination that the virtue rightly controls; cf *In Ethic.* II, *lect.* 10. In the present instance the vice

REPLY: That vice which is more opposed to a virtue is named privatively from the virtue;[b] for example, illiberality is more opposed to liberality than prodigality is. In the case of the virtue of gratitude, there is a possibility of a vice opposed to it by excess, when, for example, repayment is made for things for which it should not be, or is made sooner than it should be.[3] But since, as has been determined,[4] gratitude aims at surpassing a favour received, the vice more opposed to it is the one that sins by defect. Consequently, ingratitude has its name properly from being a lack of gratitude. Now every lack or privation has its species by reference to the positive perfection opposed; the difference between blindness and deafness, for instance, is the difference between sight and hearing. Thus, just as gratitude is a specific virtue, ingratitude is the one specific sin.

Yet it does have varying degrees, corresponding to the rank of those acts required for gratitude. Among these the first is that a person admit that he has received a favour; the second, that he praise it and express his thanks; the third, that he repay it in the proper circumstances and according to his means. Because, however, the last stage in the coming to be of anything is the first to go in its dissolution, the first degree of ingratitude is for a person to fail to return a favour; the second, to let it pass unnoticed, giving no sign that he received it; the third and most serious is to deny it outright, either by forgetting it or in any other way.

Because the meaning of a negative is implied in its opposite affirmative, the first degree of ingratitude involves the repayment of good with evil; the second, reviling a kindness; the third, counting a favour as though it were an injury.

Hence: 1. There is a *de facto* ingratitude towards God in every sin, in the sense namely that a person does something that could be a form of ingratitude. But formal ingratitude as such exists only where there is explicit contempt for a gift received; this is the specific sin.[c]

2. There is nothing against the specifying note of some special sin being merely a concomitant element in several kinds of sin. This is the way a note of ingratitude is discernible in many classes of sin.[d]

---

opposed to gratitude by excess remains nameless; it is simply fulsome gratitude. It is clearly less wrong, since it does attend to the essential in gratitude, namely awareness of the debt to be repaid; but it misses the mark in some secondary way. Ingratitude cultivates a natural reluctance to be dependent and to acknowledge indebtedness; it strikes at gratitude directly. See also *In Ethic.* IV, lect. 4; 2a2æ. 119, 3.

[c]The point is the same as that made earlier on obedience and disobedience.

[d]*materialiter* is translated 'concomitantly' because it is the moral value, specifying note in that which engages an act that gives 'form' or species to the act. Other elements are simply 'materially' present, i.e. not as engaging the act; they are concomitants. For some other act they may be specifying notes; see 1a2æ. 18, 10.

3. Ad tertium dicendum quod illa tria non sunt diversæ species sed diversi gradus unius specialis peccati.

articulus 3. utrum ingratitudo semper sit peccatum mortale

AD TERTIUM sic proceditur: 1. Videtur quod ingratitudo semper sit peccatum mortale. Deo enim maxime debet aliquis esse gratus. Sed peccando venialiter homo non est ingratus Deo alioquin omnes homines essent ingrati. Ergo nulla ingratitudo est peccatum veniale.

2. Præterea, ex hoc aliquod peccatum est mortale quod contrariatur caritati, ut supra dictum est.[1] Sed ingratitudo contrariatur caritati, ex qua procedit debitum gratitudinis, ut supra dictum est.[2] Ergo ingratitudo semper est peccatum mortale.

3. Præterea, Seneca dicit, *Hæc beneficii inter duos lex est, alter statim oblivisci debet dati, alter accepti nunquam*.[3] Sed propter hoc, ut videtur, debet oblivisci ut lateat eum peccatum recipientis, si contingat eum esse ingratum; quod non oporteret, si ingratitudo esset leve peccatum. Ergo ingratitudo semper est peccatum mortale.

SED CONTRA est quod nulli est danda via peccandi mortaliter. Sed, sicut Seneca dicit, *Interdum et ipse qui juvatur fallendus est, ut habeat nec a quo acceperit sciat;*[4] quod videtur viam ingratitudinis recipienti præbere. Ergo ingratitudo non semper est peccatum mortale.

RESPONSIO: Dicendum quod, sicut ex supra dictis patet,[5] ingratus dicitur aliquis dupliciter. Uno modo per solam omissionem; puta quia non recognoscit vel non laudat vel non retribuit vices pro beneficio accepto. Et hoc non semper est peccatum mortale, quia, ut supra dictum est,[6] debitum gratitudinis est ut homo etiam aliquid liberaliter tribuat ad quod non tenetur. Et ideo si illud prætermittit, non peccat mortaliter. Est tamen peccatum veniale, quia hoc provenit ex negligentia quadam aut ex aliqua indispositione hominis ad virtutem. Potest tamen contingere quod etiam talis ingratitudo sit mortale peccatum vel propter interiorem contemptum, vel etiam propter conditionem ejus quod subtrahitur, quod ex necessitate debetur benefico* sive simpliciter sive in aliquo necessitatis casu.

Alio modo dicitur aliquis ingratus quia non solum prætermittit implere gratitudinis debitum, sed etiam contrarium agit. Et hoc etiam secundum conditionem ejus quod agitur, quandoque est peccatum mortale, quandoque veniale.

---

*Piana: *beneficio*, the favour done
[1]1a2æ. 72, 5; 2a2æ. 24, 12   [2]106, 6 ad 2

3. The three mentioned are not different species, but different degrees of the one specific sin.

article 3. whether the sin of ingratitude is always mortal

THE THIRD POINT: 1. Ingratitude appears to be always a mortal sin. To God above all we must be grateful. Now a person is not ungrateful to God when he sins venially; otherwise everyone would be guilty of ingratitude.[a] It follows that no ingratitude is a venial sin.

2. Further, as already indicated,[1] what makes a sin mortal is its opposition to charity. Since, as noted before,[2] the debt of gratitude has its source in charity, ingratitude is contrary to charity and so is always a mortal sin.

3. Further, Seneca says, *The rule for doing favours is that one person quickly forget what he has given, and the other long remember what he has received.*[3] It would seem that the benefactor ought to forget so that should the recipient be ungrateful, his sin would be unnoticed. Such a course would be unnecessary were ingratitude a slight sin. It is therefore always mortal.

ON THE OTHER HAND, no one must be given the opportunity to sin mortally. Yet Seneca claims that *sometimes it is necessary to deceive a person who receives help, in order that he may have it and still not know its source.*[4] This would seem to provide the recipient with an opportunity for ingratitude, which, therefore, is not always a mortal sin.

REPLY: As is already clear,[5] a person is termed an ingrate in two senses. First, by reason merely of omission, for example because he takes no notice of a favour, is silent about it or does nothing to reciprocate. This is not always a mortal sin, since, as noted,[6] the debt of gratitude means that a person give and give generously something to which he is not strictly obliged. If he fails to do so, then, he does not sin mortally. Still the sin is venial, arising as it does from a kind of negligence or a distaste for the way of virtue. There might even be times when it is a mortal sin, either because of inner contempt or because of the kind of thing that is withheld, when namely it is strictly due to the benefactor, either absolutely or in some particular moment of hardship.

In a second sense a person is called an ingrate when he not merely fails to honour the debt of gratitude but acts in a way directly opposite. Here too the sin is sometimes mortal, sometimes venial, depending on what it is he does.

---

[3] *De benef.* II, 10   [4] op. cit. II, 9   [5] art. 2   [6] 106, 6
[a] The supposition of this argument is the teaching that without some extraordinary privilege of grace no one can avoid all venial sins; cf Denz. 1573; 1a2æ. 109, 9.

Sciendum tamen quod ingratitudo quæ provenit ex peccato mortali habet perfectam ingratitudinis rationem; illa vero quæ provenit ex peccato veniali, imperfectam.

1. Ad primum ergo dicendum quod per peccatum veniale non est aliquis ingratus Deo secundum perfectam ingratitudinis rationem. Habet tamen aliquid ingratitudinis inquantum peccatum veniale tollit aliquem actum virtutis per quem homo Deo obsequitur.

2. Ad secundum dicendum quod ingratitudo quæ est cum peccato veniali non est contraria caritati sed est præter ipsam quia non tollit habitum caritatis sed aliquem actum ipsius excludit.

3. Ad tertium dicendum quod idem Seneca dicit, *Errat, si quis æstimat cum dicimus eum qui beneficium dedit, oblivisci oportere, excutere nos illi memoriam rei præsertim honestissimæ. Cum ergo dicimus, Meminisse non debet, hoc volumus intelligi, Prædicare non debet, nec jactare.*[7]

4. Ad quartum dicendum quod ille qui ignorat beneficium non est ingratus si beneficium non recompenset, dummodo sit paratus recompensare si nosset. Est autem laudabile quandoque ut ille cui providetur beneficium ignoret, tum propter inanis gloriæ vitationem sicut beatus Nicolaus aurum furtim in domum projiciens vitare voluit humanum favorem;[8] tum etiam quia in hoc ipso amplius beneficium facit quod consulit verecundiæ ejus qui beneficium accipit.

articulus 4. utrum ingratis sint beneficia subtrahenda

AD QUARTUM sic proceditur: 1. Videtur quod ingratis sint beneficia subtrahenda. Dicitur enim *Sap., Ingrati spes tanquam hybernalis glacies tabescet.*[1] Non autem ejus spes tabesceret, si non esset ei beneficium subtrahendum. Ergo sunt subtrahenda beneficia ingratis.

2. Præterea, nullus debet alteri præbere occasionem peccandi. Sed ingratus beneficium recipiens sumit occasionem ingratitudinis. Ergo non est ingrato beneficium dandum.

3. Præterea, *In quo quis peccat, per hoc et torquetur*, ut dicitur *Sap.*[2] Sed ille qui ingratus est beneficio accepto peccat contra beneficium. Ergo est beneficio privandus.

---

[7]*De benef.* VII, 22
[8]The legend of St Nicholas, found in the liturgical lessons for his feast, Dec. 6
[1]*Wisdom* 16, 29   [2]*Wisdom* 11, 17
[b]From art. 2 ad 1 we should recall that the special sin of ingratitude is one of contempt for a favour received. Only where there is such contempt is there the formal sin of ingratitude, venial or mortal. Since contempt in its full sense must be serious, only a mortal sin of ingratitude can be ingratitude in the full sense. Any sin against a benefactor, as St Thomas has also noted in art. 2, would be an implicit form of ingratitude.

Take note, however: ingratitude that results from a mortal sin completely fulfils the definition of ingratitude; one arising from a venial sin, incompletely.[b]

Hence: 1. Through venial sin a person is not ungrateful to God in the full sense of ingratitude. Still there is a note of ungratefulness in that a venial sin precludes an act of virtue through which a person shows honour to God.

2. A venial sin of ingratitude is not contrary to charity but rather is outside the actual influence of charity; it does not destroy the habitual possession of charity but forestalls some one act.[c]

3. But the same Seneca says, *It would be a mistake to think that the statement 'one who has done a kindness should forget about it' means that he should blot it out of his memory, especially when his deed is one of great nobility. When I say that he should not remember it, I intend simply that he should not make it public or boast about it.*[7]

4.[d] One unaware of a kindness is not ungrateful for not returning it, provided that he has the willingness to repay any favour he is aware of. At times it is the wiser course for the recipient to be left in ignorance, both in order to forestall vanity—an example, St Nicholas secretly tossing gold into a house wanted to avoid human acclaim;[8] and because a kindness is even greater when it includes consideration for the sensibilities of the recipient.

article 4. whether favours should be denied to the ungrateful

THE FOURTH POINT: 1. It would seem that favours should be withheld from the ungrateful. In *Wisdom* it is said that *the hope of the unthankful shall melt away as the winter's ice*.[1] This would not be so unless were he to be deprived of all favours. Therefore favours should be withheld from all ingrates.

2. Further, no one should give to another an occasion for sinning, and the ingrate who receives a kindness just turns it into an occasion for ingratitude. No good turn, then, should be done for him.

3. Further, *By what things a man sinneth, by the same also he is tormented.*[2] Since the sin of the ingrate is against the favour he receives, he should be deprived of it.

---

[c]Charity is the power to fulfil the commandment to love God totally, with one's whole heart and mind and strength; it seeks to direct every action towards this totality. A venially sinful act falls outside this orientation of charity; it supplants the opportunity to love God or neighbour in a particular act.

[d]This is one of the infrequent places in the *Summa* where there is a response to the *sed contra*; it serves as a reminder of the structure of the *Summa*; see Vol. I of this series, ed. T. Gilby, Appendix I; below III, 4, note *a*.

SED CONTRA est quod dicitur *Luc.* quod *Altissimus benignus est super ingratos et malos.*³ Sed per ejus imitationem nos filios ejus esse oportet, ut ibidem dicitur. Ergo non debemus ingratis beneficia subtrahere.

RESPONSIO: Dicendum quod circa ingratum duo consideranda sunt. Primo quidem, quid ipse dignus* sit pati. Et sic certum est quod meretur beneficii subtractionem.

Alio modo considerandum est quid oporteat beneficum facere. Primo namque non debet esse facilis ad ingratitudinem judicandam, quia *frequenter aliquis,* ut Seneca dicit, *qui non reddidit, gratus est,*⁴ quia forte non occurrit ei facultas aut debita opportunitas reddendi. Secundo debet tendere ad hoc quod de ingrato gratum faciat; quod si non potest primo beneficio facere, forte faciet secundo. Si vero ex beneficiis multiplicatis ingratitudinem augeat et pejor fiat, debet a beneficiorum exhibitione cessare.

1. Ad primum ergo dicendum quod auctoritas illa loquitur quantum ad id quod ingratus dignus est pati.

2. Ad secundum dicendum quod ille qui ingrato beneficium exhibet non dat ei occasionem peccandi sed magis gratitudinis et amoris. Si vero ille qui accipit ingratitudinis exinde occasionem sumat, non est danti imputandum.

3. Ad tertium dicendum quod ille qui beneficium dat, non statim se debet exhibere punitorem ingratitudinis sed prius pium medicum, ut scilicet iteratis beneficiis ingratitudinem sanet.

---

*Piana: *quid est quod ipse dignus est pati*; sense the same

INGRATITUDE

ON THE OTHER HAND, in *Luke* we read that *the highest is kind to the unthankful and evil*,[3] and in the same place that by imitation we should show ourselves his children. We should not, then, keep back favours from the ungrateful.

REPLY: Two points must be considered about the ungrateful. First, what punishment he deserves. Certainly he merits withdrawal of favours.

In another way one must take account of how a benefactor is to act towards him. First, he should not be quick to judge that there has been ingratitude, because, as Seneca remarks, often someone *does not reciprocate, yet is grateful*;[4] it may be that the person simply has not had the means or the right opportunity. Secondly, the benefactor should exert his efforts to transform the ingrate; if one good turn is not enough, perhaps a second will be. Still, when the ingratitude only increases and worsens with repeated kindnesses, they must be discontinued.

Hence: 1. This text is speaking from the point of view of what punishment the unthankful deserve.

2. The one who does a good turn for an ingrate does not provide him with an occasion of sin, but of gratitude and love. When the recipient uses favours as an occasion for sinning, it is through no fault of the giver.

3. A benefactor should not immediately become the avenger of ingratitude, but first a kindly physician, seeking by repeated kindness to remedy it.

---

[3] *Luke* 6, 35   [4] *De benef.* III, 7

Quæstio 108. de vindicatione

DEINDE CONSIDERANDUM EST de vindicatione. Et circa hoc quæruntur quatuor:

1. utrum vindicatio sit licita;
2. utrum sit specialis virtus;
3. de modo vindicandi;
4. in quos sit vindicta exercenda.

articulus 1. *utrum vindicatio sit licita*

AD PRIMUM sic proceditur.[1] 1. Videtur quod vindicatio non sit licita. Quicumque enim usurpat sibi quod Dei est, peccat. Sed vindicta pertinet ad Deum, dicitur enim *Deut.* secundum aliam litteram, *Mihi vindicta, et ego retribuam*.[2] Ergo omnis vindicatio est illicita.

2. Præterea, ille de quo vindicta sumitur, non toleratur. Sed mali sunt tolerandi, quia super illud *Cant.*, *Sicut lilium inter spinas*,[3] dicit Glossa, *Non fuit bonus, qui malos tolerare non potuit*.[4] Ergo vindicta non est sumenda de malis.

3. Præterea, vindicta per pœnas fit, ex quibus causatur timor servilis. Sed lex nova non est lex timoris, sed amoris, ut Augustinus dicit.[5] Ergo ad minus in Novo Testamento nulla vindicta fieri debet.

4. Præterea, ille dicitur vindicare se qui injurias suas ulciscitur. Sed, ut videtur, non licet etiam judici in se delinquentes punire; dicit enim Chrysostomus *Super Matth.*, *Discamus exemplo Christi nostras injurias magnanimiter sustinere, Dei autem injurias nec usque ad auditum sufferre*.[6] Ergo vindicatio videtur esse illicita.

---

[1] cf 2a2æ. 158, 3. 3a. 15, 9. *De malo* XII, 1 & 3 ad 5. *In Romanos* 12, *lect.* 3
[2] *Deuteronomy* 32, 35   [3] *Canticle of Canticles* 2, 2
[4] *Ordinaria*, from Gregory, Homil. *in Evang.* 38, PL 76, 1286
[5] *Contra Adimantum* 17. PL 42, 158
[6] *Opus imperf. in Matth.* 5 on 4, 10. PG 56, 668. Pseudo-Chrysostom.
[a] In 2a2æ. 80, which assigns the potential parts of justice, gratitude and vengeance are coupled. Both are concerned with a repayment owed in terms of the deeds done by others: gratitude in terms of the good done to us; vengeance, in terms of the evil.
[b] 'Vengeance' does not have the ring of virtue about it, yet in exact usage it is the best word here. *Vindicatio* comes from Cicero's list of virtues (see art. 2 *sed contra*). As a juridical term it meant laying legal claim to a thing; as a virtue Cicero intends it as a kind of self-defence from injuries and a way of redress. *Vindicta*, originally referring to the rod laid on a slave about to be freed in the ceremony of manumission, came to signify the means taken to avenge a wrong, a punishment. In

Question 108. vengeance

NEXT, WE MUST discuss vengeance;[a] there are four points of inquiry:

1. whether vengeance[b] is lawful;
2. a special virtue;
3. the way in which it is carried out;
4. those against whom it is to be directed.

article 1. whether vengeance is permissible

THE FIRST POINT:[1] 1. Vengeance seems to be unlawful. He sins who takes on himself what belongs to God. Vengeance, however, belongs to God, for in *Deuteronomy*, according to one reading, it is written, *Revenge is mine and I will repay.*[2c] All vengeance, therefore, is unlawful.

2. Further, we do not bear with a person against whom we take vengeance. We must, however, bear with the wicked; on the verse, *As the lily among the thorns,*[3] the *Gloss* comments, *The one who could not put up with the wicked was not good himself.*[4] Therefore not even with regard to the wicked is vengeance to be taken.

3. Further, vengeance is achieved through punishment, which in turn is a cause of slavish fear. Since Augustine asserts that the New Law is a law not of fear but of love,[5] at least under the New Testament there should be no vengeance.

4. Further, to avenge oneself is to retaliate for wrongs to oneself. Yet apparently not even a judge is allowed to punish those wronging himself; thus Chrysostom, *From Christ's example let us learn to bear injuries to ourselves with greatness of soul, but not to suffer wrongs against God even by giving ear to them.*[6] Vengeance, then, would seem to be unlawful.

English 'vindicate' and 'vindication' have all but lost the meaning of avenging, and refer to clearing a claim, demonstrating a point, etc. (The usage 'vindictive' or 'vindicative justice' survives, connoting justice as retributive.) 'Vengeance' has the meaning of both the act of avenging and the object of the act, the punishment exacted. It should be noted that 'to avenge' has the connotation of a just retribution for an injury; 'to revenge' connotes retaliating with resentment and malice. An equivalent distinction is made here in the Reply of art. 1.

The issue of this Question is the virtue of retaliating for a wrong done; and it is personal retaliation, a kind of self-defence, rather than the public administration of punishment (cf art. 2 ad 2); St Thomas does, however, make remarks on the whole subject of redressing wrongs.

[c]The Vulgate text of *Deuteronomy* itself has *Mea est ultio*; but the Vulgate text of *Romans* 12, 19 cites *Deuteronomy* as it is here, with *vindicta* in place of *ultio*.

5. Præterea, peccatum multitudinis magis est nocivum quam peccatum unius tantum; dicitur enim *Eccl.*, *A tribus timuit cor meum zelaturam civitatis, et collectionem populi*.[7] Sed de peccato multitudinis non est vindicta sumenda, quia super illud *Matt.*, *Sinite utraque crescere, ne forte eradicetis triticum*,[8] dicit *Glossa* quod *multitudo non est excommunicanda, nec princeps*.[9] Ergo nec alia vindicatio est licita.

SED CONTRA nihil est expectandum a Deo, nisi quod est bonum et licitum. Sed vindicta de hostibus est expectanda a Deo, dicitur enim *Luc.*, *Deus non faciet vindictam electorum suorum clamantium ad se die ac nocte?*[10] quasi diceret, *immo faciet*. Ergo vindicatio non est per se mala et illicita.

RESPONSIO: Dicendum quod vindicatio fit per aliquod pœnale malum inflictum peccanti. Est ergo in vindicatione considerandus vindicantis animus. Si enim ejus intentio feratur principaliter in malum illius de quo vindictam sumit, et ibi quiescat, est omnino illicitum. Quia delectari in malo alterius pertinet ad odium quod caritati repugnat qua omnes homines debemus diligere. Nec aliquis excusatur si malum intendat illius qui sibi injuste intulit malum, sicut non excusatur aliquis per hoc quod odit se odientem. Non enim debet homo in alium peccare propter hoc quod ille peccavit prius in ipsum; hoc enim est vinci a malo, quod Apostolus prohibet *Ad Rom.*, dicens, *Noli vinci a malo, sed vince in bono malum*.[11]

Si vero intentio vindicantis feratur principaliter ad aliquod bonum, ad quod pervenitur per pœnam peccantis, puta ad emendationem peccantis vel saltem ad cohibitionem ejus et quietem aliorum et ad justitiæ conservationem et Dei honorem, potest esse vindicatio licita, aliis debitis circumstantiis servatis.

1. Ad primum ergo dicendum quod ille qui secundum gradum sui ordinis vindictam exercet in malos non usurpat sibi quod Dei est, sed utitur potestate sibi divinitus concessa. Dicitur enim *ad Rom.*, de principe terreno, quod *Dei minister est, vindex in iram ei qui male agit*.[12] Si autem præter ordinem divinæ institutionis aliquis vindictam exerceat, usurpat sibi quod Dei est, et ideo peccat.

2. Ad secundum dicendum quod mali tolerantur a bonis in hoc quod ab eis proprias injurias patienter sustinent secundum quod oportet; non autem tolerant eos, ut sustineant injurias Dei et proximorum. Dicit enim

---

[7]*Ecclesiasticus* 26, 5–6
[8]*Matthew* 13, 29
[9]*Ordinaria*; Augustine,*Quæst. in Matthæum*, XII on 13, 30. PL 35, 1370
[10]*Luke* 18, 7
[11]*Romans* 12, 21
[12]*Romans* 13, 4

5. Further, the sin of the many is more injurious than the sin of one person; *Of three things my heart has been afraid, the accusations of a city and the gathering together of the people.*[7] Yet vengeance may not be taken on the sin of a whole group, since the *Gloss* on the words in *Matthew, Lest perhaps ... you root up the wheat ... suffer both to grow*,[8] comments, *Neither a whole people nor its ruler should be excommunicated.*[9] Neither, then, is any other kind of vengeance lawful.

ON THE OTHER HAND we should expect from God only what is good and lawful. But vengeance upon enemies is to be expected from God; in *Luke* there is the rhetorical question, *And will not God revenge his elect who cry to him day and night?*[10] Therefore vengeance is not in itself evil and unlawful.

REPLY: Vengeance is accomplished by some punishment[d] being inflicted upon one who has given offence. In vengeance, therefore, the attitude of the avenger must be considered. Should his intention be centred chiefly upon the evil done to the recipient and is satisfied with that, then the act is entirely unlawful. Taking delight in evil done to another is in fact a type of hatred, the opposite of that charity with which we are bound to love all. Nor is there any excuse just because the evil is intended towards one who has himself unjustly inflicted injury, even as there is no excuse for hating someone who already hates us. A person has no right to sin against another because the other first sinned against him; this is to be overcome by evil, which St Paul forbids, *Be not overcome by evil, but overcome evil by good.*[11]

Vengeance, however, can be lawful—so long as all proper conditions are safeguarded—if the intention of the avenger is aimed chiefly at a good to be achieved by punishing a wrongdoer; thus, for example, at the correction of the wrongdoer, or at least at restraining him and relieving others; at safeguarding the right and doing honour to God.

Hence: 1. One who exacts vengeance of the wicked in keeping with his own station does not arrogate to himself what is God's; rather he simply exercises a God-given power. St Paul says of the earthly ruler, *He is God's minister, an avenger to execute wrath upon him that doeth evil.*[12] However, if in wreaking vengeance someone exceeds the divinely established order, he usurps what is God's and sins.

2. The good bear with the wicked by patience in sustaining the wrongs done them personally to the extent required; they do not bear with them to the point of allowing wrongs against God or neighbour. Chrysostom

---

[d]*pœnale malum* refers to punishment. In moral considerations of evil, *malum culpæ* is the evil of fault; *malum pœnæ*, the evil of punishment. Fault is the disordered act of the will; punishment, the deprival, against his will, of something the sinner wishes to have or retain; see 1a. 45, 5 & 6. Vol. 8. ed. T. Gilby.

Chrysostomus, *In propriis injuriis esse quempiam patientem, laudabile est; injurias autem Dei dissimulare, nimis est impium.*[13]

3. Ad tertium dicendum quod lex Evangelii est lex amoris. Et ideo illis qui ex amore bonum operantur, qui soli proprie ad Evangelium pertinent, non est timor incutiendus per pœnas, sed solum illis qui ex amore non moventur ad bonum, qui etsi numero sint de Ecclesia non tamen merito.

4. Ad quartum dicendum quod injuria quæ infertur personæ alicui, quandoque redundat in Deum et in Ecclesiam; et tunc debet aliquis propriam injuriam ulcisci, sicut patet de Elia, qui fecit ignem descendere super eos qui venerant ad ipsum capiendum, ut legitur IV *Reg.*;[14] et similiter Eliseus maledixit pueris eum irridentibus, ut habetur IV *Reg.*;[15] et Sylvester papa excommunicavit eos qui eum in exilium miserunt.[16] Inquantum vero injuria in aliquem illata ad ejus personam pertinet, debet eam tolerare patienter, si expediat. Hujusmodi enim præcepta patientiæ intelligenda sunt secundum præparationem animi, ut Augustinus dicit in libro *De serm. Domini in monte.*[17]

5. Ad quintum dicendum quod quando tota multitudo peccat, est de ea vindicta sumenda vel quantum ad totam multitudinem, sicut Ægyptii submersi sunt in mari Rubro, persequentes filios Israel, ut habetur *Exod.*;[18] et sicut Sodomitæ universaliter perierunt; vel quantum ad magnam multitudinis partem, sicut patet *Exod.* in pœna eorum qui vitulum adoraverunt.[19] Quandoque vero si speretur multorum correctio, debet severitas vindictæ exerceri in aliquos paucos principaliores, quibus punitis cæteri terreantur; sicut Dominus *Num.* mandavit suspendi populi principes pro peccato multitudinis.[20]

Si autem non tota multitudo peccavit sed pro parte, tunc si possunt mali secerni a bonis, debet in eos vindicta exerceri. Si tamen hoc fieri possit sine scandalo aliorum; alioquin parcendum est multitudini et detrahendum severitati. Et eadem ratio est de principe quem sequitur multitudo. Tolerandum enim est peccatum ejus, si sine scandalo multitudinis puniri non posset, nisi forte esset tale peccatum principis quod magis noceret multitudini vel spiritualiter vel temporaliter quam scandulum quod exinde timeretur.

---

[13]loc cit note 6 above
[14]IV *Kings* 1, 9
[15]ibid 2, 23
[16]*Decretum Magistri Gratiani* II, XXIII, 4, 30. The reference is to the 12th century canonist, Gratian, whose *Concordantia discordantium canonum*, a co-ordination of patristic texts, papal and conciliar decrees, came to be accepted, along with the Decretals of Gregory IX, as the *Corpus Juris Canonici.*
[17]*De serm. Dom.* I, 19 & 20. PL 34, 1260, 1262
[18]*Exodus* 14, 22   [19]op cit. 32, 27
[20]*Numbers* 25, 4

notes, *It is commendable when someone is patient about injury to himself; it is wicked to take no notice of wrongs against God.*[13]

3. The law of the Gospel is indeed the law of love. This is why there is no need to instil fear through punishment in those who live rightly out of love (and these alone belong in truth to the New Testament[e]), but in those who are not drawn to the good out of love and who belong to the Church in name but not in life.

4. A personal wrong can sometimes rebound upon God or the Church; then the individual should himself seek redress for the injury done him. These are examples: Elias made fire come down upon those who had come to seize him;[14] Eliseus cursed the youths who made fun of him;[15] Pope Sylvester excommunicated those who exiled him.[16] When an injury is in fact strictly personal, one should bear with it patiently, but only if this can be done sensibly; the precepts of patience cited here are to be understood as referring to one's inner willingness,[f] as Augustine states.[17]

5. When an entire community sins, vengeance should be taken on the whole group or on a notable segment; examples of the first are the Egyptians pursuing the children of Israel and being drowned in the Red Sea,[18] and the utter destruction of the Sodomites; of the second, the punishment of those who adored the golden calf.[19] When, however, there is some hope for the correction of the group, severe vengeance should be limited to a few principal figures, so that through their punishment the rest may be made fearful; an example, the Lord ordering the leaders of the people to be hanged for the sins of all.[20]

When the community as a whole has not sinned, but only a part of it, then it is possible to separate the wicked from the good and make them the object of vengeance. This is true, however, only if it can be done without scandal[g] to the rest; otherwise the whole community is to be spared and severity mitigated. The same reasoning applies to a leader whom a community has followed. His sin has to be tolerated if it cannot be punished without scandal to the many, unless the sin were so heinous that it did more spiritual or temporal damage to the group than any scandal from his being punished could do.

---

[e] See 1a2æ. 107, 1 & ad 2 & ad 3.
[f] *præparationem animi*, Augustine's expression, used regularly to refer to the way a Christian is held to evangelical ideals, especially regarding love of enemies and patience. One must have an habitual willingness to put these ideals into practice if necessity requires, for then the necessity makes such ideals matters of precept, e.g. to come to the aid of an enemy who is in dire need. But to seek opportunities actively to practise these ideals is a matter of counsel, not of precept; cf 1a2æ. 108, 3 ad 2; 4 & ad 4; 2a2æ. 40, 1 ad 2; 43, 8 ad 4; 140, 2 ad 2.
[g] 'scandal', in its proper theological sense, is whatever occasions spiritual ruin for another; cf 2a2æ. 43.

articulus 2. *utrum vindicatio sit specialis virtus*

AD SECUNDUM sic proceditur: 1. Videtur quod vindicatio non sit specialis virtus ab aliis distincta. Sicut enim remunerantur boni pro his quæ bene agunt, ita puniuntur mali pro his quæ male agunt. Sed remuneratio bonorum non pertinet ad aliquam virtutem specialem sed est actus commutativæ justitiæ. Ergo pari ratione vindicatio non debet poni specialis virtus.

2. Præterea, ad actum illum non debet ordinari specialis virtus ad quem homo sufficienter disponitur per alias virtutes. Sed ad vindicandum mala sufficienter disponitur homo per virtutem fortitudinis et per zelum. Non ergo vindicatio debet poni specialis virtus.

3. Præterea, cuilibet speciali virtuti aliquod speciale vitium opponitur. Sed vindicationi non videtur opponi aliquod vitium speciale. Ergo non est specialis virtus.

SED CONTRA est quod Tullius ponit eam partem justitiæ.[1]

RESPONSIO: Dicendum quod, sicut Philosophus dicit in *Ethic.*,[2] aptitudo ad virtutem inest nobis a natura, licet complementum virtutis sit per assuetudinem vel per aliquam aliam causam. Unde patet quod virtutes perficiunt nos ad prosequendum debito modo inclinationes naturales quæ pertinent ad jus naturale. Et ideo ad quamlibet inclinationem naturalem determinatam ordinatur aliqua virtus specialis.

Est autem quædam specialis inclinatio naturæ ad removendum nocumenta, unde et animalibus datur vis irascibilis separatim a vi concupiscibili. Repellit autem homo nocumenta per hoc quod se defendit contra injurias ne ei inferantur, vel jam illatas injurias ulciscitur non intentione nocendi sed intentione removendi nocumenta. Hoc autem pertinet ad vindicationem; dicit enim Tullius quod *vindicatio est per quam vis aut injuria, et omnino quidquid obscurum est*, idest, ignominiosum, *defendendo aut ulciscendo propulsatur*.[3] Unde vindicatio est specialis virtus.

1. Ad primum ergo dicendum quod, sicut recompensatio debiti legalis pertinet ad justitiam commutativam, recompensatio autem debiti moralis, quod nascitur ex particulari beneficio exhibito, pertinet ad virtutem gratiæ; ita etiam punitio peccatorum secundum quod pertinet ad publicam justitiam est actus justitiæ commutativæ; secundum autem quod pertinet ad immunitatem alicujus personæ singularis a qua injuria propulsatur pertinet ad virtutem vindicationis.

---

[1]*Rhet.* II, 53 [2]*Ethics* II, I. 1103a23
[3]*Rhet.* II, 53
[a]cf 1a2æ. 63, 1–4; 94, 2 & 3; 2a2æ. 47, 6; *De veritate* XI, 1; *De virtutibus* 8. The

article 2. whether vengeance is one specific virtue

THE SECOND POINT: 1. Vengeance does not seem to be a special virtue distinct from others. As the good are rewarded for good deeds, so the wicked are punished for acting evilly. Now rewarding the good does not involve some new specific virtue, but is simply an act of commutative justice. For a like reason vengeance should not be proposed as a special virtue.

2. Further, there is no call for a special virtue in regard to an act towards which man is already sufficiently disposed through other virtues. As to seeking redress for injuries, a person is well enough prepared by the virtue of courage and by zeal. Vengeance, then, ought not to be accounted a special virtue.

3. Further, whereas there is a specific vice against every specific virtue, opposed to vengeance there seems to be no specific vice. Vengeance, then, is not a specific virtue.

ON THE OTHER HAND, Cicero counts it as a part of justice.[1]

REPLY: As Aristotle teaches in the *Ethics*,[2] while completeness in virtue comes about by habituation or some other cause, the predisposition for virtue is innate. Hence it is clear that virtues bring about a proper development of tendencies that are innate and that are included in natural law.[a] Accordingly, to every distinct bent of nature, there corresponds some specific virtue.

There is a specific innate tendency to get rid of what is harmful; a sign of this in brute animals is that there is a contending power distinct from the impulse power.[b] A human being repels what is harmful by self-defence, either warding off injuries, or, if they have already been inflicted, avenging them, not with the intention of doing harm but of repelling a wrong. This is what vengeance is about; Cicero says, *By vengeance we resist force or wrong and in general anything sinister* (i.e. hostile) *either by self-defence or by retaliating.*[3] Vengeance, therefore, is a specific virtue.

Hence: 1. To acquit a legal debt is the concern of commutative justice; a moral debt, arising from personal favours, the concern of gratitude. In a like way, the punishment of offences where public order is at stake, is the concern of commutative justice; vengeance has place where the issue is the right to personal safety of the individual from whom an evil is repulsed.

---

innate origins of virtue and their relationship to natural law is one key to St Thomas's conception of the moral order and its intrinsic finalism.

[b] cf 1a. 81, 2 on this distinction of powers in the sense appetite, and Vol. 21 of this series, J. P. Reid, ed., for the terminology 'impulse' and 'contending' as translations of *concupiscibilis* and *irascibilis*.

2. Ad secundum dicendum quod fortitudo disponit ad vindictam removendo prohibens, scilicet timorem periculi imminentis. Zelus autem secundum quod importat fervorem amoris importat primam radicem vindicationis, prout aliquis vindicat injurias Dei vel proximorum, quas ex caritate reputat quasi suas. Cujuslibet autem virtutis actus ex radice caritatis procedit, quia, ut Gregorius dicit in quadam homilia, *nihil habet viriditatis ramus boni operis, si non procedat ex radice caritatis.*[4]

3. Ad tertium dicendum quod vindicationi opponuntur duo vitia. Unum quidem per excessum, scilicet peccatum crudelitatis vel sævitiæ, quæ excedit mensuram in puniendo. Aliud autem est vitium quod consistit in defectu, sicut cum aliquis est nimis remissus in puniendo. Unde dicitur *Prov., Qui parcit virgæ, odit filium suum.*[5] Virtus autem vindicationis consistit in hoc ut homo secundum omnes circumstantias debitam mensuram in vindicando conservet.

articulus 3. *utrum vindicatio debeat fieri per pœnas apud homines consuetas*

AD TERTIUM sic proceditur:[1] 1. Videtur quod vindicatio non debeat fieri per pœnas apud homines consuetas. Occisio enim hominis est quædam eradicatio ejus. Sed Dominus mandavit *Matt.* 13 quod zizania, per quæ significantur filii nequam, non eradicarentur.[2] Ergo peccatores non sunt occidendi.

2. Præterea, quicumque mortaliter peccant eadem pœna videntur digni. Si ergo aliqui peccantes mortaliter morte puniuntur, videtur quod omnes tales deberent morte puniri. Quod patet esse falsum.

3. Præterea, cum aliquis pro peccato punitur manifeste, ex hoc peccatum ejus manifestatur, quod videtur esse nocivum multitudini, quæ ex exemplo peccati sumit occasionem peccandi. Ergo videtur quod non sit pœna mortis pro aliquo peccato infligenda.

SED CONTRA est quod in lege divina hujusmodi pœnæ* determinantur, ut ex supra dictis patet.[3]

---

*Leonine: *his hujusmodi pœnæ*, for these (crimes) these
[4]*Homil. in Evang.* 27. PL 76, 1205
[5]*Proverbs* 13, 24
[1]cf 2a2æ. 64, 2; 65, 1-3
[2]*Matthew* 13, 29
[3]1a2æ. 105, 2, ad 9 & 10
[c]On courage see 2a2æ. 123, 1-4, and vol. 42 of this series. On the phrase 'removing an obstacle' (*removens prohibens*) see *In Meta.* V, *lect.* 3; to be a *removens prohibens* is to be a cause only in an incidental sense (*per accidens*), a cause that allows a direct cause to have its effect; see also 1a2æ. 76, 1.

2. Courage opens the way for vengeance by removing an obstacle, the fear namely of a pressing danger.[c] For its part, zeal,[d] as it means the fervour of love, functions as a first root of vengeance in the sense that one seeks to right wrongs against God or neighbour because charity causes him to see these wrongs as done to himself.[e] In any case, the acts of all virtues stem from charity as their root;[f] in one of his homilies Gregory says, *The branch, a good work, is withered unless it grows out of its root, charity.*[4]

3. There are in fact two vices against vengeance. By excess there is the sin of cruelty or ferocity, going beyond measure in punishing. The other is a vice by way of defect,[g] as when someone fails to inflict punishment at all— *He that spares the rod spoils the child.*[5] For its part, the virtue of vengeance means that in redressing wrongs a person keep to a right measure with proper regard for all circumstances.[h]

article 3. whether vengeance should be carried out by means of conventional forms of punishment[a]

THE THIRD POINT:[1] 1. Vengeance, it seems, should not be exercised through the usual forms of human punishment. Obviously, to put a person to death is to uproot him, and to uproot the cockle, symbol of the *children of the wicked one*, is against our Lord's command in *Matt.*[2] Offenders, therefore, are not to be put to death.

2. Further, it seems that all who sin mortally merit the same punishment, so that if some of these receive capital punishment, all should. This is obviously false.

3. Further, public punishment publicizes a crime. This would seem to have a harmful effect on the community, namely that the example of sin would become the occasion for more sin. Therefore it seems that for no sin should capital punishment be inflicted.

ON THE OTHER HAND, there are prescriptions of divine law with regard to these penalties, as shown above.[3]

---

[d]On zeal as an effect of love see 1a2æ. 28, 4.
[e]On love as personally unitive see 1a2æ. 26, 4; 27, 1 & ad 2; 2; 2a2æ. 23, 1; 25 & 26.
[f]cf 2a2æ. 23, 8 ad 2.
[g]See above 107, 2 note *b*. The vice opposite to vengeance by defect is nameless; as the privation of vengeance it is more opposed to vengeance and the natural inclination perfected by vengeance; but it is a lesser evil than cruelty. On cruelty see 2a2æ. 149.
[h]On moral circumstances see above 10, 4 note *a*.
[a]The scope of this article is clearly broader than vengeance as personal self-defence and touches on the meaning of criminal punishment.

RESPONSIO: Dicendum quod vindicatio intantum licita est et virtuosa inquantum tendit ad cohibitionem malorum. Cohibentur autem aliqui a peccando qui affectum virtutis non habent, per hoc quod timent amittere aliqua quæ plus amant quam illa quæ peccando adipiscuntur, alias timor non compesceret peccatum. Et ideo per subtractionem omnium quæ homo maxime diligit, est vindicta de peccatis sumenda.

Hæc autem sunt quæ homo maxime diligit, vitam, incolumitatem corporis, libertatem sui, et bona exteriora, puta divitias, patriam et gloriam. Et ideo, ut Augustinus refert, *De civ. Dei, Octo genera pœnaru min legibus esse scribit Tullius*; scilicet *mortem*, per quam tollitur vita; *verbera* et *talionem*, ut scilicet oculum pro oculo perdat; per quæ amittit quis corporis incolumitatem; *servitutem*, et *vincula*, per quæ perdit libertatem; *exilium*, per quod perdit patriam; *damnum*, per quod perdit divitias; *ignominiam*, per quam perdit gloriam.[4]

1. Ad primum ergo dicendum quod Dominus prohibet eradicari zizania, quando timetur ne simul cum eis eradicetur et triticum. Sed quandoque possunt eradicari mali per mortem non solum sine periculo sed etiam cum magna utilitate bonorum. Et ideo in tali casu potest pœna mortis peccatoribus infligi.

2. Ad secundum dicendum quod omnes peccantes mortaliter digni sunt morte æterna quantum ad futuram retributionem quæ est secundum veritatem divini judicii. Sed pœnæ præsentis vitæ sunt magis medicinales, et ideo illis solis peccatis pœna mortis infligitur quæ in gravem perniciem aliorum cedunt.

3. Ad tertium dicendum quod quando simul cum culpa innotescit et pœna vel mortis vel quæcumque alia quam homo horret, ex hoc ipso voluntas ejus a peccando abstrahitur. Quia plus terret pœna quam alliciat exemplum culpæ.

articulus 4. utrum vindicta sit exercenda in eos qui involuntarie peccaverunt

AD QUARTUM sic proceditur:[1] 1. Videtur quod vindicta sit exercenda in eos qui involuntarie peccaverunt. Voluntas enim unius non consequitur voluntatem alterius. Sed unus punitur pro alio, secundum illud *Exod., Ego sum Deus zelotes, visitans iniquitatem patrum in filios, in tertiam et quartam generationem.*[2] Unde et pro peccato Cham, Chanaan filius ejus maledictus est, ut habetur *Gen.*[3] Giezi etiam peccante, lepra transmittitur ad posteros, ut habetur IV *Reg.*[4] Sanguis etiam Christi pœnæ reddit obnoxios successores Judæorum, qui dixerunt *Matt., Sanguis ejus super nos, et super filios*

---

[4]*De civ. Dei* XXI, 11. PL 41, 725
[1]cf 1a2æ. 87, 7 & 8

REPLY: Vengeance is lawful and virtuous to the extent that its purpose is to check evil. Some people, having no liking for virtue, are kept from sinning solely through fear of losing things dearer to them than what they would get out of sinning; only in this way may fear curb sin. Reprisal for sin, consequently, should consist in depriving a person of the things dearest to him.

Such things are these: life, soundness of body, personal liberty and outward advantages like wealth, homeland and reputation. Thus according to Augustine, *Cicero writes that there are eight types of penalty in law*, namely *death* (this deprives a man of his life); *flogging* and *retaliation, i.e. an eye for an eye* (these mean loss of bodily integrity); *bondage* and *chains* (these take away personal liberty); *exile* (the loss of homeland); *damages* (these cost a man his wealth); *disgrace* (the ruin of his reputation).[4]

Hence: 1. Our Lord forbade the cockle to be uprooted when there was any fear that the wheat would be torn up with it. Sometimes, however, it is possible to get rid of the wicked by death, not only without peril to good people, but even to their great advantage. In such an instance capital punishment can be inflicted upon the wicked.

2. All who sin mortally are deserving of eternal death, speaking of the retribution in the after-life that comes under the infallibility of God's judgment. Since in this life, however, punishments have more of a medicinal purpose, the death penalty is to be exacted only for crimes which involve dire injury to others.

3. When along with the sin its punishment is made plain, namely death or other things terrifying to men, then any leaning towards the sin is checked. The punishment terrifies more than sin attracts.[b]

article 4. whether vengeance is to be taken on those whose offence is involuntary

THE FOURTH POINT:[1] 1. Seemingly vengeance is to be taken even on those who have offended unintentionally. While the will-act of one person does not automatically follow another's, yet, in keeping with the text, *I am... God... jealous, visiting the iniquity of the fathers upon the children, unto the third and fourth generation*,[2] one person is punished for another's offence. Cham's son Chanaan was cursed for the sin of Cham[3]. For the sin of Giezi leprosy passed to his descendants.[4] The blood of Christ made the descendants of those Jews who cried out, *His blood be upon us and upon our*

---

[2] *Exodus* 20, 5
[3] *Genesis* 9, 25
[4] IV *Kings* 5, 27
[b] A point of view that seems challenged by the history of crime and punishment.

nostros.⁵ Legitur etiam quod pro peccato Achan populus Israel traditus est in manus hostium, ut habetur *Josue*.⁶ Et pro peccato filiorum Heli idem populus corruit in conspectu Philistinorum, ut habetur I *Reg*.⁷ Ergo aliquis involuntarius est puniendus.

2. Præterea, illud solum est voluntarium quod est in potestate hominis. Sed quandoque pœna infertur pro eo quod non est in ejus potestate; sicut propter vitium lepræ aliquis removetur ab administratione ecclesiæ; et propter pravitatem* aut malitiam civium ecclesia perdit cathedram episcopalem. Ergo non solum pro peccato voluntario vindicta infertur.

3. Præterea, ignorantia causat involuntarium. Sed vindicta quandoque exercetur in aliquos ignorantes; parvuli enim Sodomitarum, licet haberent ignorantiam invincibilem, cum parentibus tamen perierunt, ut legitur *Gen*.⁸ Similiter etiam parvuli pro peccato Dathan et Abiron pariter cum eis absorpti sunt, ut habetur *Num*.⁹ Bruta etiam animalia, quæ carent ratione, jussa sunt interfici pro peccato Amalecitarum, ut habetur I *Reg*.¹⁰ Ergo vindicta quandoque exercetur in involuntarios.

4. Præterea, coactio maxime repugnat voluntario. Sed aliquis qui timore coactus aliquod peccatum committit, non propter hoc reatum pœnæ evadit. Ergo vindicta quandoque exercetur in involuntarios.

5. Præterea, Ambrosius dicit *Super Lucam*, quod *navicula in qua erat Judas, turbabatur;* unde *et Petrus, qui erat firmus meritis suis, turbabatur alienis*.¹¹ Sed Petrus non volebat peccatum Judæ. Ergo quandoque involuntarius punitur.

SED CONTRA est quod pœna debetur peccato. Sed omne peccatum est voluntarium, ut dicit Augustinus.¹² Ergo in solos voluntarios exercenda est vindicta.

RESPONSIO: Dicendum quod pœna dupliciter potest considerari; uno modo secundum rationem pœnæ. Et secundum hoc pœna non debetur nisi peccato, quia per pœnam reparatur æqualitas justitiæ, inquantum ille qui peccando nimis secutus est suam voluntatem, aliquid contra suam voluntatem patitur. Unde cum omne peccatum sit voluntarium, etiam originale, ut supra habitum est,¹³ consequens est quod nullus punitur hoc modo, nisi pro eo quod voluntarie factum est.

Alio modo potest considerari pœna, inquantum est medicina, non solum

---

*Leonine: *paupertatem*, poverty

⁵*Matthew* 27, 25
⁶*Josue* 7
⁷I *Kings* 4, 2, 10
⁸*Genesis* 19, 25
⁹*Numbers* 26, 27
¹⁰I *Kings* 15, 2
¹¹*Expos. Luc.* IV on 5, 3. PL 15, 1717
¹²*De lib. arb.* III, I. PL 32, 1271
¹³1a2æ. 81, I

children,[5] liable to punishment. For the sin of Achan we read that the people of Israel were delivered into the hands of their enemies,[6] and for the sins of Heli they fell before the Philistines.[7] A person is to be punished, therefore, even where there is no voluntary offence.

2. Further, only what is under a person's control is voluntary. Yet in some instances a penalty is assessed for what is beyond control, for example someone is removed from jurisdiction over a church because of leprosy, or a church may lose its status as an episcopal seat because of the corruption and wickedness of the people. Thus vengeance is not exacted only for voluntary offences.

3. Further, while ignorance is a cause of the involuntary, there are cases of vengeance against those who were in ignorance. The children of the Sodomites, even though invincibly ignorant, still perished with their parents, as we read in *Gen.*[8] Similarly, for the sin of Dathan and Abiron, children also were swallowed up with them.[9] In 1 *Kings* it was even commanded that dumb animals be slaughtered because of the sin of the Amalekites.[10] Vengeance, then, is at times exacted without reference to voluntariness.

4. Further, force is the absolute opposite of voluntariness. Yet one under duress who commits a sin out of fear is not thereby exempt from being liable to penalty. Hence vengeance is wrought even upon those whose offence is involuntary.

5. Further, Ambrose *On Luke* asserts that *the boat holding Judas was in distress, and so Peter, safe in terms of his own merits, was imperilled because of those of another.*[11] Now Peter certainly did not will Judas's sin; thus this is another case of punishment where there was no wilful offence.

ON THE OTHER HAND, it is sin that calls for punishment, and *every sin is voluntary*, says Augustine.[12] Therefore vengeance is to be taken only against those offending intentionally.

REPLY: There are two ways of looking at punishment, and first in its intrinsic meaning. So regarded, punishment is due only for sin. The reason is that punishment consists in a restoration of the balance of justice, i.e. one who has indulged his own will by sinning is repressed by something contrary to his will. In these terms, since every sin, even original sin, is voluntary,[a] as we have determined,[13] it necessarily follows that no one is punished except for a voluntary act.

We can, however, also look at punishment as medicinal, and then not

---

[a]On St Thomas's explanation of the voluntariness of original sin, see also vol. 26 ed. T. C. O'Brien, Appendix 7.

sanativa peccati praeteriti sed etiam praeservativa a peccato futuro, vel etiam promotiva in aliquod bonum. Et secundum hoc aliquis interdum punitur sine culpa, non tamen sine causa. Sciendum tamen quod nunquam medicina subtrahit majus bonum, ut promoveat minus bonum, sicut medicina carnalis nunquam caecat oculum, ut sanet calcaneum. Quandoque tamen infert nocumentum in minoribus, ut in melioribus auxilium praestet. Et quia bona spiritualia sunt maxima bona, bona autem temporalia sunt minima, ideo quandoque punitur aliquis in temporalibus bonis absque culpa; cujusmodi sunt plures poenae praesentis vitae divinitus inflictae ad humiliationem vel probationem. Non autem punitur aliquis in spiritualibus bonis sine propria culpa neque in praesenti neque in futuro, quia ibi poenae non sunt medicinae, sed consequuntur spiritualem damnationem.

1. Ad primum ergo dicendum quod unus homo poena spirituali nunquam punitur pro peccato alterius, quia poena spiritualis pertinet ad animam, secundum quam quilibet est liber sui. Poena autem temporali quandoque unus punitur pro peccato alterius, triplici ratione. Primo quidem quia unus homo temporaliter est res alterius; et ita in poenam ejus etiam ipse punitur; sicut filii secundum corpus sunt quaedam res patris et servi quaedam res dominorum.

Alio modo inquantum peccatum unius derivatur in alterum vel per imitationem, sicut filii imitantur peccata parentum et servi peccata dominorum, ut audacius peccent; vel per modum meriti, sicut peccata subditorum merentur peccatorem praelatum, secundum illud *Job, Qui regnare facit hominem hypocritam propter peccata populi.*[14] Unde et pro peccato David populum numerantis populus Israel punitus est, ut habetur II *Reg.*[15] Sive etiam per aliqualem consensum seu dissimulationem; sicut etiam interdum boni simul puniuntur temporaliter cum malis, quia eorum peccata non redarguerunt, ut Augustinus dicit.[16]

Tertio ad commendandum unitatem humanae societatis, ex qua unus debet pro alio sollicitus esse ne peccet et ad detestationem peccati, dum poena unius redundat in omnes quasi omnes essent unum corpus, ut Augustinus dicit de peccato Achan.[17]

Quod autem Dominus dicit, *Visitans peccata parentum in filios in tertiam et quartam generationem*, magis videtur ad misericordiam quam ad severitatem pertinere, dum non statim vindictam adhibet sed expectat in posterum, ut vel saltem posteri corrigantur. Sed crescente malitia posterorum, quasi necesse est ultionem inferri.

---

[14] *Job* 34, 30
[15] II *Kings* 24
[16] *De civ. Dei* I, 9. PL 41, 21
[17] *Quaest. in Heptateuch.* VI, 8 on *Joshua* 7, 1. PL 34, 778
[b] See also 2a2ae, 125, 4.

simply as a cure for past sins, but as a preventive of future sins, or even as an inducement to some good. In these terms, a person is at times punished without there being a sin, but not without there being a reason. Here, however, we must be sure that no remedy ever destroy a greater good in order to bring about a lesser good, even as medicine never blinds an eye in order to heal a blister. Sometimes, however, a cure does inflict secondary ills in order to further some more important good. Seeing that spiritual goods are of supreme importance, while the temporal are of slight moment, a person who is sinless at times suffers the loss of earthly goods; this is the meaning of many of the hardships of life inflicted by God to humble and test us.[b] But no one who has not sinned personally is ever punished by being deprived of spiritual goods, either in this life or the next, where punishments are not medicinal but the consequence of spiritual damnation.

Hence: 1. No one is ever punished for another's sin by any spiritual penalty, which affects the soul wherein everyone is his own man. For another's sin, however, one person is sometimes punished by a temporal punishment, and there are three reasons. First, because on a temporal level one person is as it were the property of another—children physically are as the possessions of their parents, or slaves of their master—and so the one is punished really in order to punish the other.

Secondly, in that the very sin of the one reaches the other. This can happen either because of imitation—for example children following the sinful example of parents, or slaves of their master, and consequently sinning even more flagrantly. Or it can be a matter or just deserts, as when sinful subjects get what they deserve in a wicked superior; thus the text of *Job, Who maketh a man that is a hypocrite to reign for the sins of the people?*;[14] and the example in II *Kings*,[15] the people of Israel being punished for David's sin of numbering the people. Or, finally, it can be because of a kind of tacit consent or dissimulation; for example in the *City of God*[16] Augustine says that the good are punished on this earth along with the wicked because they did not reproach the sins of the wicked.

Thirdly, to emphasize the unity of the human family, which is the basis for each being bound to take care that his brother not sin, and to inculcate hatred for sin, since the punishment of the one redounds harmfully upon all—all being as it were one body, as Augustine says about Achan's sin.[17]

The word of the Lord, *Visiting the iniquity of the fathers upon the children unto the third and fourth generation*, seems rather to be an allusion to mercy than to severity, in the sense that God does not immediately exact vengeance but postpones it in order that at least the descendants might be corrected. Yet when instead their wickedness only worsens, vengeance becomes, in a sense, inevitable.

2. Ad secundum dicendum quod, sicut Augustinus dicit,[18] judicium humanum debet imitari divinum judicium in manifestis Dei judiciis, quibus homines spiritualiter damnat pro proprio peccato. Occulta vero Dei judicia, quibus temporaliter aliquos punit absque culpa, non potest humanum judicium imitari; quia homo non potest comprehendere horum judiciorum rationes, ut sciat quid expediat unicuique. Et ideo nunquam secundum humanum judicium aliquis debet puniri sine culpa pœna flagelli, ut occidatur vel mutiletur vel verberetur. Pœna autem damni punitur aliquis etiam secundum humanum judicium, etiam sine culpa sed non sine causa; et hoc tripliciter. Uno modo ex hoc quod aliquis ineptus redditur sine sua culpa ad aliquod bonum habendum vel consequendum sicut propter vitium lepræ aliquis removetur ab administratione ecclesiæ; et propter bigamiam vel judicium sanguinis aliquis impeditur a sacris ordinibus. Secundo quia bonum in quo damnificatur, non est proprium bonum sed commune, sicut quod aliqua ecclesia habeat episcopatum pertinet ad bonum totius civitatis, non autem ad bonum clericorum tantum. Tertio quia bonum unius dependet ex bono alterius; sicut in crimine læsæ majestatis filius amittit hæreditatem pro peccato parentis.

3. Ad tertium dicendum quod parvuli divino judicio simul puniuntur temporaliter cum parentibus, tum quia sunt res parentum, et in eis etiam parentes puniuntur; tum etiam quia hoc in eorum bonum cedit, ne si reservarentur, essent imitatores paternæ malitiæ et sic graviores pœnas mererentur. In bruta vero animalia et quascumque alias irrationales creaturas vindicta exercetur, quia per hoc puniuntur illi quorum sunt. Et iterum propter detestationem peccati.

4. Ad quartum dicendum quod coactio timoris non facit simpliciter involuntarium, sed habet voluntarium mixtum, ut supra habitum est.[19]

5. Ad quintum dicendum quod hoc modo pro peccato Judæ cæteri apostoli turbabantur, sicut pro peccato unius punitur multitudo ad unitatem commendandam, ut dictum est.[20]

---

[18]*Quæst. in Heptateuch.* VI, 8 on *Joshua* 7, 1. PL 34, 778
[19]1a2æ. 6, 6
[20]above ad 1
[c]*pœna flagelli*, the term *flagellum* is used in the *Summa* for any severe corporal punishment; literally it is a scourge or whip and the expression suggests flogging. The contrast is with *pœna damni*, the loss of rights, privileges or possessions.

2. As Augustine observes,[18] human judgment ought to be patterned after the divine as to the manifest judgments of God that decree spiritual condemnation for spiritual sin. But human judgment cannot mirror the secret judgments of God that lay earthly penalties upon some people where there is no sin; it is impossible for a man so to fathom the meaning of these judgments as to be sure of what is in the best interest of each person. No man, then, should ever decide that an innocent person be punished by an afflictive punishment,[c] such as death, mutilation, or flogging. As to the punishment of forfeiture, the fact is that some are punished under human sentence even when there has been no offence, but not where there is no cause; and this for any of three reasons. First, because without any fault of his own a person is rendered incapable of possessing or acquiring some good; examples are removal from office in the church because of leprosy, or exclusion from holy orders because of impediments like second marriage or handing down a death sentence.[d] Secondly, when the good forfeited is not private but public; a church being an episcopal seat, for example, is an advantage not for the clergy alone but for the whole town. Thirdly, when the good of the one is derived from that of another; thus in the case of treason a son loses his inheritance because of his father's crime.

3. Under God's judgment, children are punished temporally together with their parents, first in that they are like the property of the parents, and thus it is the parents who are really being punished. Again, because this eventually leads to good for the children, in that, should they go untouched, they might follow the example of their parents and come to deserve worse punishments. Vengeance is visited upon dumb animals or even other non-rational creatures because their owners are thereby punished. And also to instil hatred for sin.

4. Force arising from fear does not cause an act to be altogether involuntary but only partially so, as indicated earlier.[19]

5. The other Apostles were in distress because of Judas's sin for the same reason that any community is punished because of the sin of an individual, namely as pointed out earlier,[20] to stress the bond that unites them.

---

[d]These last are canonical irregularities still in force; *Codex Jur. Canon.* 984, 4 & 6. *Bigamia* in this usage means two or more successive valid marriages.

DEINDE CONSIDERANDUM EST de veritate et de vitiis oppositis.

Quæstio 109. de veritate

Circa veritatem autem quæruntur quatuor:

1. utrum veritas sit virtus;
2. utrum sit virtus specialis;
3. utrum sit pars justitiæ;
4. utrum magis declinet in minus.

articulus 1. *utrum veritas sit virtus*

AD PRIMUM sic proceditur:[1] 1. Videtur quod veritas non sit virtus. Prima enim virtutum est fides, cujus objectum est veritas. Cum ergo objectum sit prius habitu et actu, videtur quod veritas non sit virtus, sed aliquid prius virtute.

2. Præterea, sicut Philosophus dicit in *Ethic.*,[2] ad veritatem pertinet quod aliquis confiteatur existentia circa seipsum et neque majora neque minora. Sed hoc non semper est laudabile neque in bonis, quia, ut dicitur *Prov.*, *laudet te alienus, et non os tuum*;[3] nec etiam in malis, quia contra quosdam dicitur *Isa.*, *Peccatum suum quasi Sodoma prædicaverunt, nec absconderunt.*[4] Ergo veritas non est virtus.

3. Præterea, omnis virtus aut est theologica aut intellectualis aut moralis. Sed veritas non est virtus theologica, quia non habet Deum pro objecto, sed res temporales; dicit enim Tullius quod *veritas est per quam immutata ea quæ sunt, aut fuerint, aut futura sunt, dicuntur.*[5] Similiter etiam non est virtus intellectualis, sed finis earum. Neque etiam est virtus moralis, quia non consistit in medio inter superfluum et diminutum; quanto enim aliquis plus dicit verum, tanto melius est. Ergo veritas non est virtus.

SED CONTRA est quod Philosophus in *Ethic.* ponit veritatem inter cæteras virtutes.[6]

---

[1] *In Ethic.* IV, *lect.* 15
[2] *Ethics* IV, 7. 1127a5
[3] *Proverbs* 27, 2
[4] *Isaiah* 3, 9
[5] *Rhetorica* II, 53
[6] *Ethics* II, 7. 1108a20; IV, 7. 1127a29
[a] The virtues considered in Questions 109–19 are parts of justice in that they are concerned with a form of debt, but not with strict debt; rather one of honour or decency (see Question 80). Truth attends to an obligation that is indispensable to

NEXT[a] WE LOOK at truth[b] (109) and its opposites (110-13)

Question 109. truth

There are four points of inquiry about truth:
1. whether it is a virtue;
2. a specific virtue;
3. a part of justice;
4. whether it leans more towards understatement.

article 1. whether truth is a virtue

THE FIRST POINT:[1] 1. Truth does not seem to be a virtue. Faith is absolutely the first virtue, and truth is its objective. Since an objective is prior both to a habit and to its act, truth is not a virtue but something antecedent to virtue.

2. Further, as Aristotle teaches, truth is that which *makes a person acknowledge the facts about himself and nothing more or nothing less.*[2] Yet this is not always commendable, either as to good points, since *Proverbs* says, *Let another praise thee and not thy own mouth;*[3] or as to bad points, since *Isaiah* speaks out against those *who have proclaimed abroad their sin as Sodom and they have not hid it.*[4] Hence truth is not a virtue.

3. Further, every virtue is either theological, intellectual[c] or moral. Truth is not a theological virtue, since it does not have God as its objective, but temporal matters; Cicero says, *It is through truth that we speak of present or past of future events without distortion.*[5] Nor is it an intellectual virtue, but the end for all of them. Nor is it a moral virtue, since it does not stand as a mean between excess and defect; the more a person speaks the truth, the better. In no sense, then, is truth a virtue.

ON THE OTHER HAND, in the *Ethics* Aristotle lists it among the virtues.[6]

---

a civilized community of men; friendliness (114) and liberality (117) have a lesser indebtedness about them; they are required for a better realization of civility.
[b]The Latin *veritas* and the English 'truth' both have several meanings. The two principal ones are: i. a disposition to speak the truth, ii. a conformity to reality or to a model, such conformity existing either in a thing, a thought or a statement. Truth in the second sense is considered in 1a. 16: here the disposition to speak the truth or manifest it in deed is considered—truthfulness or veracity, candour, honesty, sincerity, modesty (see 2a2æ. 168, 1 ad 3; 169, 1 ad 3). We keep the term 'truth' because the play on its twofold signification is part of the argumentation of the Question.
[c]On the meaning of 'intellectual virtue' see 1a2æ. 57-8.

RESPONSIO: Dicendum quod veritas dupliciter accipi potest. Uno modo, secundum quod veritate aliquid dicitur verum, et sic veritas non est virtus, sed objectum vel finis virtutis. Sic enim accepta veritas non est habitus, qui* est genus virtutis, sed æqualitas quædam intellectus, vel signi ad rem intellectam et significatam† vel etiam rei ad suam regulam, ut in Primo habitum est.[7]

Alio modo potest dici veritas qua aliquis verum dicit, secundum quod per eam aliquis dicitur verax. Et talis veritas, sive veracitas necesse est quod sit virtus, quia hoc ipsum quod est dicere verum est bonus actus. Virtus autem est quæ bonum facit habentem, et opus ejus bonum reddit.

1. Ad primum ergo dicendum quod ratio illa procedit de veritate primo modo dicta.

2. Ad secundum dicendum quod confiteri id quod est circa seipsum, inquantum est confessio veri est bonum ex genere. Sed hoc non sufficit ad hoc quod sit virtutis actus; sed ad hoc requiritur quod ulterius debitis circumstantiis vestiatur, quæ si non observentur, erit actus vitiosus. Et secundum hoc vitiosum est quod aliquis sine debita causa laudet seipsum etiam de vero; vitiosum est etiam quod aliquis peccatum suum publicet, quasi se de hoc laudando vel qualitercumque inutiliter manifestando.

3. Ad tertium dicendum quod ille qui dicit verum profert aliqua signa conformia rebus, scilicet vel verba vel aliqua facta exteriora aut quascumque res exteriores. Circa hujusmodi autem res sunt solæ virtutes morales, ad quas scilicet pertinet usus exteriorum membrorum secundum quod fit per imperium voluntatis. Unde veritas non est virtus theologica neque intellectualis sed moralis.

Est autem in medio inter superfluum et diminutum dupliciter: uno quidem modo ex parte objecti; alio modo ex parte actus. Ex parte quidem objecti, quia verum secundum suam rationem importat quamdam æqualitatem; æquale autem est medium inter majus et minus. Unde ex hoc ipso quod aliquis dicit verum de seipso, medium tenet inter eum qui majora dicit de seipso, et inter eum qui minora. Ex parte autem actus medium tenet, inquantum verum dicit quando oportet et secundum quod oportet. Superfluum autem convenit illi qui importune ea quæ sua sunt manifestat; defectus autem competit illi qui occultat quando manifestare oportet.

articulus 2. utrum veritas sit specialis virtus

AD SECUNDUM sic proceditur:[1] 1. Videtur quod veritas non sit specialis virtus. Verum enim et bonum convertuntur. Sed bonitas non est specialis

---

*Leonine: *quod* for *qui*
†Piana: *signatam* for *significatam*; same meaning
[7] 1a. 16, 1 & 2; 21, 2   [1] IV *Sent.* 16, 4, 1, ii. *In Ethic.* IV, lect. 15
[d]*bonum ex genere*, see above 107, 2 note *a*.
[e]On circumstances, see above 101, 4 note *a*.

REPLY: 'Truth' can have two meanings. In the first it is the quality by which a thing is said to be 'true', and it is not a virtue but the objective or the end for virtue. Nor is it a habit, the genus of virtue, but rather it is the correspondence of mind or sign to the reality thought or signified; or else it is the correspondence of a thing to its measure, as we have shown in the *Prima Pars*.[7]

In its second sense 'truth' can be taken as that by which a person speaks the truth; it is the reason for his being called 'truthful'. So understood, truth or truthfulness has to be a virtue, for to speak the truth is a morally good act and that which makes its possessor and his actions good is a virtue.

Hence: 1. This argument takes truth in the first sense indicated.

2. To acknowledge facts about oneself is an act good in its kind,[d] because it is the acknowledgment of what is true. This is not enough, however, to make this act virtuous; it must also be fitted to proper circumstances,[e] otherwise it will be a bad action. On this basis it is sinful for someone to praise himself without due cause even over something true; and also to broadcast his own sin, whether as though praising himself for it or making it known uselessly for any reason.

3. One who expresses the truth puts forward some signs that correspond to reality, words, namely, or gestures, or something else perceptible. Since such externals are exclusively the concern of moral virtues—which even deal with the use of bodily members as these are subject to control of the will—truth is neither a theological nor an intellectual virtue, but a moral virtue.

In fact it does hold to a mean between excess and defect, and that in two ways, namely from the standpoint of its objective and of its act. It does so by reason of its objective because in its essence[f] truth means a kind of balance, a median between too much and too little. Accordingly, a person speaking the truth about himself sticks to the middle ground between one who speaks boastingly of self and one who speaks slightingly. Secondly, truth observes a mean because of its act, i.e. expressing the truth at the time and in the manner called for. Here excess is in the one who brings up things about himself at the wrong moment; defect, in the one who hides things when he should be candid.

article 2. whether truth is a special virtue

THE SECOND POINT:[1] 1. Truth seems not to be a special virtue. While the true and the good are convertible terms, goodness is not a special virtue;

---

[f]'essence' for *rationem*. The meaning or nature of truth is the point; it has this specification from its objective.

virtus; quinimo omnis virtus est bonitas, quia bonum facit habentem. Ergo veritas non est specialis virtus.

2. Præterea, manifestatio ejus quod ad ipsum hominem pertinet, est actus veritatis de qua nunc loquimur. Sed hoc pertinet ad quamlibet virtutem; quilibet enim virtutis habitus manifestatur per proprium actum. Ergo veritas non est specialis virtus.

3. Præterea, veritas vitæ dicitur, qua quis recte vivit, de qua dicitur *Isa., Memento quæso, quomodo ambulaverim coram te in veritate et in corde perfecto.*[2] Sed qualibet virtute recte vivitur, ut pater per definitionem virtutis supra positam.[3] Ergo veritas non est specialis virtus.

4. Præterea, veritas videtur idem esse simplicitati, quia utrique opponitur simulatio. Sed simplicitas non est specialis virtus, quia facit intentionem rectam, quod requiritur in omni virtute. Ergo etiam veritas non est specialis virtus.

SED CONTRA est quod in II *Ethic.*, connumeratur aliis virtutibus.[4]

RESPONSIO: Dicendum quod ad rationem virtutis humanæ pertinet quod opus hominis bonum reddat. Unde ubi in actu hominis invenitur specialis ratio bonitatis, necesse est quod ad hoc disponatur homo per specialem virtutem. Cum autem bonum, secundum Augustinum,[5] consistat in ordine, necesse est specialem rationem boni considerari ex determinato ordine. Est autem quidam specialis ordo secundum quod exteriora nostra vel verba vel facta debite ordinantur ad aliquid sicut signum ad signatum, et ad hoc perficitur homo per virtutem veritatis. Unde manifestum est quod veritas est specialis virtus.

1. Ad primum ergo dicendum quod verum et bonum subjecto quidem convertuntur, quia omne verum est bonum et omne bonum est verum. Sed secundum rationem invicem se excedunt, sicut intellectus et voluntas invicem se excedunt, nam intellectus intelligit voluntatem et multa alia, et voluntas appetit ea quæ pertinent ad intellectum et multa alia. Unde verum secundum rationem propriam, qua* est perfectio intellectus, est quoddam particulare bonum inquantum appetibile quoddam est; et

---

*Piana: *quæ* for *qua*
[2]*Isaiah* 38, 3
[3]1a2æ. 55, 4
[4]*Ethics* II, 7. 1108a20
[5]*De nat. boni* 8. PL 42, 553
[a]see 1a. 5, 5.
[b]The proper concern of truth is here implicit: our words, gestures, clothing, style of life are signs of what we think and of what we are. Keeping these signs in their proper reference according to right circumstances is the act of truthfulness. The

rather every virtue is a form of goodness, since it makes its possessor good. Neither, then, is truth a specific virtue.

2. Further, the act of truth as it is now being discussed is to make plain what sort of person one is. This is characteristic of every virtue, however, the virtuous act being evidence of the presence of the habitual disposition. Truth is not, therefore, a special virtue.

3. Further, the expression 'truth of life' refers to uprightness of life and Isaiah alludes to it in these words, *I beseech thee* . . . *remember how I have walked before thee in truth and with a perfect heart.*[2] Now the very definition of virtue determined above[3] shows every virtue to be a source of living rightly. Truth, then, is not one special kind of virtue.

4. Further, truth seems identical with simplicity, since deceit is contrary to both. Simplicity is not a specific virtue; it merely makes for an upright intention, a requisite in every virtue. Equally, then, truth is not a specific virtue.

ON THE OTHER HAND, in the *Ethics* it is listed among the other virtues.[4]

REPLY: Part of the meaning of human virtue is that it is the source of a person's good actions. Wherever, therefore, some specifically good quality is verified in human activity, there is need that a person be properly disposed towards this by a specific virtue. Since the good,[a] following Augustine's description,[5] is marked by proper order, a specific kind of good must be discerned on the basis of any determinate form of order. There is a specific aspect of order in keeping our spoken words or observable actions in their proper reference as signs to the thing they signify.[b] The virtue of truth brings this about in a person and so is clearly a special virtue.

Hence: 1. When taken as substantives 'true' and 'good' are convertible terms meaning that everything true is good and everything good is true. However, in the quality they signify each has a meaning wider than the other, even as is the case with mind and will, since the mind knows not only the will but also many other things and the will seeks not only what is of mental interest, but much else. Accordingly, in terms of its own distinctive meaning, as the fulfilment of mind, truth is one sort of good, i.e. one sort of will-objective; in like manner, on the basis of its own distinctive meaning as the goal of appetite, the good is one sort of truth, i.e. one sort

---

virtue thus includes such qualities as honesty, simplicity, sincerity. The balance described in this and the following Questions is keyed to what human concourse requires. Truth does not make indiscriminate self-revelation virtuous; but it does avoid projecting a false image of self. The meaning of the virtue clashes directly with the aims of contemporary image-making industries.

similiter bonum secundum propriam rationem prout est finis appetitus est quoddam verum inquantum est quoddam intelligibile. Quia ergo virtus includit rationem bonitatis, potest esse quod veritas sit specialis virtus sicut verum est speciale bonum. Non autem potest esse quod bonitas sit specialis virtus, cum magis secundum rationem sit genus virtutis.

2. Ad secundum dicendum quod habitus virtutum et vitiorum sortiuntur speciem ex eo quod est per se intentum, non autem ab eo quod est per accidens et præter intentionem. Quod autem aliquis manifestet quod circa ipsum est, pertinet quidem ad virtutem veritatis sicut per se intentum; ad alias autem virtutes potest pertinere ex consequenti, præter principalem intentionem. Fortis enim intendit fortiter agere; quod autem fortiter agendo aliquis manifestet fortitudinem quam habet, hoc consequitur præter ejus principalem intentionem.

3. Ad tertium dicendum quod veritas vitæ est veritas secundum quam aliquid est verum, non veritas secundum quam aliquis dicit verum. Dicitur autem vita vera, sicut et quælibet alia res, ex hoc quod attingit suam regulam et mensuram, scilicet divinam legem per cujus conformitatem rectitudinem habet. Et talis veritas sive rectitudo communis est ad quamlibet virtutem.

4. Ad quartum dicendum quod simplicitas dicitur per oppositum duplicitati, qua scilicet aliquis aliud habet in corde et aliud ostendit exterius. Et sic simplicitas ad hanc virtutem pertinet. Facit autem intentionem rectam, non quidem directe, (quia hoc pertinet ad omnem virtutem), sed excludendo duplicitatem qua homo unum prætendit et aliud intendit.

articulus 3. utrum veritas sit pars justitiæ

AD TERTIUM sic proceditur:[1] 1. Videtur quod veritas non sit pars justitiæ. Justitiæ enim proprium esse videtur quod reddat alteri debitum. Sed ex hoc quod aliquis dicit verum, non videtur alteri debitum reddere, sicut fit in omnibus præmissis justitiæ partibus. Ergo veritas non est pars justitiæ.

2. Præterea, veritas pertinet ad intellectum. Justitia autem est in voluntate, ut supra habitum est.[2] Ergo veritas non est pars justitiæ.

3. Præterea, triplex distinguitur veritas secundum Hieronymum, scilicet veritas vitæ, et veritas justitiæ et veritas doctrinæ.[3] Sed nulla istarum est pars justitiæ. Nam veritas vitæ continet in se omnem virtutem, ut dictum est;[4] veritas autem justitiæ est idem justitiæ, unde non est pars ejus; veritas

---
[1] cf *In Ethic.* IV, lect. 15
[2] 2a2æ. 58, 4
[3] The distinction is not found in St Jerome; it was used by William of Auxerre, Hugh of St Cher and other medievals; see also 2a2æ. 43, 7 obj. 4.

of intelligible objective.[c] Therefore, it is possible for truth to be a specific virtue, even as the true is a specific sort of good, because virtue itself stands for a specific quality of goodness. There is, conversely, no possibility for just 'goodness' being a specific virtue, since the quality of goodness rather expresses the generic meaning of virtue.[d]

2. Virtuous and evil habits have their species from what a person intends directly, not from what is incidental and apart from his intention. In this regard, that a person show himself for what he is engages the virtue of truth as to direct intent; it is the concern of other virtues only as a natural sequel, apart from the principal intent. For example, the intention of the man of courage is to be brave; that he thereby reveals his own bravery is an unintended consequence.

3. Truth of life is the kind of truth by which something exists as true, not by which someone speaks what is true. Like everything else one's life is called true on the basis of its reaching its rule and norm, namely divine law; by measuring up to this, a life has uprightness. This is the kind of truth, i.e. uprightness, common to every virtue.

4. Simplicity takes its name in opposition to the duplicity by which a person holds one thing inwardly and outwardly expresses something else. For this reason simplicity is one facet of the virtue of truth. As for its good effect upon intent, this it has not directly, since every virtue has this function, but by excluding the duplicity by which a person pretends one thing and intends another.

article 3. whether truth is a part of justice

THE THIRD POINT:[1] 1. Truth does not seem to be a part of justice. While it is proper to justice to give another his due, speaking the truth does not seem to involve this as do the parts of justice already discussed. Therefore it is not a part of justice.

2. Further, as already indicated,[2] truth involves mind; justice is in the will. Therefore truth is not a part of justice.

3. Further, following Jerome,[3] we can discern three kinds of truth: truth in life, truth in justice, truth in teaching. Not one of them is a part of justice. As noted,[4] truth in life embraces every virtue; truth in justice is

---

[4]art. 2 ad 3
[c]Through this kind of interrelationship St Thomas consistently explains the interaction and mutual causality of mind and will in human action. The point runs throughout his moral theory; see 1a. 87, 4; 1a2æ. 8–17; *De veritate* XXII, 12–15.
[d]On the meaning of good in the definition of virtue, see 1a2æ. 55, 4 ad 1 & 2.

autem doctrinæ pertinet magis ad virtutes intellectuales. Ergo veritas nullo modo est pars justitiæ.

SED CONTRA est quod Tullius ponit veritatem inter partes justitiæ.[5]

RESPONSIO: Dicendum quod, sicut supra dictum est[6] ex hoc aliqua virtus justitiæ annectitur, sicut secundaria principali, quod partim quidem cum justitia convenit, partim autem deficit ab ejus perfecta ratione. Virtus autem veritatis convenit quidem cum justitia in duobus. Uno quidem modo in hoc quod est ad alterum; manifestatio enim, quam diximus esse actum voluntatis, est ad alterum inquantum scilicet ea quæ circa ipsum sunt unus homo alteri manifestat. Alio modo, inquantum justitia æqualitatem quamdam in rebus constituit. Et hoc etiam facit virtus veritatis; adæquat enim signa rebus existentibus circa ipsum.

Deficit autem a propria ratione justitiæ quantum ad rationem debiti. Non enim hæc virtus attendit debitum legale, quod attendit justitia, sed potius debitum morale, inquantum scilicet ex honestate unus homo alteri debet veritatis manifestationem.

Unde veritas est pars justitiæ inquantum annectitur ei sicut virtus secundaria principali.

1. Ad primum ergo dicendum quod quia homo est animal sociale, naturaliter unus homo debet alteri id sine quo societas humana servari non posset. Non autem possent homines ad invicem convivere nisi sibi invicem crederent, tanquam sibi invicem veritatem manifestantibus. Et ideo virtus veritatis aliquo modo attendit rationem debiti.

2. Ad secundum dicendum quod veritas secundum quod est cognita pertinet ad intellectum; sed homo per propriam voluntatem, per quam utitur et habitibus et membris, profert exteriora signa ad veritatem manifestandam et secundum hoc manifestatio veritatis est actus voluntatis.

3. Ad tertium dicendum quod veritas de qua nunc loquimur, differt a veritate vitæ, ut dictum est art. præc.[7] Veritas autem justitiæ dicitur dupliciter. Uno modo secundum quod ipsa justitia est rectitudo quædam regulata secundum regulam divinæ legis. Et secundum hoc differt veritas justitiæ a veritate vitæ; quia veritas vitæ est secundum quam aliquis recte vivit in seipso; veritas autem justitiæ est secundum quam aliquis rectitudinem legis in judiciis quæ sunt ad alterum servat et secundum hoc veritas justitiæ non pertinet ad veritatem de qua nunc loquimur, sicut nec veritas vitæ.

Alio modo potest intelligi veritas justitiæ secundum quod aliquis ex

---

[5]*Rhet.* II, 53   [6]2a2æ, 89
[7]art. 2 ad 3

justice itself, not its part; truth in teaching rather engages the intellectual virtues. In no sense, then, is truth a part of justice.

ON THE OTHER HAND, this is what Cicero makes of it.[5]

REPLY: As previously stated,[6] any virtue is allied to justice as a subordinate to its principal, when it coincides in part with justice, but in part falls short of the full meaning. The virtue of truth has two points in common with justice. The first is that justice has reference to another person, and what we have determined the act of truth to be, namely a communication, has reference to someone else, in that one person makes known to someone else things about himself. The second is that justice establishes a certain objective equality. So does truth, making as it does signs match facts.

Truth falls short of the exact meaning of justice from the standpoint of the quality of indebtedness. This virtue does not dispatch a legal debt, the interest of justice, but rather a debt of honour, in that it is out of honourableness that one person owes it to another to express the truth.[a]

Consequently, truth is a part of justice, i.e. allied to it as a secondary to a principal virtue.

Hence: 1: Since man is by nature a social being, there is a natural indebtedness of one person to another in regard to those things without which life together in society could not be maintained. People could not live with one another were there not a mutual trust that they were being truthful to one another. The virtue of truth, therefore, in some sense is concerned with a form of indebtedness.

2. Truth in knowledge is the sphere of mind. The manifestation of the truth is an act of will, however, in that it is by personal will, which underlies the deliberate use of bodily members and habits of soul, that anyone employs outward signs to make known the truth.

3. We have already pointed out[7] how truth in its present sense is different from truth in life. As to truth in justice, this can have two meanings. The first is that justice itself is a certain rightness measured by conformity to divine law. In this regard truth in justice is different from truth in life: truth in life means that someone keeps his own life upright; truth in justice, that someone keeps the requirements of law in the judgments he passes on others.[b] In this sense truth in justice does not enter into the meaning of the truth at issue here, any more than does truth in life.

In a second sense truth in justice can be taken to indicate that out of

---

[a] For legal and moral debt, see Appendix 1.
[b] *judicium* here and in the following paragraph refers to an act of strict justice; it is considered in 2a2æ. 60, where it means a judge's sentence, or strict legal testimony, or a personal judgment about the strict rights of another.

justitia veritatem manifestat; puta cum aliquis in judicio veritatem confitetur, aut verum testimonium dicit. Et hæc veritas est quidam particularis actus justitiæ, et non pertinet directe ad hanc veritatem de qua nunc loquimur, quia scilicet in hac manifestatione veritatis principaliter homo intendit jus suum alteri reddere. Unde Philosophus in *Ethic.*, de hac virtute* determinans dicit, *Non de veridico in confessionibus dicimus, neque quæcumque ad justitiam, vel injustitiam contendunt.*[8]

Veritas autem doctrinæ consistit in quadam manifestatione verborum,† de quibus est scientia. Unde nec ista veritas directe pertinet ad hanc virtutem, sed solum veritas qua aliquis et vita et sermone talem se demonstrat, qualis est, et non alia quam circa ipsum‡ sint, nec majora, nec minora. Verumtamen quia scibilia,§ inquantum sunt a nobis cognita circa nos sunt et ad nos pertinent, secundum hoc veritas doctrinæ potest ad hanc virtutem pertinere; et quæcumque alia veritas qua quis manifestat verbo vel facto quod cognoscit.

articulus 4. utrum virtus veritatis magis declinet in minus

AD QUARTUM sic proceditur:[1] 1. Videtur quod virtus veritatis non declinet in minus. Sicut enim aliquis dicendo majus incurrit falsitatem, ita et dicendo minus; non enim magis est falsum quatuor esse quinque, quam quatuor esse tria. Sed *omne falsum est secundum se malum, et fugiendum*, ut Philosophus dicit in *Ethic.*[2] Ergo veritatis virtus non plus declinat in minus quam in majus.

2. Præterea, quod una virtus magis declinet ad unum extremum quam ad aliud, contingit ex hoc quod virtutis medium est propinquius uni extremo quam alteri; sicut fortitudo est propinquior audaciæ quam timiditati. Sed veritatis medium non est propinquius uni extremo quam alteri, quia veritas, cum sit æqualitas quædam, in medio punctuali consistit. Ergo veritas non magis declinat in minus.

3. Præterea, in minus videtur a veritate recedere qui veritatem negat;* in majus autem qui veritati aliquid superaddit. Sed magis repugnat veritati qui veritatem negat quam qui superaddit, quia veritas non compatitur secum negationem veritatis, compatitur autem secum superadditionem. Ergo videtur quod veritas magis debeat declinare in majus quam in minus.

SED CONTRA est quod Philosophus dicit in *Ethic.*, quod *homo secundum hanc virtutem magis a vero declinat in minus.*[3]

---

*Leonine; *veritate*, truth
†Leonine: *verorum*, truths
‡Piana: *ipsa*, those things
§Piana: *moralia*, moral matters, for *scibilia*
*Piana: adds *veritati aliquid subtrahens*, holding back something of the truth

respect for justice someone makes known the truth, expressing it or bearing true testimony in a legal case. This kind of truth is one special act of justice and does not have direct bearing upon the truth now being discussed, seeing that in the sense indicated the communication of the truth is intended as a matter of giving another his legal rights. This is why, in fixing the nature of the present virtue, Aristotle states, *We are not speaking of someone speaking the truth in solemn avowals, or of litigants in a case of justice or injustice.*[8]

Truth in teaching comprises the expression in words about matters of scientific knowledge. Accordingly, this kind of truth is not directly related to the virtue, but that truth alone in which a person by his life and his speech shows himself as he is and not otherwise, either by exaggeration or suppression. Notice, however, that since it is we who know them, matters of science are facts about ourselves and they concern us. Consequently, it is possible for truth in teaching, and any other truth by which in word or deed we communicate what we know, to come under this virtue.

article 4. whether the virtue of truth leans more to understatement

THE FOURTH POINT:[1] 1. The virtue of truth does not seem to favour understatement. We are as guilty of falsehood for saying too little as for saying too much; it is no more false to say four is five than to say it is three. As Aristotle says, *Every kind of falsehood is evil in itself and must be avoided.*[2] Hence the virtue of truth no more favours saying too little than saying too much.

2. Further, when it does happen that a virtue leans more to one extreme, it is because this is closer to the virtuous mean; courage, for example, is closer to daring than to timidity. Such is not the case, however, with the virtue of truth, since truth itself as a kind of equality stands in the dead centre. Truth, therefore, does not lean towards understatement.

3. Further, one who denies the truth seems to deviate on the minus side; one who embellishes the truth errs on the plus side. To deny it runs more counter to the truth than to add to it, since denying it is incompatible with truth, whereas merely supplementing it is not. Seemingly, then, truth should rather lean towards going too far than holding back.

ON THE OTHER HAND, Aristotle holds that through this virtue *any slanting of the truth is rather on the side of understatement.*[3]

---

[8] *Ethics* IV, 7. 1127a33
[2] *Ethics* IV, 7. 1127a28
[1] cf *In Ethic.* IV, lect. 15
[3] ibid 1127b7

RESPONSIO: Dicendum quod declinare in minus a veritate contingit dupliciter. Uno modo affirmando, puta cum aliquid non manifestat totum bonum quod in ipso est, puta scientiam vel sanctitatem vel aliquid hujusmodi, quod fit sine præjudicio veritatis. Quia in majori etiam est minus; et secundum hoc hæc virtus declinat in minus. Hoc enim, ut Philosophus dicit ibidem, *videtur esse prudentius, propter onerosas superabundantias*.[4] Homines enim qui majora de seipsis dicunt quam sint, sunt aliis onerosi, quasi excellere alios volentes: homines autem qui minora de seipsis dicunt, gratiosi sunt, quasi aliis condescendentes per quamdam moderationem. Unde Apostolus dicit II *ad Cor.*, *Si voluero gloriari, non ero insipiens, veritatem enim dicam; parco autem, ne quis me existimet supra id quod videt in me, aut audit aliquid* ex me.*[5] Alio modo potest aliquis declinare in minus negando, scilicet ut neget sibi inesse quod inest. Et sic non pertinet ad hanc virtutem declinare in minus, quia per hoc incurreret falsum. Et tamen hoc ipsum esset minus repugnans veritati, non quidem secundum propriam rationem veritatis, sed secundum rationem prudentiæ, quam oportet salvari in omnibus virtutibus. Magis enim repugnat prudentiæ, quia periculosius est et onerosius aliis, quod aliquis existimet vel jactet se habere quod non habet, quam quod existimet vel dicat se non habere quod habet.

Et per hoc patet responsio ad objecta.

---

*Piana omits

REPLY: To play down the truth can take place in two ways, and first through what we affirm. For example, a person does not make known all his endowments, his learning or holiness and the like. The greater already including the less, such conduct is without prejudice to the truth. And in this sense truth favours understatement, for this, Aristotle says, *seems the wiser course in order to avoid wearisome details.*[4] People who exaggerate about themselves are bores, intent on outdoing others; people who are reticent about themselves are agreeable, in their reserve treating others as equals. And so St Paul says, *Though I should have a mind to glory, I shall not be foolish: for I will say the truth. But I forbear, lest any man should think of me above that which he seeth in me or anything he heareth from me.*[5]

A person can play down the truth in another way by denial, namely by disclaiming what really is true of himself. So taken, understatement forms no part of this virtue, since it amounts to falsehood. Even so there is something here not altogether alien to truth, not of course in line with the strict meaning of the virtue, but in terms of the interests of prudence, which must be safeguarded in all cases of virtue. As being more hazardous and tiresome to others, it is more against prudence for a person to imagine or to boast that he possesses traits that he lacks than to pretend the opposite.

The response to the first set of arguments is clear from all this.

---

[4] ibid 1127b8   [5] II *Corinthians* 12, 6

SUMMA THEOLOGIÆ, 2a2æ. 110, 1

DEINDE CONSIDERANDUM EST de vitiis oppositis veritati:
et primo, de mendacio;
secundo, de simulatione sive hypocrisi;
tertio, de jactantia et opposito vitio.

Quæstio 110. de mendacio

Circa mendacium quæruntur quatuor:

1. utrum mendacium semper opponitur veritati, quasi continens falsitatem;
2. de speciebus mendacii;
3. utrum mendacium semper sit peccatum;
4. utrum semper sit peccatum mortale.

articulus 1. utrum mendacium semper opponatur veritati

AD PRIMUM sic proceditur:[1] 1. Videtur quod mendacium non semper opponatur veritati. Opposita enim non possunt esse simul. Sed mendacium simul potest esse cum veritate. Qui enim verum loquitur quod falsum esse credit mentitur, ut Augustinus dicit.[2] Ergo mendacium non opponitur veritati.

2. Præterea, virtus veritatis non solum consistit in verbis, sed etiam in factis, quia, secundum Philosophum in *Ethic.*, *Secundum hanc virtutem aliquis verum dicit et in sermone, et in vita.*[3] Sed mendacium consistit solum in verbis: dicitur enim quod mendacium est *falsa vocis significatio.*[4] Sic ergo videtur quod mendacium non directe opponatur virtuti veritatis.

3. Præterea, Augustinus dicit quod *culpa mentientis est fallendi cupiditas.*[5] Sed hoc non opponitur veritati, sed magis benevolentiæ vel justitiæ. Ergo mendacium non opponitur veritati.

---

[1] cf III *Sent.* 38, 1
[2] *De mendac.* 3. PL 40, 489. See note b
[3] *Ethics* IV, 7. 1127a24   [4] Peter Lombard, III *Sent.* 38
[5] *De mendac.* 3. PL 40, 489

[a] 'lying' for *mendacium* because the consideration is of the sin and the vice opposed to truth; in the Question, however, *mendacium* is also used to refer to the lie told, the objective of the sin.

[b] The *De Mendacio* of Augustine, written in 395, is a theological disquisition on the intrinsic malice of the lie and on its kinds; the *Contra Mendacium*, written in 420, is a response to a particular theological question, whether one may feign heresy in order to discover heretics. Except for art. 3, reply and ad 4, each time St Thomas quotes Augustine he cites *Contra Mendacium*; the text is actually from the *De*

NEXT, THE VICES against truthfulness:

> first, lying[a] (110);
> secondly, deception or hypocrisy (111);
> thirdly, boasting and its own opposite (112–13).

Question 110. lying

The points of inquiry about lying are four:

1. whether as containing falsehood a lie is always against truth;
2. species of the lie;
3. whether lying is always a sin;
4. and a mortal sin.

article 1. whether to lie is always against truth

THE FIRST POINT:[1] 1. Lying, it seems, does not always run counter to truth. While opposites cannot co-exist, it is possible for a lie to co-exist with truth. For it is lying when someone speaks the truth believing he speaks a falsehood, as Augustine notes.[2] So a lie is not the opposite of truth.[b]

2. Further, the virtue of truth involves not only words but deeds as well, because, following Aristotle's statement, *Through this virtue a person expresses the truth in both his speech and his actions.*[3] A lie, however, is found in words only, being described as the *false meaning of words*.[4] There is, then, no direct opposition between lying and truth.

3. Further, Augustine claims that *the sin of the liar is the desire to deceive*,[5] and this is not so much against truth as against charity or justice. Lying is not, therefore, opposed to the virtue of truth.

Mendacio, as are the quotations without citation in art. 3 ad 3 and art. 4 ad 5. The core position of Augustine in both works, that a lie is intrinsically evil and no cause, no intention can make it good or permit it, is clearly present in this Question, esp. in art. 3. In the teaching of both doctors there is the firm yet necessarily delicate affirmation both of intrinsic, objective, moral good and evil and of the decisive importance of personal intention. Augustine's strong statement is worth quoting: *When deeds are themselves already sinful—robbery, rape, blasphemy and the like—who is there who will say that where there are good reasons, they become not sins, or what is more absurd, justifiable sins . . . unless he is one bent on subverting all human values, all morals and law?* Contra Mendacium 7, PL 40, 528, 529. See Deman, T., *La Traitement scientifique de la morale chrétienne selon saint Augustin* (Montreal, Paris, 1957) 39–41.

SED CONTRA est quod dicit Augustinus, *Nemo dubitet mentiri eum qui falsum enuntiat causa fallendi. Quapropter enuntiatio falsi cum voluntate ad fallendum prolata, manifestum est mendacium.*[6] Sed hoc opponitur veritati. Ergo mendacium veritati opponitur.

RESPONSIO: Dicendum quod actus moralis ex duobus speciem sortitur, scilicet ex objecto et ex fine. Nam finis est objectum voluntatis, quæ est primum movens in moralibus actibus. Potentia autem a voluntate mota habet suum objectum, quod est proximum objectum voluntarii actus et se habet in actu voluntatis ad finem, sicut materiale ad formale, ut ex supra dictis patet.[7]

Dictum[8] est autem quod virtus veritatis, et per consequens opposita vitia, in manifestatione consistit, quæ fit per aliqua signa. Quæ quidem manifestatio sive enuntiatio est rationis actus conferentis signum ad signatum. Omnis enim repræsentatio consistit in quadam collatione, quæ proprie pertinet ad rationem; unde etsi bruta animalia aliquid manifestent, non tamen manifestationem intendunt, sed naturali instinctu aliquid agunt, ad quod manifestatio sequitur.

Inquantum tamen hujusmodi manifestatio sive enuntiatio est actus moralis oportet quod sit voluntarius et ex intentione voluntatis dependens. Objectum autem proprium manifestationis sive enuntiationis est verum vel falsum. Intentio vero voluntatis inordinatæ potest ad duo ferri. Quorum unum est ut falsum enuntietur; aliud est effectus proprius falsæ enuntiationis, ut scilicet aliquis fallatur.

Si ergo ista tria concurrant, scilicet quod falsum sit id quod enuntiatur et quod adsit voluntas falsum enuntiandi et iterum intentio fallendi, tunc est falsitas materialiter, quia falsum dicitur; et formaliter propter voluntatem falsum dicendi; et effective propter voluntatem falsitatem imprimendi. Sed tamen ratio mendacii sumitur a formali falsitate, ex hoc scilicet quod aliquis habet voluntatem falsum enuntiandi; unde et mendacium nominatur ex eo quod contra mentem dicitur.[9]

Et ideo si quis falsum enuntiet, credens id esse verum, est quidem

---

[6]*De mendac.* 4. PL 40, 491
[7]1a2æ. 18, 6
[8]109, 2 ad 2; 3
[9]The etymology is found in William of Auxerre, *Summa aurea*, III, 18, 1, 2.
[c]On the sources of the moral good or evil in an act, see Vol. 18, ed. T. Gilby, esp. Appendices 10–14. The present article is a singular example of St Thomas's own application of the principles set out in 1a2æ. 18–20.
[d]Compare this with art. 3 in order to see the difference between the intended expression of falsehood and the intention to deceive another. The intended expression of falsehood is what constitutes lying as inherently sinful, since words are communicative and should communicate truth meant. The actual deception resulting is

ON THE OTHER HAND there are Augustine's words, *No one should doubt that he lies who states what is false for the purpose of deceiving. Therefore it is plain that a false statement uttered with intent to deceive is a lie.*[6] Since this is against truth, so is lying.

REPLY: The moral act gets its species from two sources, objective and end.[c] As to end, this is the objective of the will, the prime mover in moral acts. As to objective, each power moved by the will has its own. This is both the immediate objective of the voluntary act and is related to the act of willing the end as matter is related to form, points we have made clear earlier.[7]

We have also determined[8] that the virtue of truth (and for that matter its opposed vices) has its activity in a communication accomplished through certain signs. This communication or statement is an act of reason referring sign to thing signified. (Every representation consists in a kind of comparison, and this properly calls for reasoning, so that while animals communicate something, they do not do so by intent, but rather act out of sheer instinct, the communication being the chance result.)

In so far as the communication or statement in question is a moral act it must be voluntary and dependent on an intention of will. The objective proper to communication or statement is truth or falsity; but the intentions open to a disordered will are two. The first is that something false be expressed; the second is the direct result of expressing falsity, namely that someone be deceived.

When these three, therefore, are all present—namely falsehood in what is expressed, the willingness to express it, as well as the intention to deceive—then there is a factual falsehood because something false is stated, and a moral act of falsehood because of the willingness to say what is false, and falsehood as a moral effect because of the will to communicate it. Still, the meaning of lying is taken from falsehood in its moral species, namely from someone having the intent to express what is false.[d] An indication of this is that the term *mendacium* derives from the lie's being speech *contra mentem*.[9]

Therefore, should someone utter a false statement believing it to be

---

another moral aspect. Here and in art. 3 St Thomas is following the strict line of Aristotle and Augustine that lying is intrinsically evil. Honest communication among men is necessary to the survival of society; it is not the presence or absence of the right to particular information in an individual hearer that fixes the malice of lying; it is the innate order of words to communicate truth. By this strict interpretation of lying certain moral dilemmas arise, e.g. the conflict between the moral evil of a lie and the good of, say, preserving one's life. Many, often tedious, discussions on ways around such dilemmas (e.g. mental reservation, equivocation, etc.) have marked the history of moral theology). On Church condemnation of moral laxism with regard to lying, see Denz. 2124-8.

falsum materialiter sed non formaliter, quia falsitas est præter intentionem dicentis. Unde non habet perfectam rationem mendacii; id enim quod præter intentionem est* per accidens est, unde non potest esse specifica differentia.

Si vero aliquis formaliter falsum dicat, habens voluntatem falsum dicendi, licet sit verum id quod dicitur, inquantum tamen hujusmodi actus est voluntarius et moralis habet per se falsitatem et per accidens veritatem. Unde ad speciem mendacii pertingit.

Quod autem aliquis intendat falsitatem in opinione alterius constituere fallendo ipsum, non pertinet ad speciem mendacii, sed ad quamdam perfectionem ipsius, sicut et in rebus naturalibus aliquid speciem sortitur si formam habeat, etiamsi desit formæ effectus; sicut patet in gravi, quod violenter sursum detinetur ne descendat secundum exigentiam suæ formæ.

Sic ergo patet quod mendacium directe et formaliter opponitur virtuti veritatis.

1. Ad primum ergo dicendum quod unumquodque magis judicatur secundum id quod est in eo formaliter et per se quam secundum id quod est in eo materialiter et per accidens. Et ideo magis opponitur veritati inquantum est virtus moralis quod aliquis dicat verum intendens dicere falsum, quam quod dicat falsum intendens dicere verum.

2. Ad secundum dicendum quod, sicut Augustinus dicit,[10] voces præcipuum locum tenent inter alia signa. Et ideo cum dicitur quod mendacium est falsa vocis significatio, nomine vocis intelligitur omne signum. Unde ille qui aliquod falsum nutibus significare intenderet non esset a mendacio immunis.

3. Ad tertium dicendum quod cupiditas fallendi pertinet ad perfectionem mendacii non autem ad speciem ipsius, sicut nec aliquis effectus pertinet ad speciem suæ causæ.

articulus 2. utrum mendacium sufficienter dividatur per mendacium officiosum, jocosum et perniciosum

AD SECUNDUM sic proceditur:[1] 1. Videtur quod mendacium insufficienter dividatur per mendacium officiosum, jocosum et perniciosum. Divisio enim est danda secundum ea quæ per se conveniunt rei, ut patet per Philosophum in *Meta*.[2] Sed intentio effectus est præter speciem actus moralis, et per accidens se habet ad ipsum, ut videtur; unde et infiniti effectus possunt consequi ex uno actu. Sed hæc divisio datur secundum intentionem effectus: nam mendacium jocosum est quod fit causa ludi;

---

*Piana: *præter intentionem dicentis*, outside the speaker's intention

true, there is a factual, but not a moral falsehood, since falsity is not the speaker's intention. Neither, then, is there a lie in any complete sense; what is outside one's intention is incidental and so cannot be a specific difference.

When an utterance false in a moral sense does take place because of willingness to speak falsely—even though what is spoken is in fact true—the action as voluntary and moral is inherently a falsehood and contains truth only incidentally. Therefore in its moral species it is a lie.

As to the intent to introduce falsity into another's mind by deceiving him, this does not enter into the very species of lying, but is a kind of finishing touch; an example: in the beings of nature a thing receives its species by having its form, even though the effect of that form be lacking, as in the case of a heavy object being suspended in air by an outside force so that it does not fall as its form requires.

From these considerations it is clear that lying is directly and in its species contrary to the virtue of truth.

Hence: 1. Judgment about anything should follow what is in it formally and expressly rather than materially and incidentally. On this basis there is more of an opposition to the moral virtue of truth where someone utters truth intending falsity, than where one utters falsity intending truth.

2. As Augustine says,[10] among all signs words occupy first place. In the saying, then, that lying is a false meaning in words, by 'words' every sort of sign is meant. Hence were one to intend to convey something false by nodding he would not be innocent of lying.

3. The desire to deceive stands as the complement of lying, not as forming its species; it is the same with any effect—it does not enter into the species of its cause.

article 2. whether the division of the lie into the useful, the humorous and the malicious lie is broad enough

THE SECOND POINT:[1] 1. It seems that the division of the lie into the useful, the humorous and the malicious is incomplete. We should base a division on essential notes; Aristotle makes this clear in the *Metaphysics*.[2] Intention of effect seems to be something over and above the species of a moral act, and in fact countless effects may issue from one act. Now the division proposed has as its basis the effect intended: the humorous lie, to amuse;

---

[10]*De doctr. christ.* II, 3. PL 34, 37
[1]III *Sent.* 38, 2 & 5. *In Psalm.* 5. *De duobus præceptis caritatis*
[2]*Meta.* VII, 12. 1038a9; a55

mendacium autem officiosum est quod fit causa utilitatis; mendacium autem perniciosum est quod fit causa nocumenti. Ergo inconvenienter hoc modo dividitur mendacium.

2. Præterea, Augustinus dividit mendacium in octo partes: quorum primum est *in doctrina religionis*; secundum est *quod nulli prosit, et obsit alicui*; tertium est *quod prodest ita uni, ut alteri obsit*; quartum est *quod fit sola mentiendi fallendique libidine*; quintum est *quod fit placendi cupiditate*; sextum est *quod nulli obest et prodest alicui ad conservandum pecuniam*; septimum est *quod nulli obest et prodest alicui ad vitandam mortem*; octavum *quod nulli obest et prodest alicui ad vitandam immunditiam corporalem*.[3] Ergo videtur quod prima divisio mendacii sit insufficiens.

3. Præterea, Philosophus in *Ethic.*,[4] dividit mendacium in jactantiam, quæ verum excedit in dicendo, et ironiam, quæ deficit a vero in minus. Quæ duo sub nullo prædictorum membrorum continentur. Ergo videtur quod divisio prædicta mendacii sit incompetens.

SED CONTRA est quod super illud *Ps.*, *Perdes omnes qui loquuntur mendacium*,[5] dicit glossa quod *sunt tria genera mendaciorum: quædam enim sunt pro salute et commodo alicujus; est etiam aliud genus mendacii quod fit joco; tertium vero mendacii genus est quod fit ex malignitate*.[6] Primum autem horum trium dicitur officiosum, secundum jocosum, tertium perniciosum. Ergo mendacium in tria prædicta dividitur.

RESPONSIO: Dicendum quod mendacium tripliciter dividi potest. Uno modo secundum ipsam mendacii rationem, quæ est propria et per se mendacii divisio, et secundum hoc mendacium in duo dividitur: scilicet in mendacium quod transcendit veritatem in majus, quod pertinet ad jactantiam; et in mendacium quod deficit a veritate in minus, quod pertinet ad ironiam, ut patet per Philosophum in *Ethic.*[7] Hæc autem divisio ideo per se est ipsius mendacii, quia mendacium, inquantum hujusmodi opponitur veritati, ut dictum est.[8] Veritas autem æqualitas quædam est, cui per se opponitur majus et minus.

Alio modo potest dividi mendacium inquantum habet rationem culpæ secundum ea quæ aggravant vel diminuunt culpam mendacii ex parte finis intenti. Aggravat autem culpam mendacii, si aliquis per mendacium intendat alterius nocumentum, quod vocatur mendacium perniciosum. Diminuitur autem culpa mendacii, si ordinetur ad aliquod bonum, vel

---

[3]*De mendac.* 14. PL 40, 505   [4]*Ethics* IV, 7. 1127a20; a28   [5]*Psalm* 5, 7
[6]*Lombardi.* PL 191, 97   [7]*Ethics* IV, 7. 1127a20; a28   [8]art. 1
[a]This and the following paragraph are another case of accounting for 'authorities' or authoritative texts (see 101, 4, note *c*). In terms of his own principles (see 1a2æ. 18, 5-11; 72, 1, 3, 5 & 9; 73, 3, 6, 7, 8) St Thomas classifies both divisions as

the pernicious, to do harm; the useful, to be of help. This is not, then, a sound division.

2. Further, we have Augustine's eight-member division of the lie: the first, *in religious teaching;* the second, *serving no one but harming someone;* the third, *working to someone's advantage by hurting another;* the fourth, *told for the sheer pleasure of lying and deceiving;* the fifth, *told with a desire to amuse;* the sixth, *going against no one, but saving someone's money;* the seventh, *hurting nobody, but saving somebody's life;* the eighth, *harming no one, but saving someone's purity.*[3] Hence the division proposed is incomplete.

3. Further, in the *Ethics*[4] Aristotle divides lies into those of boasting and of false modesty, the first violating truth by exaggerating; the second, by disclaiming. Since its members include neither kind, the division proposed seems inadequate.

ON THE OTHER HAND, a gloss on the verse, *Thou wilt destroy all that speak a lie,*[5] comments, *There are three kinds of lie; some lies are for another's advantage and well-being; another kind is uttered in jest; a third, from evilmindedness.*[6] The first is the useful lie; the second, the humorous; the third, the pernicious. The lie is therefore divided into the three kinds mentioned.

REPLY: There are three possible bases for division of the lie. The first is its intrinsic nature, and this makes for a proper and essential division. Here the division of the lie is twofold; namely into the lie that transgresses truth by excess, i.e. boasting; and the lie that falls short of the truth, i.e. false modesty. Aristotle makes this point clear in the *Ethics.*[7] The reason this is an essential division is the essential opposition of the lie to truth;[8] truth itself consists in an exactness to which either too much or too little is directly opposed.

In a second way the lie that is sinful can be divided on the basis of factors that worsen or lessen its sinfulness by reason of the end intended.[a] On the one hand the malice of the lie is worsened should anyone intend by it to injure another; and this is what is called a pernicious lie. On the other hand, the fault is lightened should the purpose be some good, whether pleasurable, the case with the humorous lie; or practical,[b] the case with the

---

accidental, i.e. the end intended by the liar (*finis operantis*) is an accident (circumstance) in relation to the specific morality of the lie deriving from its objective. The second and third divisions differ from each other: in the second the gravity deriving from end is the divisor; in the third, the intention distinguishes the members, with the gravity varying within each part of the division.

[b] On the division of the good into the noble, the delightful and the practical or useful, see 1a. 5, 6; 2a2æ. 145, 3; Vol. 18, ed. T. Gilby, Appendix 3, esp. pp. 136-7.

delectabile, et sic est mendacium jocosum; vel utile, et sic est mendacium officiosum, quo intenditur juvamentum alterius vel remotio nocumenti. Et secundum hoc dividitur mendacium in tria prædicta.

Tertio modo dividitur mendacium universalius secundum ordinem ad finem, sive ex hoc addatur vel diminuatur ad culpas mendacii, sive non; et secundum hoc divisio est octo membrorum, quæ dicta est.[9] In qua quidem tria prima membra continentur sub mendacio pernicioso. Quod quidem fit vel contra Deum, et ad hoc pertinet primum mendacium quod est in doctrina religionis. Vel est contra hominem, sive sola intentione nocendi alicui, et sic est mendacium secundum, quod scilicet nulli prodest, et obest alicui; sive etiam intendatur in nocumento unius utilitas alterius, et hoc est tertium mendacium, quod uni prodest, et alteri obest. Inter quæ tria primum est gravissimum, quia semper peccata contra Deum sunt graviora, ut supra dictum est.[10] Secundum autem est gravius tertio, quod diminuitur ex intentione utilitatis alterius.

Post hæc autem tria, quæ superaddunt ad gravitatem culpæ mendacii, ponitur quartum, quod habet propriam quantitatem sine additione vel diminutione. Et hoc est mendacium quod fit ex sola mentiendi libidine, quod procedit ex habitu; unde et Philosophus dicit in IV *Ethic.*, quod *mendax, eo quod talis est secundum habitum, ipso mendacio gaudet.*[11]

Quatuor vero subsequentes modi diminuunt de culpa mendacii; nam quintum est mendacium jocosum, quod fit placendi cupiditate; alia vero tria continentur sub mendacio officioso. In quo intenditur quod est alteri utile: vel quantum ad res exteriores, et sic est sextum mendacium, quod prodest alicui ad pecuniam conservandum; vel est utile corpori; et hoc est septimum mendacium, in quo impeditur mors hominis; vel etiam utile est ad honestatem virtutis, et hoc est octavum mendacium in quo impeditur illicita pollutio corporalis.

Patet autem quod quanto bonum intentum est melius tanto magis minuitur culpa mendacii. Et ideo si quis diligenter consideret, secundum ordinem prædictæ enumerationis est ordo gravitatis culpæ in istis mendaciis. Nam bonum utile præfertur delectabili, et vita corporalis præfertur pecuniæ, honestas autem ipsi corporali vitæ.

Et per hoc patet responsio ad objecta.

articulus 3. utrum omne mendacium sit peccatum

AD TERTIUM sic proceditur:[1] 1. Videtur quod non omne mendacium sit peccatum. Manifestum enim est quod evangelistæ scribendo Evangelium non peccaverunt. Videntur tamen aliquid falsum dixisse, quia verba

---

[9]obj. 2   [10]1a2æ. 73, 3; 2a2æ. 94, 3

useful lie, intended for another's advantage or protection. This is the basis for the division of the lie into these three members.

The third basis for dividing the lie is broader, namely an order to end whether or not this increases or diminishes the blame of the lie. Augustine's eight-member division[9] proceeds along these lines. The first three members are comprised by the malicious lie. The first is against God, a lie in religious teaching. Against another human being the lie is either solely for the sake of injuring, and this is the second member, namely one which profits no one but goes against someone; or it is one in which there is intent to help by harming someone else, and this is the third member, to help one person at the expense of another. The first of these three is most serious, sins against God always being worse, as shown earlier;[10] and the second is worse than the third, wherein the intention of helping someone is an extenuating element.

After these three, worsening the inherent gravity of lying, comes the fourth member, that has its proper and unvarying degree of guilt. This is the lie uttered out of sheer delight in lying, as it issues from a habit; thus Aristotle notes that the liar *takes delight in a lie because he is a liar by disposition.*[11]

The next four members decrease the culpability in lying, the fifth being the humorous lie told to entertain; the other three being included in the useful lie. Here what is intended is helpful to someone else; as to his possessions, the sixth member—to help someone save money; or as to his physical well-being, the seventh member—to save someone from death; or even as to the integrity of his virtue, the eighth member—to prevent bodily defilement.

Clearly, the better the good intended, the lighter the blame of a lie. Therefore anyone who considers carefully will note the correspondence between the degrees of gravity and the order in which the lies in the second two divisions are listed. For among goods the practical takes precedence over the pleasurable; bodily well-being over money; the life of virtue over physical life.

These considerations make clear the response to the first set of arguments.

article 3. whether every lie is sinful

THE THIRD POINT:[1] 1. Apparently not every lie is sinful. The evangelists obviously did not sin in writing the Gospels. Yet they seem to have written

---

[11]*Ethics* IV, 7. 1127b15
[1]III *Sent.* 38, 3. *In De Trinitate* III, 1. *In Ethic.* IV, *lect.* 15. 2a2æ. 69, 1 & 2

Christi et etiam aliorum frequenter aliter unus, et aliter retulit alius; unde videtur quod alter eorum dixerit falsum. Non ergo omne mendacium est peccatum.

2. Præterea, nullus remuneratur a Deo pro peccato. Sed obstetrices Ægypti remuneratæ sunt a Deo propter mendacium; dicitur enim *Exod.* quod *ædificavit illis Deus domos*.[2] Ergo mendacium non est peccatum.

3. Præterea, gesta sanctorum narrantur in Sacra Scriptura ad informationem vitæ humanæ. Sed de quibusdam sanctissimis viris legitur quod sunt mentiti; sicut legitur *Gen.* quod Abraham dixit de uxore sua quod soror sua esset:[3] Jacob etiam mentitus est dicens se esse Esau, et tamen benedictionem adeptus est, ut habetur *Gen.*[4] Judith etiam commendatur, quæ tamen Holoferni mentita est.[5] Non ergo omne mendacium est peccatum.*

4. Præterea, minus malum est eligendum ut vitetur majus malum; sicut medicus præscindit membrum ne corrumpatur totum corpus. Sed minus nocumentum est quod aliquis generet falsam opinionem in animo alicujus quam quod aliquis occidat vel occidatur. Ergo licite potest homo mentiri, ut unum præservet ab homicidio et alium præservet a morte.

5. Præterea, mendacium est si quis non impleat quod promisit. Sed non omnia promissa sunt implenda; dicit enim Isidorus, *In malis promissis rescinde fidem.*[6] Ergo non omne mendacium est peccatum.

6. Præterea, mendacium ob hoc videtur esse peccatum, quia per ipsum homo decipit proximum; unde Augustinus dicit, *Quisquis esse aliquod genus mendacii quod peccatum non sit putaverit, decipiet seipsum turpiter, cum honestum se deceptorem arbitratur aliorum.*[7] Sed non omne mendacium est deceptionis causa, quia per mendacium jocosum nullus decipitur; non enim ad hoc dicuntur hujusmodi mendacia ut credatur, sed propter delectationem solam; unde et hyperbolicæ locutiones quandoque etiam in Scriptura Sacra inveniuntur. Non ergo omne mendacium est peccatum.

SED CONTRA est quod dicitur *Eccli., Noli velle mentiri omne mendacium.*[8]

RESPONSIO: Dicendum quod illud quod est secundum se malum ex genere, nullo modo potest esse bonum et licitum, quia ad hoc quod aliquid sit bonum requiritur quod omnia recte concurrant. Bonum enim est ex integra causa, malum vero est ex singularibus defectibus, ut Dionysius dicit.[9] Mendacium autem est malum ex genere; est enim actus cadens super indebitam materiam. Cum enim voces naturaliter sint signa intellectuum,

---

*Piana: *Non ergo omne peccatum est mendacium,* not every sin is a lie
[2]*Exodus* 1, 21   [3]*Genesis* 12, 13; 20, 2
[4]*Genesis* 17   [5]cf *Judith* 15

something false, since often the words of Christ or of others are quoted differently by different evangelists. Not every lie, then, is a sin.

2. Further, no one receives a reward from God for sin. Yet for their lie the Egyptian midwives did; *Exodus* says, *God built them houses.*[2] Hence lying is not a sin.

3. Further, the lives of holy men are set down in Scripture as a pattern on how to live, and we read that the holiest of them lied: Abraham saying that his wife was his sister;[3] Jacob, that he was Esau, yet still receiving the blessing;[4] Judith lied to Holofernes, yet was commended.[5] Not every lie, then, is a sin.

4. Further, a lesser evil must be accepted when there is question of avoiding a greater—a doctor amputates a leg to prevent infection of the whole body. Now there is certainly less harm in a false idea being engendered in someone's mind than in his being the perpetrator or the victim of murder. Hence for someone to lie in order to save one person from murdering and another from being murdered is permissible.

5. Further, failure to keep a promise amounts to a lie. Not all promises, however, are to be kept, since Isidore says, *Where a promise is wicked, go back on your word.*[6] Thus not all lies are sins.

6. Further, a lie would seem to be sinful in that by it a person deceives his neighbour; *It is shameful self-deception when anyone imagines that some sort of lie is not a sin, for he counts himself honest when in reality he is a deceiver of others.*[7] Yet not every lie is a cause of deception; no one is fooled by the humorous lie, told as it is not to be believed but to be enjoyed; and hyperbole occurs even in Scripture. Thus not every sort of lie is sinful.

ON THE OTHER HAND, *Be not willing to make any manner of lie.*[8]

REPLY: There is no way in which something inherently bad can become good and lawful. For anything to be good requires that all its elements be present together in right order; Denis says, *the good consists in integrity of elements; evil in any of them being missing.*[9] Now lying is inherently evil, an action that involves a disordered objective. Words by their nature being signs of thought, it is contrary to their nature and out of order for anyone

---

[6] *Synonyma de lamentatione animæ peccatricis.* PL 83, 858. Isidore, Archbishop of Seville (*c.* 560–636), Doctor of the Church, is especially known as an encyclopedist, through his principal work, *Etymologiæ*, used in the Middle Ages as a source book and for its etymologies, many of them rather far-fetched. The *Synonyma* is a moralizing work.

[7] *De mendac.* 21. PL 40, 516   [8] *Ecclesiasticus* 7, 14
[9] *De div. nom.* 4, 30. PG 3, 729

innaturale est et indebitum quod aliquis voce significet id quod non habet in mente. Unde Philosophus dicit in *Ethic.* quod *mendacium est per se pravum et fugiendum; verum autem est bonum et laudabile.*[10] Unde omne mendacium est peccatum, sicut etiam Augustinus asserit.[11]

1. Ad primum ergo dicendum quod nec in Evangelio, nec in aliqua Scriptura canonica fas est opinari aliquod falsum asseri, nec quod scriptores earum mendacium dixerint, quia periret fidei certitudo, quæ auctoritati Sacræ Scripturæ innititur. In hoc vero quod in Evangelio et in aliis Scripturis Sacris verba aliquorum diversimode recitantur non est mendacium. Unde Augustinus dicit: *Nullo modo hinc laborandum esse judicat qui prudenter intelligit ipsas sententias esse necessarias cognoscendæ veritati, quibuslibet verbis fuerint explicatæ. Et in hoc apparet,* ut ibidem subdit, *non debere nos arbitrari mentiri quemquam, si pluribus reminiscentibus rem quam audierunt vel viderunt non eodem modo atque eisdem verbis eadem res fuerit indicata.*[12]

2. Ad secundum dicendum quod obstetrices non sunt remuneratæ pro mendacio, sed pro timore Dei et benevolentia ex qua processit mendacium. Unde signanter dicitur *Exod.* 1, *Et quia timuerunt obstetrices Deum, ædificavit illis domos.*[13] Mendacium vero postea sequens non fuit meritorium.

3. Ad tertium dicendum quod in Sacra Scriptura, ut Augustinus dicit,[14] inducuntur aliquorum gesta, quasi exempla perfectæ virtutis; de quibus non est æstimandum eos fuisse mentitos. Si quæ tamen in eorum dictis appareant quæ mendacia videantur, intelligendum est ea figuraliter et prophetice dicta esse. Unde Augustinus dicit, *Credendum est illos homines qui propheticis temporibus digni auctoritate fuisse commemorantur, omnia quæ scripta sunt de illis, prophetice gessisse atque dixisse.*[15]

Abraham tamen, ut Augustinus dicit in *Quæst. super Gen.,*[16] dicens Saram esse suam sororem, veritatem voluit celari, et non mendacium dici: soror enim dicitur, quia filia patris* erat. Unde et ipse Abraham dicit *Gen., Vere soror mea est, fiila patris mei, et non matris meæ filia,*[17] quia scilicet ex parte patris ei attinebat.

Jacob vero mystice dixit se esse Esau primogenitum Isaac, quia videlicet primogenita illius de jure ei debebantur. Usus autem est hoc modo loquendi per spiritum prophetiæ ad designandum mysterium, quia videlicet minor populus, scilicet gentilium, substituendus erat in locum primogeniti, scilicet in locum Judæorum.

---

*Leonine: *fratris*, brother
[10]*Ethics* IV, 7. 1127a28
[11]*Contra mendac.* 1. PL 40, 519; 21. PL 40, 547; *Enchir.* 18. PL 40, 240; 22. PL 40, 243
[12]*De consensu evangelistarum* II, 12. PL 34, 1090
[14]*De mendac.* 5. PL 40, 492
[13]*Exodus* 1, 21
[15]loc. cit.

to convey in words something other than what he thinks. This is why Aristotle in the *Ethics* teaches that *the lie is evil in itself and to be shunned, while truth is good and worthy of praise*.[10] Therefore, *every lie is sinful*, as Augustine maintains.[11]

Hence: 1. That either in the Gospels or anywhere else in the canonical Scriptures falsehood is asserted or that their authors lied is inadmissible;[a] it would put an end to the certainty of faith, which rests on the authoritativeness of Sacred Scripture.[b] There is no lie in the Gospels and other sacred books in which people's words are variously set down. Augustine states, *Anyone wisely realizing that he must get at the sense in order to understand the truth, will conclude that he is not to be troubled no matter in what words the sense is expressed*. And he continues, *It is clear that we must not imagine someone to be lying if several persons fail to describe identically and verbatim something they variously recall having seen or heard*.[12]

2. The midwives were not in fact rewarded for their lie, but for the fear of God and the good-heartedness behind it; notice that *Exodus* says pointedly, *And because the midwives feared God he built them houses*.[13] The ensuing lie, however, was not deserving of reward.

3. As Augustine says,[14] the deeds of some are brought forward in Scripture as examples of virtue in the highest degree; we must not think that these people lied. When something sounds like a lie in their statements, these must be interpreted as figurative and prophetic. *We must believe that whatever is related about those who, in prophetical times, are mentioned as being worthy of credence, was done and said of them by way of prophecy*.[15]

In particular: in saying Sarah was his sister Abraham, as Augustine says,[16] wished to hide the truth, not to lie; he called her his sister because she was his father's daughter. So Abraham himself says, *She is truly my sister, the daughter of my father, not the daughter of my mother*,[17] seeing that she was related to him on his father's side.

Jacob's assertion that he was Esau, Isaac's firstborn, has a mystical sense, namely that Esau's birthright was his by right. He employed this manner of speech under the influence of the spirit of prophecy to point to a mystery, namely that a younger people, the gentiles, were to take the place of the first-born, the Jews.

---

[16]*Quæst. Heptat.* I, 26 on *Gen.* 12, 12. PL 34, 554. *Contra mendac.* 10. PL 40, 533
[17]*Gen.* 20, 12
[a]Modern biblical science has a wider idea of scriptural inerrancy than the medieval; problems such as these and those in ad 3 would be faced through the interpretative function of form criticism.
[b]A strong statement of the primacy given by St Thomas to Scripture as the rule of faith.

Quidam vero commendantur in Scriptura non propter perfectam virtutem, sed propter quamdam virtutis indolem; scilicet quia apparebat in eis aliquis laudabilis affectus ex quo movebantur ad quædam indebita facienda. Et hoc modo Judith laudatur, non quia mentita est Holoferni, sed propter affectum quem habuit ad salutem populi, pro qua periculis se exposuit. Quamvis etiam dici possit quod verba ejus veritatem habent secundum aliquem mysticum intellectum.

4. Ad quartum dicendum quod mendacium non solum habet rationem peccati ex damno quod infertur proximo, sed ex sua inordinatione, ut dictum est.[18] Non licet autem aliqua illicita inordinatione uti ad impediendum nocumenta et defectus aliorum; sicut non licet furari ad hoc quod homo eleemosynam faciat, nisi forte in casu necessitatis in quo omnia sunt communia. Et ideo non est licitum mendacium dicere ad hoc quod aliquis alium a quocumque periculo liberet. Licet tamen veritatem occultare prudenter sub aliqua dissimulatione, ut Augustinus dicit.[19]

5. Ad quintum dicendum quod ille qui aliquid promittit, si habeat animum faciendi quod promittit non mentitur, quia non loquitur contra id quod gerit in mente. Si vero non faciat quod promisit, tunc videtur infideliter agere per hoc quod animum mutat. Potest tamen excusari ex duobus. Uno modo, si promisit id quod manifeste est illicitum, quia promittendo peccavit, mutando autem propositum bene facit. Alio modo, si sunt mutatæ conditiones personarum et negotiorum. Ut enim Seneca dicit in libro *De benefic.*,[20] ad hoc quod homo teneatur facere quod promisit, requiritur quod omnia immutata permaneant. Alioquin nec fuit mendax in promittendo, quia promisit quod habebat in mente sub intellectis debitis conditionibus; nec etiam est infidelis non implendo quod promisit, quia eædem conditiones non extant. Unde et Apostolus non est mentitus, qui non ivit Corinthum, quo se iturum esse promiserat, ut dicitur II *Cor.*[21] et hoc propter impedimenta quæ supervenerant.

6. Ad sextum dicendum quod operatio aliqua potest considerari dupliciter: uno modo secundum seipsam; alio modo ex parte operantis. Mendacium ergo jocosum ex ipso genere operis habet rationem fallendi, quamvis ex intentione dicentis non dicatur ad fallendum, nec fallat ex modo dicendi. Nec est simile de hyperbolicis aut quibuscumque figuratis locutionibus quæ in Sacra Scriptara inveniuntur, quia, sicut Augustinus dicit, *quidquid figurate fit aut dicitur, non est mendacium. Omnis enim enuntiatio ad id quod enuntiat referenda est; omne autem figurate aut factum aut dictum hoc enuntiat quod significat eis quibus intelligendum prolatum est.*[22]

---

[18]In the Reply
[19]*Contra mendac.* 10. PL 40, 553
[20]*De benef.* IV, 35
[21]II *Corinthians* 1, 15
[22]*De mendac.* 5. PL 40, 492

Moreover, some biblical personages are praised not because of real virtue, but for having at least a sense of virtue, i.e. for giving evidence of some praiseworthy sentiment that prompted them into doing untoward deeds. This, then, is the sense in which Judith is praised, i.e. not for her lie to Holofernes, but for her zeal for her people's welfare, which led her to expose herself to danger. Note, too, that it is possible to say her words contained truth according to some mystical interpretation.

4. As has been determined,[18] a lie has the quality of sinfulness not merely as being something damaging to a neighbour, but as being disordered in itself. Now it is not permissible to employ any unlawful wrongdoing in order to prevent injury to another or another's failings. For example, no one may steal in order to give alms, except in the case of dire necessity when all things are common property anyway. For this reason, then, it is unlawful for anyone to lie in order to rescue another, no matter what the peril; one may, however, prudently mask the truth,[c] as Augustine explains.[19]

5. One who makes a promise does not lie as long as he has made up his mind to do what he promises, since his words do not conflict with what he has in his mind. If he does not in fact keep his promise, he would seem to act faithlessly by changing his mind. Still he might be excused on two counts. First, if he promised what is plainly unlawful; then the promise was itself sinful and his change of intent a good act. Secondly, if there has been a change in the condition of the parties and of the object of the promise. As Seneca maintains,[20] for a man to be held to live up to a promise, it is required that the situation remain unchanged. If not, he was neither untruthful in promising—since his pledge matched his thoughts, but only under the presupposition of all appropriate conditions; nor is he faithless in failing to keep the promise once the original terms no longer prevail. For this reason St Paul was not guilty of lying by not going to Corinth as he had promised,[21] because of obstacles that came up.

6. We can look on any action in two ways: first, in its own nature; secondly, from the standpoint of the person performing it. Hence the humorous lie has the quality of deceiving, even though from its author's intent it is not uttered to deceive, nor does in fact deceive, because of the tone in which it is spoken. And we should not put the hyperbole and other figures of speech found in Sacred Scripture in the same category, because, as Augustine says, *Anything spoken or done figuratively is no lie. Every statement is to be related to what it is declaring, and everything done or spoken figuratively does declare what it means to those to whom it is tendered for their understanding.*[22]

---

[c]Note the distinction here and in III, 1 ad 4 between expressing what is false and being silent about or masking the truth.

articulus 4. utrum omne mendacium sit peccatum mortale

AD QUARTUM sic proceditur:¹ 1. Videtur quod omne mendacium sit peccatum mortale. Dicitur enim, *Perdes omnes qui loquuntur mendacium*;² et *Sap.* I, *Os quod mentitur, occidit animam.*³ Sed perditio et mors animæ non est nisi peccatum mortale.* Ergo omne mendacium est peccatum mortale.

2. Præterea, omne quod est contra præceptum Decalogi est peccatum mortale. Sed mendacium est contra hoc præceptum Decalogi, *Non falsum testimonium dices.*⁴ Ergo omne mendacium est peccatum mortale.

3. Præterea, Augustinus dicit, *Nemo mentiens in eo quod mentitur servat fidem; nam hoc utique vult ut cui mentitur fidem sibi habeat, quam tamen ei mentiendo non servat; omnis autem fidei violator iniquus est.*⁵ Nullus autem dicitur fidei violator vel iniquus propter peccatum veniale. Ergo nullum mendacium est peccatum veniale.

4. Præterea, merces æterna non perditur nisi pro peccato mortali. Sed pro mendacio perditur merces æterna commutata in temporalem. Dicit enim Gregorius quod *in remuneratione obstetricum cognoscitur quid mendacii culpa mereatur; nam benignitatis earum merces, quæ eis potuit in æterna vita retribui, pro admissa culpa mendacii in terrenam est remunerationem declinata.*⁶ Ergo etiam mendacium officiosum, quale fuit obstetricum, quod videtur esse levissimum, est peccatum mortale.

5. Præterea, Augustinus dicit quod *perfectorum præceptum est, omnino non solum non mentiri, sed nec velle mentiri.*⁷ Sed facere contra præceptum est peccatum mortale. Ergo omne mendacium perfectorum est peccatum mortale. Pari ergo ratione et omnium aliorum, alioquin essent pejoris conditionis quam alii.

SED CONTRA est quod Augustinus dicit,⁸ *Duo sunt genera mendaciorum, in quibus non est magna culpa; sed tamen non sunt sine culpa, cum aut jocamur aut proximo consulendo mentimur.*⁹ Sed omne peccatum mortale habet gravem culpam. Ergo mendacium jocosum et officiosum non sunt peccata mortalia.

RESPONSIO: Dicendum quod peccatum mortale proprie est quod repugnat caritati, per quam anima vivit Deo conjuncta, ut dictum est.¹⁰ Potest autem mendacium contrariari caritati tripliciter: uno modo secundum se; alio modo secundum finem intentum; tertio modo per accidens.

---

*Leonine: *per peccatum mortale*
¹2a2æ. 70, 4. III *Sent.* 38, 4. *In Psalm.* 5
³*Wisdom* I, 11
⁵*De doctr. christ.* I, 36. PL 34, 34
²*Psalm* 5, 7
⁴*Exodus* 20, 16,
⁶*Moral.* XVIII 3. PL 76, 41

article 4. *whether every lie is a mortal sin*

THE FOURTH POINT:[1] 1. Every lie seems to be mortally sinful. *Thou wilt destroy all that speak a lie;*[2] and, *The mouth that belieth killeth the soul.*[3] Only a mortal sin is the ruin and death of the soul, and so every lie is a mortal sin.

2. Further, since everything against a commandment of the Decalogue is a mortal sin, and lying is against the precept, *Thou shalt not bear false witness,*[4] it is mortal sin.

3. Further, Augustine says, *Every liar in lying breaks faith; for what he wants is that his hearer have faith in him; yet by lying, he himself does not keep faith. Everyone who breaks faith is wicked.*[5] Since no one is called a breaker of faith or a wicked person for a venial sin, no lie is a venial sin.

4. Further, only for a mortal sin do we lose our eternal reward, and we lose it for a lie, an earthly reward being substituted. Gregory says, *We learn from the reward of the midwives what the sin of lying deserves, since the reward that they merited for their kindness and that they should have received in eternal life, faded into an earthly prize because of the lie they were guilty of.*[6] Consequently, even a useful lie like that of the midwives, which seems most innocent, is a mortal sin.

5. Further, *The commandment for those who are perfect is not just not to lie, but not even to wish to lie.*[7] To act against a commandment is a mortal sin. Every lie of the perfect,[a] then, is a mortal sin, and, with equal reason, a lie by anybody else; unless we are to say that other people are of a worse spiritual condition.

ON THE OTHER HAND, Augustine comments on a *Psalm*[8] that *there are two kinds of lie in which, even if there is some blame, it is not great, namely when we are joking or when we lie in our neighbour's interest.*[9] Since great blame is attached to every mortal sin, the humorous and the useful lie are not mortal sins.

REPLY: We have already determined[10] that by definition a mortal sin is one that is incompatible with the charity that gives the soul life by uniting it to God.[b] There are three possibilities for a lie to go counter to charity: first, because of what it is; secondly, because of an end intended; thirdly, because of intervening circumstances.

---

[7]*De mendac.* 17. PL 40, 510
[8]*Psalm* 5, 7
[9]*Enarrat. in Ps.* 5, 7. PL 36, 86
[10]1a2æ. 72, 5. 2a2æ. 24, 12; 35, 3
[a]*perfecti* in Augustine's statement and in St Thomas's vocabulary refers to those who have reached a high state in the spiritual life because of progress in charity; see 2a2æ. 24, 9; 184, 1-4.
[b]See above 105, 1, note c.

Secundum se quidem caritati contrariatur ex ipsa falsa significatione. Quæ quidem sit sit circa res divinas, contrariatur caritati Dei, cujus veritatem aliquis tali mendacio occultat vel corrumpit. Unde hujusmodi mendacium non solum opponitur virtuti caritatis,* sed etiam virtuti fidei et religionis; et ideo hoc mendacium est gravissimum et mortale.

Si vero falsa significatio sit circa aliquid cujus cognitio pertineat ad hominis bonum, puta quæ pertinent ad perfectionem scientiæ et informationem morum, tale mendacium, inquantum infert damnum falsæ opinionis proximo contrariatur caritati quantum ad dilectionem proximi, unde est peccatum mortale. Si vero falsa opinio ex mendacio generata sit circa aliquid de quo non referat utrum sic vel aliter cognoscatur, tunc ex tali mendacio non damnificatur proximus; sicut si quis fallatur in aliquibus particularibus contingentibus ad se non pertinentibus. Unde tale mendacium secundum se non est peccatum mortale.

Ratione vero finis intenti aliquod mendacium contrariatur caritati. Puta quod dicitur aut in injuriam Dei, quod semper est peccatum mortale utpote religioni contrarium; aut in nocumentum proximi quantum ad personam, divitias vel famam; et hoc etiam est peccatum mortale, cum nocere proximo sit peccatum mortale. Ex sola autem intentione peccati mortalis aliquis mortaliter peccat. Si vero finis intentus non sit contrarius caritati, nec mendacium secundum hanc rationem erit peccatum mortale. Sicut apparet in mendacio jocoso in quo intenditur aliqua levis delectatio et in mendacio officioso in quo intenditur etiam utilitas proximi.

Per accidens autem potest contrariari caritati ratione scandali vel cujuscumque damni consequentis. Et sic erit etiam peccatum mortale, dum scilicet aliquis non veretur propter scandalum publice mentiri.

1. Ad primum ergo dicendum quod illæ auctoritates intelliguntur de mendacio pernicioso, ut exponit *Glossa*[11] super illud, *Perdes omnes qui loquuntur mendacium.*[12]

2. Ad secundum dicendum quod cum omnia præcepta Decalogi ordinentur ad dilectionem Dei et proximi, sicut supra dictum est,[13] intantum mendacium est contra præceptum Decalogi inquantum est contra dilectionem Dei et proximi. Unde signanter prohibetur contra proximum falsum testimonium.

3. Ad tertium dicendum quod etiam peccatum veniale largo modo potest dici iniquitas, inquantum est præter æquitatem justitiæ. Unde dicitur 1 *Joan.*, *Omne peccatum est iniquitas;*[14] et hoc modo loquitur Augustinus.

---

*Leonine: *veritatis*, the virtue of truth
[11]*Ordinaria*; *Lombardi*. PL 191, 98
[12]*Psalm* 5, 7
[13]1a2æ. 100, 5 ad 1. 2a2æ. 44, 1 ad 3

That a lie in its nature be against charity depends upon its own false meaning. When this relates to the things of God, the lie is opposed to charity towards him, whose truthfulness is obscured or subverted by such a lie. For this reason this kind of lie is not only against the virtue of charity, but also against faith and religion, and as such is a most serious, mortal sin.

When the false meaning related to a matter the knowledge of which has bearing on the well-being of another person—for example his growth in learning or his moral training—then the lie in question is against charity towards the neighbour, doing the injury of misleading him. On the other hand when the false impression engendered by a lie relates to something the knowledge of which makes no difference one way or another—for example when someone is misled about bits of news that do not matter to him—the neighbour is not harmed by such a lie. Consequently this kind of lie is not a sin mortal in kind.

Because of an end intended, a particular lie may be a mortal sin. For example, it may be spoken to do injury to God, which is always a mortal sin as against religion; or to harm a neighbour in his person, his possessions or his good name; this also is a mortal sin, since to do harm to one's neighbour is a mortal sin and we sin mortally even by simply intending something gravely sinful. On the other hand, should the end intended itself not be against charity, the lie involved will not, in terms of end, be a mortal sin. Clear instances of this are the humorous lie with its intention of some harmless pleasure and the useful lie with its intention of service to another.

By reason of intervening circumstances, also, a lie can be against charity, i.e. by reason of scandal or some other damage ensuing. Then the lie will be a mortal sin, its author not being deterred from lying openly by the possibility of scandal.

Hence: 1. The two texts are usually referred to the pernicious lie, as in the *Gloss*[11] on the Psalm verse, *Thou wilt destroy all that speak a lie.*[12]

2. Since, as already noted,[13] all the Ten Commandments have the love of God and of neighbour as their purpose, a lie is against the Decalogue in the measure that it is against the love of God and of neighbour. This is why bearing false witness against a neighbour is explicitly forbidden.

3. Even a venial sin can be termed iniquity in a broad sense, since it is diverted from the true measure of righteousness.[c] Wherefore *John* says, *Every sin is iniquity*,[14] and Augustine here is speaking in the same sense.

---

[14] 1 *John* 3, 4

[c] *præter æquitatem justitiæ* is not a reference to the virtue of justice, but to that right order of soul brought about by grace and charity; see 1a2æ. 113, 1. Venial sin is an act outside of the harmony in which all man's acts are meant to contribute to the right order of charity; see 1a2æ. 88, 2.

4. Ad quartum dicendum quod mendacium obstetricum potest dupliciter considerari. Uno modo quantum ad affectum benevolentiæ in Judæos et quantum ad reverentiam divini timoris, ex quibus commendatur in eis indoles virtutis; et sic debetur eis remuneratio æterna. Unde Hieronymus exponit[15] quod Deus ædificavit illis domos spirituales.

Alio modo potest considerari quantum ad ipsum exteriorem actum mendacii. Quo quidem non potuerunt æternam remunerationem mereri, sed forte aliquam remunerationem temporalem, cujus merito non repugnabat deformitas illius mendacii, sicut repugnabat merito remunerationis æternæ. Et sic intelligenda sunt verba Gregorii, non quod per illud mendacium merentur amittere remunerationem æternam quam jam ex præcedenti affectu meruerant, ut ratio procedebat.

5. Ad quintum dicendum quod quidam dicunt[16] quod perfectis viris omne mendacium est peccatum mortale. Sed hoc irrationabiliter dicitur. Nulla enim circumstantia aggravat in infinitum, nisi quæ transfert in aliam speciem. Circumstantia autem personæ non transfert in aliam speciem, nisi forte ratione alicujus annexi, puta si sit contra votum ipsius; quod non potest dici de mendacio officioso vel jocoso. Et ideo mendacium officiosum vel jocosum non est peccatum mortale in viris perfectis, nisi forte per accidens ratione scandali. Et ad hoc potest referri quod Augustinus dicit, *perfectis esse præceptum non solum non mentiri, sed nec velle mentiri*.[17] Quamvis hoc Augustinus non assertive, sed sub dubitatione dicat; præmittit enim, *Nisi forte ita ut perfectorum*,[18] etc.

Nec obstat quod ipsi ponuntur in statu conservandæ veritatis, quia* veritatem tenentur conservare ex suo officio in judicio vel doctrina. Contra quæ si mentiantur, erit mendacium quod est peccatum mortale; in aliis autem non oportet quod mortaliter peccent mentiendo.

---

*Leonine: *qui ad*; for *quia*
[15]*Comment. in Isaiam* XVIII on 65. PL 24, 672.
[16]e.g. Alexander of Hales, *Summa Theologica* II–II (Quaracchi III, 406); Peter of Poitiers, *Sententiarum Libri V*, 4, 5. PL 211, 1154

4. There are two possible ways of looking at the sin of the midwives. The first regards their kindly sentiments towards the Jews and their reverential fear of God. These are the grounds for commending the sense of virtue in them and for an eternal reward being their due. This is why Jerome comments[15] that the houses God built for them were spiritual. The second possibility is to look at their outward act, the lie. This could not be title to an eternal reward but perhaps to some temporal one, with which the moral irregularity of the lie is not in conflict, as it is with meriting an eternal reward. The words of Gregory are to be taken in this sense and not, as the argument implies, to mean that by their lying they deserved to lose the eternal reward they had already merited by their previous kindliness.

5. Some theologians[16] maintain that for the perfect every lie is a mortal sin. But this position is not well reasoned. No circumstance worsens a sin infinitely unless it change the species. The circumstance of a person's status[d] does not do this, except perhaps when there is something else involved, for example a vow, and this is not the case in regard to the humorous or the useful lie. So in these there is no mortal sin for the perfect, except in the event of scandal. This possibility is the point of Augustine's words, *For the perfect the commandment is not only not to lie, but not even to want to.*[17] Although in fact Augustine did not even propose this definitively, but as a hypothesis, prefacing it with, *Unless perhaps in the case of the perfect*, etc.[18]

Nor is our point refuted by the fact that they are placed in a state where they are guardians of the truth, i.e. bound *ex officio* to safeguard the truth in judging and teaching. If in fact they lie in these circumstances, their sin will be mortal; but in other matters it does not follow that by lying they sin mortally.

---

[17]*De mendac.* 17. PL 40, 510 [18]ibid
[d]On the moral circumstance *quis*, the person of the one acting, see 1a2æ. 7, 3; 73, 10.

Quæstio 111. de simulatione et hypocrisi

POSTEA CONSIDERANDUM EST de simulatione et hypocrisi. Et circa hoc quæruntur quatuor:

1. utrum omnis simulatio sit peccatum;
2. utrum hypocrisis sit simulatio;
3. utrum opponatur veritati;
4. utrum sit peccatum mortale.

articulus 1. utrum omnis simulatio sit peccatum

AD PRIMUM sic proceditur:[1] 1. Videtur quod non omnis simulatio sit peccatum. Dicitur enim *Luc.* quod *Dominus se finxit longius ire.*[2] Et Abrosi us dicit de Abraham in libro *De patriarchis* quod captiose loquebatur cum servulis,[3] cum dixit *Gen., Ego et puer illuc usque properantes, postquam adoraverimus, revertemur ad vos.*[4] Fingere autem et captiose loqui ad simulationem pertinet. Sed non est dicendum quod in Christo et in Abraham fuerit peccatum. Ergo non omnis simulatio est peccatum.

2. Præterea, nullum peccatum est utile. Sed, sicut Hieronymus dicit, *utilem simulationem, et in tempore assumendam, Jehu regis Israel nos doceat exemplum, qui interfecit sacerdotes Baal, fingens se idola colere velle,*[5] ut habetur IV *Reg.*[6] Et David *immutavit faciem suam coram Achis rege Geth,* ut habetur I *Reg.*[7] Ergo non omnis simulatio est peccatum.

3. Præterea, bonum est malo contrarium. Si ergo simulare bonum est malum, ergo simulare malum erit bonum.

4. Præterea, *Isa.* contra quosdam dicitur, *Peccatum suum quasi Sodoma prædicaverunt nec absconderunt.*[8] Sed abscondere peccatum ad simulationem pertinet. Ergo non uti simulatione interdum est reprehensibile. Vitare autem peccatum nunquam est reprehensibile. Ergo simulatio non est semper peccatum.

SED CONTRA est quod *Isa.,* super illud, *In tribus annis,* etc.,[9] dicit *Glossa, In comparatione duorum malorum levius est aperte peccare quam sanctitatem simulare.*[10] Sed aperte peccare semper est peccatum. Ergo simulatio semper est peccatum.

RESPONSIO: Dicendum quod, sicut dictum est,[11] ad virtutem veritatis pertinet ut quis talem se exhibeat exterius per signa exteriora qualis est.

---

[1] cf. IV *Sent.* 16, 4, 1, i [2] *Luke* 24, 28 [3] *De Abraham* I, 8. PL 14, 469
[4] *Genesis* 22, 5 [5] *Interl.* 1 (2, 11). PL 26, 364 [6] IV *Kings* 10, 18

Question 111. deception and hypocrisy

NEXT, DECEPTION AND hypocrisy; there are four points of inquiry:
1. whether all deception is sinful;
2. whether hypocrisy is a form of deception;
3. whether it is against truth;
4. and a mortal sin.

article 1. whether in every case deception is sinful

THE FIRST POINT:[1] 1. Not every case of deception, it seems, is sinful. We read of our Lord that *he made as though he would go further.*[2] Ambrose says of Abraham that *he was speaking craftily to the young man*[3] when he said, *I and the boy will speed as far as yonder and after we have worshipped we will return to you.*[4] While both actions are instances of deception, we may not say that either Christ or Abraham was sinning. Therefore deception is not sinful in every case.

2. Further, no sin is truly useful. Still Jerome says, *The example of Jehu, King of Israel, who slew the priests of Baal, pretending a desire to worship their idols, should teach us that there is a use and a time for guile.*[5] (The incident is in IV *Kings.*[6]) Also, *David changed his countenance before Achis, king of Geth.*[7] Hence, not every form of deception is sinful.

3. Further, good and evil being opposed, if feigning good is an evil, feigning evil is a good.

4. Further, in *Isaiah* there is this condemnation, *They have proclaimed abroad their sin as Sodom and they have not hid it.*[8] Since to hide one's sin is a cause of deception, it must follow that not to employ deception is in some instances reprehensible. Since avoiding sin is never reprehensible, deception is not always a sin.

ON THE OTHER HAND, on the verse of *Isaiah, In three years,* etc.,[9] the *Gloss* comments, *If we are to compare the evil of each, it is less serious to sin openly than to feign holiness.*[10] To sin openly is always a sin. So too, then, is deception.

REPLY: As noted,[11] it belongs to the virtue of truth that a person openly show his true self in outward signs. These consist not only in words, but

---
[7] 1 *Kings* 21, 13
[8] *Isaiah* 3, 9
[9] *Isaiah* 16, 14
[10] *Ordinaria*; also Jerome, *Comment. in Isaiam* VI, on 16, 14. PL 24, 248
[11] above 109, 3 ad 3

Signa autem exteriora non solum sunt verba sed etiam facta. Sicut ergo veritati opponitur quod aliquis per verba exteriora aliud significet quam quod habet apud se, quod ad mendacium pertinet ita etiam opponitur veritati quod aliquis per aliqua signa factorum vel rerum aliquid* significet contrarium ejus quod in eo est, quod proprie simulatio dicitur. Unde simulatio proprie est mendacium quoddam in exteriorum signis factorum consistens. Non refert autem utrum aliquis mentiatur verbo vel quocumque alio facto, ut supra habitum est.[12] Unde cum omne mendacium sit peccatum, ut supra dictum est,[13] consequens est etiam quod omnis simulatio est peccatum.

1. Ad primum ergo dicendum quod, sicut Augustinus dicit, *non omne quod fingimus mendacium est; sed quando id fingimus quod nihil significat, tunc est mendacium. Cum autem fictio nostra refertur ad aliquam significationem, non est mendacium sed aliqua figura veritatis.*[14] Et subjungit exemplum de figuratis locutionibus, in quibus fingitur quædam res, non ut asseratur ita esse, sed eam proponimus ut figuram alterius quod asserere volumus. Sic ergo Dominus in Evangelio *finxit se longius ire*, quia composuit motum suum quasi volentis longius ire ad aliud figurate significandum, scilicet quod ipse ab eorum fide longe erat, ut Gregorius dicit.[15] Vel, ut Augustinus dicit,[16] quia cum longius recessurus esset ascendendo in cœlum, per hospitalitatem quodammodo retinebatur in terra.

Abraham etiam figurate locutus est. Unde Ambrosius dicit de Abraham quod *prophetavit quod ignorabat; ipse enim solus disponebat redire, immolato filio; sed Dominus per os ejus locutus est quod parabat.*[17]

Unde patet quod neuter simulavit.

2. Ad secundum dicendum quod Hieronymus utitur large nomine simulationis pro quacumque fictione. Commutatio autem faciei David fuit fictio figuralis, sicut glossa exponit[18] in titulo Ps., *Benedicam Dominum in omni tempore.*[19] Simulationem vero Jehu non est necesse excusari a peccato vel mendacio, quia malus fuit utpote ab idololatria Jeroboam non recedens. Commendatur tamen et temporaliter remuneratur a Deo, non pro simulatione sed pro zelo quo destruxit cultum Baal.

3. Ad tertium dicendum quod quidam[20] dicunt quod nullus potest se simulare esse malum, quia per opera bona nullus simulat se malum; si autem opera mala faciat, malus est. Sed hæc ratio non cogit. Potest enim aliquis se simulare malum per opera quæ in se non sunt mala, sed habent in se quamdam speciem mali. Et tamen ipsa simulatio est mala tum ratione mendacii tum ratione scandali. Et quamvis per hoc fiat malus, non tamen fit

---

*Leonine: *de se*, of themselves; instead of *aliquid*
[12]above 110, 1 ad 2   [13]above 110, 3
[14]*Quæst. evang.* II, 51, on *Luke* 24, 28. PL 35, 1362
[16]*Homil. in evang.* II, 23. PL 76, 1181

also in deeds. Therefore just as it is against truth for anyone by words to convey a meaning other than what he thinks, which is what lying is, so also it is against truth for a person to communicate by actions or otherwise a meaning at odds with the facts about himself, which is properly what deception is. In other words deception is a lie consisting in the signification of outward acts. As noted earlier,[12] it does not matter whether someone lie by word or by some sort of deed, and since every lie is sinful, as already determined,[13] so also is every act of deception.

Hence: 1. As Augustine remarks, *To pretend is not always to lie, but only when there is nothing behind the meaning of the pretence. When, however, our pretence has reference to some further meaning, there is no lie, but truth in a figure.*[14] And as an example he cites figures of speech, wherein one thing is portrayed not as though being asserted itself, but as a figure of something else we wish to convey.

Accordingly, our Lord in the text cited, *made as though to go further*, i.e. he acted like a person intending to go on, in order to communicate another idea under this figure, namely that the truth about himself was far removed from their way of thinking; this is Gregory's explanation.[15] Augustine's is[16] that while he was about to depart far from them by the Ascension, their hospitality held him back as it were on earth.

Abraham also spoke in a figure, *He prophesied unwittingly. While he did plan, once Isaac was sacrificed, to return alone, the Lord put on his lips what was divinely arranged*, says Ambrose.[17]

Clearly, then, neither Christ nor Abraham was guilty of deception.

2. Jerome uses *simulatio* in a broad sense for any sort of ruse. David's change of countenance was one that served as a figure, as a gloss[18] on the Psalm title, *I will bless the Lord at all times*,[19] interprets it. There is no need to try to explain away the sin or the lie in the deception of Jehu; he was wicked, not departing from the idolatry of Jeroboam. Still, he received praise and an earthly reward from God, not for his deceit but for the zeal that destroyed the cult of Baal.

3. Some theologians[20] state that it is impossible for anyone to simulate being evil, arguing that he does not do so by good works and should he perform evil works, he becomes really evil. But their reasoning is inconclusive. It is quite possible for someone to pretend that he is bad through acts that are really not bad, but that only seem bad. Nevertheless the deception itself is evil, because of both the lie involved and the scandal.

---

[16] loc cit note 14
[17] loc cit note 3
[18] *Interlinear.; Lombardi.* PL 191, 338
[19] *Psalm* 23
[20] e.g. Alexander of Hales, *Summa Theologica.* (Quaracchi III, 786)

malus illa malitia quam simulat, et quia ipsa simulatio secundum se mala est, non ratione ejus de quo est, sive sit de bono sive sit de malo, peccatum est.

4. Ad quartum dicendum quod sicut aliquis verbo mentitur, quando significat quod non est, non autem quando tacet quod est, quod aliquando licet, ita etiam simulatio est, quando aliquis per exteriora signa factorum vel rerum significat aliquid quod non est, non autem si aliquis prætermittat significare quod est. Unde aliquis potest peccatum suum occultare absque simulatione. Et secundum hoc intelligendum est quod Hieronymus dicit ibidem,[21] quod secundum remedium post naufragium est peccatum abscondere, ne scilicet exinde aliis scandalum generetur.

articulus 2. utrum hypocrisis sit idem quod simulatio

AD SECUNDUM sic proceditur:[1] 1. Videtur quod hypocrisis non sit idem quod simulatio. Simulatio enim consistit in quodam factorum mendacio. Sed hypocrisis potest etiam esse, si aliquis ostendat exterius quæ interius agit, secundum illud *Matt., Cum facis eleemosynam noli tuba canere ante te, sicut hypocritæ faciunt.*[2] Ergo hypocrisis non est idem simulationi.

2. Præterea, Gregorius dicit *Moral., Sunt nonnulli qui et sanctitatis habitum tenent, et perfectionis meritum exequi non valent. Hos nequaquam credendum est in hypocritarum numerum currere, quia aliud est infirmitate aliud malitia peccari.*[3] Sed illi qui tenent habitum sanctitatis et meritum perfectionis non exequuntur sunt simulatores, quia exterior habitus sanctitatis opera perfectionis significat. Non ergo simulatio est idem quod hypocrisis.

3. Præterea, hypocrisis in sola intentione consistit. Dicit enim Dominus de hypocritis *Matt.* quod *omnia opera sua faciunt, ut ab hominibus videantur*;[4] et Gregorius *Moral.* quod *nunquam quid agant, sed quomodo de actione qualibet hominibus possint placere, considerant.*[5] Sed simulatio non consistit in sola intentione, sed in exteriori operatione: unde super illud *Job, Simulatores et callidi provocant iram Dei,*[6] dicit glossa quod *simulator aliud simulat et aliud agit; castitatem præfert et lasciviam sequitur; ostentat paupertatem et marsupium replet.*[7] Ergo hypocrisis non est idem quod simulatio.

SED CONTRA est quod Isidorus dicit, *Hypocrita Græco sermone in Latino simulator interpretatur; qui cum intus malus sit, ut bonum se palam ostendit; hypo enim falsum, crisis judicium interpretatur.*

---

[21]loc cit note 10, on 3, 9. PL 24, 66
[1]cf IV *Sent.* 16, 4, 1, 1   [2]*Matthew* 6, 2   [3]*Moral.* XXXI, 13. PL 76, 586
[4]*Matthew* 13, 5   [5]*Moral.* XXXI, 13. PL 76, 586   [6]*Job* 36, 13
[7]*Interlinear.* on *Isaiah* 9, 17   [8]*Etymolog.* x. PL 82, 379
[a]The etymology of Isidore here and in the Reply is unfounded. The Greek verb

While a person thereby becomes evil, it is not with the kind of evil his deception suggests; rather the deception is wrong in itself, not by reason of its content, and it is a sin whatever it is about, good or evil.

4. A person lies verbally when he gives expression to what is not true, not when he is silent about what is true, a course sometimes permissible. Similarly, there is deception when a person expresses what is not true through the meaning of actions or objects, but not when he refrains from conveying what is true. Consequently, it is possible for one to conceal his own sin without deceiving. This is how Jerome is to be interpreted when, in the same context,[21] he says that the second remedy after shipwreck is to hide one's sin, i.e. so that it does not become a scandal for others.

article 2. whether hypocrisy is the same as deception

THE SECOND POINT:[1] 1. Hypocrisy does not seem to be identical with deception. Deception consists in a kind of lying in act, while there can be hypocrisy even when someone outwardly reveals what is truly going on inwardly—*When thou dost an almsdeed, sound not a trumpet before thee as the hypocrites do.*[2] Thus the two are not the same.

2. Further there are Gregory's words, *Some there are who wear the habit of holiness but are unable to reach the merit of perfection. We must by no means presume that they have joined the ranks of the hypocrites, since it is one thing to sin from weakness; another, from malice.*[3] Still those who wear the garb of holiness but do not achieve the merit of perfection are deceivers, the outer robe of sanctity being a symbol of the works of perfection. Therefore deception and hypocrisy are not the same thing.

3. Further, hypocrisy is solely a matter of intent. Our Lord says of hypocrites, *All their works they do for to be seen of men;*[4] and Gregory, *They are never concerned about what it is they do, but about how from their every act they can gain people's favour.*[5] In contrast, deception is not just a matter of intent but of outward performance; hence on the verse of *Job*, *Dissemblers and crafty men prove the wrath of God*,[6] a gloss comments that *the deceiver feigns one thing and does something else; parading chastity, he delights in lewdness; making a show of poverty, he stuffs his purse.*[7] Hypocrisy, then, is not the same as deception.

ON THE OTHER HAND, Isidore has it that *'Hypocrita'* in Greek corresponds to *'simulator'* in Latin, and means one who, being inwardly evil, outwardly poses as good, ὑπό signifying *'false'* and κρίσις judgment.[8a]

ὑποκρίνομαι means first *to reply or give answer*; then is applied to actors, *to speak a dialogue, to play a part*; then is transferred to mean *to dissemble, to play the hypocrite*. Similarly ὑποκριτής means *a respondent, an interpreter*; then *an actor or player*; then a *pretender* or *hypocrite*.

RESPONSIO: Dicendum quod, sicut Isidorus dicit ibidem, *nomen hypocritæ tractum est a specie eorum qui in spectaculis contecta facie incedunt, distinguentes vultum vario colore, ut ad personæ quam simulant colorem perveniant, modo in specie viri, modo in specie fœminæ, ut in ludis populum fallant.*[9] Unde Augustinus dicit quod *sicut hypocritæ simulatores aliarum personarum* agunt partes illius quod non sunt *non enim qui agit partes Agamemnonis, vere ipse est, sed simulat eum, sic in Ecclesiis, et in omni vita humana, quisquis se vult videri quod non est, hypocrita est; simulat enim se justum, non exhibet.*[10]

Sic igitur dicendum est quod hypocrisis simulatio est, non autem omnis simulatio sed solum illa qua quis simulat personam alterius sicut cum peccator simulat personam justi.

1. Ad primum ergo dicendum quod opus exterius naturaliter significat intentionem. Quando ergo aliquis per bona opera quæ facit ex suo genere ad Dei servitium pertinentia non quærit Deo placere sed hominibus, simulat rectam intentionem quam non habet. Unde Gregorius dicit quod *hypocritæ per causas Dei deserviunt intentioni sæculi, quia per ipsa quoque quæ se agere sancta ostendunt, non conversionem quærunt hominum, sed auras favorum.*[11] Et ita simulant mendaciter intentionem rectam quam non habent, quamvis non simulant aliquod rectum opus quod non agunt.

2. Ad secundum dicendum quod habitus sanctitatis, puta religionis vel clericatus, significat statum quo quis obligatur ad opera perfectionis. Et ideo cum quis habitum sanctitatis assumit intendens se ad statum perfectionis transferre, si per infirmitatem deficiat, non est simulator vel hypocrita, quia non tenetur manifestare suum peccatum sanctitatis habitum deponendo. Si autem ad hoc sanctitatis habitum assumeret ut se justum ostentaret, esset hypocrita et simulator.

3. Ad tertium dicendum quod in simulatione sicut in mendacio duo sunt: unum quidem sicut signum et aliud sicut signatum. Mala ergo intentio in hypocrisi consideratur sicut signatum quod non respondet signo; exteriora autem vel verba vel opera vel quæcumque sensibilia considerantur in omni simulatione et mendacio sicut signa.

articulus 3. utrum hypocrisis opponatur virtuti veritatis

AD TERTIUM sic proceditur:[1] 1. Videtur quod hypocrisis non opponatur virtuti veritatis. In simulatione enim sive hypocrisi est signum et signatum. Sed quantum ad utrumque non videtur opponi alicui speciali virtuti. Hypocrita enim simulat quamcumque virtutem et etiam per quæcumque

---

[9] *Etymolog.* X. PL 82, 379
[10] *De serm. Dom.* II, 2. PL 34, 1271. St Thomas paraphrases

REPLY: Isidore's information is that *The word 'hypocrite' is derived from the guise of those who in the theatre come on to the stage with their faces disguised by make-up to suit the look of the person they are portraying, now appearing as a man, now as a woman, in order to take in the audience with their acting.*[9] So also Augustine notes, *Just as stage players (hypocritæ) take off other people*, i.e. play the part of someone they are not, *the one who plays the part of Agamemnon not really being he, but pretending to be—so in the Church and in all of human life one wishing to appear to be what he is not is a hypocrite. He plays the good man without being one.*[10]

From this we conclude that hypocrisy is deception; not, however, just any form of deception, but only that whereby one poses as someone else, as in the case of a sinful person pretending to be virtuous.

Hence: 1. In the ordinary course outward action reflects intent. Consequently a person who, in works that of themselves are of God's service, seeks not divine by human favour, is in fact making a pretence of a virtuous intent that he does not have. Hence Gregory's remark, *Hypocrites make God's interests serve a worldly purpose, because by making a show of holy conduct they seek, not to turn men to God, but to direct to themselves the shifting winds of approval.*[11] Thus they lyingly affect the honourable intention that they lack, even when they do not make a show of doing a good deed without doing it.

2. The garb of holiness, for example religious or clerical habit, is a symbol of a state of life wherein one obliges oneself to the works of perfection. Therefore in the case of someone putting on the garb of holiness with the intention of entering a state of perfection, he is no deceiver or hypocrite should he fail through human frailty; he is not bound to broadcast his sin by putting aside the habit. He would be a hypocrite and a deceiver were he to put it on in order to pass himself off as righteous.

3. In deception as in lying there are two elements: one, the sign; the other, the thing signified. In hypocrisy the bad intention stands as the thing signified that does not match the sign; in all deception and lying words, deeds or whatever appears outwardly are regarded as signs.

article 3. whether hypocrisy is against the virtue of truth

THE THIRD POINT:[1] 1. Hypocrisy does not seem to be against the virtue of truth. Hypocrisy and deception include sign and thing signified, but from neither standpoint does there seem to be opposition to any specific virtue. For the hypocrite pretends to all kinds of virtues and by using all kinds of

---

[11]*Moral.* XXXI, 13. PL 76, 587
[1]IV *Sent.* 16, 4, 1 Sol. 2.

virtutis opera, puta per jejunium, orationem et eleemosynam, ut habetur *Matt.*² Ergo hypocrisis non opponitur specialiter virtuti veritatis.

2. Præterea, omnis simulatio ex aliquo dolo videtur procedere, unde et simplicitati opponitur. Dolus autem opponitur prudentiæ, ut supra habitum est.³ Ergo hypocrisis quæ est simulatio non opponitur veritati sed magis prudentiæ vel simplicitati.

3. Præterea, species moralium considerantur ex fine. Sed finis hypocrisis est acquisitio lucri vel inanis gloriæ; unde super illud *Job*,⁴ *Quæ est spes hypocritæ, si avare rapiat*,⁴ etc., dicit *Glossa, Hypocrita, qui latine dicitur simulator, avarus raptor est, qui dum inique agens desiderat de sanctitate venerari, laudem vitæ rapit alienæ.*⁵ Cum ergo avaritia vel inanis gloria non directe opponatur veritati, videtur quod nec simulatio, sive hypocrisis.

SED CONTRA est quia omnis simulatio est mendacium quoddam, ut dictum est.⁶ Mendacium autem directe opponitur veritati. Ergo et simulatio sive hypocrisis.

RESPONSIO: Dicendum quod secundum Philosophum in *Meta*.⁷ contrarietas est oppositio secundum formam, a qua scilicet res speciem habet. Et ideo dicendum est quod simulatio sive hypocrisis potest opponi alicui virtuti dupliciter: uno modo, directe; alio modo, indirecte. Directa quidem oppositio ejus sive ejus contrarietas est attendenda secundum ipsam speciem actus, qui accipitur secundum proprium objectum. Unde cum hypocrisis sit quædam simulatio qua quis simulat se habere personam quam non habet, ut dictum est,⁸ consequens est quod directe opponatur veritati, per quam aliquis exhibet se talem vita et sermone qualis est, ut dicitur in *Ethic*.⁹

Indirecta autem oppositio sive contrarietas hypocrisis potest attendi secundum quodcumque accidens, puta secundum aliquem finem remotum vel secundum aliquod instrumentum actus vel quodcumque aliud hujusmodi.

1. Ad primum ergo dicendum quod hypocrita simulans aliquam virtutem assumit eam ut finem, non quidem secundum existentiam, quasi volens eam habere, sed secundum apparentiam, quasi volens videri eam habere; ex quo non habet quod opponatur illi virtuti, sed quod opponatur veritati, inquantum vult decipere homines circa illam virtutem. Opera autem illius virtutis non assumit quasi per se intenta sed instrumentaliter, quasi signa illius virtutis. Unde ex hoc non habet directam oppositionem ad illam virtutem.

---

²*Matthew* 6, 1–5; 17–18   ³2a2æ. 55, 4   ⁴*Job* 27, 8
⁵*Ordinaria*, from Gregory, *Moral*. XVIII, 6. PL 76, 44

acts of virtue—like fasting, prayer, and almsgiving.[2] Consequently, hypocrisy is not specifically against truthfulness.

2. Further, all deception seems to issue from some form of guile and so is contrary to simplicity, since guile is against prudence,[3] hypocrisy, as a form of deception, is not against truth, but rather against prudence or simplicity.

3. Further, species in moral matters are accounted for from ends. The end of hypocrisy is to get money or vainglory, so that the *Gloss* on *Job*, *What is the hope of the hypocrite if through covetousness he take by violence*,[4] comments, *A hypocrite, in Latin* simulator, *is a grasping thief who, while acting wickedly, craves to be esteemed for holiness, and so steals the praise due to another way of living*.[5] Since neither greed nor vainglory is against truth, neither, it seems, is deception or hypocrisy.

ON THE OTHER HAND, every form of deception is a kind of lie, as already determined.[6] Lying is the direct opposite to truth. So therefore are deception or hypocrisy.

REPLY: Following Aristotle,[7] contrariety is a type of opposition based on the form by which a thing has its species. Thus there are two possible ways of opposition between deception or hypocrisy and any virtue, namely direct and indirect. Direct opposition or contrariety is to be determined on the basis of the species of an act, which in turn derives from the proper objective. Hence, in that hypocrisy, as noted,[8] is a type of deception whereby someone pretends to be a kind of person that he is not, its direct opposition is to truth, whereby in work and word a person shows himself as he is, as the *Ethics* teaches.[9]

An indirect opposition or contrariety on the part of hypocrisy can be counted on the basis of any sort of secondary element, some ulterior motive, for example, or some means employed for the act, etc.

Hence: 1. The hypocrite in making a show of virtue does not adopt it as end in its reality, as though intending to possess it, but in its appearances, intending to be thought to possess it. The import of this is not opposition to the virtue feigned, but to truth, in that the hypocrite intends deception of others regarding the virtue in question. As to virtuous acts, he employs them not for their own value but for the sheer expediency of their being signs of virtue. Neither, then, on this basis is their direct opposition to the virtue feigned.

---

[6]art. 1
[7]*Metaphysics* IX, 4. 1055a5
[8]art. 2
[9]*Ethics* IV, 7. 1127a24

2. Ad secundum dicendum quod, sicut supra dictum est,[10] prudentiæ directe opponitur astutia ad quam pertinet adinvenire quasdam vias apparentes et non existentes ad propositum consequendum. Executio autem astutiæ est proprie per dolum in verbis, per fraudem autem in factis. Et sicut astutia se habet ad prudentiam, ita dolus et fraus ad simplicitatem. Dolus autem vel fraus ordinatur ad decipiendum principaliter et quandoque secundario ad nocendum. Unde ad simplicitatem pertinet directe se præservare a deceptione; et secundum hoc, ut supra dictum est,[11] virtus simplicitatis est eadem virtuti veritatis, sed differt sola ratione, quia veritas dicitur secundum quod signa concordant signatis; simplicitas autem dicitur secundum quod non tendit in diversa, ut scilicet aliud intendat interius et aliud prætendat exterius.

3. Ad tertium dicendum quod lucrum vel gloria est finis remotus simulatoris sicut et mendacis. Unde ex hoc fine speciem non sortitur, sed ex fine proximo, qui est ostendere se alium quam sit. Unde quandoque contingit quod aliquis fingit de se magna nullius alterius gratia sed sola libidine simulandi, sicut Philosophus dicit in *Ethic.*[12] et sicut etiam supra de mendacio dictum est.[13]

articulus 4. utrum hypocrisis semper sit peccatum mortale

AD QUARTUM sic proceditur:[1] 1. Videtur quod hypocrisis semper sit peccatum mortale. Dicit enim Hieronymus, *Isa.*,[2] in *Glossa* quod *in comparatione duorum malorum levius est aperte peccare quam sanctitatem simulare.*[3] Et super illud *Job., Sicut autem Domino placuit,* etc.,[4] *Glossa* dicit quod *simulata æquitas non est æquitas, sed duplex peccatum*[5] et super illud *Thren., Major effecta est iniquitas populi mei peccato Sodomorum,*[6] dicit *Glossa, Scelera animæ planguntur, quæ in hypocrisim labitur, cujus major est iniquitas peccato Sodomorum.*[7] Peccata autem Sodomorum sunt peccata mortalia. Ergo et hypocrisis semper est peccatum mortale.

2. Præterea, Gregorius dicit *Moral.*,[8] quod hypocritæ ex malitia peccant. Sed hoc est gravissimum, quia pertinet ad peccatum in Spiritum Sanctum. Ergo hypocrita semper mortaliter peccat.

3. Præterea, nullus meretur iram Dei et exclusionem a Dei visione nisi propter peccatum mortale. Sed per hypocrisim aliquis meretur iram Dei, secundum istud *Job, Simulatores et callidi provocant iram Dei.*[9]

---

[10]2a2æ. 55, 3
[11]109, 2 ad 4
[12]*Ethics* IV, 7. 1127b9
[13]110, 2
[1]cf IV *Sent.* 16, 4, 1, iii
[2]*Isaiah* 16, 14

2. As noted earlier,[10] there is direct opposition to prudence in craftiness with its capacity for devising specious, not genuine ways of achieving a goal. The carrying out of this craftiness comes about, strictly speaking, in speech by guile, in act by fraud. As craftiness is related to prudence, so guile and fraud to simplicity. They have deception as their principal end; injury, occasionally as a secondary end. Hence to guard against being deceitful is the direct concern of simplicity; this is why, as noted earlier,[11] simplicity in reality is the same virtue as truth, with just this nuance in their meanings: truth connotes agreement of sign with thing signified; simplicity connotes straightforwardness, i.e. that it does not intend one thing inwardly and outwardly make a pretence of something else.

3. Gain and glory are ulterior motives for the deceiver just as they are for the liar and as such do not cause the species of the act; the immediate end does, namely to present oneself as other than one is. This is why it may well happen that someone creates fantasies about himself with no other purpose than the sheer pleasure of deceiving, as Aristotle notes,[12] and as has already been pointed out in connection with lying.[13]

article 4. *whether hypocrisy is always a mortal sin*

THE FOURTH POINT:[1] 1. Hypocrisy seems to be a mortal sin in every case. From Jerome on *Isaiah*,[2] the *Gloss* notes, *Comparing the two evils, it is less serious to sin openly than to pretend virtue.*[3] The *Gloss* on *Job, As it hath pleased the Lord*, etc.,[4] notes, *Counterfeit goodness is not goodness at all but a double sin.*[5] The *Gloss* on *Lamentations, The iniquity of my people is made greater than the sin of Sodom*,[6] notes, *His lament is for the sins of the soul of the hypocrite, which are graver in their wickedness than those of Sodom.*[7] Since the sins of Sodom are mortal, so then is every sin of hypocrisy.

2. Further, Gregory maintains[8] that hypocrites sin out of malice, and malice, as a sin against the Holy Spirit, is the worst kind of sin. The hypocrite, then, always sins mortally.

3. Further, no one deserves the wrath of God and exclusion from the vision of God except for mortal sin. Now by hypocrisy one merits both; the first because *dissemblers and crafty men prove the wrath of God*;[9] the

---

[3] *Ordinaria*; from Jerome, *In Isaiam* VI, on 16, 14. PL 24, 248
[4] *Job* 1, 21
[5] *Ordinaria* on *Col.* 3, 23; *Glossa Lombardi*. PL 192, 285
[6] *Lamentations* 4, 6
[7] *Ordinaria*
[8] *Moral.* XXXI, 13. PL 76, 587
[9] *Job* 36, 13

Excluditur etiam hypocrita a visione Dei, secundum illud *Job, Non veniet in conspectu ejus omnis hypocrita*.[10] Ergo hypocrisis semper est peccatum mortale.

Sed contra est quod hypocrisis est mendacium operis, cum sit simulatio quædam. Non autem omne mendacium oris* est peccatum mortale. Ergo nec omnis hypocrisis.
2. Præterea, intentio hypocritæ est ad hoc quod videatur bonus. Sed hoc non opponitur caritati. Ergo hypocrisis non est secundum se peccatum mortale.
3. Præterea, hypocrisis nascitur ex inani gloria, ut Gregorius dicit.[11] Sed inanis gloria non semper est peccatum mortale. Ergo nec hypocrisis.

RESPONSIO: Dicendum quod in hypocrisi duo sunt, scilicet defectus sanctitatis et simulatio ipsius. Si ergo hypocrita dicatur ille cujus intentio fertur ad utrumque, ut scilicet aliquis non curet sanctitatem habere sed solum sanctus apparere, sicut consuevit accipi in Sacra Scriptura, sic manifestum est quod est peccatum mortale; nullus enim totaliter privatur sanctitate nisi per peccatum mortale.

Si autem dicatur hypocrita ille qui intendit simulare sanctitatem, a qua deficit per peccatum mortale, tunc quamvis sit in peccato mortali, ex quo privatur sanctitate, non tamen semper ipsa simulatio est ei peccatum mortale, sed quandoque veniale.

Quod discernendum est ex fine. Qui si repugnat caritati Dei vel proximi, erit peccatum mortale; puta cum simulat sanctitatem ut falsam doctrinam disseminet; vel ut adipiscatur ecclesiasticam dignitatem indignus vel quæcumque alia temporalia bona in quibus finem constituit.

Si vero finis intentus non repugnet caritati erit peccatum veniale, puta cum aliquis in ipsa fictione delectatur; de quo dicitur *Ethic.* quod *magis videtur vanus quam malus*.[12] Eadem enim ratio est de mendacio et simulatione.

---

*Piana: *operis*, work
[10]*Job* 13, 16
[11]*Moral.* xxxi, 45. PL 76, 621
[12]*Ethics* IV, 7. 1127b11
[a]Occasionally in the Summa several arguments *sed contra* are given; it is the usual procedure in the *Quæstiones Disputatæ*. The use here is a reminder of the structure of the article as it reflects the Scholastic method, and of the significance of the argument *sed contra* as a position alternative to the first set of arguments (objections), not primarily an 'argument from authority' in line with the Reply. See Vol. 1 of this series, Appendix 1, T. Gilby. F. A. Blanche, 'Le Vocabulaire de l'argu-

second because *no hypocrite shall come before his presence*.¹⁰ Therefore hypocrisy is always mortal.

On the other hand: 1. Hypocrisy is a lie in action, since it is a form of deception. Not every lie in words is a mortal sin. Neither is hypocrisy.
 2. Further, it is the hypocrite's intention to be well thought of. This is not against charity. Therefore hypocrisy is not a sin mortal of its kind.
 3. Further Gregory has it¹¹ that hypocrisy is the offspring of vainglory. Vainglory is not itself always mortal; thus neither is hypocrisy.ᵃ

REPLY: There are two factors in hypocrisy, namely the absence of holiness and the pretence of its presence. If by a hypocrite we mean one whose intention is marked by the duplicity of having no regard for holiness while merely appearing to be holy—the usual usage in Scripture—then it is clearly a mortal sin. No one is totally lacking in holiness except by reason of mortal sin.ᵇ

If, however, we take a hypocrite to be one who intends to feign the holiness he lacks because of mortal sin, then even though he is in a state of mortal sin and so wanting in holiness, the deception itself is not always a mortal sin for him but at times is venial.

We should judge which of the two it is by the end involved.ᶜ When this is incompatible with charity towards God or neighbour, the sin will be mortalᵈ—when for example he puts on the guise of holiness in order to spread false teaching or to gain some ecclesiastical rank of which he is unworthy or any temporal advantage on which he settles as his final end.ᵉ

When the end intended is not contrary to charity, the sin will be venial— for example when someone simply finds delight in deceiving;ᶠ of such a person Aristotle says that *he seems empty-headed rather than wicked*.¹² The same criterion applies to deception as to lying.

---

mentation et la structure de l'article dans les ouvrages de Saint Thomas', *Revue des Sciences Philosophiques et Théologiques* XIV (1925) 167–87.
ᵇInfused virtue is meant here, the existence of which depends on the grace and charity lost by mortal sin; see 1a2æ. 63, 3; 88, 1 & 2; 110, 3 & 4; 2a2æ. 24, 11 & 12.
ᶜEnd here means an end intended over and above the objective of hypocrisy itself; a *finis operantis* or ulterior motive; see 1a2æ. 18, 6–9 and Vol. 18 of this series, Appendix 14, T. Gilby.
ᵈSee above 105, 1, note *c*.
ᵉSee 1a2æ. 71; 88, 2 & 4; adhering to any temporal good as ultimate is the constitutive of mortal sin.
ᶠOn the force of this, see 112, 1 ad 2 and note *a*.

Contingit tamen quandoque quod aliquid simulat perfectionem sanctitatis, quæ non est de salutis necessitate. Et talis simulatio nec semper est peccatum mortale, nec semper est cum peccato mortali.

Et per hoc patet responsio ad objecta.

---

gThe reference is to the holiness of a higher degree of charity, consisting in the practice of the evangelical counsels; see 1a2æ. 108, 4; 2a2æ. 27, 5; 184, 1-4.

DECEPTION AND HYPOCRISY

Note that there can also be a case of someone pretending that high degree of holiness which is beyond what is required for salvation.[g] This form of deception is neither always a mortal sin nor does it presuppose one.

From these considerations the response to both sets of arguments is evident.

DEINDE CONSIDERANDUM EST de jactantia et ironia quæ sunt partes mendacaii secundum Philosophum in *Ethic.*[1]

Quæstio 112. de jactantia

Primo autem circa jactantiam quæruntur duo:

1. cui virtuti opponatur;
2. utrum sit peccatum mortale.

articulus 1. *utrum jactantia opponatur virtuti veritatis*

AD PRIMUM sic proceditur:[2] 1. Videtur quod jactantia non opponatur virtuti veritatis. Veritati enim opponitur mendacium. Sed quandoque potest esse jactantia etiam sine mendacio, sicut cum aliquis suam excellentiam ostentat; dicitur enim *Esther* I, *Assuerus facit grande convivium ut ostenderet divitias gloriæ suæ ac regni sui ac magnitudinem atque jactantiam potentiæ suæ.*[3] Ergo jactantia non opponitur virtuti veritatis.

2. Præterea, jactantia ponitur a Gregorio *Moral.*[4] ung de quatuor speciebus superbiæ, cum scilicet quis jactat se habere quod non habet. Unde dicitur *Jer., Audivimus superbiam Moab superbus est valde, sublimitatem ejus et arrogantiam et superbiam et altitudinem cordis ejus. Ego scio, ait Dominus, jactantiam ejus et quod non sit juxta eam virtus ejus.*[5] Et Gregorius dicit quod *jactantia oriatur ex inani gloria.*[6] Superbia autem et inanis gloria opponuntur virtuti humilitatis. Ergo jactantia non opponitur veritati sed humilitati.

3. Præterea, jactantia ex divitiis causari videtur, unde dicitur *Sap., Quid nobis profuit superbia, aut divitiarum jactantia quid contulit nobis?*[7] Sed superfluitas divitiarum videtur pertinere ad peccatum avaritiæ, quod opponitur justitiæ vel liberalitati. Non ergo jactantia opponitur veritati.

SED CONTRA est quod Philosophus dicit in *Ethic.*[8] jactantiam opponi veritati.

RESPONSIO: Dicendum quod jactantia proprie importare videtur quod homo verbis se extollat; illa enim quæ vult homo longe jactare in altum elevat. Tunc autem proprie aliquis se extollit, quando de se supra se

---

[1] cf *Ethics* IV, 7. 1127a20
[2] *In Ethic.* IV, *lect.* 15
[3] *Esther* I, 3

NEXT WE EXAMINE boasting (112) and false modesty (113), parts of lying according to Aristotle.[1]

Question 112. boasting

First, in regard to boasting there are two points of inquiry:

1. on the virtue it is against;
2. whether it is a mortal sin.

article 1. whether boasting is opposed to the virtue of truth

THE FIRST POINT:[2] 1. Boasting does not seem to be against the virtue of truth. Lying is the opposite of truthfulness and boasting is possible without lying, as when someone draws attention to an excellence he really has; *Assuerus made a great feast that he might show the riches of the glory of his kingdom and the greatness and boasting of his power.*[3] Boasting, then, is not against truth.

2. Further, boasting is listed by Gregory[4] as one of the four species of pride, namely when a person lays claim to having what in fact he lacks. Thus we read, *We have heard the pride of Moab; he is exceeding proud; his haughtiness and his arrogancy and his pride and his loftiness of heart.*[5] Gregory also says that *boasting issues from vainglory.*[6] Yet pride and vainglory stand in opposition to humility and thus boasting is opposed, not to truth, but to humility.

3. Further, riches seem to give rise to boasting; *What hath pride profited us? or what advantage hath the boasting of riches brought us?*[7] Excessive wealth, however, seems to be connected with the sin of greed that is contrary to justice or liberality. So boasting is not against truth.

ON THE OTHER HAND, Aristotle in the *Ethics*[8] opposes boasting to truth.

REPLY: In its proper sense boasting (*jactantia*) denotes a person's raising himself high with words, for things that are to be thrown (*jactare*) far are lofted. Strictly speaking someone raises himself on high when he says that he is more than he is. This happens in two ways. Sometimes a person

---

[4] *Moral.* XXIII, 6. PL 76, 258
[5] *Jeremiah* 48, 29
[6] *Moral.* XXXI, 45. PL 76, 621
[7] *Wisdom* 5, 8
[8] *Ethics* II, 7. 1108a21. IV, 7. 1127a21; a23

aliquid dicit. Quod quidem contingit dupliciter. Quandoque enim aliquis loquitur de se, non quidem supra id quod in se est, sed supra id quod de eo homines opinantur. Quod Apostolus refugiens dicit II *ad Cor.*, *Parco, ne quis existimet me supra id quod videt in me, aut audit aliquid ex me*.[9] Alio modo aliquis per verba se extollit, loquens de se supra id quod in se est secundum rei veritatem.

Et quia magis est aliquid judicandum secundum quod in se est quam secundum quod est in opinione aliorum, inde est quod magis proprie dicitur jactantia quando aliquis effert se supra id quod in ipso est quam quando effert se supra id quod est in opinione aliorum; quamvis utroque modo jactantia dici possit. Et ideo jactantia proprie dicta opponitur veritati per modum excessus.

1. Ad primum ergo dicendum quod ratio illa procedit de jactantia secundum quod excedit opinionem.

2. Ad secundum dicendum quod jactantiæ peccatum considerari potest dupliciter; uno modo secundum speciem actus et sic opponitur veritati, ut dictum est.[10] Alio modo secundum causam suam, ex qua etsi non semper, tamen frequentius accidit. Et sic procedit quidem ex superbia sicut ex causa interius motiva et impellente. Ex hoc enim quod aliquis interius per arrogantiam supra seipsum elevatur sequitur plerumque quod exterius majora quædam de se jactet, licet quandoque non ex arrogantia sed ex quadam vanitate aliquis ad jactantiam procedat et in hoc delectetur, quia talis est secundum habitum.

Et ideo arrogantia, per quam aliquis supra seipsum extollitur, est species superbiæ; non tamen est idem jactantiæ sed ut frequentius ejus causa. Et propter hoc Gregorius jactantiam ponit inter superbiæ species. Tendit autem jactator plerumque ad hoc quod gloriam consequatur per suam jactantiam; et ideo secundum Gregorium ex inani gloria oritur secundum rationem finis.

3. Ad tertium dicendum quod opulentia etiam jactantiam causat dupliciter. Uno modo occasionaliter, inquantum de divitiis aliquis superbit, unde et signanter *Prov. opes* dicuntur *superbæ*.[11] Alio modo per modum finis, quia, ut dicitur in *Ethic.*,[12] aliqui seipsos jactant non solum propter gloriam sed etiam propter lucrum, qui de seipsis fingunt ea ex quibus lucrari possunt, puta quod sint medici, vel sapientes, vel divini.

---

[9] II *Corinthians* 12, 6
[10] In the Reply; 110, 2
[11] *Proverbs* 8, 18
[12] *Ethics* IV, 7. 1127b17

overdoes it in speaking about himself not in regard to what he really is but in regard to what others think him to be. St Paul, refusing to do even this, says, *I forbear, lest any man should think of me above that which he seeth in me, or anything he heareth of me.*[9] In a second way a person exalts himself in words by speaking of himself in a way that exceeds what is actual fact.

Since any matter should be judged as it is in itself not as it is in someone's opinion, it follows that the term boasting, even though it applies to both cases given, is more properly used of one who raises himself beyond what he really is rather than beyond what people think he is. On this basis boasting in its exact meaning is against truthfulness by way of excess.

Hence: 1. This argument uses boasting as it means excess in relation to the opinion people have.

2. We can view the sin of boasting in two ways and first from the standpoint of the kind of act it is. Herein lies its opposition to truthfulness, as has been determined.[10] Secondly, we may regard it in reference to the cause from which it issues, if not invariably, at least more often than not. This is the way it stems from pride as from a cause inwardly prompting and impelling. When because of arrogance a person inwardly has an excessive opinion of self, it often follows that outwardly he boasts of grand things about himself. Yet sometimes it is not from arrogance but from some other sort of vanity that a person resorts to boasting and finds delight in it, since he is vain by disposition.[a]

Consequently, arrogance, by which someone extols himself excessively, is a species of pride; it is not, however, identical with boasting but is quite often the cause. This is why Gregory lists it among the species of pride. Often, too, the boaster seeks to gain recognition through his bragging and this is why, following Gregory, it issues from vainglory, i.e. as from its end.

3. Great wealth is also a cause of boasting; in two ways. In the first as providing the occasion for it, someone being puffed up about his riches. Thus *riches* in *Proverbs* are pointedly described as *proud.*[11] Secondly, as a final cause, since, as it is put in the *Ethics*,[12] some boast, not for the sake of glory, but also for gain, passing themselves off in roles that can make them rich, as physicians, savants or seers, for example.

---

[a]*To every habit those things that are proper, i.e. connatural, are pleasurable. In Ethic.* III, *lect.* 10, n. 494. Ease and delight in operation form part of the Aristotelean theory of habits, whether virtues or vices, since a habit or firm disposition is the bent or training of a faculty towards a specific kind of operation. See 1a2æ. 49.

articulus 2. utrum jactantia sit peccatum mortale

AD SECUNDUM sic proceditur: 1. Videtur quod jactantia sit peccatum mortale. Dicitur enim *Prov.*, *Qui se jactat et dilatat, jurgia concitat.*[1] Sed concitare jurgia est peccatum mortale; *detestatur enim Deus eos qui seminant discordias*, ut habetur *Prov.*[2] Ergo jactantia est peccatum mortale.
 2. Præterea, omne quod prohibetur in lege Dei, est peccatum mortale. Sed super illud *Eccl.*, *Non te extollas in cogitatione animæ tuæ*,[3] dicit glossa, *Jactantiam et superbiam prohibet*.[4] Ergo jactantia est peccatum mortale.
 3. Præterea, jactantia est mendacium quoddam. Non est autem mendacium officiosum vel jocosum, quod patet ex fine mendacii, quia, ut Philosophus dicit in *Ethic.*, *jactator fingit de se majora existentibus, quandoque nullius gratia, quandoque gratia gloriæ vel honoris, quandoque autem gratia argenti*.[5] Et sic patet quod neque est mendacium jocosum neque officiosum; unde relinquitur quod semper sit perniciosum. Videtur ergo quod semper sit peccatum mortale.

SED CONTRA est quod *jactantia oritur ex inani gloria* secundum Gregorium.[6] Sed inanis gloria non semper est peccatum mortale, sed quandoque veniale, quod vitare est valde perfectorum. Dicit enim Gregorius quod *valde est perfectorum, sic ex ostenso opere auctoris gloriam quærere, ut de illata laude privata nesciant exultatione gaudere*.[7] Ergo jactantia non semper est peccatum mortale.

RESPONSIO: Dicendum quod, sicut supra dictum est,[8] peccatum mortale est quod caritati contrariatur, dupliciter ergo jactantia considerari potest. Uno modo secundum se prout est mendacium quoddam, et sic quandoque est peccatum mortale, quandoque veniale. Mortalequi dem quando aliquis jactanter de se profert quod est contra gloriam Dei, sicut ex persona regis Tyri dicitur *Ezech.*, *Elevatum est cor tuum, et dixisti: Deus ego sum*.[9] Vel etiam contra caritatem proximi, sicut cum aliquis jactando seipsum, prorumpit in contumelias aliorum, sicut habetur *Luc.* de Pharisæo, qui dicebat, *Non sum sicut cæteri hominum, raportes, injusti, adulteri, velut etiam hic publicanus*.[10] Quandoque vero est peccatum veniale, quando scilicet aliquis de se talia jactat quæ neque sunt contra Deum, neque contra proximum.
 Alio modo potest considerari secundum suam causam, scilicet superbiam vel appetitum lucri aut inanis gloriæ. Et sic si procedat ex superbia vel inani gloria, quæ sit peccatum mortale, etiam ipsa jactantia erit peccatum

---
[1] *Proverbs* 28, 25
[2] *Proverbs* 6, 16

article 2. whether boasting is a mortal sin

THE SECOND POINT: 1. The sin of boasting seems to be mortal. *He that boasteth and puffeth himself stirreth up quarrels.*[1] This is a mortal sin; *God hateth those that sow discord.*[2] Therefore boasting is a mortal sin.

2. Further, whatever is forbidden in God's law is a mortal sin. Now on the verse, *Extol not thyself in the thoughts of thy soul,*[3] a gloss comments, *This is proscribing boastfulness and pride.*[4] Therefore boasting is a mortal sin.

3. Further, a boast is a type of lie, but neither a useful nor a humorous one, as is clear from its purpose as a lie. *The boaster lays claim to more than he has at times for no special reason; at times for the sake of glory or honour; at times for money,* as Aristotle says.[5] Being neither a humorous nor a useful lie, it can obviously only be malicious and seems, therefore, always to be a mortal sin.

ON THE OTHER HAND, according to Gregory, *Boasting stems from vainglory,*[6] which is not always mortal, but sometimes venial, and avoiding it belongs to those far advanced in perfection. For *it belongs to the very perfect so to seek by outward deeds the glory of their divine author that they themselves are unable even to feel any personal gratification in praise offered.*[7] Boasting is therefore not always a mortal sin.

REPLY: Keeping in mind[8] that a mortal sin is one opposed to charity,[a] we can look at boasting in two ways. First in its own right as it is a type of lie, and from this standpoint it is sometimes mortal, sometimes venial. It is mortal when someone boastingly claims for himself something that runs contrary to God's glory—an example, spoken in the person of the king of Tyre, *Thy heart is lifted up and thou hast said; I am God.*[9] Or it can be something against love of neighbour, for example when someone spews out invective against another in order to brag about himself, as the Pharisee did: *I am not as the rest of men, extortioners, unjust, adulterers, as also is this publican.*[10] At times, however, the sin is venial, namely when someone boasts about things that are against neither God nor neighbour.

In another way boasting can be viewed from the standpoint of its cause, pride namely or the craving for money or vainglory. In this way if it issues from either a pride or a vainglory that is itself mortal, the boasting

---

[3]*Ecclesiasticus* 6, 2
[5]*Ethics* IV, 7. 1127b9
[7]ibid VIII, 48. PL 75, 853
[9]*Ezekiel* 28, 2
[a]See above 105, 1, note *c*.

[4]*Interlinear*
[6]*Moral.* XXXI, 45. PL 76, 621
[8]1a2æ. 72, 5; 2a2æ. 24, 12; 35, 3
[10]*Luke* 18, 11

mortale; alioquin erit peccatum veniale. Sed quandoque aliquis prorumpit in jactantiam propter appetitum lucri, et hoc videtur jam pertinere ad proximi deceptionem et damnum; et ideo talis jactantia magis est peccatum mortale. Unde et Philosophus dicit in *Ethic.*[11] quod turpior est qui se jactat causa lucri, quam qui se jactat causa gloriæ vel honoris. Non tamen semper est peccatum mortale, quia potest esse tale lucrum ex quo alius non damnificatur.

1. Ad primum ergo dicendum quod ille qui jactat se ad hoc quod jurgia concitet, peccat mortaliter. Sed quandoque contingit quod jactantia est causa jurgiorum non per se sed per accidens, unde ex hoc jactantia non est peccatum mortale.

2. Ad secundum dicendum quod glossa illa loquitur de jactantia secundum quod procedit ex superbia quæ est peccatum mortale.

3. Ad tertium dicendum quod non semper jactantia importat mendacium perniciosum, sed solum* quando est contra caritatem Dei aut proximi, aut secundum se aut secundum suam causam. Quod autem aliquis se jactet quasi ex hoc ipso delectatus est quoddam vanum, ut Philosophus dicit.[12] Unde reducitur ad mendacium jocosum, nisi forte hoc divinæ dilectioni præferret, ut propter hoc Dei præcepta contemneret. Sic enim esset contra caritatem Dei, in quo solo mens nostra debet quiescere sicut in ultimo fine. Videtur autem ad mendacium officiosum pertinere, cum aliquis ad hoc se jactat ut gloriam vel lucrum acquirat; dummodo hoc sit sine damno aliorum, quia hoc jam pertineret ad mendacium perniciosum.

---

*Piana: *sola*

will also be mortal; otherwise it will be venial. But sometimes a person comes out with a boast because of greed for money, and this would seem of itself to involve deception and damage to neighbour and so most of the time be mortally sinful. This is why Aristotle says[11] that the one who boasts for the sake of profit is more contemptible than one who does so for glory or honour. Note, however, that it is not always a mortal sin, because it is possible for the gain involved to be such as to be no great loss to anyone.

Hence: 1. One who boasts in order to incite strife sins mortally. Still it may happen that boasting is a cause of disputes not directly but indirectly, and then it is not a mortal sin.

2. This gloss is referring to boasting as the sequel of a pride that is forbidden and is a mortal sin.

3. A boast does not always imply a pernicious lie, but only when, either in itself or in its cause, it is against the love of God and neighbour. For someone to boast because he enjoys it is silliness, as Aristotle says,[12] and so amounts to a humorous lie, unless, of course, he should so place this above the love of God that for its sake he rejects God's commandments. Then the boasting would be against the love for God whereby our soul should rest in him alone as final end.[b] Only a lie of expediency would seem to be involved were someone to boast in order to gain glory or riches, provided there be no injury to others, because then the lie would be pernicious.

---

[11]*Ethics* IV, 7. 1127b12   [12]ibid b11
[b]See above III, 4 note *e*.

Quæstio 113. de ironia

DEINDE CONSIDERANDUM EST de ironia.
Circa quam quæruntur duo:
1. utrum ironia sit peccatum;
2. de comparatione ejus ad jactantiam.

articulus 1. utrum ironia per quam aliquis de se fingit minora sit peccatum

AD PRIMUM sic proceditur:[1] 1. Videtur quod ironia, per quam aliquis de se fingit minora, non sit peccatum. Nullum enim peccatum procedit ex divina confortatione; ex qua procedit quod aliquis de se minora dicat, secundum illud *Prov.*, *Visio quam locutus est vir cum quo est Deus, et qui Deo secum morante confortatus, ait: Stultissimus sum virorum*;[2] et *Amos* dicitur, *Respondit Amos, Non sum propheta.*[3] Ergo ironia, per quam aliquis minora de se dicit, non est peccatum.

2. Præterea, Gregorius dicit in epistola, *Bonarum mentium est suas ibi culpas agnoscere, ubi culpa non est.*[4] Sed omne peccatum repugnat bonitati mentis. Ergo ironia non est peccatum.

3. Præterea, fugere superbiam non est peccatum. Sed aliqui *minora de seipsis dicunt, fugientes tumidum*, ut Philosophus dicit in *Ethic.*[5] Ergo ironia non est peccatum.

SED CONTRA est quod Augustinus dicit, *Cum humilitatis causa mentiris, si non eras peccator antequam mentireris, mentiendo efficeris.*[6]

RESPONSIO: Dicendum quod hoc quod aliqui minora de se dicant potest contingere dupliciter. Uno modo salva veritate, dum scilicet majora quæ sunt in seipsis reticent, quædam vero minora detegunt et de se proferunt, quæ tamen in se esse recognoscunt, et sic minora de se dicere non pertinet ad ironiam; nec est peccatum secundum genus suum, nisi per alicujus circumstantiæ corruptionem.

---

[1] cf *In Ethic.* IV, *lect.* 15   [2]*Proverbs* 30, 1   [3]*Amos* 7, 14
[4]*Regist. epist.* 64, *Ad Augustinum episcopum Anglorum.* PL 77,1195; found also in Gratian, *Decretum* I, 5, 4
[5]*Ethics* IV, 7. 1127b22   [6]*Serm. ad pop.* CLXXXI, 4. PL 38, 981
[a]*ironia*, from ειρωνεία, a term attached particularly to Socrates' affectation of ignorance in his style of argument with the Sophists. (See also *Oxford English Dictionary* V: 484.) Aristotle uses the term in *Nicomachean Ethics* II, c. 7, 1108a22,

Question 113. false modesty

NEXT, FALSE MODESTY[a] is to be examined.
There are two points of inquiry.

1. whether it is sinful;
2. how it compares with boasting.

article 1. whether false modesty, by which a person belittles himself, is sinful

THE FIRST POINT:[1] 1. False modesty, by which a person makes little of himself, does not seem to be a sin. No sin can be the result of God's strengthening us, yet this has led people to belittle themselves—*The vision which the man spoke, with whom is God, and who being strengthened by God abiding with him, said, I am the most foolish of men*;[2] also, *Amos answered, I am not a prophet*.[3] False modesty is, therefore, no sin.

2. Further, Gregory states, *To acknowledge one's faults even where there may be no fault is a mark of goodness of heart*.[4] Since goodness of heart shuns all sin, false modesty is not a sin.

3. Further, to take flight from pride is no sin. But in the *Ethics* Aristotle says that some *avoid pride by playing themselves down*.[5] Hence this is not a sin.

ON THE OTHER HAND, Augustine says, *Should you lie to humble yourself, even were you not a sinner beforehand, you would become one by the lie*.[6]

REPLY: There are two possible ways for people to belittle themselves. In the first the truth is respected, i.e. they remain silent about outstanding qualities in themselves, but reveal and even assert characteristics that, while less impressive, are none the less true. This manner of understatement does not involve a self-disparagement sinful in kind; it may become sinful only where there is failure with regard to some circumstance.[b]

---

to describe a kind of mock modesty opposed to truth; also in IV, 3, 1124b30, in his well-known portrait of the magnanimous man, who will use this affected ignorance or modesty in his dealings with common people. The primary English use of the term irony for mild sarcasm does not convey the point of this Question, the morality of self-depreciation. Refer this Question back to 109, 4 and also to the consideration of humility, 2a2æ. 161.

[b]See 1a2æ. 18, 10; 72, 9 on the possibility of moral circumstances being the source of a specific good or evil in an action. Here the implication is that, for example, there are times when a person would be at fault for not bringing out the best about himself.

Alio modo aliquis dicit minora a veritate declinans, puta cum asserit de se aliquid vile quod in se non recognoscit aut cum negat de se aliquid magnum, quod tamen percipit in seipso esse. Et sic pertinet ad ironiam et est semper peccatum.

1. Ad primum ergo dicendum quod duplex est sapientia et duplex stultitita. Est enim quædam sapientia secundum Deum, quæ humanam vel mundanam stultitiam habet adjunctam, secundum illud 1 *Cor.*, *Si quis inter vos sapiens videtur esse in hoc sæculo, stultus fiat, ut sit sapiens.*[7] Alia vero est sapientia mundana, quæ, ut ibidem subditur, *stultitia est apud Deum.*[8] Ille ergo qui a Deo confortatur, confitetur se esse stultissimum secundum reputationem humanam, quia scilicet humana contemnit quæ hominum sapientia quærit. Unde et ibidem subditur, *Et sapientia hominum non est mecum;*[9] et postea subdit, *Et novi sanctorum scientiam.*[10]

Vel potest dici *sapientia hominum** quæ humana ratione acquiritur; *sapientia* vero *sanctorum* quæ ex divina inspiratione habetur.

Amos autem negavit se esse prophetam origine, quia scilicet non erat de genere prophetarum. Unde ibidem subdit, *Nec filius prophetæ.*[11]

2. Ad secundum dicendum quod ad bonitatem mentis pertinet ut homo ad justitiæ perfectionem tendat, et ideo in culpam reputat non solum si deficiat a communi justitia, quod vere culpa est, sed etiam si deficiat a justitiæ perfectione, quod quandoque culpa non est. Non autem culpam dicit quod pro culpa non recognoscit; quod ad ironiæ mendacium pertineret.

3. Ad tertium dicendum quod homo non debet unum peccatum facere ut aliud vitet, et ideo non debet mentiri qualitercumque ut vitet superbiam. Unde Augustinus dicit, *Non ita caveatur arrogantia, ut veritas relinquatur,*[12] et Gregorius dicit quod *incaute sunt humiles qui se mentiendo illaqueant.*[13]

articulus 2. utrum ironia sit minus peccatum quam jactantia

AD SECUNDUM sic proceditur:[1] 1. Videtur quod ironia non sit minus peccatum quam jactantia. Utrumque enim est peccatum, inquantum declinat a veritate, quæ æqualitas est quædam. Sed ab æqualitate non magis declinat qui excedit quam qui diminuit. Ergo ironia non est minus peccatum quam jactantia.

2. Præterea, secundum Philosophum[2] ironia quandoque est jactantia. Jactantia autem non est ironia. Ergo ironia non est minus peccatum quam jactantia.

---

*Leonine: *sapientia hominum esse quæ*
[7] 1 *Corinthians* 3, 18
[8] ibid. 19
[9] *Proverbs* 30, 2

Secondly, someone may belittle himself by turning from the truth, for example were he to allege something base about himself that he knows not to be true, or to deny outright some good quality he knows he possesses. This would be a case of the false modesty that is always a sin.

Hence: 1. There are two kinds of wisdom and two kinds of foolishness. There is a godly wisdom that has attached to it a human or worldly foolishness—*If any man among you seems to be wise, let him become a fool that he may be wise*.[7] There is another, a worldly wisdom, which, Paul adds, is *foolishness with God*.[8] Thus one who is strengthened by God professes himself to be an utter fool by human standards, because he spurns what the wisdom of men prizes. In this sense *Proverbs* continues, *the wisdom of men is not with me*,[9] and adds, and *I have known the science of the saints*.[10]

Note, however, that *human wisdom* may simply signify a wisdom acquired by man's reason; the *wisdom of the saints*, a wisdom possessed through divine inspiration.

Amos denied that he was a prophet by birth, not being of the race of prophets; hence the text goes on, *nor am I the son of a prophet*.[11]

2. Goodness of heart involves striving for perfect righteousness. Consequently, a person counts as fault not only failure in the righteousness required for all, which is truly sin, but also failure in the righteousness of perfection; this sometimes is not a sin. He does not, however, call sin something he does not regard as sin; this would be the lie of false modesty.

3. Since a person ought not to commit one sin in order to avoid another, he must not lie in any way in order to shun pride. Thus Augustine states, *Pride is not to be avoided in such a way that truth is abandoned*;[12] and Gregory, *It is a rash humility that entangles itself with lies*.[13]

article 2. whether false modesty is less sinful than boasting

THE SECOND POINT:[1] 1. False modesty would seem to be no less a sin than boasting. Each is a sin because a deviation from truth, which consists in exactness. Too much is not a greater departure from exactness than is too little. Therefore false modesty is not less sinful than boasting.

2. Further, Aristotle says[2] that sometimes false modesty is really a form of boasting; but the converse is not true. Therefore false modesty is not the lighter sin.

---

[10] ibid. 3. Text *I have not*
[11] *Amos* 7, 14
[12] *In Joann. Evang.* XLIII, on 8, 54. PL 35, 1712
[13] *Moral.* XXVI, 5. PL 76, 351
[1] cf *In Ethic.* IV, lect. 15
[2] *Ethics* IV, 7. 1127b22

3. Præterea, *Prov.*, *Quando submiserit vocem suam, ne credideris ei, quoniam septem nequitiæ sunt in corde illius.*[3] Sed submittere vocem pertinet ad ironiam. Ergo in ea est multiplex nequitia.

SED CONTRA est quod Philosophus dicit in *Ethic.* quod *irones et minus dicentes gratiores secundum mores videntur.*[4]

RESPONSIO: Dicendum quod, sicut dictum est,[5] unum mendacium est gravius altero. Quandoque quidem ex materia de qua est, sicut mendacium quod fit in doctrina religionis est gravissimum, quandoque autem ex motivo ad peccandum, sicut mendacium perniciosum est gravius quam officiosum vel jocosum. Ironia autem et jactantia circa idem mentiuntur vel verbis vel quibuscumque exterioribus signis, scilicet circa conditionem personæ; unde quantum ad hoc æqualia sunt. Sed ut plurimum jactantia ex turpiori motivo procedit, scilicet ex appetitu lucri vel honoris; Ironia vero ex hoc quod fugit, licet inordinate, per elationem aliis gravis esse. Et secundum hoc Philosophus dicit quod jactantia est gravius peccatum quam ironia.[6]

Contingit tamen quandoque quod aliquis minora de se fingit ex aliquo alio motivo, puta ad dolose decipiendum. Et tunc ironia est gravior.

1. Ad primum ergo dicendum quod ratio illa procedit de ironia et jactantia secundum quod mendacii gravitas consideratur ex seipso vel ex materia ejus. Sic enim dictum est quod æqualitatem habent.

2. Ad secundum dicendum quod duplex est excellentia: una quidem in temporalibus rebus, alia vero in spiritualibus. Contingit autem quandoque quod aliquis per verba exteriora vel signa prætendit quidem defectum in exterioribus rebus, puta per aliquam vestem abjectam aut per aliquid hujusmodi, et per hoc ipsum intendit ostendere aliquam excellentiam spiritualem; sicut Dominus de quibusdam dicit *Matt.* quod *exterminant facies suas, ut appareant hominibus jejunantes.*[7] Unde isti simul incurrunt vitium ironiæ et jactantiæ, tamen secundum hoc diversa, et propter hoc gravius peccant. Unde et Philosophus dicit in *Ethic., et superabundantia, et valde defectus jactantium est.*[8] Propter quod et de Augustino legitur[9] quod neque vestes nimis pretiosas neque nimis abjectas habere volebat, quia in utroque homines suam gloriam quærunt.

3. Ad tertium dicendum quod, sicut dicitur *Eccl.*, *Est qui nequiter se humiliat, et interiora ejus plena sunt dolo.*[10] Et secundum hoc Salomon loquitur de eo qui ex dolosa humilitate nequiter* vocem suam submittit.

---

*Leonine omits
[3]*Proverbs* 26, 25
[5]110, 2 & 4
[7]*Matthew* 6, 16

[4]*Ethics* IV, 7. 1127b22
[6]*Ethics* IV, 7. 1127a31; b32
[8]*Ethics* IV, 7. 1127b29

3. Further, *When he shall speak low, trust him not: because there are seven mischiefs in his heart.*[3] A mark of false modesty is speaking softly, and so it contains a manifold wickedness.

ON THE OTHER HAND, Aristotle says in the *Ethics* that *people who underrate and say less about themselves are regarded as having more pleasant manners.*[4]

REPLY: As already established,[5] one lie is more serious than another. Sometimes this is from its content, a lie in religious teaching being the gravest of all; sometimes, from the sinful motivation involved, the pernicious lie being more grievous than the useful or the humorous. Both false modesty and boasting, whether through actions or any outward signs, are lies about the same content, namely a person's qualities and so on this score are equal. Most of the time, however, boasting issues from a baser motive, the craving for money or honour. False modesty, on the other hand, is motivated by what it shuns, even though misguidedly, namely to be a bore to others by bragging. On this basis Aristotle states that boasting is a worse fault than false modesty.[6]

Of course it may happen that on occasion someone belittles himself for some other motive, for example to deceive by cunning. Then false modesty is more serious.

Hence: 1. This argument reasons about false modesty and boasting by regarding the gravity a lie has in itself, i.e. from its subject matter. We have concluded that on this score they are equal.

2. Excellence is of two kinds, the first in temporal, the second in spiritual matters. Occasionally there is a case of someone in word or deed affecting a lowly worldly status, by shabby attire for example, or something similar, intending thereby to vaunt some spiritual superiority; as our Lord says, *they disfigure their faces that they may appear unto men to fast.*[7] Thus in one and the same act but on different grounds they are guilty of both false modesty and boasting, and consequently sin the more gravely. In this sense Aristotle notes, *The mark of the boaster is either exaggeration or gross understatement.*[8] For this reason it is related of Augustine[9] that he never wanted clothes that were either too fine or too shabby, since people seek recognition through both kinds.

3. *Ecclesiasticus* says, *There is one that humbleth himself wickedly and his interior is full of deceit;*[10] and the words of Solomon cited refer to one who speaks in soft tones wickedly, out of a deceitful humility.

---

[9]From Possidus, *Vita Sancti Augustini*, 22. PL 32, 51. St Possidus, bishop of Calama in Numidia (d. c. 437), friend and disciple of Augustine; attached to his biography of Augustine was the important *Indiculus* of Augustine's writings.
[10]*Ecclesiasticus* 19, 23

DEINDE CONSIDERANDUM EST de amicitia, quæ affabilitas dicitur, et de ejus vitiis oppositis, quæ sunt adulatio et litigium.

Quæstio 114. de amicitia

Circa amicitiam autem seu affabilitatem quæruntur duo:
1. utrum sit specialis virtus;
2. utrum sit pars justitiæ.

articulus 1. *utrum amicitia sit specialis virtus*

AD PRIMUM sic proceditur:[1] 1. Videtur quod amicitia non sit specialis virtus. Dicit enim Philosophus *Ethic.* quod *amicitia perfecta est quæ est propter virtutem*.[2] Quælibet autem virtus est amicitiæ causa, quia *bonum omnibus est amabile*, ut Dionysius dicit.[3] Ergo amicitia non est specialis virtus, sed consequens omnem virtutem.

2. Præterea, Philosophus dicit in *Ethic.* quod *non in amando, vel inimicando recipit singula ut oportet*.[4] Sed quod aliquis signa amicitiæ ostendat ad eos quos non amat videtur pertinere ad simulationem, quæ repugnat virtuti. Ergo hujusmodi amicitia non est virtus.

3. Præterea, virtus *in medietate* constituitur prout sapiens determinabit*, sicut dicitur *Ethic.*[5] Sed *Eccli.* dicitur, *Cor sapientum ubi tristitia, et cor stultorum ubi lætitia*;[6] unde ad virtuosum† pertinet maxime a delectatione sibi cavere, ut dicitur in *Ethic.*[7] Hæc autem amicitia *per se quidem desiderat condelectare, contristare autem reveretur*, ut Philosophus dicit in *Ethic.*[8] Ergo hujusmodi amicitia non est virtus.

SED CONTRA, præcepta legis dantur de actibus virtutum. Sed *Eccli.* dicitur, *Congregationi pauperum affabilem te facito*.[9] Ergo affabilitas, quæ hic amicitia dicitur, est quædam specialis virtus.

---

*Piana: *immediate*, immediately, for *in medietate*
†Piana: *vitiosum*, the wicked
[1] cf *In Ethic.* IV, lect. 14
[2] *Ethics* VIII, 3. 1156b7
[3] *De div. nom.* 4. PG 3, 708
[4] *Ethics* IV, 6. 1126b23
[5] *Ethics* II, 6. 1106b36
[6] *Ecclesiastes* 7, 5
[7] *Ethics* II, 9. 1109b7
[8] *Ethics* IV, 6. 1127a2
[9] *Ecclesiasticus* 4, 7

FRIENDLINESS

NEXT WE TURN TO friendliness,[a] i.e. affability, and the vices against it, namely flattery (115) and quarrelling (116).

Question 114. friendliness

Regarding friendliness or affability there are two points of inquiry:
1. whether it is a specific virtue;
2. and a part of justice.

article 1. whether friendliness is a specific virtue

THE FIRST POINT:[1] 1. Friendliness does not seem to be a special virtue. In the *Ethics* Aristotle says, *Genuine friendship has virtue as its motive.*[2] But every virtue is a cause of friendship, since, as Denis says, *For everyone goodness is a cause of love.*[3] Friendship is not, therefore, a specific virtue but follows upon every virtue.

2. Further, Aristotle notes of the courteous man that *he accepts everything in good grace, whether from his friends or from others.*[4] Yet for anyone to show marks of friendship towards those for whom he has no liking would seem to involve deception, against truthfulness. This sort of friendliness, then, is no virtue at all.

3. Further, *virtue consists in a mean to be determined by the prudent man.*[5] Ecclesiastes says that *the heart of the wise is where there is mourning, and the heart of fools where there is mirth;*[6] hence it is the part of the virtuous man to be especially wary about pleasure.[7] As Aristotle says, however, *friendliness seeks above all to afford pleasure and shrinks from giving displeasure.*[8] Thus it is no virtue.

ON THE OTHER HAND, precepts of the Law are laid down about acts of virtue, and *Ecclesiasticus* says, *Make thyself affable to the congregation of the poor.*[9] Affability, termed here friendliness, is therefore one specific virtue.

---

[a]Art. 1 ad 1 should be read first for the sense in which *amicitia* is used here. In *Nicomachean Ethics* IV, 6, 1127a9, Aristotle remarks that the man who possesses this virtue has no special name. The middle state between obsequiousness and surliness is like what is meant by friendship, but without affection or passion towards those whom it regards. The virtue is concerned with maintaining a proper manner towards all in regard to the pleasant and the unpleasant in social contact simply out of propriety. It has tones of the courtesy, politeness, geniality, affability, even correct aloofness or disapproval that are called for by honourableness and ease in the civilized association of people. See also III *Sent.* 33, 3, 4, ii ad 2.

RESPONSIO: Dicendum quod, sicut dictum est[10], cum virtus ordinetur ad bonum, ubi occurrit specialis ratio boni, ibi oportet esse specialem rationem virtutis. Bonum autem in ordine consistit, sicut supra dictum est.[11] Oportet autem hominem convenienter ad alios homines ordinari in communi conversatione tam in factis quam in dictis, ut scilicet ad unumquemque se habeat secundum quod decet. Et ideo oportet esse quamdam specialem virtutem quæ hanc convenientiam ordinis observet. Et hæc vocatur amicitia sive affabilitas.

1. Ad primum ergo dicendum quod Philosophus in *Ethic.* de duplici amicitia loquitur. Quarum una consistit principaliter in affectu quo unus alium diligit,[12] et hæc potest consequi quamcumque virtutem; quæ autem ad hanc amicitiam pertinent, supra de caritate dicta sunt.[13] Aliam vero amicitiam ponit[14] quæ consistit in solis exterioribus verbis vel factis. Quæ quidem non habet perfectam rationem amicitæ sed quamdam ejus similitudinem, inquantum scilicet quis decenter habet se ad illos cum quibus conversatur.

2. Ad secundum dicendum quod omnis homo naturaliter omni homini est amicus quodam generali amore, sicut etiam dicitur *Eccli.* quod *omne animal diligit simile sibi.*[15] Et hunc amorem repræsentant signa amicitiæ, quæ quis exterius ostendit in verbis vel factis, etiam extraneis vel ignotis; unde non est ibi simulatio. Non enim ostendit eis signa perfectæ amicitiæ, quia non eodem modo se habet familiariter ad extraneos sicut ad eos qui sunt sibi speciali amicitia juncti.

3. Ad tertium dicendum quod cor sapientium dicitur esse ubi tristitia, non quidem ut ipse* proximo tristitiam inferat; dicit enim Apostolus *ad Rom., Si propter cibum frater tuus contristatur, jam non secundum caritatem ambulas;*[16] sed ut contristatis consolationem conferat, secundum illud *Eccl., Non desis plorantibus in consulatione, et cum lugentibus ambula.*[17] Cor autem stultorum est ubi lætitia, non quidem ut ipsi alios lætificent, sed ut ipsi aliorum lætitia perfruantur.

Pertinet ergo ad sapientem ut condelectationem afferat his cum quibus conversatur, non quidem lascivam quam virtus cavet, sed honestam, secundum illus *Ps., Ecce quam bonum et quam lugentibus jucundum habitare fratres in unum.*[18] Quandoque tamen propter aliquod bonum consequens vel propter aliquod malum excludendum, non refugiet virtuosus eos quibus convivit, contristare, ut Philosophus dicit in *Ethic.*[19] Unde et Apostolus dicit, *ad Cor., Si contristavi vos in epistola, non me pænitet*; et postea,

---

*Piana: *ipsi* for *ipse*
[10]109, 2
[11]ibid
[12]*Ethics*, VIII–IX
[13]2a2æ. 23, 1; 25–33
[14]*Ethics* IV, 6. 1126b17
[15]*Ecclesiasticus* 13, 19
[16]*Romans* 14, 15
[17]*Ecclesiasticus* 7, 38

REPLY: As noted earlier,[10] virtue having moral goodness as its end, there must be a specific form of virtue wherever a specific form of goodness is to be found. One quality of goodness, as noted before,[11] is right order. In their ordinary dealings with others, people ought to be agreeable both in word and in act, so that each one observes the decencies towards his fellow men. Therefore there is need of a specific virtue to maintain this propriety of order. Such a virtue is called friendliness or affability.

Hence: 1. In the *Ethics* Aristotle discusses two forms of *amicitia*. The first is chiefly a matter of interior sentiment by which one person loves another.[12] This can be the consequence of any virtue whatever; we have treated of its meaning in discussing charity.[13] But he points out as well another form of *amicitia*,[14] consisting solely in outward words or actions. This is not friendship in its proper sense, but has a resemblance to it in that a person acts with good manners towards those with whom he comes in contact.

2. By nature every man stands as friend to every other man with a kind of universal love; as *Ecclesiasticus* says, *Every beast loveth its kind*.[15] The marks of friendship shown outwardly in word and act towards strangers or people unknown express this sort of love; thus there is no deceit involved. Marks of a personal friendship are not shown, since we do not treat strangers with the same intimacy as those bound to us in personal friendship.[b]

3. The heart of the wise is said to be where there is mourning not in the sense that he brings sorrow to others—St Paul says, *If because of thy meat thy brother be grieved, thou walkest not now according to charity*;[16] but that he brings solace to those who grieve—*Be not wanting in comforting them that weep and walk with them that mourn*.[17] Nor is the heart of fools where there is mirth in the sense that they gladden others, but that they intrude on the joy belonging to others.

Consequently it is the part of the wise in regard to his associates to share not in dissolute pleasures, which virtue shuns, but in wholesome ones; *Behold how good and how pleasant it is for the brethren to dwell together in unity*.[18] Even so, at times, as Aristotle points out,[19] the virtuous man, in order either to achieve some good or to prevent some evil, will not shirk from giving pain to his associates; St Paul also remarks, *Although*

---

[18]*Psalm* 132, 1   [19]*Ethics* IV, 6. 1126b33
[b]The contrast of the universal yet personal relationship of charity to all men is noteworthy (see 2a2æ. 25, 1, 6, 8, 9); as is the impersonal quality of this virtue of friendliness. An interesting question proposes itself: is there in man's community of nature a foundation for a relationship among men that is analogous to that of charity? or is justice, which is not directly related to a person but to his rights, the only bond that could naturally relate every man to all men?

Gaudeo, non quia contristati estis, sed quia contristati estis ad pœnitentiam.[20] Et ideo his qui sunt proni ad peccandum, non debemus hilarem vultum ostendere ad eos delectandum, ne videamur eorum peccato consentire et quodammodo peccandi* audaciam ministrare. Unde dicitur *Eccli., Filiæ, tibi sunt? Serva corpus earum, et non ostendas hilarem faciem tuam ad illas.*[21]

articulus 2. *utrum hujusmodi amicitia sit pars justitiae*

AD SECUNDUM sic proceditur: 1. Videtur quod hujusmodi amicitia non sit pars justitiæ. Ad justitiam enim pertinet reddere debitum alteri. Sed hoc non pertinet ad hanc virtutem sed solum delectabiliter aliis convivere. Ergo hujusmodi virtus non est pars justitiæ.

2. Præterea, secundum Philosophum in *Ethic., hujusmodi virtus consistit circa delectationem vel tristitiam, quæ est in convictu.*[1] Sed moderari maximas delectationes pertinet ad temperantiam, ut supra habitum est.[2] Ergo hæc virtus est magis pars temperantiæ quam justitiæ.

3. Præterea, æqualia inæqualibus exhibere contra justitiam est, ut supra habitum est.[3] Sed sicut Philosophus dicit in *Ethic.*, hæc virtus *similiter ad notos, et ignotos, et consuetos et inconsuetos operatur.*[4] Ergo hæc virtus non est pars justitiæ sed magis ei contrariatur.

SED CONTRA est quod Macrobius ponit amicitiam partem justitiæ.[5]

RESPONSIO: Dicendum quod hæc virtus est pars justitiæ, inquantum adjungitur ei sicut principali virtuti. Convenit enim cum justitia in hoc quod ad alterum est, sicut et justitia. Deficit autem a ratione justitiæ, quia non habet plenam debiti rationem, prout aliquis alteri obligatur vel debito legali, ad cujus solutionem lex cogit, vel etiam aliquo debito proveniente ex aliquo beneficio suscepto. Sed solum attendit quoddam debitum honestatis, quod magis est ex parte ipsius virtuosi quam ex parte alterius, ut scilicet faciat alteri quod decet eum facere.

1. Ad primum ergo dicendum quod, sicut supra dictum est,[6] quia homo naturaliter est animal sociale, debet ex quadam honestate veritatis manifestationem aliis hominibus, sine qua societas hominum durare non posset. Sicut autem non posset homo vivere in societate sine veritate, ita nec sine

---

*Piana: *peccati* for *peccandi*
[20] II *Corinthians* 7, 8   [21]*Ecclesiasticus* 7, 26
[1]*Ethics* IV, 6. 1126b30
[2]1a2æ. 60, 5; 61, 3
[3]2a2æ. 61, 2
[4]*Ethics* IV, 6. 1126b25
[5]*Commentarius ex Cicerone in Somnum Scipionis* I, cf 8. Ambrosius Theodosius

I made you sad by my epistle, I do not repent; and further on, *I am glad not because you were made sorrowful, but because you were made sorrowful unto penance.*[20] The point is that we ought not show a smiling face towards those who are bent on sin, lest we appear to approve and in a sense embolden them. Wherefore, *Hast thou daughters? Have a care of their body and show not thy countenance gay towards them.*[21]

article 2. whether this sort of friendliness is a part of justice

THE SECOND POINT: 1. Friendliness of this sort does not seem to be a part of justice. While justice involves paying a debt to others, this virtue does not, but rather attends simply to getting along with others. Thus it is not a part of justice.

2. Further, in Aristotle's thought, *this virtue has its function with regard to the pleasures and pains of contact with other people.*[1] As noted before,[2] however, to control the most intense pleasures is the work of temperance. This virtue, then, is more a part of temperance than of justice.

3. Further, as established earlier,[3] to show equality where there is inequality is against justice. This virtue, as Aristotle describes it, *reacts without discrimination towards those known and those unknown, acquaintances and strangers.*[4] Instead, then, of being a part of justice, this virtue is its contrary.

ON THE OTHER HAND, Macrobius lists it as a part of justice.[5]

REPLY: This virtue is a part of justice in that it is allied to justice as to a principal virtue. The reason is that in common with justice it is between persons. Yet friendliness is not the equivalent of justice because its concern is not strict indebtedness, i.e. where one has an obligation to another based either on a legal debt, the payment of which is enforced by law, or even upon a debt stemming from favours received. Rather it sees to a kind of debt in decency, which has its binding power not so much from outside as from within the virtuous man himself, namely that he should act towards others as it befits him to act.

Hence: 1. As has been stated,[6] because man by nature is a social being, in common decency he owes plain truth to others, since without this human society could not survive. But even as men cannot live together without truthfulness, neither can they without agreeableness, since, as

---

Macrobius, a non-Christian Latin writer of the 4th century, anti-Aristotelean defender of Platonism. The work cited was a kind of encyclopedia; his principal work, *Saturnalia*, was also known to the medievals.
[6] 109, 3 ad 1

delectatione, quia, sicut Philosphus dicit in *Ethic.*, *nullus potest per diem morari cum tristi, nec cum non delectabili.*[7] Et ideo homo tenetur ex quodam naturali debito honestatis, ut aliis delectabiliter convivat; nisi propter aliquam causam necesse sit aliquando alios utiliter contristare.

2. Ad secundum dicendum quod ad temperantiam pertinet refrenare delectationes sensibiles. Sed hæc virtus consistit circa delectationes in convictu quæ ex ratione proveniunt, inquantum unus ad alterum decenter se habet; et has delectationes non oportet refrenare tanquam noxias.

3. Ad tertium dicendum quod verbum illud Philosophi non est intelligendum quod aliquis eodem modo debeat colloqui et convivere notis et ignotis, quia, ut ipse ibidem subdit, *non similiter convenit consuetos et extraneos curare, aut contristare.*[8] Sed in hoc attenditur similitudo quod ad omnes oportet facere quod decet.

---

[7] *Ethics* VIII. 5. 1157b15

Aristotle remarks, *No one can put up with the gloomy or disagreeable man all day long.*[7] Thus a person is bound by a certain natural debt in decency to get along amicably with others, except when for good cause there is need to be purposefully harsh.

2. It is the part of temperance to check the pleasures of sense. The virtue here in question addresses itself rather to social pleasantness, whereby one person behaves civilly towards others; social amenities derive from reason and there is no need to repress them as though perilous.

3. Aristotle's statement should not be taken to mean that a person must converse and deal with intimates and strangers indiscriminately, since he adds, *It is not proper to please or displease friends and strangers in the same way.*[8] What remains constant is the need to act with appropriate courtesy towards all.

---

[8]*Ethics* IV, 6. 1126b27

DEINDE CONSIDERANDUM EST de vitiis oppositis prædictæ virtuti. Et primo, de adulatione; secundo, de litigio.

Quæstio 115. de adulatione

Circa adulationem quæruntur duo:
  1. utrum adulatio sit peccatum;
  2. utrum sit peccatum mortale.

articulus 1. utrum adulatio sit peccatum

AD PRIMUM sic proceditur:[1] 1. Videtur quod adulatio non sit peccatum. Adulatio enim consistit in quodam sermone laudis alteri exhibito intentione placendi. Sed laudare aliquem non est malum, secundum illud *Prov.*, *Surrexerunt filii ejus, et beatissimam prædicaverunt, vir ejus et laudavit eam.*[2] Similiter etiam velle placere aliis non est malum, secundum illud 1 *Cor.*, *Per omnia omnibus placeo.*[3] Ergo adulatio non est peccatum.

2. Præterea, bono malum est contrarium, et similiter vituperium laudi. Sed vituperare malum non est peccatum. Ergo neque laudare bonum, quod videtur ad adulationem pertinere. Ergo adulatio non est peccatum.

3. Præterea, adulationi detractio contrariatur unde Gregorius dicit quod remedium contra adulationem est detractio. *Sciendum est*, inquit, *quod ne immoderatis laudibus elevemur, plerumque miro nostri rectoris moderamine detractionibus lacerari permittimur, ut quos vox laudantis elevat, lingua detrahentis humiliet.*[4] Sed detractio est malum, ut supra habitum est.[5] Ergo adulatio est bonum.

SED CONTRA est quod super illud *Ezech.*, *Væ qui consuunt pulvillos sub omni cubito manus*,[6] dicit glossa, *idest, suavem adulationem*.[7] Ergo adulatio est peccatum.

RESPONSIO: Dicendum quod, sicut supra dictum est,[8] amicitia prædicta vel affabilitas, etsi principaliter delectare intendat eos quibus convivit, tamen ubi necesse est propter aliquod bonum exequendum vel malum vitandum non veretur contristare. Si ergo aliquis in omnibus velit ad delectationem alteri loqui, excedit modum in delectando et ideo peccat per excessum. Et si quidem hoc faciat sola intentione delectandi, vocatur placidus, secundum Philosophum.[9] Si autem faciat hoc intentione alicujus lucri consequendi, vocatur blanditor sive adulator.

---

[1] cf *In Ethic.* IV, lect. 14   [2] *Proverbs* 31, 28   [3] 1 *Corinthians* 10, 33

NEXT, VICES AGAINST the virtue just discussed; first, flattery (115), then, quarrelling (116).

Question 115. flattery

There are two points of inquiry about flattery:

1. whether it is a sin;
2. and a mortal sin.

article 1. whether flattery is a sin

THE FIRST POINT:[1] 1. Flattery does not seem to be sinful. It means speech in praise of another with the intention of pleasing. Now to praise someone is no bad thing—*Her children rose up and called her blessed; her husband, and he praised her*;[2] nor is the wish to please—*I in all things please all men.*[3] Thus flattery is no sin.

2. Further, evil is the opposite of good, and similarly blame the opposite of praise. To blame evil is not a sin. Neither, then, is it a sin to praise good, and this is what flattery does. So it is no sin.

3. Further, because detraction is the opposite of flattery, Gregory calls the first a remedy against the second: *Observe that by the wondrous arrangements of God, we are often allowed to be lacerated by detractions lest we be puffed up by fulsome praise; so that when the voice of the flatterer puffs us up, the tongue of the detractor deflates us.*[4] Detraction being evil, as noted,[5] flattery must be good.

ON THE OTHER HAND, on the verse of *Ezekiel*, *Woe to them that sew cushions under every elbow*,[6] a gloss comments, i.e. *smooth flattery.*[7] Flattery is, therefore, sinful.

REPLY: As noted,[8] the friendliness or civility in question, while chiefly intent upon being agreeable towards associates, still does not shy away from giving pain when this is necessary to achieve some good or avert some evil. The implication is that when someone seeks in every situation to speak so as to please others, he goes too far in being agreeable and so sins by excess. When this is done with the single purpose of pleasing, he is called by Aristotle[9] an ingratiator; but when for the sake of some gain, a fawner or flatterer.

---

[4]*Moral.* XXII, 9. PL 76, 223 [5]2a2æ. 73, 2 [6]*Ezekiel* 13, 18
[7]*Interlinearic* [8]114, 1 ad 3 [9]*Ethics* IV, 6. 1127a7

Communiter tamen nomen adulationis attribui solet omnibus qui supra debitum modum virtutis volunt alios verbis vel factis delectare in communi conversatione.

1. Ad primum, ergo dicendum quod laudare aliquem contingit et bene et male, prout scilicet debitæ circumstantiæ vel servantur vel prætermittuntur. Si enim aliquis aliquem velit delectare laudando ut ex hoc eum consoletur ne in tribulationibus deficiat vel etiam ut in bono proficere studeat, aliis debitis circumstantiis observatis, pertinebit hoc ad prædictam virtutem amicitiæ. Pertinet autem ad adulationem, si quis velit aliquem laudare in quibus non est laudandus, quia forte mala sunt, secundum illud *Ps.*, *Laudatur peccator in desideriis animæ suæ*;[10] vel quia non sunt certa, secundum illud *Eccl.*, *Ante sermonem non laudes virum*;[11] et iterum *Eccl.*, *Non laudes virum in specie sua*;[12] vel etiam si timeri* possit ne humana laude ad inanem gloriam provocetur, unde dicitur *Eccli.*, *Ante mortem ne laudes hominem.*[13]

Similiter etiam velle placere hominibus propter caritatem nutriendam ut in ea homo spiritualiter proficere possit, laudabile est. Quod autem aliquis velit placere hominibus propter inanem gloriam vel propter lucrum vel etiam in malo, hoc esset peccatum secundum illud *Ps.*, *Deus dissipabit ossa eorum qui hominibus placent*;[14] et Apostolus dicit *Gal.*, *Si adhuc hominibus placerem, Christi servus non essem.*[15]

2. Ad secundum dicendum quod etiam vituperare malum, si non adhibeantur debitæ circumstantiæ, est vitiosum, et similiter laudare bonum.

3. Ad tertium dicendum quod nihil prohibet duo vitia esse contraria; et ideo sicut detractio est malum ita et adulatio, quæ contrariatur ei quantum ad ea quæ dicuntur, non autem directe quantum ad finem. Quia adulator quærit delectationem ejus cui adulatur; detractor autem non quærit ejus contristationem, cum aliquando occulte detrahat, sed magis quærit ejus infamiam.

articulus 2. utrum adulatio sit peccatum mortale

AD SECUNDUM sic proceditur:[1] 1. Videtur quod adulatio sit peccatum mortale. Quia secundum Augustinum in *Enchir.*, *malum dicitur, quid nocet.*[2] Sed adulatio maxime nocet, secundum illud *Ps.*, *Quoniam laudatur peccator in desideriis animæ suæ, et iniquus benedicitur; exacerbavit Dominum peccator.*[3] Et ideo Hieronymus dicit quod *nihil est quod tam facile corrumpat mentes hominum quam adulatio.*[4] Et super illud *Ps.*, *Convertantur statim erubescentes,*

---

*Piana: *timere* for *timeri*
[10]*Psalm* 9, 24   [11]*Ecclesiasticus* 27, 8   [12]*Ecclesiasticus* 11, 2

In its broadest sense, however, flattery is the term applied to all cases of wishing in one's daily contacts always to please in word or act without regard for the virtuous mean.

Hence: 1. Depending on whether the proper circumstances are observed or ignored, to praise someone can be good or bad. When a person seeks to gladden another by pleasing him in order to give comfort against failure in adversity, or to give heart for keeping on with some good work, then, all other circumstances being safeguarded, the act will be one of the virtue of friendliness. Flattery occurs when one wishes to praise another where no praise is called for: perhaps something evil is involved—*The sinner is praised in the desires of his heart*;[10] or something dubious—*Praise not a man before he speaketh*;[11] and *Praise not a man for his beauty*;[12] or there may be reason to fear that human praise will be an incitement to vanity—*Praise not any man before his death*.[13]

Equally, to be pleasant towards others in order to foster charity, i.e. that someone may make spiritual progress, is commendable. But for one to seek to please everyone for the sake of vainglory or gain or in some evil affair would be sinful; *God hath scattered the bones of them that please men*;[14] *If I yet pleased men, I should not be the servant of Christ*.[15]

2. To reproach someone evil when the proper circumstances are ignored is also a sin; and likewise to praise someone good.

3. There being nothing against two vices standing as contraries, flattery is an evil just as detraction is. Their opposition is in their content and not directly in their purpose. For the flatterer seeks to please the one he flatters; the detractor does not seek to affront, since he sometimes reviles behind the other's back, but rather to malign.[a]

article 2. whether flattery is a mortal sin

THE SECOND POINT:[1] 1. Apparently flattery is mortally sinful. According to Augustine, *a thing is evil because it is harmful*[2] and flattery is extremely harmful, *For the sinner is praised in the desires of his soul and the unjust man is blessed; the sinner hath provoked the Lord*.[3] Wherefore Jerome says of flattery, *Nothing so readily corrupts men's souls*;[4] and on the verse, *Let them be presently turned away blushing for shame that they say to me: 'Tis well,*

---

[13]ibid. 11, 30
[15]*Galatians* 1, 10
[1]cf *De malo* VII, 1 ad 11
[3]*Psalm* 9, 24
[4]*Ep.* 148, *Ad Celantiam matronam*. PL 22, 1212
[14]*Psalm* 52, 6
[2]*Enchir.* 12. PL 40, 237

[a]The distinctive marks of detraction are that it is secret, behind another's back, and that its purpose is to assail another's reputation; see 2a2æ. 73, 1.

*qui dicunt mihi euge, euge,*⁵ dicit *Glossa, Plus nocet lingua adulatoris quam gladius persecutoris.*⁶ Ergo adulatio est gravissimum peccatum.

2. Præterea, quicumque verbis nocet, non minus nocet sibi quam aliis; unde dicitur in *Ps., Gladius eorum intret in corda ipsorum.*⁷ Sed ille qui alteri adulatur, inducit eum ad peccandum mortaliter; unde super illud *Ps., Oleum peccatoris non impinguet caput meum,* dicit *Glossa, Falsa laus adulatoris mentes a rigore veritatis emollit ad noxia.*⁹ Ergo multo magis adulator in se mortaliter peccat.

3. Præterea, in *Decretis* scribitur, *Clericus qui adulationibus et proditionibus vacare deprehenditur, degradetur ab officio.*¹⁰ Sed talis pœna non infligitur nisi pro peccato mortali. Ergo adulatio est peccatum mortale.

SED CONTRA est quod Augustinus in *Serm. de purgat.* inter peccata minuta numerat, *si quis cuiquam majori personæ aut ex voluntate, aut ex necessitate adulari voluerit.*¹¹

RESPONSIO: Dicendum quod, sicut supra dictum est,¹² peccatum mortale est quod caritati contrariatur. Adulatio autem quandoque quidem caritati contrariatur, quandoque autem non.

Contrariatur siquidem caritati tripliciter. Uno modo ratione ipsius materiæ, puta cum aliquis laudat alicujus peccatum, hoc enim contrariatur dilectioni Dei, contra cujus justitiam homo loquitur, et contra dilectionem proximi, quem in peccato fovet. Unde est peccatum mortale, secundum illud *Isa., Væ qui dicitis malum bonum.*¹³

Alio modo ratione intentionis, puta cum quis alicui adulatur ad hoc quod fraudulenter ei noceat, vel corporaliter vel spiritualiter. Et hoc etiam est peccatum mortale, et de hoc habetur *Prov., Meliora sunt vulnera diligentis quam fraudulenta oscula odientis.*¹⁴

Tertio modo per occasionem, sicut cum laus adulatoris fit alteri occasio peccandi, etiam præter adulatoris intentionem. Et in hoc considerare oportet utrum sit occasio data vel accepta, et qualis ruina subsequatur; sicut potest patere ex his quæ supra de scandalo dicta sunt.¹⁵

Si autem aliquis ex sola aviditate delectandi alios, vel etiam ad evitandum aliquod malum vel consequendum aliquid in necessitate, alicui adulatus fuerit, non est contra caritatem. Unde non est peccatum mortale sed veniale.

1. Ad primum ergo dicendum quod auctoritates illæ loquuntur de

---

⁵*Psalm* 69, 4
⁶*Ordinaria; Lombardi.* PL 191, 644
⁷*Psalm* 36, 15
⁸*Psalm* 140, 5
⁹*Interlinear.; Lombardi.* PL 191, 1237

FLATTERY

'tis well,[5] the *Gloss* comments, *The tongue of the flatterer does more harm than the sword of the oppressor.*[6] Flattery is, therefore, a most serious sin.

2. Further, he who does harm by speech hurts himself no less than others; *Let their sword enter into their own hearts.*[7] What the flatterer does to another is to seduce him into mortal sin, so that on the Psalm, *Let not the oil of the sinner fatten on my head,*[8] a gloss notes, *The counterfeit praise of the flatterer softens the mind away from hard-headed truth and into harm.*[9] With all the more reason the flatterer's own sin is itself mortal.

3. Further, in the *Decretals* it is written, *A cleric who is found out in the practice of flattery and scheming is to be degraded,*[10] a penalty that is imposed only for a mortal sin. Hence flattery is a mortal sin.

ON THE OTHER HAND, among those he counts to be *slight sins*, Augustine lists *for someone to wish out of choice or necessity to flatter some more important person.*[11]

REPLY: As already determined,[12] a sin is mortal for being contrary to charity.[a] This flattery sometimes is, sometimes is not.

There are three ways in which it is against charity. First through its subject-matter, when, for example, someone praises another's sin. This is against both charity towards God—it amounts to contradicting his righteousness; and charity towards neighbour—it is encouraging his sin. Therefore it is mortally sinful; *Woe to you that call evil good.*[13]

Secondly, through intent, when, for example, one flatters in order to do harm to another deceitfully in body or in soul. This also is a mortal sin; *Better are the wounds of a friend than the deceitful kisses of an enemy.*[14]

Thirdly, in that the praise of the flatterer is an occasion of sin for another, even when this is not directly intended. In this case one must judge whether the occasion was given or taken, and what sort of downfall results, following the norms decided on in reference to scandal.[15]

However, it is not against charity if someone has flattered another out of a sheer passion to please or in order to avert some harm, or even, in case of need, to gain some advantage. Then it would not be a mortal sin, but venial.

Hence: 1. The texts cited[b] refer to the flatterer who praises another's

---

[10] Gratian, *Decretum* I, 46, 3
[11] *Sermones supposititii* 104. PL 39, 1946
[12] 1a2æ. 72, 5; 2a2æ. 24, 12; 35, 3
[13] *Isaiah* 5, 20   [14] *Proverbs* 27, 6
[15] 2a2æ. 43, 4
[a] See above 105, 1 note c.
[b] See 101, 4, note c, on *auctoritates*.

adulatore qui laudat peccatum alicujus. Talis enim adulatio dicitur plus nocere quam gladius persecutoris, quia in potioribus bonis nocet, scilicet in spiritualibus. Non autem nocet ita efficaciter, quia gladius persecutoris occidit effective quasi sufficiens causa mortis; nullus autem adulando potest esse alteri sufficiens causa peccandi, ut ex supra dictis patet.[16]

2. Ad secundum dicendum quod ratio illa procedit de eo qui adulatur intentione nocendi. Ille enim plus nocet sibi quam aliis, quia sibi nocet tanquam sufficiens causa peccandi, aliis autem occasionaliter tantum.

3. Ad tertium dicendum quod auctoritas illa loquitur de eo qui proditorie alteri adulatur ut eum decipiat.

---

[16] 1a2æ. 73, 8 ad 3; 75, 3; 80, 1; 2a2æ. 43, 1 ad 3

sin. This type of flattery is said to be more harmful than the sword of the oppressor because its harm is to more important goods, the spiritual.[c] Still its hurt is not so decisive; the sword of the oppressor kills outright as the sufficient cause of death; by flattery no one can be the sufficient cause of another's sin, as noted earlier.[16]

2. The argument applies to one flattering with the intent to do harm. He does hurt himself more than others, since he injures himself as the sufficient cause of his own sin; others, only as an occasion of sin.

3. The text refers to one who flatters another treacherously for the sake of deceiving.

---

[c]See 2a2æ. 73, 3.

Quæstio 116. de litigio

POSTEA CONSIDERANDUM EST de litigio. Et circa hoc quæruntur duo:
 1. utrum opponatur virtuti amicitiæ;
 2. de comparatione ejus ad adulationem.

articulus 1. *utrum litigium opponatur virtuti amicitiæ vel affabilitatis*

AD PRIMUM sic proceditur:[1] 1. Videtur quod litigium non opponatur virtuti amicitiæ vel affabilitatis. Litigium enim ad discordiam pertinere videtur, sicut et contentio. Sed discordia opponitur caritati, sicut dictum est.[2] Ergo et litigium.
 2. Præterea, *Prov.* dicitur, *Homo iracundus incendit litem.*[3] Sed iracundia opponitur mansuetudini. Ergo et lis sive litigium.
 3. Præterea, *Jac.* dicitur, *Unde bella et lites in vobis? Nonne ex concupiscentiis vestris, quæ militant in membris vestris?*[4] Sed sequi concupiscentias videtur opponi temperantiæ. Ergo videtur quod litigium non opponatur amicitiæ, sed temperantiæ.

SED CONTRA est quod Philosophus in *Ethic.*[5] litigium opponit amicitiæ.

RESPONSIO: Dicendum quod proprie litigium in verbis consistit, cum scilicet unus verbis alterius contradicit. In qua quidem contradictione duo possunt attendi. Quandoque enim contingit contradictio propter personam dicentis, cui contradicens consentire recusat propter defectum amoris animos unientis, et hoc videtur ad discordiam pertinere caritati contrariam.
 Quandoque vero contradictio oritur ratione personæ, quam aliquis contristare non veretur. Et sic fit litigium quod prædictæ amicitiæ vel affabilitati opponitur, ad quam pertinet delectabiliter aliis convivere. Unde Philosophus dicit in *Ethic.* quod illi *qui ad omnia contrariantur, causa ejus quod est contristare, neque quoscumque* curantes, discoli et litigiosi vocantur.*[6]
 1. Ad primum ergo dicendum quod contentio magis proprie pertinet ad contradictionem discordiæ; litigium autem ad contradictionem quæ fit intentione contristandi.

---

*Leonine: *quodcumque*, anything
[1] cf *In Ethic.* IV, lect. 14   [2] 2a2æ. 37, 1
[3] *Proverbs* 26, 21   [4] *James* 4, 1
[5] *Ethics* IV, 6. 1126b16   [6] *Ethics* IV, 6. 1126b14
[a] The distinction is somewhat tenuous. Quarrelsomeness is a disregard for good

Question 116. quarrelling

NEXT, QUARRELLING, UNDER two points of inquiry:
1. whether it is against friendliness;
2. how it compares with flattery.

article 1. whether quarrelling is against friendliness or affability

THE FIRST POINT:[1] 1. Quarrelling does not seem opposed to friendliness or affability. Like contentiousness it appears to be an aspect of discord, and since, as noted,[2] this is against charity, so is quarrelling.

2. Further, *an angry man stirs up strife*;[3] anger being against mildness, so is quarrelling.

3. Further, *From whence are wars and quarrels among you? Are they not hence, from your concupiscences which war in your members?*[4] Since obeying concupiscence seems to be against temperance, quarrelling seems not to be against friendliness, but against temperance.

ON THE OTHER HAND, Aristotle views quarrelsomeness as the opposite of friendliness.[5]

REPLY: In its strict sense quarrelling is verbal, i.e. someone contradicting the statement of another. In such contradicting there are two possibilities. Sometimes it is directed against the person of the one making the statement, the contradictor refusing to concur because of a lack of the love that should make men one in spirit. In this case discord, the opposite of charity, would seem to be involved.

Sometimes, however, the contradicting comes about because there is no hesitancy about being disagreeable to the person speaking.[a] This is the origin of quarrelling as it runs counter to the friendliness or affability that is concerned with agreeableness in human relations. Wherefore Aristotle states in the *Ethics*, *Those who, just to be disagreeable, speak against everything, with no regard for anyone, are called peevish*[b] *and quarrelsome*.[6]

Hence: 1. It is true that in a strict sense contentiousness enters into the contradiction characteristic of discord; quarrelling operates where the intent is to be disagreeable.

---

manners and because of this offends another person. The discord opposed to charity is directly intended as an affront to a person not loved by the love of charity.
[b]'peevish' for *discoli*, transliteration from δύσκολοι '*hard to satisfy with food; hard to please; fretful; peevish*'.

2. Ad secundum dicendum quod directa oppositio vitiorum ad virtutes non attenditur secundum causas, cum contingat unum vitium ex diversis causis oriri, sed attenditur secundum speciem actus. Licet autem quandoque litigium ex ira oriatur, potest tamen etiam ex multis aliis causis oriri. Unde non oportet quod directe opponatur mansuetudini.

3. Ad tertium dicendum quod Jacobus loquitur ibi de concupiscentia secundum quod est generale, malum ex quo omnia vitia oriuntur, prout dicit *Glossa ad Rom.*,[7] *Bona est lex, quæ dum concupiscentiam prohibet, omne malum prohibet.*[8]

articulus 2. utrum litigium sit gravius peccatum quam adulatio

AD SECUNDUM sic proceditur: 1. Videtur quod litigium sit minus peccatum quam contrarium vitium, scilicet placiditas vel adulatio. Quanto enim aliquod peccatum plus nocet, tanto pejus esse videtur. Sed adulatio plus nocet quam litigium; dicitur enim *Isa.*, *Popule meus, qui beatum te dicunt, ipsi te decipiunt, et viam gressuum tuorum dissipant.*[1] Ergo adulatio est gravius peccatum quam litigium.

2. Præterea, in adulatione videtur esse quædam dolositas, quia aliud adulator dicit ore aliud habet in corde. Litigiosus autem caret dolo, quia manifeste contradicit. Ille autem qui cum dolo peccat, turpior est, ut Philosophus dicit in *Ethic.*[2] Ergo gravius peccatum est adulatio quam litigium.

3. Præterea, verecundia est timor de turpi, ut patet per Philosophum in *Ethic.*[3] Sed magis verecundatur homo esse adulator quam litigiosus. Ergo litigium est minus peccatum quam adulatio.

SED CONTRA est quod tanto aliquod peccatum videtur esse gravius, quanto spirituali statui magis repugnat. Sed litigium magis repugnare videtur statui spirituali; dicitur enim I *Tim.* quod *oportet episcopum non litigiosum esse*;[4] et II *Tim.*, *Servum Domini non oportet litigare.*[5] Ergo litigium videtur esse gravius peccatum quam adulatio.

RESPONSIO: Dicendum quod de utroque istorum peccatorum loqui possumus dupliciter. Uno modo considerando speciem utriusque peccati, et secundum hoc tanto aliquod vitium est gravius quanto magis repugnat oppositæ virtuti. Virtus autem amicitiæ principalius tendit ad delectandum quam ad contristandum. Et ideo litigiosus, qui superabundat in contristando, gravius peccat quam placidus vel adulator, qui superabundat in delectando.

---

[7] *Romans* 7, 7

2. Since the one vice may issue from a variety of causes, you do not account for direct opposition between vices and virtues on the basis of their causes, but of the specific nature of their acts. Granted that quarrelling may at times spring from anger, it may derive as well from other causes. Hence its opposition to mildness need not be direct.

3. James is here using 'concupiscence' as a bent towards sin, the source of all vices, as *The Gloss* on *Romans*[7] says, *The Law is good, its prohibition of concupiscence applying to every kind of evil.*[8]

article 2. whether quarrelling is a sin more serious than flattery

THE SECOND POINT: 1. Quarrelling seems less serious than the contrary vice, compliancy or flattery. The more harmful a sin, the worse it is. Flattery, then, being more harmful than quarrelling—*O my people, they that call thee blessed, the same deceive thee and destroy the ways of thy steps*[1]— is a worse sin.

2. Further, flattery seems to be a form of deceit, the flatterer having one thing on his lips, another in his heart. The quarreller, on the other hand, is forthright in contradicting bluntly. Since Aristotle says[2] that to sin deceitfully is more base, flattery is a more serious sin than quarrelling.

3. Further, as is clear from Aristotle,[3] shame is a fear of anything base. People are more ashamed to appear as flatterers than as quarrellers, and so quarrelling is the lesser sin.

ON THE OTHER HAND, the more inconsistent a sin with one's spiritual station, the worse it seems. In view of the texts—*It behoveth a bishop to be not quarrelsome;*[4] and, *The servant of the Lord must not wrangle*[5]—quarrelling seems more inconsistent with some spiritual states, and thus a graver sin than flattery.

REPLY: We can discuss each of these sins from two standpoints, and first from their specific nature. On this basis one vice is worse than another when it goes more against the virtue both oppose. Friendliness is intent chiefly upon giving pleasure rather than on giving pain. Therefore quarrellers, whose excess is in disagreeableness, sin in a worse way than fawners or flatterers, who go too far in seeking to please.

---

[8]*Ordinaria; Lombardi.* PL 191, 1416
[1]*Isaiah* 3, 12
[2]*Ethics* VII, 6. 1149b13
[3]*Ethics* IV, 9. 1128b11; b22
[4]1 *Timothy* 3, 2
[5]II *Timothy* 2, 24

Alio modo possunt considerari secundum aliqua* exteriora motiva, et secundum hoc quandoque adulatio est gravior, puta quando intendit per deceptionem indebitum honorem vel lucrum acquirere. Quandoque vero litigium est gravius, puta quando homo intendit vel veritatem impugnare vel dicentem in contemptum adducere.

1. Ad primum ergo dicendum quod sicut adulator potest nocere occulte decipiendo, ita litigiosus potest interdum nocere manifeste impugnando. Gravius autem est, cæteris paribus, manifeste alicui nocere quasi per violentiam quam occulte. Unde rapina est gravius peccatum quam furtum, ut supra dictum est.[6]

2. Ad secundum dicendum quod non semper in actibus humanis illud est gravius quod est turpius. Decor enim hominis est ex ratione, et ideo turpiora sunt peccata carnalia, quibus caro dominatur rationi, quamvis peccata spiritualia sint graviora, quia procedunt ex majori contemptu. Similiter peccata quæ fiunt ex dolo sunt turpiora inquantum videntur ex quadam infirmitate procedere et ex quadam, falsitate rationis, cum tamen peccata manifesta quandoque sint ex majori contemptu. Et ideo adulatio, quasi cum dolo existens, videtur esse turpior, sed litigium, quasi ex majori contemptu procedens, videtur esse gravius.

3. Ad tertium dicendum quod, sicut dictum est[7] verecundia respicit turpitudinem peccati; unde non semper magis verecundatur homo de graviori peccato sed de magis turpi peccato. Et inde est quod magis verecundatur homo de adulatione quam de litigio, quamvis litigium sit gravius.

---

*Piana: omits *aliqua*
[6] 2a2æ. 66, 9

The two vices can also be viewed on the basis of their ulterior motives.[a] From this standpoint flattery is at times the worse, where, for example, there is intent to wheedle undeserved honour or profit through deception. At other times quarrelling is the worse, where, for example, the intent is to impugn the truth or to bring contempt on the person speaking.

Hence: 1. Just as flatterers can do harm by secretive deceit, so quarrellers can sometimes do harm by overt aggressiveness. Other things being equal, it is worse to do injury flagrantly as by violence than secretly; thus robbery is more serious than theft, as pointed out earlier.[6]

2. With human acts it is not always true that the more base is the more wicked. The noble in man is rooted in his intelligence and so the baser sins are those wherein the flesh gains mastery over reason. Sins of the spirit, however, are more grievous, issuing as they do from deeper malice. In a similar way sins committed out of deceit are the more base in that they seem to arise from a certain weakness and a distortion of reason; yet at times flagrant sins issue from a worse contempt. Consequently, flattery seems more vile as being linked with deceit, but quarrelling more serious as being prompted by greater contempt.

3. As noted earlier,[7] shame is a reaction to the baseness of a sin, so that a person is not always more ashamed of a more serious sin but of a more degrading one. For this reason there is a greater shame in regard to flattery than in regard to quarrelling, even though the second is the more serious.

---

[7] 1a2æ. 41, 4; ad 2 & ad 3; 42, 3 ad 4; see also 2a2æ. 144
[a] The meaning here again is end intended by the sinner, over and above the intrinsic meaning of the sin; see above 111, 4 note *c*.

DEINDE CONSIDERANDUM EST de liberalitate et vitiis oppositis, scilicet avaritia et prodigalitate.

Quæstio 117. de liberalitate

Circa liberalitatem autem quæruntur sex:

1. utrum liberalitas sit virtus;
2. quæ sit materia ejus;
3. de actu ipsius;
4. utrum magis ad eum dare quam accipere pertineat;
5. utrum liberalitas sit pars justitiæ;
6. de comparatione ejus ad alias virtutes.

articulus 1. *utrum liberalitas sit virtus*

AD PRIMUM sic proceditur:[1] 1. Videtur quod liberalitas non sit virtus. Nulla enim virtus contrariatur naturali inclinationi. Inclinatio autem naturalis est ad hoc ut aliquis plus sibi quam aliis provideat. Cujus contrarium pertinet ad liberalem, quia ut Philosophus dicit in *Ethic.*, *liberalis non est respicere ad seipsum, ita quod sibi minora derelinquit.*[2] Ergo liberalitas non est virtus.

2. Præterea, per divitias homo suam vitam sustentat; et ad felicitatem divitiæ organice deserviunt, ut dicitur in *Ethic.*[3] Cum ergo omnis virtus ordinetur ad felicitatem, videtur quod liberalis non sit virtuosus, de quo Philosophus dicit in *Ethic.* quod *non est acceptivus pecuniæ, neque custoditivus, sed emissivus.*[4]

3. Præterea, virtutes habent connexionem ad invicem. Sed liberalitas non videtur connexa aliis virtutibus. Multi enim sunt virtuosi qui non possunt esse liberales, quia non habent quod dent; multi etiam liberaliter dant vel expendunt, qui tamen alias sunt vitiosi. Ergo liberalitas non est virtus.

SED CONTRA est quod Ambrosius dicit quod *in Evangelio multas doctrinas accepimus justæ liberalitatis.*[5] Sed in Evangelio non docentur nisi ea quæ ad virtutem pertinent. Ergo liberalitas est virtus.

RESPONSIO: Dicendum quod, sicut Augustinus dicit, *bene uti his quibus male uti possumus, pertinet ad virtutem.*[6] Possumus autem bene et male uti

---

[1]*In Hebræos* 13, *lect.* 1
[3]ibid. I, 8. 1099b1
[2]*Ethics* IV, 1. 1120b5
[4]ibid. IV, 1. 1120b15

LIBERALITY

NEXT WE DISCUSS liberality and the opposed vices, avarice (118) and prodigality (119).

Question 117. liberality

There are six points of inquiry about liberality:

1. whether it is a virtue;
2. its objective;
3. its act;
4. whether the generous man is more intent on giving than on receiving;
5. whether liberality is a part of justice;
6. how it compares with other virtues.

article 1. whether liberality is a virtue

THE FIRST POINT:[1] 1. Liberality does not seem to be a virtue. No virtue is at cross-purposes with the bent of nature, and the inclination of nature is to take care of self before others. Yet being generous involves the opposite, as Aristotle notes—*to be unselfish even to the point of giving himself the worst of it is characteristic of the generous man.*[2] Consequently, liberality is not a virtue.

2. Further, money is the means of maintaining one's life and is even instrumental in the pursuit of happiness, as Aristotle indicates.[3] Since the set purpose of every virtue is happiness, the generous man seem unvirtuous in that *he is not interested in acquiring or holding on to money, but in giving it away,* according to Aristotle.[4]

3. Further, while the virtues are interconnected, liberality seems to have no connexion with virtues. Many virtuous people cannot be generous, having nothing to give; many who otherwise are wicked give or spend lavishly. Liberality, then, is not a virtue.

ON THE OTHER HAND, Ambrose writes, *In the Gospel we receive many instructions about a just generosity.*[5] The Gospel teaches only what is in the interest of virtue. Therefore, liberality is a virtue.

REPLY: As Augustine says, *The part of virtue is to use well those things we could use badly.*[6] We have the capacity to use well or badly not only what is

---

[5]*De offic.* I, 30. PL 16, 70
[6]*De lib. arbit.* II, 19. PL 32, 1268

non solum his quæ intra nos sunt, puta potentiis et passionibus animæ, sed etiam his quæ extra nos sunt, scilicet rebus hujus mundi concessis nobis ad sustentationem vitæ. Et ideo cum bene uti his rebus pertineat ad liberalitatem, consequens est quod liberalitas virtus sit.

1. Ad primum ergo dicendum quod, sicut Ambrosius[7] et Basilius[8] dicunt, superabundantia divitiarum datur aliquibus a Deo, ut meritum bonæ dispensationis acquirant. Pauca autem uni sufficiunt. Et ideo liberalis plura laudabiliter in alios expendit quam in seipsum. Debet autem homo semper magis sibi providere in spiritualibus bonis, in quibus unusquisque sibi præcipue subvenire potest. Et tamen etiam in rebus temporalibus non pertinet ad liberalem ut sic aliis intendat, quod omnino se et suos despiciat. Unde Ambrosius dicit, *Est illa probanda liberalitas, ut proximos seminis tui non despicias, si egere cognoscas*.[9]

2. Ad secundum dicendum quod ad liberalem non pertinet sic divitias emittere ut non sibi remaneat unde sustentetur et unde virtutis opera exequatur, quibus ad felicitatem pervenitur. Unde Philosophus dicit in *Ethic.* quod *liberalis non negligit propria, volens per hoc quibusdam sufficere*.[10] Et Ambrosius dicit *Offic.* quod *Dominus non vult simul effundi opes, sed dispensari; nisi forte ut Elisæus, qui boves suos occidit et pavit pauperes ex eo quod habuit, ut nulla cura teneretur domestias*;[11] quod pertinet ad statum perfectionis spiritualis vitæ, de quo infra dicetur.[12]

Est tamen sciendum quod hoc ipsum quod est sua liberaliter largiri, inquantum est actus virtutis ad beatitudinem ordinatur.

3. Ad tertium dicendum quod, sicut Philosophus dicit in *Ethic.*,[13] illi qui consumunt multas res in intemperantiis, non sunt liberales, sed prodigi. Et similiter quicumque effundit quæ habet, propter quæcumque alia peccata. Unde et Ambrosius dicit, *Si adjuves eum qui possessiones aliorum eripere conatur, non probatur largitas. Nec illa perfecta est liberalitas, si jactantiæ causa magis quam misericordiæ largiaris*.[14] Et ideo illi qui carent aliis virtutibus, licet in aliqua mala opera multa expendant, non sunt liberales.

Nihil etiam prohibet aliquos multa in bonos usus expendere, et habitum liberalitatis non habere; sicut et aliarum virtutum opera faciunt homines, antequam habitum virtutis habeant, licet non eodem modo quo virtuosi, ut supra dictum est.[15]

Similiter etiam nihil prohibet aliquos virtuosos, licet sint pauperes, esse

---

[7] *Serm.* 81. PL 17, 613–14
[8] *On Luke* 12, 18. Homil. 6. PG 31, 263 & 275. St Basil the Great (*c.* 330–379), one of the Cappadocian Fathers, bishop of Cæsarea, opponent of Arianism; some of his homilies were known in the West from the translations of Rufinus (*c.* 345–410).
[9] *De offic.* I, 30. PL 16, 72
[10] *Ethics* IV, 1. 1120b2

within ourselves, the powers and emotions of the soul, for example, but also what is outside of ourselves, the creatures of this world given us to maintain life. Because its concern is their good use, liberality is a virtue.

Hence: 1. As Ambrose[7] and Basil[8] say, a surplus of wealth is granted to some people by God so that they may gain the merit of good stewardship. Accordingly, since one person can get along on little, the generous man commendably spends more on others than on self. A person's obligation to take better care of self than of others applies to his spiritual well-being, wherein it is possible for every man to show the main concern for himself. Still, even in regard to temporalities it is no part of generosity for someone to be so solicitous of others as to have no regard at all for self or family. Hence Ambrose, *Generosity is commendable as long as you do not neglect your own kin, should you know they are in want.*[9]

2. It is not the mark of the generous man so to dispose of his funds that he is without the means of livelihood or of a life of virtuous deeds leading to happiness. This is why Aristotle notes, *In the desire to help others the generous man does not neglect his own interests.*[10] Ambrose writes, *Our Lord does not want a person to pour out his riches all at once, but to distribute them sensibly, unless perhaps like Elisha he slay his ox and feed the poor from the proceeds, in order to be free of domestic cares,*[11] but this has reference to the state of perfection in the spiritual life, about which later.[12]

Note, however, that a generous distribution of possessions, being itself an act of virtue, does have final happiness as its purpose.

3. As Aristotle notes,[13] those who squander great sums in dissipation are not generous but wasteful, and the same can be said of anyone who uses up his resources for any other sinful purpose. Thus Ambrose says, *If you assist someone seeking to rob others of their possessions you are not to be saluted as big-hearted. Neither is it genuine generosity to be open-handed not in order to show mercy, but to show off.*[14] The point is that those we find lacking in other virtues are not really generous either, even though they expend much in their evil-doing.

Again, there is nothing against some people laying out great sums for good purposes and yet lacking the virtuous disposition of liberality; this coincides with other cases, noted earlier,[15] where people, before possessing the virtuous habit, perform the works of other virtues, but not in the same way as the virtuous do.

Also, there is nothing against some virtuous people being generous even

---

[11]*De offic.* I, 30. PL 16, 72
[12]2a2æ. 184-9
[13]*Ethics* IV, 1. 1121b8
[14]*De offic.* I, 30. PL 16, 71
[15]2a2æ. 32, 1 ad 1

liberales. Unde Philosophus dicit in *Ethic.*, *Secundum substantiam*, idest facultatem divitiarum, *liberalitas dicitur; non enim consistit in multitudine datorum, sed in dantis habitu*.[16] Et Ambrosius dicit quod *affectus divitem collationem aut pauperem facit, et pretium rebus imponit*.[17]

articulus 2. *utrum liberalitas sit circa pecunias*

AD SECUNDUM sic proceditur:[1] 1. Videtur quod liberalitas non sit circa pecunias. Omnis enim virtus moralis est circa operationes vel passiones. Esse autem circa operationes est proprium justitiæ, ut dicitur in *Ethic.*[2] Ergo cum liberalitas sit virtus moralis, videtur quod sit circa passiones et non circa pecunias.

2. Præterea, ad liberalem pertinet quarumcumque divitiarum usus. Sed divitiæ naturales sunt veriores quam divitiæ artificiales, quæ in pecuniis consistunt, ut patet per Philosophum in *Politic*.[3] Ergo liberalitas non est principaliter circa pecunias.

3. Præterea, diversarum virtutum diversæ sunt materiæ, quia habitus distinguuntur secundum objecta. Sed res exteriores sunt materia justitiæ distributivæ et commutativæ. Ergo non sunt materia liberalitatis.

SED CONTRA est quod Philosophus dicit in *Ethic.* quod *liberalitas videtur esse medietas quædam circa pecunias*.[4]

RESPONSIO: Dicendum quod secundum Philosophum in *Ethic.*[5] ad liberalem pertinet emissivum esse. Unde et alio nomine liberalitas largitas nominatur, quia quod largum est, non est retentivum sed est emissivum. Et ad hoc idem pertinere videtur etiam nomen liberalitatis, cum enim aliquis a se emittit, quodammodo illud a sua custodia et dominio liberat, et animum suum ab ejus affectu liberum esse ostendit.

Ea vero quæ emittenda sunt ab uno homine in alium sunt bona possessa, quæ nomine pecuniæ significantur, et ideo propria materia liberalitatis est pecunia.

1. Ad primum ergo dicendum quod, sicut dictum est,[6] liberalitas non attenditur in quantitate dati, sed in affectu dantis. Affectus autem dantis disponitur secundum passiones amoris et concupiscentiæ et per consequens

---

[16]*Ethics* IV, 1. 1120b7   [17]*De offic.* I, 30. PL 16, 72
[1]cf 2a2æ. 31, 1 ad 2; 58, 9 ad 2; 118, 3 ad 2; 134, 4 ad 1; *In Ethic.* IV, lect. 1; *De malo* XIII, 1
[2]*Ethics* V, 1. 1129a3   [3]*Politics* I, 3. 1256b30
[4]*Ethics* IV, 1. 1119b22   [5]*Ethics* IV, 1. 1120b15
[6]art. 1 ad 3
[a]*materia* and *objecta* are here translated by 'objective'. The matter of a virtue is that about which it is concerned, and the term of its act; but it is the formal reference

though they are poor. On this point Aristotle notes, *Generosity has its meaning by reference to a person's substance*, i.e. his means, *for it has its being not in the amount given but in the disposition of the giver.*[16] Ambrose observes, *The sentiment is what determines whether a gift is handsome or niggardly and gives the gift its value.*[17]

article 2. whether liberality is concerned with money

THE SECOND POINT:[1] 1. Liberality does not seem to be about money. The interest of any moral virtue is either actions or emotions. Since concern for outward actions is peculiar to justice, as Aristotle establishes,[2] emotions, not money, would seem to engage liberality as a moral virtue.

2. Further, the use of any sort of wealth is proper to the generous man and, as Aristotle makes plain,[3] natural wealth is more real than artificial wealth, i.e. money. Generosity, then, is not chiefly about money.

3. Further, since they are the bases for distinguishing habits, the objectives of diverse virtues are diverse. Material things are the objective of justice,[a] both distributive and commutative, and not, therefore, of liberality.

ON THE OTHER HAND, Aristotle declares, *Liberality seems to be a right mean in regard to money.*[4]

REPLY: Following Aristotle in IV *Ethics*,[5] it is the part of the generous man to be open-handed; another word for liberality is bountifulness, because the bountiful do not hold back but let go. The same point seems to be contained in the term 'liberality', since when someone lets something go, he liberates it, from his care and control, as it were, and shows that his spirit is free (*liberum*) from attachment to it.

Since things that are allowed to pass over from one person in favour of another are possessions, designated by the term 'money', money is the proper objective of liberality.

Hence: 1. As noted,[6] liberality is judged not in terms of the amount given, but of the giver's attitude. This in turn is conformed to the emotions of love and desire and consequently of pleasure or sorrow[b] with regard to

---

of the matter to the virtue (*formalis ratio objecti*) that makes it the objective motivating the specific act of the virtue. There can be an indication of a generic matter within which diverse formalities specify distinct virtues, as in the case of commutative and distributive justice. See 1a. 77, 3, 1a2æ. 54, 2; Vol. 18 of this series, T. Gilby, ed., Appendix 11.
[b]Pleasure and sadness are 'consequent' passions or emotions, presupposing a love and desire towards what is a good for the subject; see 1a2æ. 25.

delectationis et tristitiæ, ad ea quæ dantur. Et ideo immediata materia liberalitatis sunt interiores passiones, sed pecunia exterior est objectum ipsarum passionum.

2. Ad secundum dicendum quod, sicut Augustinus dicit, *Totum quicquid homines in terra habent, et omnia quorum sunt domini, pecunia vocatur; quia antiqui quæ habebant, in pecoribus habebant.*[7] Et Philosophus dicit in *Ethic.* quod *pecunias omnia dicimus quorum dignitas numismate mensuratur.*[8]

3. Ad tertium dicendum quod justitia constituit æqualitatem in exterioribus rebus, non autem ad eam proprie pertinet moderari interiores passiones. Unde aliter pecunia est materia liberalitatis et aliter justitiæ.

articulus 3. *utrum uti pecunia sit actus liberalitatis*

AD TERTIUM sic proceditur:[1] 1. Videtur quod uti pecunia non sit actus liberalitatis. Diversarum enim virtutum diversi sunt actus. Sed uti pecunia convenit aliis virtutibus, sicut justitiæ et magnificentiæ. Non ergo est proprius actus liberalitatis.

2. Præterea, ad liberalem non solum pertinet dare sed etiam accipere et custodire. Sed acceptio et custodia non videntur ad usum pecuniæ pertinere. Ergo inconvenienter dicitur proprius actus liberalitatis usus pecuniæ.

3. Præterea, usus pecuniæ non solum consistit in hoc quod pecunia detur, sed in hoc quod expendatur. Sed expendere pecuniam refertur ad ipsum expendentem; et sic non videtur esse actus liberalitatis. Dicit enim Seneca, *Non est liberalis aliquis ex hoc quod sibi donat.*[2] Ergo non quilibet usus pecuniæ pertinet ad liberalitatem.

SED CONTRA est quod Philosophus dicit in *Ethic.*, *Unoquoque optime utitur qui habet circa singula virtutem. Ergo divitiis utetur optime qui habet circa pecunias virtutem.*[3] Iste autem est liberalis. Ergo bonus usus pecuniarum est actus liberalitatis.

RESPONSIO: Dicendum quod species actus sumitur ex objecto, ut supra habitum est.[4] Objectum autem sive materia liberalitatis est pecunia et quidquid pecunia mensurari potest, ut dictum est.[5] Et quia quælibet virtus convenienter se habet ad suum objectum, consequens est ut cum liberalitas sit virtus, actus ejus sit proportionatus pecuniæ. Pecunia autem cadit sub ratione bonorum utilium, quia omnia exteriora bona ad usum hominis sunt ordinata. Et ideo actus proprius liberalitatis est pecunia vel divitiis uti.

1. Ad primum ergo dicendum quod ad liberalitatem pertinet bene uti

---

[7]*Sermo de disciplina christiana* 6. PL 40, 672
[8]*Ethics* IV, 1. 1119b26

what is given. For this reason the immediate objective of liberality is the inner emotions, but money is the objective of these emotions.

2. As Augustine explains, *all that man possesses and has control over on earth is called 'pecunia' from the fact that in ancient times men's possessions were their flocks* (pecord).[7] And Aristotle notes in IV *Ethics, We term money anything that can be measured in cash.*[8]

3. Justice achieves a balance in regard to material things, and its interest is not strictly the moderation of the inner emotions. Money is the objective of liberality in one way, therefore, of justice, in another.[c]

article 3. *whether the act of liberality is the use of money*

THE THIRD POINT:[1] 1. The act of liberality does not seem to be the use of money. While different virtues have different acts, the use of money is an act that relates to other virtues, justice and magnificence for instance. It is not, therefore, the act distinctive of liberality.

2. Further, not only giving, but receiving and saving are characteristic of liberality. But receiving and safeguarding do not seem to involve using money. To say, then, that this is its distinctive act is inaccurate.

3. Further, the use of money means not only giving it but also spending it. Since spending is in the interest of the spender, it does not seem to be an act of generosity. Seneca says, *No one is generous for giving to himself.*[2] Consequently, not all the uses of money engage liberality.

ON THE OTHER HAND, Aristotle writes, *The one who uses a thing best is the one who has virtue in regard to that thing. Therefore, where it is a question of money the one who has virtue in this regard will put it to its best use.*[3] This describes the generous man, and so the good use of money is the act proper to liberality.

REPLY: As already established,[4] the species of an act derives from its objective. In the case of liberality we have determined[5] that its objective or matter is money and whatever else has monetary value. Since every virtue matches its own objective, liberality as a virtue has the kind of act suited to money. Money, in turn, comes under the heading of goods to be used,[a] because all material goods have as end their use by man. Therefore the act distinctive of liberality is the using of money or riches.

Hence: 1. Wealth being its proper objective, generosity has as its

---

[1]cf *In Ethic.* IV, *lect.* 1
[2]*De benef.* V, 9
[4]1a2æ. 18, 2
[c]See 1a2æ. 59, 4 & 5.
[a]See above, 110, 2 note *a*.

[3]*Ethics* IV, 1. 1120a5
[5]art. 2

divitiis inquantum hujusmodi, eo quod divitiæ sunt propria materia liberalitatis. Ad justitiam autem pertinet uti divitiis secundum aliam rationem, scilicet secundum rationem debiti,* prout scilicet res exterior debetur alteri. Ad magnificentiam autem† pertinet uti divitiis secundum quamdam specialem rationem, id est secundum quod assumuntur in alicujus operis magni expletionem. Unde et magnificentia quodammodo se habet ex additione ad liberalitatem, ut infra dicetur.[6]

2. Ad secundum dicendum quod ad virtuosum pertinet non solum convenienter uti sua materia vel instrumento, sed etiam præparare opportunitates ad bene utendum. Sicut ad fortitudinem militis pertinet non solum exercere‡ gladium in hostes, sed etiam exacuere gladium et in vagina conservare. Sic etiam ad liberalitatem pertinet non solum uti pecunia, sed etiam eam præparare et conservare ad idoneum usum.

3. Ad tertium dicendum quod sicut dictum est[7] propinqua materia liberalitatis sunt interiores passiones, secundum quas homo afficitur circa pecuniam. Et ideo ad liberalitatem pertinet præcipue ut homo propter inordinatem affectionem ad pecuniam non prohibeatur a quocumque debito usu ejus.

Est autem duplex usus pecuniæ: unus ad seipsum, qui videtur ad sumptus vel expensas pertinere; alius autem quo quis utitur ad alios, qui§ pertinet ad dationes. Et ideo ad liberalitatem pertinet ut neque propter immoderatum amorem pecuniæ aliquis impediatur a convenientibus expensis, neque a convenientibus dationibus. Unde *circa dationes et sumptus liberalitas consistit*, secundum Philosophum in *Ethic*.[8]

Verbum autem Senecæ est intelligendum de liberalitate, secundum quod se habet ad dationes, non enim dicitur aliquis liberalis ex hoc quod sibi aliquid‖ donat.

articulus 4. *utrum ad liberalem maxime pertineat dare*

AD QUARTUM sic proceditur:[1] 1. Videtur quod ad liberalem non maxime pertineat dare. Liberalitas enim a prudentia dirigitur, sicut et quælibet alia virtus moralis. Sed maxime videtur ad prudentiam pertinere divitias conservare. Unde et Philosophus dicit in *Ethic*. quod *illi qui non acquisierunt pecuniam, sed susceperunt acquisitam ab aliis, liberalius eam expendunt, quia sunt inexperti indigentiæ*.[2] Ergo videtur quod dare non maxime pertineat ad liberalem.

---

*Piana: has simply, *divitiis secundum rationem debiti*
†Leonine: *etiam* for *autem*
‡Leonine: *exserere*, unsheath
§Leonine: *quod*
‖Piana: *aliquis*

function the good use of wealth for what it is. For its part justice is concerned with money under another title, namely that of indebtedness, i.e. something being owed to another. As for magnificence, its function is to make good use of money in relation to a highly specialized interest, namely expenditure for the accomplishment of some grand enterprise.[b] In this sense magnificence stands as a kind of superlative generosity, as we will point out further on.[6]

2. The part of the virtuous man is not only to use the objective or the means of virtue properly, but even to create opportunities for so doing. For example, the courage of the military man involves not only wielding his sword against enemies, but also keeping it sharpened and ready in its scabbard. Thus it is the mark of liberality not only to use money but to accumulate and to save it for appropriate uses.

3. As noted,[7] the immediate objective of liberality is the emotions that mark a person's attitude towards money. On this basis it is the concern of liberality chiefly that a person be not deterred from any appropriate use of money by reason of uncontrolled attachment to it.

Now the use of money is twofold: one, on one's own behalf, and this seems to come under the term 'spending' or 'expenses'; the other, on someone else's behalf, under the term 'giving'. Consequently, it is the mark of the generous man not to be held back through disordered love of money from either proper spending or giving. In this sense Aristotle states that *generosity is operative with regard to both giving and spending.*[8]

Seneca's statement is to be understood in reference to the relationship of liberality to giving, i.e. no one is called generous for making a gift to himself.

article 4. whether giving is the chief interest of the generous man

THE FOURTH POINT:[1] 1. Giving does not seem to be the primary characteristic of the generous man. Liberality, like any other moral virtue, is guided by prudence, and above all it seems the part of prudence to save money. Thus Aristotle says, *Those who have not earned their money but have come into it are more generous spenders for never having known want.*[2] It would therefore not seem that the generous man is intent above all on giving.

---

[6] 2a2æ. 128, 1 ad 1
[7] art. 2 ad 1
[8] *Ethics* IV, 1. 1120a8
[1] cf *In Ethic.* IV, lect. 1
[2] *Ethics* IV, 1. 1120b11
[b] *magnificentia* in this usage means munificence.

2. Præterea, de hoc quod aliquis maxime intendit, nullus tristatur neque ab eo cessat. Sed liberalis quandoque tristatur de his quæ dedit, neque etiam dat omnibus ut dicitur in *Ethic.*³ Ergo ad liberalem non maxime pertinet dare.

3. Præterea, ad illud implendum quod quis maxime intendit, homo utitur viis quibus potest. Sed *liberalis non est petitivus*, ut Philosophus dicit in *Ethic.*,⁴ cum per hoc posset sibi præparare facultatem aliis donandi. Ergo videtur quod non maxime intendat ad dandum.

4. Præterea, magis homo obligatur ad hoc quod provideat sibi quam aliis. Sed expendendo aliquid providet sibi; dando autem providet aliis. Ergo ad liberalem magis pertinet expendere quam dare.

SED CONTRA est quod Philosophus dicit in *Ethic.* quod *liberalis est superabundare in datione.*⁵

RESPONSIO: Dicendum quod proprium est liberalis uti pecunia. Usus autem pecuniæ est in emissione ipsius. Nam acquisitio pecuniæ magis assimilatur generationi quam usui; custodia vero pecuniæ inquantum ordinatur ad facultatem utendi assimilatur habitui. Emissio autem alicujus rei quanto fit ad aliquid distantius, tanto a majori virtute procedit, sicut patet in his quæ projiciuntur. Et ideo ex majori virtute procedit quod aliquis emittat pecuniam dando eam aliis, quam expendendo eam circa seipsum. Proprium est autem virtutis ut præcipue* tendat in id quod perfectius est; nam *virtus est perfectio quædam*, ut dicitur in *Physic.*⁶ Et ideo liberalis maxime laudatur ex datione.

1. Ad primum ergo dicendum quod ad prudentiam pertinet custodire pecuniam, ne surripiatur aut inutiliter expendatur. Sed utiliter eam expendere non est minoris prudentiæ quam utiliter eam conservare, sed majoris, quia plura sunt attendenda circa usum pecuniæ, qui assimilatur motui, quam circa conservationem, quæ assimilatur quieti.

Quod autem illi qui susceperunt pecunias ab aliis acquisitas liberalius expendant, quasi existentes inopiæ inexperti, si propter solam hanc inexperientiam liberaliter expenderent, non haberent virtutem liberalitatis. Sed quandoque hujusmodi inexperientia se habet solum sicut tollens impedimentum liberalitatis, ita quod promptius liberaliter agant. Timor enim inopiæ ex ejus experientia procedens, impedit quandoque eos qui acquisierunt pecuniam, ne eam consumant liberaliter agendo, et similiter amor quo eam amant tanquam proprium effectum, ut Philosophus dicit in *Ethic.*⁷

---

*Piana: *præcise*, precisely
³*Ethics* IV, 1. 1121a1 ⁴ibid. 1120a33 ⁵ibid. 1120b4

LIBERALITY

2. Further, no one regrets or fails to do that which is uppermost in his intention. The generous man, however, at times regrets his giving, nor does he give to everyone, as Aristotle points out.[3] Giving is not, therefore, his principal interest.

3. Further, a person uses every means at his disposal to accomplish his highest purpose. As Aristotle says, however, *the generous man is reluctant to ask for anything*,[4] even though by doing so he could acquire the wherewithal for giving. Thus giving seems not to be his chief aim.

4. Further, a person is more urgently bound to care for self than for others. Since by spending he provides for self, by giving, for others, the first has priority over the second for the generous man.

ON THE OTHER HAND, Aristotle states that *to be lavish in giving is characteristic of the generous man*.[5]

REPLY: The act distinctive of the generous man is to use money. The use of money means letting it go. For the acquiring of money is more like a coming to be than a use, and the saving of it more like a habit,[a] since the purpose is the power to use the money. The release of something proceeds from the greater power (*virtus*) the further the distance it is to go, as the example of throwing shows. In this way there is greater virtue behind the releasing of money in giving to others than in spending it on self. Since it is distinctive of virtue, *being itself a form of perfection*,[6] that it strive especially towards the more perfect, the generous man is praised especially for giving.

Hence: 1. Prudence has to protect money against theft or senseless spending. But it takes not less but more prudence to spend wisely than to save wisely, since there are more factors to consider in using a thing, which is compared to movement, than in keeping it, which is compared to rest.

On the point that those who have come into their money spend more generously for never having known want, should their inexperience be the sole reason for their generous spending, they would not possess the virtue of liberality. Sometimes this same lack of experience, however, serves simply to clear the way for truly generous actions. For the fear of need born from experience sometimes inhibits those who have earned their money from using it up in generous acts, even as does their fondness for money inasmuch as it is the fruit of their own toils.[7]

---

[6] *Physics* VII, 30, 246a13, 247a2. cf 246b27
[7] *Ethics* IV, 1. 1120b13
[a] *habitus* in this sense is a disposition or training of a faculty to act with readiness and facility in a certain way; see Vol. 22 of this series. A. Kenny, ed.

2. Ad secundum dicendum quod, sicut dictum est,[8] ad liberalitatem pertinet convenienter uti pecunia et per consequens convenienter dare, quod est quidam pecuniæ usus. Quælibet autem virtus tristatur de contrario sui actus et vitat ejus impedimenta. Ei autem quod est convenienter dare, duo opponuntur, scilicet non dare quod convenienter est dandum et dare aliquid inconvenienter. Unde de utroque tristatur liberalis, sed de primo magis, quia plus opponitur proprio actui. Et ideo etiam non dat omnibus, impediretur enim actus ejus, si quibuslibet daret, non enim haberet unde aliis daret quibus dare convenit.

3. Ad tertium dicendum quod dare et accipere se habent sicut agere et pati. Non est autem idem principium agendi et patiendi. Unde quia liberalitas est principium dationis, non pertinet ad liberalem ut sit promptus ad recipiendum et multo minus ad petendum. Unde versus, Si quis in hoc mundo multis vult gratus haberi, det, capiat, quærat plurima, pauca, nihil. Ordinat autem ad dandum aliqua secundum convenientiam liberalitatis scilicet fructus propriarum possessionum, quos sollicite procurat, ut eis liberaliter utatur.

4. Ad quartum dicendum quod ad expendendum in seipsum natura inclinat; unde hoc quod pecuniam quis profundat in alios pertinet proprie ad virtutem.

articulus 5. utrum liberalitas sit pars justitiæ

AD QUINTUM sic proceditur:[1] 1. Videtur quod liberalitas non sit pars justitiæ. Justitia enim respicit debitum. Sed quanto est aliquid magis debitum tanto minus liberaliter datur. Ergo liberalitas non est pars justitiæ, sed ei repugnat.

2. Præterea, justitia est circa operationes, ut supra habitum est.[2] Sed liberalitas est præcipue circa amorem et concupiscentiam pecuniarum, quæ sunt passiones. Ergo magis videtur liberalitas ad temperantiam pertinere quam ad justitiam.

3. Præterea, ad liberalitatem pertinet præcipue convenienter dare, ut dictum est.[3] Sed convenienter dare pertinet ad beneficentiam et misericordiam, quæ pertinent ad caritatem, ut supra dictum est.[4] Ergo liberalitas magis est pars caritatis quam justitiæ.

SED CONTRA est quod Ambrosius dicit, *Justitia ad societatem generis humani refertur. Societatis enim ratio dividitur in duas partes, justitiam scilicet et*

---

[8]In the Reply & art. 3   [1]cf 2a2æ. 58, 12 ad 1; 157, 1; *De malo* XIII, 1
[2]1a2æ. 60, 2 & 3; 2a2æ. 58, 8 & 9   [3]art. 4   [4]2a2æ. 31, 1
[b]*actio-passio*, one of the nine Aristotelean categories of accidental being; *actio* refers to a physical doing that passes outside the agent and effects change in a subject;

2. As already determined,[8] the concern of liberality is to use money properly, and so—since this is one way of using it—to give it properly. Every virtue is pained by anything contrary to its own act and is bent on avoiding obstacles to it. As to proper giving, the ways of going against it are two, namely withholding what rightfully should be given and giving something improperly. Hence, should either occur, the generous man is pained, but more so over the first for being more against the act typical of him. It also follows that he does not give to just anybody, since if he did his own act would be thwarted by not having the means to give to whom he should.

3. Giving and receiving are related as acting and being acted upon, and action and passion do not have the same source.[b] Hence liberality being the source of giving, the generous man is not quick to accept things and much less to ask for them. There is a saying to the effect that if you wish to be well-liked by many in this world, give a lot, take little, ask for nothing. As is appropriate to liberality, however, the generous man does make provision for giving certain things, namely the fruits of his own possessions, which he manages carefully in order to put them to generous use.

4. Nature itself prompts us to spend on ourselves; virtue properly is engaged when it comes to spending on others.[c]

article 5. whether liberality is a part of justice

THE FIRST POINT:[1] 1. Liberality seems not to be a part of justice. Justice regards debt. The more indebtedness there is the less is payment an act of generosity. Instead of being a part, then, liberality is quite the opposite of justice.

2. Further, the sphere of justice is actions;[2] of liberality, fondness and desire for money, which are emotions. Liberality would seem, then, rather to be a part of temperance than of justice.

3. Further, we have already determined[3] that the act chiefly characteristic of liberality is giving properly. This act in turn is part of the beneficence and mercy that, as noted earlier,[4] are functions of charity. Consequently, liberality is more a part of charity than of justice.

ON THE OTHER HAND, Ambrose says, *Justice has to do with the association of men*. For human association has two sides, that of justice and that of

---

passio is the action as received by the subject acted upon. The use here is as a simile for the comparison in question. See *In Meta.* XI, lect. 9.

[c]See 1a2æ. 50, 5; 56, 6; *De virtutibus in communi* 5. The will itself is the connatural inclination to the proper good of the person, a key point in St Thomas's conception of the psychological and ontological sub-structure of the moral life.

beneficentiam, quam eamdem liberalitatem et benignitatem vocant.[5] Ergo liberalitas ad justitiam pertinet.

RESPONSIO: Dicendum quod liberalitas non est species justitiæ, quia justitia exhibet alteri quod est ejus, sed liberalitas exhibet id quod suum est. Habet tamen quamdam convenientiam cum justitia in duobus. Primo quidem, quia principaliter est ad alterum sicut et justitia. Secundo quia est circa res exteriores sicut et justitia, licet secundum aliam* rationem, ut dictum est.[6] Et ideo liberalitas a quibusdam[7] ponitur pars justitiæ, sicut virtus annexa ei ut principali.

1. Ad primum ergo dicendum quod liberalitas etsi non attendat debitum legale quod attendit justitia, attendit tamen debitum quoddam morale quod attenditur ex quadam ipsius decentia, non ex hoc quod sit alteri obligatus. Unde minimum habet de ratione debiti.

2. Ad secundum dicendum quod temperantia est circa concupiscentiam corporalium delectationum. Concupiscentia autem pecuniæ et delectatio non est corporalis sed magis animalis. Unde liberalitas non pertinet proprie ad temperantiam.

3. Ad tertium dicendum quod datio beneficentiæ et misericordiæ procedit ex eo quod homo est aliqualiter affectus circa eum cui dat. Et ideo talis datio pertinet ad caritatem sive ad amicitiam. Sed datio liberalitatis provenit ex eo quod dans est aliqualiter affectus circa pecuniam, dum eam non concupiscit neque amat. Unde non solum amicis sed etiam ignotis dat quando oportet. Unde non pertinet ad caritatem sed magis ad justitiam, quæ est circa res exteriores.

articulus 6. utrum liberalitas sit maxima virtutum

AD SEXTUM sic proceditur: 1. Videtur quod liberalitas sit maxima virtutum. Omnis enim virtus hominis est quædam similitudo divinæ bonitatis. Sed per liberalitatem homo maxime assimilatur Deo *qui dat omnibus affluenter, et non improperat,* ut dicitur *Jac.*[1] Ergo liberalitas est maxima virtutum.

2. Præterea, secundum Augustinum, *in his quæ non mole magna sunt, idem est esse majus, quod melius.*[2] Sed ratio bonitatis maxime videtur ad liberalitatem pertinere, quia bonum diffusivum est, ut patet per Dionysium.[3]

---

*Piana: omits *aliam*
[5]*De offic.* I, 28. PL 16, 66   [6]art. 2 ad 3
[7]Andronicus of Rhodes, *De affectibus*; see 2a2æ. 80. Andronicus (1st cent. B.C.) is known chiefly as a compiler and editor of Aristotle's works.
[1]*James* I, 5
[2]*De Trin.* VI, 8. PL 42, 929
[3]*De div. nom.* IV, 20. PG 3, 720

beneficence, called also liberality or kind-heartedness.[5] Consequently, liberality is related to justice.

REPLY: Liberality is not a species of justice in that justice gives another what belongs to him; liberality, what belongs to oneself.
 Still, on two counts it does have a certain affinity with justice. First, like justice it is chiefly interpersonal. Secondly, like justice, but for a different reason,[6] its concern is materialities. Therefore liberality is listed by some authors[7] as a part of justice, i.e. as a virtue related to justice as to a principal virtue.
 Hence: 1. While it is true that liberality does not, like justice, acquit a legal debt, still it does attend to a form of moral debt, one that a person respects not because he is under obligation to another but out of his own sense of decency. Thus liberality implies indebtedness in a very minor sense.
 2. Temperance has to do with desire for physical pleasures. Desire and pleasure where money is the object are not physical but mental.[a] Therefore liberality is not properly a part of temperance.
 3. Giving in the beneficent and the merciful is prompted by a particular regard for the recipient. This kind of giving is part of charity or friendship. On the other hand, the giving proper to liberality derives from the giver's attitude towards money, that he neither covets nor loves it. Hence he gives it not only to friends but even to strangers, whenever it is appropriate to do so. This is why liberality is annexed not to charity but rather to justice, which is concerned with materialities.

article 6. whether liberality is the highest of virtues

THE SIXTH POINT: 1. Liberality seems to be the greatest of all the virtues. Every virtue in man is a likeness to God's own perfection. Since through liberality most of all a person becomes like God—*Who giveth to all men abundantly and upbraideth not*[1]—it is the greatest virtue of all.
 2. Further, following Augustine, *in things which are great in a non-quantitative sense, to be greater and to be better mean the same.*[2] Now the quality of being good seems especially to fit liberality, the good being generous of itself, as Denis makes plain.[3] Ambrose too points out that

---

[a] *animalis* in this usage is synonymous with *animata*, i.e. of soul. 1a2æ. 72, 2 associates *delectatio animalis* with *delectatio spiritualis*, a delight in the apprehension alone of something valued, e.g. in receiving praise. It is in contrast with *delectatio corporalis* or *naturalis* or *carnalis*, a pleasure that takes place completely in the sense of touch. The distinction will also be used in 118, 6. See 1a2æ. 31, 3 & ad 1; 31, 6 ad 1, 7; 2a2æ. 123, 8; 168, 2; *De malo* XIV, 1; *In Ethic.* III, lect. 19.

Unde et Ambrosius dicit quod *justitia censuram tenet, liberalitas bonitatem*.[4] Ergo liberalitas est maxima virtutum.

3. Præterea, homines honorantur et amantur propter virtutem. Sed Boëthius dicit, *Largitas maxime claros** *facit*.[5] Et Philosophus dicit in *Ethic.* quod *inter virtuosos maxime liberales amantur*.[6] Ergo liberalitas est maxima virtutum.

SED CONTRA est quod Ambrosius dicit quod *justitia excellentior videtur liberalitate, sed liberalitas gratior*.[7] Philosophus etiam dicit in 1 *Rhetor.* quod *fortes et justi maxime honorantur, et post eos liberales*.[8]

RESPONSIO: Dicendum quod quælibet virtus tendit in aliquod bonum, unde quanto aliqua virtus in majus bonum tendit tanto melior est. Liberalitas autem tendit in aliquod bonum dupliciter: uno modo primo et per se; alio modo ex consequenti.

Primo quidem et per se tendit ad ordinandum propriam affectionem circa possessionem pecuniarum et usum. Et sic secundum hoc præfertur liberalitati temperantia, quæ moderatur concupiscentias et delectationes pertinentes ad proprium corpus; et fortitudo et justitia, quæ ordinantur quodammodo in bonum commune; una quidem tempore pacis, alia vero tempore belli. Et omnibus præferuntur virtutes quæ ordinantur in bonum divinum, nam bonum divinum præeminet cuilibet bono humano. Et in bonis humanis bonum publicum præeminet bono privato; in quibus bonum corporis præeminet bono exteriorum rerum.

Alio modo ordinatur liberalitas ad aliquod bonum ex consequenti. Et secundum hoc liberalitas ordinatur in omnia bona prædicta. Ex hoc enim quod homo non est amativus pecuniæ, sequitur quod de facili utatur ea et ad seipsam et ad utilitatem aliorum et ad honorem Dei. Et secundum hoc habet quamdam excellentiam ex hoc quod utilis est ad multa.

Quia tamen unumquodque magis judicatur secundum id quod primo et per se competit ei quam secundum id quod consequenter se habet, ideo dicendum est liberalitatem non esse maximam virtutum.

1. Ad primum ergo dicendum quod datio divina provenit ex eo quod amat homines quibus dat, non autem ex eo quod afficiatur ad ea quæ dat. Et ideo magis videtur pertinere ad caritatem, quæ est maxima virtutum, quam ad liberalitatem.

2. Ad secundum dicendum quod quælibet virtus participat rationem

---

*Piana: *caros*, beloved
[4]*De offic.* I, 28. PL 16, 67
[5]*De consolatione philosophiæ* II, 5. PL 63, 690. Anicius Manlius Torquatus Severinus Boethius (*c.* 480–*c.* 524) statesman in the late Roman empire; his Latin translation

LIBERALITY

justice favours severity; liberality, goodness.[4] Liberality is therefore the greatest of all virtues.

3. Further, people are honoured and loved because of their virtue. Boethius says, *The greatest cause of honour is being generous;*[5] and Aristotle remarks, *The best liked among all virtuous people is the generous man.*[6] Liberality is therefore the greatest virtue of all.

ON THE OTHER HAND, Ambrose says, *Justice seems more lofty than liberality, but liberality is more gracious.*[7] Aristotle also mentions that *the brave and the just are honoured above all, and after them, the generous.*[8]

REPLY: Every virtue is bent upon some good and thus the greater the good, the better the corresponding virtue. As for liberality, it strives towards a good objective in two ways: first, immediately and by reason of what it is; second, by reason of its effect.

Immediately and of its nature liberality is concerned with setting right a person's attitude towards the possession and use of money. On this basis liberality takes second place both to temperance—this controls desires and delights related to one's own body; and to courage and justice—both are set upon the public good, justice in peace and courage in war. And the virtues that set us right in relation to the divine good excel all others, because the divine good has pre-eminence over all human goods. Among these, the public good has precedence over private goods; among these, in turn, the good of the body ranks over the good in material things.

In a second way liberality has a reference towards certain goods by reason of its effect. And on this basis it bears upon all the goods mentioned above. By not being a money lover a person readily uses it for both his own well-being and that of others, as well as for God's honour. This is the basis for a degree of distinction that it has, namely, its many-sided usefulness.

Yet the conclusion must be that liberality is not the greatest of all the virtues, for everything is judged more on the basis of what characterizes it immediately and in itself than on the basis of its consequences.

Hence: 1. God's giving issues more from love for those to whom he gives than from any sentiment towards what he gives. Thus his giving involves charity, the greatest of all virtues, rather than liberality.

2. Every virtue shares in the quality of the good, i.e. that it is generous

---

of Aristotelean logical works formed the *logica vetus* upon which early Scholasticism relied; other works were important for theological epistemology.
[6]*Ethics* IV, 1. 1120a21
[7]*De offic.* I, 28. PL 16, 67
[8]*Rhet.* I, 9. 1366b5

boni quantum ad emissionem proprii actus. Actus autem quarumdam aliarum virtutum meliores sunt pecunia quam emittit liberalis.

3. Ad tertium dicendum quod liberales maxime amantur, non quidem amicitia honesti, quasi sint meliores, sed amicitia utilis, quia sunt utiliores in exterioribus bonis, quæ communiter homines maxime cupiunt, et etiam propter eamdem causam clari redduntur.

---

[a] Aristotle's distinction of friendships, on the basis of different ends, into friendship in the noble (*honestum*), in the useful (*utile*) and in the pleasurable (*delectabile*)

of its own act. And the acts of certain other virtues are better than the money that the generous man gives.

3. The generous are the best liked not with that friendship in virtue that would indicate their moral superiority, but with an interested friendship,[a] suggesting that they are more helpful in regard to the material goods that people so desire. And they come to be honoured for the same reason.

---

follows the division of the good, since the good is the cause of friendship; see *Nicomachean Ethics* VIII, ch. 3, 1156a7; 1a2æ. 26, 4; 27, 1; above 106, 5 note *b*.

DEINDE CONSIDERANDUM EST de vitiis liberalitati oppositis: et primo, de avaritia; secundo, de prodigalitate.

Quæstio 118. de avaritia

Circa primum, quæruntur octo:

1. utrum avaritia sit peccatum;
2. utrum sit speciale peccatum;
3. cui virtuti opponatur;
4. utrum sit peccatum mortale;
5. utrum sit gravissimum peccatorum;
6. utrum sit carnale vel spirituale peccatum;
7. utrum sit vitium capitale;
8. de filiabus ejus.

articulus 1. utrum avaritia sit peccatum

AD PRIMUM sic proceditur:[1] 1. Videtur quod avaritia non sit peccatum. Dicitur enim avaritia, quasi æris aviditas,[2] quia scilicet in appetitu pecuniæ consistit per quam omnia exteriora bona intelligi possunt. Sed appetere exteriora bona non est peccatum; naturaliter enim homo ea appetit, tum quia subjecta sunt homini naturaliter tum quia per ea vita hominis conservatur, unde et substantia hominis dicuntur. Ergo avaritia non est peccatum.

2. Præterea, omne peccatum aut est in Deum aut in proximum aut in seipsum, ut supra habitum est.[3] Sed avaritia non est proprie peccatum contra Deum, non enim opponitur neque religioni neque virtutibus theologicis, quibus homo ordinatur in Deum. Neque etiam est peccatum in seipsum, hoc enim proprie pertinet ad gulam et luxuriam, de qua Apostolus dicit 1 *Cor.*, *Qui fornicatur, in corpus suum peccat.*[4] Similiter etiam non videtur esse peccatum in proximum, quia per hoc quod homo retinet sua, nulli facit injuriam. Ergo avaritia non est peccatum.

3. Præterea, ea quæ naturaliter adveniunt, non sunt peccata. Sed avaritia naturaliter consequitur senectutem et quemlibet defectum, ut Philosophus dicit in *Ethic.*[5] Ergo avaritia non est peccatum.

SED CONTRA est quod dicitur *Ad Heb.* ult., *Sint mores sine avaritia contenti præsentibus.*[6]

---

[1] *In Hebræos* 13, *lect.* 1. *In Ethic.* IV, *lect.* 5. *De duobus præceptis caritatis*
[2] From Isidore, *Etymolog.* PL 82, 369   [3] 1a2æ. 72, 4

NEXT WE TURN to the vices against liberality: first, avarice;[a] secondly, prodigality (119).

Question 118. avarice

Here there are eight points of inquiry:

1. whether avarice is sinful;
2. and a specific sin;
3. the virtue it is against;
4. whether it is a mortal sin;
5. and the gravest of all;
6. a sin of the flesh or of the spirit;
7. whether it is a capital sin;
8. its daughters.

article 1. whether avarice is sinful

THE FIRST POINT:[1] 1. Avarice does not seem to be a sin. The meaning of the word is greed for brass (*æris aviditas*),[2] indicating that it consists in desire for money, as this stands for all material goods. There is nothing sinful in such a desire, which is connatural to man both because in the nature of things material goods are put at his disposal and because they sustain his life, being called his 'substance'. Avarice, then, is no sin.

2. Further, as established earlier,[3] every sin is against God, self or neighbour. Avarice is in no proper sense a sin against God, being contrary neither to the virtue of religion nor to the theological virtues, by which a person stands in right relation to God. Nor is it a sin against self; strictly speaking this entails gluttony and lust, St Paul saying that *He that committeth fornication sinneth against his own body*.[4] And avarice does not seem to be against neighbour; keeping what belongs to oneself is no injury to others. Hence avarice is no sin.

3. Further, natural occurrences are not sinful. Avarice is the natural sequel to old age and to any other state of want, as Aristotle points out.[5] Therefore it is not sinful.

ON THE OTHER HAND, there is the text, *Let your manners be without covetousness, contented with such things as you have*.[6]

---

[4] 1 Corinthians 6, 18   [5] *Ethics* IV, 1. 1121b13
[6] *Hebrews* 13, 5
[a] Note that *avaritia* or *cupiditas* is discussed as the 'root of all evil' in 1a2æ. 84, 1.

RESPONSIO: Dicendum quod in quibuscumque bonum consistit in debita mensura, unde necesse est quod per excessum vel diminutionem illius mensuræ malum proveniat. In omnibus autem quæ sunt propter finem, bonum consistit in quadam mensura, nam ea quæ sunt ad finem necesse est commensurari fini, sicut medicina commensuratur sanitati, ut patet per Philosophum in 1 *Pol*.[7] Bona autem exteriora habent rationem utilium ad finem, sicut dictum est.[8] Unde necesse est quod bonum hominis circa ea consistat in quadam mensura, dum scilicet homo secundum aliquam mensuram quærit habere exteriores divitias prout sunt necessariæ ad vitam ejus secundum suam conditionem. Et ideo in excessu hujus mensuræ consistit peccatum, dum scilicet aliquis supra debitum modum vult eas vel acquirere vel retinere, quod pertinet ad rationem avaritiæ; quæ definitur esse *immoderatus amor habendi*.[9] Unde patet quod avaritia est peccatum.

1. Ad primum ergo dicendum quod appetitus rerum exteriorum est homini naturalis ut eorum quæ sunt propter finem. Et ideo intantum vitio caret, inquantum continetur sub regula sumpta ex ratione finis. Avaritia autem hanc regulam excedit, et ideo est peccatum.

2. Ad secundum dicendum quod avaritia potest importare immoderantiam circa res exteriores dupliciter. Uno modo immediate quantum ad acceptionem vel conservationem ipsarum, ut scilicet homo plus debito eas acquirat vel conservet. Et secundum hoc est directe peccatum in proximum, quia in exterioribus divitiis non potest unus homo superabundare nisi alter* deficiat, quia bona temporalia non possunt simul possideri a multis.

Alio modo potest importare immoderantiam circa interiores affectiones, quas quis ad divitias habet, puta quod immoderate aliquis divitias amet aut desideret aut delectetur in eis. Et sic avaritia est peccatum hominis in seipsum, quia per hoc deordinatur ejus affectus, licet non deordinetur corpus sicut per vitia carnalia. Ex consequenti autem est peccatum in Deum, sicut et omnia peccata mortalia, inquantum homo propter bonum temporale contemnit æternum.

3. Ad tertium dicendum quod inclinationes naturales sunt regulandæ secundum rationem quæ principatum tenet in natura humana. Et ideo quamvis senes propter naturæ defectum avidius exteriorum rerum inquirant subsidia, sicut et omnis indigens quærit suæ indigentiæ supplementum, non tamen a peccato excusantur si debitam rationis mensuram circa divitias excedant.

---

*Piana: *alteri*
[7]*Politics* I, 3. 1257b25   [8]1a2æ. 2, 1; 2a2æ. 117, 3
[9]From Hugh of St Victor, *De sacramentis* II, p. xiii, 1. PL 176, 526. Hugh of St Victor (*c*. 1096–1141) one of the great Victorine theologians, i.e. of the Abbey of St Victor in Paris, influential in the formation of Scholasticism and in mystical theology.

REPLY: In any case where the good depends on a given measure, evil necessarily results from an exceeding or falling short of the measure. As to things existing for the sake of an end, the good does consist in a determinate measure, for it is imperative that ways towards an end match the end, as Aristotle makes clear.[7] As already noted,[8] material goods have the quality of usefulness towards an end. Consequently the human good in them consists in a determinate measure, namely that a person seek to possess material wealth to the degree that it is necessary to a life suited to his station. The sin is to go beyond this measure, namely the will to acquire or to hoard material goods excessively. The meaning of avarice, defined as *unchecked love to possess*,[9] involves this and so avarice clearly is sinful.

Hence: 1. The desire for material things as they are conducive to an end is natural to man. Therefore it is without fault to the extent that it is confined within the norms set by the nature of that end. Avarice exceeds these limits and is thereby sinful.

2. There are two ways in which avarice may mean a failure in moderation with regard to material things. The first is in its immediate relation to getting or keeping them, namely that a person goes too far in getting or keeping them. In this way avarice is a sin directly against neighbour, because with material possessions it is impossible for one man to enjoy extreme wealth without someone else suffering extreme want, since the resources of this world cannot be possessed by many at one time.[b]

In a second way, avarice may mean excess in regard to inner attitudes towards wealth, for example an immoderate love, desire or enjoyment of them. On this basis avarice is a sin against self; even though, as in sins of the flesh, a person's body is not defiled, his desires are.

Like other mortal sins, avarice in its consequences is also a sin against God, namely in that for the sake of an earthly good a person rejects the eternal.[c]

3. The tendencies of nature have to be controlled in accord with reason, which has primacy in man's nature. On this account even if old people, with the breakdown of nature, do more greedily seek compensation in material possessions, just as anyone in need attempts to make up for it, still they are not excused from sin when, in regard to riches, they go beyond the measure called for by reason.[d]

---

[b]Implicit here is the point made in art. 3 that avarice so taken is a sin directly against justice. One cannot but be impressed by the unqualified principle of social and economic justice, so flatly stated in the 13th century, that still remains an unfulfilled, even revolutionary ideal.

[c]See above 105, 1 note *c*.

[d]Reason here means, first of all, the specific difference of human nature, that its essential form is a rational soul; then the faculty of reason as it serves to express what is specifically natural to man, the reasonable; see 1a2æ. 18, 1 & 5; 19, 3.

SUMMA THEOLOGIÆ, 2a2æ. 118, 2

articulus 2. utrum avaritia sit speciale peccatum

AD SECUNDUM sic proceditur:[1] 1. Videtur quod avaritia non sit speciale peccatum. Dicit enim Augustinus, *Avaritia, quæ græce philargyria dicitur, non in solo argento, vel in nummis, sed in omnibus rebus quæ immoderate cupiuntur, intelligenda est.*[2] Sed in omni peccato est cupiditas immoderata alicujus rei, quia peccatum est, spreto bono incommutabili, bonis commutabilibus inhærere, ut supra habitum est.[3] Ergo avaritia est generale peccatum.

2. Præterea, secundum Isidorum avarus dicitur quasi *avidus æris*,[4] idest, pecuniæ; unde et in Græco avaritia *philargyria* nominatur, idest, amor argenti. Sed sub argento, per quod pecunia significatur, significantur omnia bona exteriora, quorum pretium potest numismate mensurari, ut supra habitum est.[5] Ergo avaritia consistit in appetitu cujuslibet exterioris rei. Ergo videtur esse generale peccatum.

3. Præterea, super illud *Ad Rom. 7, Nam concupiscentiam nesciebam*,[6] etc., dicit *Glossa, Bona est lex quæ dum concupiscentiam prohibet, omne malum prohibet.*[7] Videtur autem lex specialiter prohibere concupiscentiam avaritiæ, unde dicitur *Exod., Non concupisces rem proximi tui.*[8] Ergo concupiscentia avaritiæ est omne malum; et ita avaritia est generale peccatum.

SED CONTRA est quod *Rom.* avaritia connumeratur inter alia specialia peccata, ubi dicitur, *Repletos omni iniquitate, malitia, fornicatione, avaritia,* etc.[9]

RESPONSIO: Dicendum quod peccata sortiuntur speciem secundum objecta, ut supra habitum est.[10] Objectum autem peccati est illud bonum in quod tendit inordinatus appetitus. Et ideo ubi est specialis ratio boni quod inordinate appetitur, ibi est specialis ratio peccati.

Alia autem est ratio boni utilis et boni delectabilis. Divitiæ autem secundum se habent rationem utilis. Ea enim ratione appetuntur inquantum in usum hominis cedunt. Et ideo speciale quoddam peccatum est avaritia secundum quod est immoderatus amor habendi possessiones, quæ nomine pecuniæ designantur, ex qua sumitur avaritiæ nomen.

Verum quia verbum habendi, quod secundum primariam impositionem ad possessiones pertinere videtur quarum sumus totaliter domini, ad multa alia derivatur, sicut dicitur homo habere sanitatem, uxorem, vestimentum et alia hujusmodi, ut patet in *Prædic.*,[11] per consequens et nomen avaritiæ

---

[1]cf II *Sent.* 42, 2, 3 ad 1. *De malo* XIII, 1
[2]*De lib. arbit.* III, 17. PL 32, 1294
[3]1a2æ. 71, 6 obj. 3
[4]*Etymolog.* PL 82, 369
[5]117, 2 ad 2
[6]*Romans* 7, 7
[7]*Ordinaria; Lombardi.* PL 191, 1416
[8]*Exodus* 20, 17
[9]*Romans* 1, 29

AVARICE

article 2. whether avarice is a specific sin

THE SECOND POINT:[1] 1. Avarice does not seem to be a special kind of sin. We should recognize avarice, in Greek φῐλαργυρια, not only with reference to silver or gold, but wherever there is unchecked desire, Augustine says.[2] Now in every case of sin there exists an unchecked desire for something, since sin means spurning the immortal good and cleaving to the mortal, as already explained.[3] So avarice is a general sin.

2. Further, following Isidore, 'avaricious' means 'greedy for gold' (*avarus æris*),[4] i.e. money; accordingly, the Greek word for avarice is φῐλαργυρια, i.e. love of silver. As already noted,[5] silver or money stands for all material goods, the value of which can be reckoned in cash. It follows that avarice exists in the desire for any sort of material thing and on this account is a general sin.

3. Further, on *Romans, For I had not known concupiscence*, etc.,[6] the comment of the *Gloss* is this, *The Law is good in that by forbidding concupiscence it rules out all evil.*[7] The Law seems particularly to forbid the concupiscence in avarice by the verse, *Thou shalt not covet thy neighbour's goods.*[8] All evil, therefore, is included in this and avarice is a general sin.

ON THE OTHER HAND, avarice is listed along with other specific sins in the text of *Romans, Being filled with all iniquity, malice, fornication, avarice,* etc.[9]

REPLY: As determined earlier,[10] sins derive their specific nature from their objectives, i.e. that particular good upon which the disordered appetite is bent. Accordingly wherever there is a specific quality of good in the objective of untoward desire, there is a specific kind of sinfulness.

Now there is one value in the useful good, a different one in the pleasurable.[a] By their nature riches possess the quality of usefulness, desired as they are because they lend themselves to the uses of man. This is why avarice is a specific kind of sin when taken as the uncontrolled love of having possessions as these are connoted by 'money' (*æris*), the term from which 'avarice' derives.

Note, however, that the term 'having' in its original application seemed to refer to the possessions over which we exercise complete ownership, but then its meaning was extended to many other things—we say, for example, that a man has his health, a wife, clothes, etc., as is clear from Aristotle's *Categories*.[11] Correspondingly, the word 'avarice' also was

---

[10] 1a2æ. 72, 1
[a] See above 110, 2 note *a*.

[11] *Categories* 12. 15b17

ampliatum est ad omnem immoderatum appetitum habendi quamcumque rem, sicut Gregorius dicit in quadam homilia quod *avaritia est non solum pecuniæ, sed etiam altitudinis, cum supra debitum* modum sublimitas ambitur*.[12] Et secundum hoc avaritia non est speciale peccatum, et hoc etiam modo loquitur Augustinus de avaritia in auctoritate inducta.[13]

1. Unde patet responsio ad primum.

2. Ad secundum dicendum quod omnes res exteriores quæ veniunt in usum humanæ vitæ nomine pecuniæ intelliguntur inquantum habent rationem boni utilis. Sunt autem quædam exteriora bona quæ potest aliquis pecunia consequi, sicut voluptates, honores et alia hujusmodi, quæ habent aliam rationem appetibilitatis. Et ideo illorum appetitus non proprie dicitur avaritia secundum quod est vitium speciale.

3. Ad tertium dicendum quod *Glossa* illa loquitur de concupiscentia inordinata cujuscumque rei. Potest enim intelligi quod per prohibitionem concupiscentiæ rerum possessarum prohibeantur quarumcumque rerum concupiscentiæ quæ per res possessas haberi possunt.

articulus 3. utrum avaritia opponatur liberalitati

AD TERTIUM sic proceditur:[1] 1. Videtur quod avaritia non opponatur liberalitati. Quia super illud *Matt., Beati qui esuriunt et sitiunt justitiam,*[2] Chrysostomus dicit[3] quod duplex est justitia, una generalis et alia specialis, cui opponitur avaritia. Et idem Philosophus dicit in *Ethic.*[4] Ergo avaritia non opponitur liberalitati.

2. Præterea, peccatum avaritiæ in hoc consistit quod homo transcendit mensuram in rebus possessis. Sed hujusmodi mensura statuitur per justitiam. Ergo avaritia directe opponitur justitiæ et non liberalitati.

3. Præterea, liberalitas est virtus media inter duo vitia contraria, ut pater per Philosophum in *Ethic.*[5] Sed avaritia non habet peccatum contrarium oppositum,† ut‡ patet per Philosophum in *Ethic.*[6] Ergo avaritia non opponitur liberalitati.

SED CONTRA est quod sicut dicitur *Eccles., Avarus non implebitur pecunia; et qui amat divitias fructum non capiet ex eis*.[7] Sed non impleri pecunia et inordinate eas amare est contrarium liberalitati, quæ in appetitu divitiarum medium tenet. Ergo avaritia opponitur liberalitati.

RESPONSIO: Dicendum quod avaritia importat immoderantiam quamdam

---

*Leonine: omits *debitum*
†Piana: *contrarium et oppositum*
‡Piana: *et* for *ut*
[12]*Homil. in Evang.* 16. PL 76, 1136   [13]obj. 1

broadened to include every sort of unchecked desire to have any sort of thing; Gregory notes, *Avarice exists not only with regard to money, but also with regard to knowledge and high position, when prominence is sought unduly.*[12] In this sense, avarice is not a specific kind of sin and this is Augustine's use in the text cited.[13]

Hence: 1. The response to the argument from Augustine is clear.

2. In so far as they have the quality of being useful goods, all materialities that contribute to a man's living are comprised in the term 'money'. But there are also certain temporal goods—pleasures, honours and the like—that we can get with money, but which have another kind of appeal. Hence desire for them is not called avarice in its proper sense as it is a specific kind of vice.

3. The *Gloss* refers to disordered concupiscence towards anything whatsoever; and there is good reason for seeing the prohibition against coveting possessions as forbidding the craving after any of the things obtainable by means of one's possessions.

article 3. whether avarice is against liberality

THE THIRD POINT:[1] 1. Avarice does not seem to be opposed to liberality. On the text, *Blessed are they that hunger and thirst after justice,*[2] Chrysostom comments[3] that justice is of two kinds, the one general, the other special, which avarice opposes. And Aristotle says the same.[4] It is not liberality, then, to which avarice is opposed.

2. Further, the sin of avarice exists where a person goes beyond the measure in regard to possessions. This measure is fixed by justice. Thus avarice is the direct contrary to justice, not to liberality.

3. Further, while, as Aristotle makes clear in the *Ethics*,[5] liberality is a virtue midway between two contrary vices, avarice has no vice opposed as its contrary, as he also shows.[6] Therefore avarice is not the opposite of liberality.

ON THE OTHER HAND, *A covetous man shall not be satisfied with money and he that loveth riches shall have no fruit from them.*[7] Not to be satisfied with money and to love it unduly are against liberality, which strikes the mean in the appetite for riches. Therefore avarice is against liberality.

REPLY: The meaning of avarice is the failure to be moderate about wealth

---

[1] cf *In Ethic.* IV, lect. 1, 3 & 5; *De malo* XIII, 1
[2] *Matthew* 5, 6
[3] *In Matt. Hom.* 15. PG 57, 227
[4] *Ethics* V, 1. 1129b27; 2. 1130a14
[5] ibid. II, 7. 1107b8; IV, 1. 1119b22, b27
[6] ibid. V, 1. 1129b1
[7] *Ecclesiastes* 5, 9

circa divitias dupliciter. Uno modo immediate, circa ipsam acceptionem et conservationem divitiarum, inquantum scilicet aliquis acquirit pecuniam ultra debitum, aliena surripiendo vel retinendo. Et sic opponitur justitiæ, et hoc modo accipitur avaritia. *Ezech.* ubi dicitur, *Principes ejus in medio ejus quasi lupi rapientes prædam ad effundendum sanguinem et avare lucra sectanda.*[8]

Alio modo importat immoderantiam circa interiores affectiones divitiarum, puta cum quis nimis amat vel desiderat divitias aut nimis delectatur in eis, etiam si nolit rapere aliena. Et hoc modo avaritia opponitur liberalitati, quæ moderatur hujusmodi affectiones, ut dictum est.[9] Et sic accipitur avaritia, II *Cor.*, *Præparent repromissam benedictionem hanc paratam esse: sic quasi benedictionem non quasi avaritiam;*[10] glossa, scilicet *ut doleant pro dato, et parum sit quod dent.*[11]

1. Ad primum ergo dicendum quod Chrysostomus et Philosophus loquuntur de avaritia primo modo dicta. Avaritiam autem secundo modo dictam nominat Philosophus illiberalitatem.

2. Ad secundum dicendum quod justitia proprie statuit mensuram in acceptionibus et conservationibus divitiarum secundum rationem debiti legalis, ut scilicet homo non accipiat nec retineat alienum. Sed liberalitas constituit mensuram rationis, principaliter quidem in interioribus affectionibus et per consequens in exteriori acceptione et conservatione pecuniarum et emissione earum secundum quod ex interiori affectione* procedunt, non observando rationem debiti legalis sed debiti moralis, quod attenditur secundum regulam rationis.

3. Ad tertium dicendum quod avaritia secundum quod opponitur justitiæ non habet vitium oppositum, quia avaritia consistit in plus habendo quam debeat secundum justitiam; et huic opponitur minus habere, quod non habet rationem culpæ sed pœnæ. Sed avaritia secundum quod opponitur liberalitati habet vitium prodigalitatis oppositum.

articulus 4. utrum avaritia semper sit peccatum mortale

AD QUARTUM sic proceditur:[1] 1. Videtur quod avaritia semper sit peccatum mortale. Nullus enim est dignus morte nisi pro peccato mortali. Sed propter avaritiam homines digni sunt morte; cum enim Apostolus *Rom.* præmisisset, *Repletus omni iniquitate, fornicatione, avaritia,* etc.,[2] subdit, *Qui talia agunt, digni sunt morte.*[3] Ergo avaritia est peccatum mortale.

---

*Piana: *quod exteriori affectione*
[8]*Ezekiel* 22, 27
[9]117, 2 ad 1; 3 ad 3; 6
[10]II *Corinthians* 9, 5
[11]*Interlinearis; Lombardi.* PL 192, 62

in two senses. The first is immediate and regards getting and keeping, namely where someone acquires money unduly by stealing it or retaining another's property. In this sense avarice is against justice, and *Ezekiel* so understands it: *Her princes in the midst of her are like wolves ravening the prey to shed blood and to run after gains through covetousness.*[8]

In a second sense avarice means the failure to moderate inner attachment to wealth, for example when someone loves or desires it too much or takes excessive pleasure in it, even if he has no wish to take what belongs to someone else. In this way avarice is against liberality, which, as noted,[9] controls such feelings. This is how avarice is taken in II *Cor.*, *That they prepare this blessing not as covetousness,*[10] a gloss adding, *lest they regret their gift and give but little.*[11]

Hence: 1. Chrysostom and Aristotle are speaking of avarice in the first sense indicated. Avarice in the second sense Aristotle calls 'illiberality'.[a]

2. Justice establishes the measure in getting and keeping wealth on the basis of the legal debt that no one take or keep what belongs to another. Liberality, for its part, puts the mean of reason into inner attitudes chiefly and then extends to the outward acts of receiving, keeping and spending money as these acts have their origin in the affections. It does so by observing not a legal but a moral debt, one honoured in keeping with the norm of reason.[b]

3. As it is opposed to justice avarice does not have its own contrary vice, for the reason that it means having more than is right in justice; the opposite of this is having less, which does not imply fault but penalty.[c] As it is against liberality avarice has prodigality as its opposing vice.

article 4. whether avarice is always a mortal sin

THE FOURTH POINT:[1] 1. Avarice seems always to be a mortal sin. No one deserves death except for a mortal sin. But people are deserving of death for avarice; St Paul, beginning with these words, *Being filled with all iniquity, fornication, avarice,*[2] continues, *They who do such things are worthy of death.*[3] So avarice is a mortal sin.

---

[1]cf *De malo* XIII, 2   [2]*Romans* 1, 29   [3]ibid. 32
[a]See also art. 8 and ad 5. St Thomas includes both forms in his discussion.
[b]The medium, the virtuous ideal realized in an act of virtue, is always a mean of reason, but in matters of justice the reasonable ideal is that which matches a norm or measure set objectively by nature or by law—the objective rights of another person (see 1a2æ. 64, 1 & 2). It clarifies the meaning of 'moral debt' to relate it to the mean of reason, a proportion determined by the inner affections and virtuous ideal of the person respecting a moral debt. A legal debt is a real mean, objectively set. See Appendix 1.
[c]See above 108, 1 note d.

2. Præterea, minimum in avaritia est quod aliquis inordinate retineat sua. Sed hoc videtur esse peccatum mortale. Dicit enim Basilius, *Est panis famelici quem tu tenes, nudi tunica quam conservas, indigentis argentum quod possides. Quocirca tot injuriaris quot exhibere valeres.*[4] Sed injuriari alteri est peccatum mortale, quia contrariatur dilectioni proximi. Ergo multo magis omnis avaritia est peccatum mortale.

3. Præterea, nullus excæcatur spirituali cæcitate nisi per peccatum mortale quod animam privat lumine gratiæ. Sed, secundum Chrysostomum[5] tenebra animæ est pecuniarum cupido. Ergo avaritia, quæ est pecuniarum cupido, est peccatum mortale.

SED CONTRA est quod 1 *Ad Cor.* super illud, *Si quis ædificaverit super hoc fundamentum,* etc.,[6] dicit *Glossa* quod *lignum, fenum et stipulam superædificat ille qui cogitat quæ mundi sunt, quomodo placeat mundo*,[7] quod pertinet ad peccatum avaritiæ. Ille autem qui ædificat lignum, fenum et stipulam non peccat mortaliter sed venialiter; de eo enim dicitur quod *salvus erit sic quasi per ignem.*[8] Ergo avaritia quandoque est veniale peccatum.

RESPONSIO: Dicendum quod, sicut dictum est[9] avaritia dupliciter dicitur. Uno modo secundum quod opponitur justitiæ, et hoc modo ex genere suo est peccatum mortale; sic enim ad avaritiam pertinet quod aliquis injuste accipiat vel retineat res alienas, quod pertinet ad rapinam vel furtum, quæ sunt peccata mortalia, ut supra habitum est.[10] Contingit tamen in hoc genere avaritiæ aliquid esse peccatum veniale propter imperfectionem actus, sicut supra dictum est.[11]

Alio modo potest accipi avaritia secundum quod opponitur liberalitati, et secundum hoc importat inordinatum amorem divitiarum. Si ergo intantum amor divitiarum crescat quod præferatur caritati, ut scilicet propter amorem divitiarum aliquis non vereatur facere contra amorem Dei et proximi, sic avaritia erit peccatum mortale. Si autem inordinatio amoris infra* hoc sistat, ut scilicet homo quamvis superflue divitias amet, non tamen præferat earum amorem amori divino, ut si propter divitias non velit aliquid facere contra Deum et proximum, sic avaritia est peccatum veniale.

1. Ad primum ergo dicendum quod avaritia connumeratur peccatis mortalibus secundum illam rationem qua est peccatum mortale.

---

*Piana: *intra*
[4]Hom. VI *On Luke* 12, 18. PG 31, 278
[5]Pseudo-Chrysostom, *Op. imperf. in Matt.*, 15 on 6, 23. PG 56, 721
[6]I *Corinthians* 3, 12
[7]*Ordinaria;* Lombardi. PL 91, 1557

2. Further, the very least form of avarice is to hold on tightly to one's possessions, and this seems to be a mortal sin. *It is the bread of the starving you hoard, the cloak of the naked you lay away, the money of the pauper you hold on to. In fact you injure as many people as you have the power to help*, says Basil.[4] To do harm to another is a mortal sin because it is against love for neighbour. Every other form of avarice, therefore, is a fortiori, a mortal sin.

3. Further, no one is blinded with a spiritual blindness except through mortal sin, which robs the soul of the light of grace. Yet, following Chrysostom,[5] money-lust is a darkness of soul. Hence avarice, the lust for money, is a mortal sin.

ON THE OTHER HAND, on the text, *If any man build upon this foundation*,[6] there is a gloss that *anyone whose thoughts are of this world, how he may* the *Gloss* comments, *build upon wood, hay and stubble*.[7] And this is what avarice does. Yet in view of the verse that *he shall be saved yet so as by fire*,[8] one who builds upon wood, hay and stubble does not sin mortally but venially.[a] In some cases, then, avarice is a venial sin.

REPLY: As indicated already,[9] avarice has two meanings. In the first, whereby it is contrary to justice, it is a sin mortal in its kind; for then it involves taking or keeping another's property unjustly, i.e. theft or robbery—both mortal sins, as I have shown earlier.[10] In this type of avarice, however, it does happen that the sin may be venial because the act of sinning is not a completely human act, as was also pointed out in discussing theft.[11]

In its other meaning avarice goes against liberality and thus involves an unchecked love for riches. When this becomes so intense that it is put ahead of charity, i.e. to a point where for the sake of money a person is not deterred from acting against the love of God or neighbour, then avarice is a mortal sin. When, however, the inordinate love is not that far out of line, the avarice is a venial sin, i.e. although loving riches too much, a person does not put them ahead of love for God, not wishing for the sake of riches to do anything against God or neighbour.

Hence: 1. Avarice is here listed with other mortal sins on the basis of that sense in which it is mortally sinful.

---

[8]1 *Corinthians* 3, 15
[9]art. 3
[10]2a2æ. 66, 9
[11]ibid. ad 3
[a]See 1a2æ. 89, 2. The text of 1 *Corinthians* was traditionally interpreted in this way, following Augustine, *City of God* XXI, 26, venial sin being purged by the fire of suffering this world's ills or by the fire of purgatory.

2. *Ad secundum dicendum* quod Basilius loquitur de illo casu, in quo aliquis tenetur ex debito legali bona sua pauperibus erogare vel propter periculum necessitatis vel etiam propter superfluitatem habitorum.

3. *Ad tertium dicendum* quod cupido divitiarum obtenebrat animam proprie, quando excludit lumen caritatis, præferendo amorem divitiarum amori divino.

articulus 5. utrum avaritia sit maximum peccatorum

AD QUINTUM sic proceditur: 1. Videtur quod avaritia sit maximum peccatorum. Dicitur enim *Eccli.*, *Avaro nihil est scelestius*; et postea subditur, *Nihil est iniquius quam amare pecuniam: hic enim et animam suam venalem habet.*[1] Et Tullius dicit, *Nihil est tam angusti animi tamque parvi quam amare pecuniam.*[2] Sed hoc pertinet ad avaritiam. Ergo avaritia est gravissimum peccatorum.

2. Præterea, tanto aliquod peccatum est gravius quanto magis caritati contrariatur. Sed avaritia maxime contrariatur caritati. Dicit enim Augustinus quod *venenum caritatis est cupiditas.*[3] Ergo avaritia est maximum peccatorum.

3. Præterea, ad gravitatem peccati pertinet quod sit incurabile; unde et peccatum in Spiritum Sanctum dicitur gravissimum, quia est irremissibile. Sed avaritia est peccatum insanabile, unde* dicit Philosophus in *Ethic.* quod *senectus et omnis impotentia illiberales facit.*[4] Ergo avaritia est gravissimum peccatorum.

4. Præterea, Apostolus dicit *Ephes.* quod *avaritia est idolorum servitus.*[5] Sed idololatria computatur inter gravissima peccata. Ergo et avaritia.

SED CONTRA est quod adulterium est gravius peccatum quam furtum, ut habetur *Prov.*[6] Furtum autem pertinet ad avaritiam. Ergo avaritia non est gravissimum peccatorum.

RESPONSIO: Dicendum quod omne peccatum ex hoc ipso quod est malum consistit in quadam corruptione sive privatione alicujus boni; inquantum autem est voluntarium consistit in appetitu alicujus boni. Dupliciter ergo ordo peccatorum potest attendi.

Uno modo ex parte boni quod per peccatum contemnitur vel corrumpitur, quod quanto majus est tanto peccatum gravius est. Et secundum hoc peccatum quod est contra Deum est gravissimum, et sub hoc est peccatum quod est contra personam hominis, sub quo est peccatum quod est contra

---

*Piana: *ut* for *unde*
[1]*Ecclesiasticus* x, 9, 10

2. Basil is speaking of the case wherein someone is bound under a legal debt to give of his goods to the poor in view either of their dire need or of his own surplus of possessions.[b]

3. Lust for money darkens the soul, strictly speaking, when it shuts out the light of charity by putting love for money above love for God.

article 5. whether avarice is the worst of sins

THE FIFTH POINT: 1. Avarice seems to be the worst of sins. *Ecclesiasticus* says, *Nothing is more wicked than a covetous man,* and continues, *There is no more wicked thing than love of money, for such a one setteth his own soul to sale.*[1] Cicero says, *Nothing is so narrow or small-minded as loving money.*[2] This is what avarice is. Thus it is the worst of sins.

2. Further, a sin is the more serious the more it goes against charity. Avarice is in extreme opposition to charity. *Greed,* says Augustine, *is poison to charity.*[3] So it is the most serious of sins.

3. Further, incurability is a mark of the gravity of a sin; thus the gravest of all, a sin against the Holy Spirit, is termed unforgivable. For its part avarice is beyond remedy, Aristotle attesting that *it is old age and weakness of any kind that make men avaricious.*[4] Hence avarice is the worst kind of sin.

4. Further, St Paul calls avarice a *serving of idols*[5] and idolatry is counted among the most serious sins. So then is avarice.

ON THE OTHER HAND, according to *Proverbs,*[6] adultery is a worse sin than theft, and theft and avarice are of the same order. Avarice, then, is not the most serious sort of sin.

REPLY: Every sin, as a form of evil, means the spoiling of some good; as voluntary, the willing of another good.[a] In consequence, the gradation of sins may be accounted for in two ways.[b]

The first is from the standpoint of the good spurned or spoiled: the higher this good is, the worse the sin. Accordingly a sin against God is the worst of all; next, a sin against the person of a neighbour; then, one

---

[2]*De officiis* I, 20
[3]LXXXIII *Quæst.* 36. PL 40, 25
[4]*Ethics* IV, 1. 1121b13
[5]*Ephesians* 5, 5
[6]*Proverbs* 6, 30
[b]See 2a2æ. 32, 1 & 5.
[a]See 1a2æ. 71, 6; Vol. 25, J. Fearon, ed., Appendix 1; also above 104, 3 and note *a*.
[b]See 1a2æ. 73, 2-5; vol. 25, Appendix 2 & 3.

res exteriores, quæ sunt ad usum hominis deputatæ, quod videtur ad avaritiam pertinere.

Alio modo potest attendi gradus peccatorum ex parte boni cui inordinate subditur appetitus humanus, quod quanto minus est tanto peccatum est deformius; turpius est enim subesse inferiori bono quam superiori. Bonum autem exteriorum rerum est infimum inter humana bona; est enim minus quam bonum corporis, quod etiam minus est quam bonum animæ, quod exceditur a bono divino. Et secundum hoc peccatum avaritiæ quo appetitus humanus subjicitur etiam exterioribus rebus habet quodam modo deformitatem majorem.

Quia tamen corruptio vel privatio boni formaliter se habet in peccato, conversio autem ad bonum commutabile materialiter, magis est judicanda gravitas peccati ex parte boni quod corrumpitur quam ex parte boni cui subjicitur appetitus. Et ideo dicendum est quod avaritia non est simpliciter maximum peccatorum.

1. Ad primum ergo dicendum quod auctoritates illæ loquuntur de avaritia ex parte boni cui subditur appetitus. Unde et in *Eccli.* pro ratione subditur quod avarus *suam animam habet venalem*,[7] quia videlicet animam suam, idest vitam suam, exponit periculis pro pecunia; et ideo subdit, *Quoniam in vita sua projecit*, idest, contempsit, *intima sua*,[8] ut scilicet pecuniam lucraretur. Tullius etiam addit hoc esse *angusti animi*,[9] ut scilicet velit pecuniæ subjici.

2. Ad secundum dicendum quod Augustinus ibi accipit cupiditatem generaliter cujuscumque temporalis boni, non secundum quod accipitur specialiter pro avaritia. Cupiditas enim cujuscumque temporalis boni est venenum caritatis inquantum scilicet homo spernit bonum divinum propter hoc quod inhæret bono temporali.

3. Ad tertium dicendum quod aliter est insanabile peccatum in Spiritum Sanctum et aliter avaritia. Nam peccatum in Spiritum Sanctum est insanabile ex parte contemptus, puta quia homo contemnit vel misericordiam vel justitiam divinam aut aliquid horum per quæ hominis peccata sanantur; et ideo talis insanabilitas pertinet ad majorem gravitatem peccati. Avaritia vero habet insanabilitatem ex parte defectus humani, in quem scilicet semper procedit humana natura. Quia quo aliquis est magis deficiens, eo magis indiget adminiculo exteriorum rerum, et ideo magis in avaritiam labitur. Unde per talem insanabilitatem non ostenditur peccatum esse gravius sed quodammodo esse periculosius.

4. Ad quartum dicendum quod avaritia comparatur idololatriæ per

---

[7]*Ecclesiasticus* 10, 10
[8]ibid. [9]*De offic.* I, 20
[c]There was a long-standing Scholastic controversy over the formal constitutive of sin: is it the turning from the true good (*privatio, aversio*) or the turning towards the

against the material things appointed for man's use. The last is what avarice seems to involve.

In a second way, the gradation of sins can be looked at from the standpoint of the good enslaving a person's appetites: the lower this is the more base the sin; it is more shameful to be captive to a lower than to a higher good. Among all human goods, the good in material things is the least; it is less than that of the body and this in turn is inferior to a good of the soul; a good of the soul is less than the divine good. By this scale the sin of avarice, with its submission of a person's appetites to material things, is in a certain way the most twisted of all sins.

Still, the spoiling or deprivation of a good is the formal element in sin; the turning to a passing good, the material element.[c] We must, then, assess the gravity of sin more from the side of the good destroyed than from that of the good enslaving the appetites. The necessary conclusion is that avarice is not the absolute worst among sins.

Hence: 1. These texts refer to avarice from the standpoint of the good to which the appetite is subjected. Thus, as to *Ecclesiasticus*, the statement that the greedy man *setteth his own soul to sale*[7] is given as a reason, namely because for money he exposes his own soul, i.e. his life, to peril. So the text goes on, *Because while he liveth he hath cast away*—i.e. held to no account—*his bowels*,[8] in order to make money. As for Cicero, he adds that a willingness to be subservient to money is the mark of a *small mind*.[9]

2. Augustine here takes *cupiditas* in a general sense, referring to any sort of earthly good, not in the restricted sense of avarice. And covetousness of any earthly good is indeed poisonous to charity in the sense that because of attachment to some earthly good a person spurns the divine.

3. A sin against the Holy Spirit[d] and avarice are beyond cure in different ways. The first, because of contempt, for example because a person rejects either the mercy or the justice of God or any of the remedies for sin. Hence to be incurable in this way is an indication that a sin is the more serious. The incurableness of avarice, however, has its basis in the constant deterioration which besets our nature. Thus, the more needy a person becomes, the more he needs the relief afforded by temporal things and so the more he slips into avarice. Consequently, this sort of incurability is no sign of a sin's being worse, but does mean that in a sense it is more perilous.

4. Avarice is compared to idolatry because of a certain resemblance, i.e.

---

apparent good (*conversio*). St Thomas seems clear enough here. The turning towards an objective gives the act its moral kind; this act is thereby the 'subject', the material in which the privation is found and which makes the act sinful. See 1a2æ. 73, 2.

[d]See above 105, 2 ad 2 and note *b*.

quamdam similitudinem quam habet ad ipsam, quia sicut idolatra subjicit se creaturæ exteriori ita etiam avarus. Non tamen eodem modo; sed idololatra quidem subjicit se creaturæ exteriori, ut exhibeat ei cultum divinum; avarus autem subjicit se creaturæ exteriori immoderate eam concupiscendo ad usum, non tamen ad cultum. Et ideo non oportet quod avaritia habeat tantam gravitatem quantam habet idololatria.

articulus 6. utrum avaritia sit peccatum spirituale

AD SEXTUM sic proceditur:[1] 1. Videtur quod avaritia non sit peccatum spirituale. Peccata enim spiritualia videntur esse circa spiritualia bona. Sed materia avaritiæ sunt bona corporalia, scilicet exteriores divitiæ. Ergo avaritia non est peccatum spirituale.

2. Præterea, peccatum spirituale contra carnale dividitur. Sed avaritia videtur esse peccatum carnale. Sequitur enim corruptionem carnis, ut patet in senibus, qui propter naturæ carnalis defectum in avaritiam incidunt. Ergo avaritia non est peccatum spirituale.

3. Præterea, peccatum carnale est per quod etiam corpus hominis deordinatur, secundum illud Apostoli 1 *Cor.*, *Qui fornicatur in corpus suum peccat.*[2] Sed avaritia etiam corporaliter hominem vexat; unde et Chrysostomus[3] *Marc.*[4] comparat avarum dæmoniaco qui in corpore vexatur. Ergo avaritia non videtur esse peccatum spirituale.

SED CONTRA est quod Gregorius[5] computat avaritiam cum vitiis spiritualibus.

RESPONSIO: Dicendum quod peccata præcipue in affectu consistunt; omnes autum affectiones animæ sive passiones terminantur ad delectationes et tristitias, ut patet per Philosophum in *Ethic.*[6] Delectationum autem quædam sunt carnales et quædam spirituales. Carnales quidem delectationes dicuntur quæ in sensu carnis complentur, sicut delectationes ciborum et venereorum; delectationes vero spirituales dicuntur quæ complentur in sola animæ apprehensione. Illa ergo peccata dicuntur carnalia quæ perficiuntur in delectationibus carnalibus; illa vero dicuntur spiritualia quæ perficiuntur in spiritualibus delectationibus absque carnali delectatione. Et hujusmodi est avaritia, delectatur enim avarus in hoc quod considerat se possessorem divitiarum. Et ideo avaritia est peccatum spirituale.

1. Ad primum ergo dicendum quod avaritia circa corporale objectum non quærit delectationem corporalem sed solum animalem, prout scilicet

[1] cf 1a2æ. 72, 2 ad 4. IV *Sent.* 15, 1, 4, iii ad 2. *In Matt.* 23. *In Ephes.* 5, lect. 2
[2] 1 *Corinthians* 6, 18

just as the idolater submits himself to an inanimate creature so does the avaricious man. They do not, however, do so in the same way: the idolater's subjection to a creature is the offering of divine worship; the greedy man's unchecked desire is to use, not to worship a creature. Thus there is no reason for avarice to have a gravity equal to that of idolatry.

article 6. whether avarice is a spiritual sin

THE SIXTH POINT:[1] 1. Avarice does not seem to be a spiritual sin. Spiritual vices would seem to be related to spiritual goods, whereas the objective of avarice is physical goods, namely wealth. Avarice is not, then, a sin of the spirit.

2. Further, in the division of sins, the spiritual and the carnal are opposite members. Being the sequel of the body's deterioration, as is clear with the aged who fall into avarice because their bodies are failing, it seems to be a carnal sin, and therefore not a spiritual one.

3. Further, a sin of the flesh is one through which a person's body is in disorder; *He that committeth fornication sinneth against his own body.*[2] Avarice torments a person even in his body, so that Chrysostom[3] compares the man of greed to the possessed man in *Mark*,[4] who was troubled in body. Avarice, then, does not seem to be a sin of the spirit.

ON THE OTHER HAND, Gregory counts avarice among the spiritual sins.[5]

REPLY: Sin has its being primarily in an affect of soul, and all the soul's affects and emotions terminate either in pleasure or sorrow, as Aristotle makes plain.[6] As for pleasures, some are carnal, some spiritual. The first take their name from being consummated in the flesh, those, for example, of food and sex; the second, from being completed simply in the soul's own experience of them.[a] Accordingly, these sins are called carnal which reach their term in pleasures of the flesh; spiritual, those which terminate in pleasures of the spirit, without fleshly delight. Avarice is of this sort, seeing that the greedy man finds his pleasure in the realization that he is the possessor of riches. Therefore avarice is a sin of the spirit.

Hence: 1. Set upon an objective relating to the body, avarice is still not a quest for the pleasures of body but of soul, namely the experience

---

[3] *In Matt.* 28. PG 57, 355
[4] *Mark* 5, 15
[5] *Moral.* xxxi, 45. PL 76, 621
[6] *Ethics* II, 3. 1104b14
[a] See above 117, 5 note *a*.

homo in hoc delectatur quod divitias possideat. Et ideo non est peccatum carnale.

Ratione tamen objecti medium est inter peccata pure spiritualia, quæ quærunt delectationem spiritualem circa objecta spiritualia, sicut superbia est circa excellentiam, et vitia pure carnalia, quæ quærunt delectationem pure corporalem circa objectum corporale.

2. Ad secundum dicendum quod motus recipit speciem secundum terminum ad quem, non autem secundum terminum a quo. Et ideo vitium dicitur carnale ex hoc quod tendit in delectationem carnalem, non autem ex eo quod procedit ex aliquo defectu carnis.

3. Ad tertium dicendum quod Chrysostomus comparat avarum dæmoniaco non quia vexetur in carne sicut dæmoniacus, sed per oppositum, quia sicut dæmoniacus ille de quo legitur *Marc.* se denudabat, ita avarus se superfluis divitiis onerat.

articulus 7. utrum avaritia sit vitium capitale

AD SEPTIMUM sic proceditur:[1] 1. Videtur quod avaritia non sit vitium capitale. Avaritia enim opponitur liberalitati sicut medio et prodigalitati sicut extremo. Sed neque liberalitas est principalis virtus neque prodigalitas vitium capitale. Ergo etiam avaritia non debet poni vitium capitale.

2. Præterea, sicut supra dictum est,[2] illa dicuntur esse vitia capitalia quæ habent principales fines ad quos ordinantur fines aliorum vitiorum. Sed hoc non competit avaritiæ, quia divitiæ non habent rationem finis, sed magis rationem ejus quod est ad finem, ut dicitur in *Ethic.*[3] Erg oavaritia non est vitium capitale.

3. Præterea, Gregorius dicit quod *avaritia quandoque oritur ex elatione, quandoque ex timore. Dum enim quidam deficere sibi ad sumptum necessaria æstimant, mentem ad avaritiam relaxant. Sunt alii qui dum potiores videri appetunt, ad alienarum rerum ambitum succenduntur.*[4] Ergo avaritia magis oritur ab aliis vitiis quam ipsa sit vitium capitale respectu aliorum.

SED CONTRA est quod Gregorius[5] ponit avaritiam inter vitia capitalia.

RESPONSIO: Dicendum quod,sicut supra dictum est,[6] vitium capitale dicitur ex quo alia vitia oriuntur secundum rationem finis, qui cum sit multum appetibilis, propter ejus appetitum homo procedit ad multa facienda vel bona vel mala.

---

[1] cf II *Sent.* 42, 2, 3; *De malo* VIII, 1; XIII, 3   [2] 1a2æ. 84, 3 & 4
[3] *Ethics* I, 5. 1096a5   [4] *Moral.* xv, 25. PL 75, 1096
[5] op. cit. XXXI, 45. PL 76, 621   [6] 1a2æ. 84, 3 & 4
[a] Although not found in Scripture, lists of capital sins or vices (sometimes in-

wherein a person delights in his possession of riches. This is why it is not a carnal sin.

Still, because of the objective, it is true that it stands midway between purely spiritual sins, which pursue an inner delight in regard to some intangible objective—as pride does with regard to personal worth—and purely carnal sins, which pursue sheer physical pleasure in some objective related to body.

2. Movement gets its species by reference to its term, not its starting point. On this basis a vice is termed carnal as being bent upon fleshly pleasure, not as originating in the frailty of the flesh.

3. Chrysostom makes the comparison of the miser with the man possessed, not because he is troubled in the flesh like the demoniac, but by way of contrast: while in *Mark* we read that the possessed man tore his clothes off, the greedy man wraps himself up in unneeded possessions.

article 7. whether avarice is a capital sin

THE SEVENTH POINT:[1] 1. Avarice does not seem to be a capital vice. Its opposites are liberality, the virtuous mean, and prodigality, the other extreme. Liberality is not a cardinal virtue nor is prodigality a capital sin. Consequently it is wrong to count avarice a capital sin.

2. Further, as determined earlier,[2] those vices are designated capital that have ends which are primary, i.e. to which the ends of other vices are subordinated. This is not the case, however, with avarice, since riches do not have the quality of end but rather of means to end, as noted in Aristotle's *Ethics*.[3] Thus avarice is not a capital sin.

3. Further, Gregory writes, *Avarice has its origins sometimes in pride, sometimes in fright. For when they think they are getting short in what they need for expenses, some people let their spirit give way to greed. Then there are some who, yearning to seem important, burn with greed for the possessions of others.*[4] Rather than being itself a capital source of other vices, avarice derives from other vices.

ON THE OTHER HAND, Gregory includes avarice in his list of capital sins.[5]

REPLY: As already established,[6] that vice is termed capital from which others originate in dependence on its end. For when an end is highly appealing, from attachment to it a person goes on to many good or evil deeds.[a]

---

accurately called the seven deadly sins) became a principal ascetical and homiletic theme from the 4th century on. Prominent in this development were Evagrius
(*footnote a continued on page 261*)

Finis autem maxime appetibilis est beatitudo vel felicitas quæ,* est ultimus finis humanæ vitæ, ut supra habitum est.⁷ Et ideo quanto aliquid magis participat conditiones felicitatis tanto magis est appetibile. Est autem una de conditionibus felicitatis ut sit per se sufficiens, alioquin non quietaret appetitum tanquam ultimus finis. Sed per se sufficientiam maxime repromittunt divitiæ, ut Boëthius dicit.⁸ Cujus ratio est, quia, sicut Philosophus dicit in *Ethic.*, *denario utimur quasi fidejussore ad dominia habenda*;⁹ et *Eccles.* dicitur quod *pecuniæ obediunt omnia*.¹⁰ Et ideo avaritia, quæ consistit in appetitu pecuniæ, est vitium capitale.

1. Ad primum ergo dicendum quod virtus perficitur secundum rationem; vitium autem perficitur secundum inclinationem appetitus sensitivi. Non autem ad idem genus principaliter respicit ratio et appetitus sensitivus. Et ideo non oportet quod principale vitium opponatur principali virtuti. Unde, licet liberalitas non sit principalis virtus, quia non respicit ad principale bonum rationis, avaritia tamen est principale vitium, quia respicit ad pecuniam, quæ habet quamdam principalitatem inter bona sensibilia ratione jam dicta.¹¹ Prodigalitas autem non ordinatur ad aliquem finem principaliter appetibilem sed magis videtur procedere ex defectu rationis. Unde Philosophus dicit in *Ethic.*¹² quod prodigus magis dicitur vanus quam malus.

2. Ad secundum dicendum quod pecunia ordinatur quidem ad aliud sicut ad finem;† inquantum tamen utilis est ad omnia sensibilia acquirenda continet quodammodo virtute omnia. Et ideo habet quamdam similitudinem felicitatis, ut dictum est.¹³

3. Ad tertium dicendum quod nihil prohibet vitium capitale interdum a quibusdam aliis oriri, ut dictum est,¹⁴ dum tamen ex eo alia vitia soleant plerumque oriri.

articulus 8. *utrum sint avaritiæ filiæ quæ dicuntur*‡

AD OCTAVUM sic proceditur:¹ 1. Videtur quod non sint avaritiæ filiæ, quæ dicuntur, scilicet proditio, fraus, fallacia, perjuria, inquietudo, violentia et contra misericordiam obduratio. Avaritia enim opponitur liberalitati, ut

---

*Piana: *qui*
†Piana: *ad alium finem*, to another end
‡Piana: *utrum proditio . . . obduratio sint avaritiæ filiæ*; i.e. title follows list in obj. 1

⁷1a2æ. 1, 8; 2, 8   ⁸*De consol. phil.* III, 3. PL 63, 732
⁹*Ethics* V, 5. 1133b10   ¹⁰*Ecclesiastes* 10, 19
¹¹In the Reply
¹²*Ethics* IV, 1. 1121a25
¹³In the Reply
¹⁴2a2æ. 36, 4 ad 1
¹cf 2a2æ. 55, 8, *De malo* XIII, 3

As is also clear from the preceding,[7] the end prized above all is beatitude or happiness, the last end of human life. Thus the more anything shares in the qualities of beatitude the more desirable it is. One of these qualities is that happiness is all-sufficing in itself, otherwise it would not stand as ultimate end fulfilling all desires. Riches especially give a promise of self-sufficiency, as Boethius remarks;[8] and Aristotle explains this, saying, *Money serves us as a guarantee of possessing all things*;[9] and *Ecclesiastes*, *All things obey money*.[10] This is the reason why avarice, the desire for money, is a capital vice.

Hence: 1. The development of virtue follows reason; the development of vice follows the propensities of sense-appetite. Reason and sense-appetite do not look to the same interests. Hence there is no necessity that a principal vice be the opposite of a principal virtue. Thus while liberality is not a principal virtue, not being concerned with a primary good of reason,[b] yet avarice is a principal vice, because it is bent upon money which has a certain primacy among the goods of sense for the reason already stated.[11] Prodigality, however, is not set upon any end of primary appeal but seems rather to issue from witlessness. Thus Aristotle says[12] that a prodigal man is empty-headed rather than wicked.

2. It is true that money is subordinated to something else as its end; still to the extent that it is useful in the quest for all material goods by its power it somehow contains them all. As noted,[13] this is how it has some likeness to beatitude.

3. As has been established,[14] there is nothing against a capital vice sometimes deriving from other vices, provided that more often than not other vices derive from it.

article 8. whether those usually listed are the daughters of avarice

THE EIGHTH POINT:[1] 1. It seems that *treachery, fraud, falsehood, perjury, restlessness, violence and callousness to mercy* are not the daughters of avarice.[a] While avarice is against liberality, treachery, fraud and falsehood

---

(*footnote a continued from page 259*)
Pontus in Egyptian monasticism and Cassian in the West. The list developed by Gregory the Great in his *Moralia* prevailed in the Middle Ages. St Thomas respects the tradition by including the capital sins in his moral synthesis, but does not give them the emphasis they had in medieval preaching and piety.

[b]The meaning of this reasoning is connected with the way in which some virtues are principal or cardinal; their concern is with some primary, i.e. more urgent and more obvious, moral value; see 1a2æ. 61, 2 & 3.

[a]Gregory, in the place cited in the *sed contra* refers to these as the army of avarice, but also as the offspring from avarice as their root. The figure of army or daughters clearly applies the meaning of a vice as capital given in art. 7.

dictum est. Proditio autem, fraus, et fallacia opponuntur prudentiæ, perjuria religioni, inquietudo spei vel caritati, quæ quiescit in amato, violentia opponitur justitiæ, obduratio misericordiæ. Ergo hujusmodi vitia non pertinent ad avaritiam.

2. Præterea, proditio, dolus et fallacia ad idem pertinere videntur, scilicet ad proximi deceptionem. Ergo non debent enumerari† tanquam diversæ filiæ avaritiæ.

3. Præterea, Isidorus ponit novem filias, quæ sunt *mendacium, fraus, furtum, perjurium,* et *turpis lucri appetitus, falsa testimonia, violentia, inhumanitas, rapacitas.*[2] Ergo prima assignatio filiarum fuit insufficiens.

4. Præterea, Philosophus in *Ethic.* ponit multa genera vitiorum pertinentium ad avaritiam, quam nominat *illiberalitatem;* videlicet *parcos, tenaces, kimibiles, illiberales*‡ *operationes operantes,* et *de meretricio pastos,* et *usurarios, aleatores,* et *mortuorum spoliatores,* et *latrones.*[3] Ergo videtur quod prædicta enumeratio sit insufficiens.

5. Præterea, tyranni maxime violentias subditis inferunt. Dicit autem Philosophus ibidem, quod *tyrannos civitates desolantes, et sacra prædantes non dicimus illiberales,*[4] id est avaros. Ergo violentia non debet poni filia avaritiæ.

SED CONTRA est quod Gregorius *Moral.* assignat avaritiæ filias prius enumeratas.[5]

RESPONSIO: Dicendum quod filiæ avaritiæ dicuntur vitia quæ ex ipsa oriuntur et præcipue secundum appetitum finis. Quia vero avaritia est superfluus amor habendi divitias, in duobus excedit. Primo enim superabundant in retinendo, et ex hac parte oritur ex avaritia obduratio contra misericordiam, quia scilicet cor ejus misericordia non emollitur ut de divitiis subveniat miseris. Secundo ad avaritiam pertinet superabundare in accipiendo. Et secundum hoc avaritia potest considerari dupliciter: uno modo secundum quod est in affectu. Et sic ex avaritia oritur inquietudo inquantum ingerit homini sollicitudinem et curas superfluas; *avarus* enim *non implebitur pecunia,* ut dicitur *Eccles.,*[6] Alio modo potest considerari in effectu et sic in acquirendo aliena utitur quandoque quidem vi, quod pertinet ad violentias; quandoque autem dolo. Qui* quidem, si fiat in

---

†Piana: *non debent omnia enumerari,* all should not be enumerated
‡Piana: *liberales* for *illiberales*
*Piana: *quod* for *qui*
[2]*Mysticorum expositiones sacramentorum seu quæstiones in VT., In Deut.* 16. PL 83, 366
[3]*Ethics* IV, 1. 1121b22, b32, 1122a7
[4]ibid. 1122a5
[5]*Moralia* XXXI, 45. PL 76, 621
[6]*Ecclesiastes* 5, 9

are against prudence; perjury, against religion; restlessness, against hope or charity with its serenity in the beloved; violence, against justice; callousness, against mercy. Therefore these vices are not allied to avarice.

2. Further, treachery, deceit and lying seem to amount to the same thing, deception of neighbour. They should not, then, be enumerated as distinct daughters of avarice.

3. Further, Isidore lists nine daughters, *lying, deceit, theft, perjury, desire for base gain, false witnessing, violence, inhumanity, rapacity.*[2] The other enumeration is thus incomplete.

4. Further, Aristotle lists many forms of vice connected with avarice (which he calls *illiberality*): the greedy are *niggardly, tight-fisted, skinflints;*[b] *involved in low-down dealings, they fatten on prostitution, are usurers, dicers, grave robbers, thieves.*[3] Thus Gregory's list is inadequate.

5. Further, tyrants above all inflict violence on their subjects; yet in the same place Aristotle remarks that *we do not simply call 'mean' the tyrants who lay cities waste and profane shrines.*[4] Violence, then, should not be counted a daughter of avarice.

ON THE OTHER HAND, this list is Gregory's[5].

REPLY: The daughters of avarice are the vices issuing from it, especially on the basis of desire for its end. Avarice being an exaggerated love for possessing riches, it is excessive on two counts. First of all it goes too far in keeping. In this regard callousness to mercy is born of avarice, in that a person's heart is not so softened by mercy as to come to the aid of the wretched out of his own resources.

Secondly, it is the part of avarice to go too far in getting. In this regard avarice can be looked on in two ways, and first as it is in the heart. Thus restlessless issues from avarice in that this engenders anxiety and undue worry in a person; *a covetous man shall not be satisfied with money.*[6]

In another way avarice can be viewed as to its effect, whereby in order to acquire wealth the man of greed employs now force—which entails

---

[b]The Greek *textus receptus* used in the Loeb Classical Library edition of the *Nicomachean Ethics* (tr. R. Rackham, 1934, p. 201 and note *a*) has *kuminopriotēs*, translated literally as 'one who saws cumminseeds in half' and idiomatically as 'skinflint'. The Latin text of Aristotle's work reconstructed for the Leonine, critical edition of St Thomas's *Sententia Libri Ethicorum* (*Opera Omnia*, XLVII, Rome, 1969) at Lib. IV, 5 has *kyminibilis*, and also in the text of St Thomas's *expositio* (vol. 2, 215–16). See Vol. 1, *Præfatio* by R. A. Gauthier on the Latin text of the *Nicomachean Ethics* used by St Thomas, a much revised and corrupted text of Robert Grosseteste's translation of *c.* 1245; see also Gauthier's, *L'Éthique à Nicomaque* (2nd. ed. 1970, 2 vol., Louvain, 1970) 125–9. G. maintains that St Thomas has absolutely no knowledge of Greek.

verbo, fallacia erit quantum ad simplex verbum, perjurium, si addatur confirmatio juramenti. Si autem dolus committatur opere, sic quantum ad res erit fraus; quantum autem ad personas erit proditio, ut patet de Juda, qui ex avaritia prodidit Christum.

1. Ad primum ergo dicendum quod non oportet filias alicujus peccati capitalis ad idem genus vitii pertinere, quia ad finem unius vitii possunt ordinari etiam peccata alterius generis. Aliud est enim peccatum habere filias, et peccatum habere species.

2. Ad secundum dicendum quod illa tria distinguuntur sicut dictum est.[7]

3. Ad tertium dicendum quod illa novem reducuntur ad septem prædicta. Nam mendacium et falsum testimonium continentur sub fallacia; falsum enim testimonium est quædam specificatio mendacii, sicut et furtum est quædam specificatio fraudis, unde sub fraude continetur. Appetitus autem turpis lucri pertinet ad inquietudinem. Rapacitas autem continetur sub violentia, cum sit species ejus. Inhumanitas autem est idem quod obduratio contra misericordiam.

4. Ad quartum dicendum quod illa quæ ponit Aristoteles sunt illiberalitatis* vel avaritiæ species magis quam filiæ. Potest enim aliquis dici illiberalis vel avarus ex eo quod deficit in dando; et si quidem parum det, vocatur parcus; si autem nihil, tenax; si autem cum magna difficultate det, vocatur kimibilis, quasi kimini venditor, quia de parvis magnam vim facit.

Quandoque autem aliquis dicitur illiberalis vel avarus, quia excedit in accipiendo, et hoc dupliciter. Uno modo quia turpiter lucratur vel vilia et servilia opera exercendo per illiberales operationes; vel quia de aliquibus vitiosis actibus lucratur, sicut de meretricio vel de aliquo hujusmodi; vel quia lucratur de eo quod gratis oportet concedere, sicut usurarii; vel quia lucratur parva cum magno labore. Alio modo quia injuste lucratur, vel vivis vim inferendo, sicut latrones, vel mortuos spoliando, vel ab amicis auferendo, sicut aleatores.

5. Ad quintum dicendum quod sicut liberalitas est circa mediocres pecunias ita et illiberalitas. Unde tyranni, qui magna per violentiam auferunt, non dicuntur illiberales sed injusti.

---

*Piana: *liberalitatis*
[7]In the Reply

violence; now deceit. Should the deceit be perpetrated verbally, where there is simple assertion, we have falsehood; where there is confirmation by oath, perjury. If the deceit is accomplished by deed, when it centres upon some object, it is fraud; on persons, treachery, as is clear from Judas's betrayal of Christ out of greed.

Hence: 1. There is no necessity that the daughters of a capital sin belong to the same class of sins, since even sins of a different species can be made to serve the end of the one vice. That a sin have daughters means one thing; species, another.

2. These three are distinct in the way indicated.[7]

3. Isidore's nine are reducible to the seven given. Lying and false-witnessing are included under falsehood; false-witnessing is a particular kind of lying, even as theft is a particular form of fraud and so is contained under it. As to desire for base gain, this is implicit in restlessness. Rapacity is included in violence as a species. Inhumanity is identical with callousness to mercy.

4. These that Aristotle lists are species rather than daughters of meanness or avarice. Someone may be called mean or greedy on the grounds of his failure in giving; if he gives little, he is called niggardly; if nothing, tight-fisted; if grudgingly, a skin-flint—from the Greek word for a vendor of cumin, i.e. one who strains mightily over next to nothing.[c]

At times someone is termed mean or greedy because he goes too far in taking; and in two ways. First, because he goes after base profits, either by performing low and menial tasks in mean dealings; or because he makes money out of the evil activities of others, as from prostitution and the like; or from something he should give for nothing, as in the case of usurers; or because he slaves to earn a pittance. The second way is making money by unjust means, either doing violence to the living, as thieves, or to the dead, as grave-robbers or extracting it from friends, as dice players.

5. Like liberality, meanness is concerned with modest sums. This is the reason why tyrants, who seize great riches by violence, are not called illiberal, but unjust.

---

[c] St Thomas's explanation, on the *Ethics* IV, 5, makes the point more clearly: *They are called kyminibiles, i.e. vendors of cumin, from their excessive closeness about money, namely because they do not wish to give the least little thing without being paid.*

Quæstio 119. de prodigalitate

DEINDE CONSIDERANDUM EST de propdigalitate. Et circa hoc quæruntur tria:

1. utrum prodigalitas avaritiæ opponatur;
2. utrum prodigalitas sit peccatum;
3. utrum sit gravius peccatum quam avaritia.

articulus 1. utrum prodigalitas opponatur avaritiæ

AD PRIMUM sic proceditur:[1] 1. Videtur quod prodigalitas non opponatur avaritiæ. Opposita enim non possunt simul* esse in eodem. Sed aliqui sunt simul prodigi et avari. Ergo prodigalitas non opponitur avaritiæ.

2. Præterea, opposita sunt circa idem. Sed avaritia secundum quod opponitur liberalitati est circa passiones quasdam, quibus homo afficitur ad pecuniam, prodigalitas autem non videtur esse circa aliquas animæ passiones; non enim afficitur circa pecunias nec circa aliquid aliud hujusmodi. Non ergo prodigalitas opponitur avaritiæ.

3. Præterea, peccatum principaliter recipit speciem a fine, ut supra habitum est.[2] Sed prodigalitas semper videtur ordinari ad aliquem finem illicitum propter quem sua bona expendit et præcipue propter voluptates; unde et *Luc.* dicitur de filio prodigo quod *dissipavit substantiam suam luxuriose vivendo*.[3] Ergo videtur quod prodigalitas magis opponatur temperantiæ et insensibilitati quam avaritiæ et liberalitati.

SED CONTRA est quod Philosophus in *Ethic.*[4] ponit prodigalitatem oppositam liberalitati et illiberalitati, quam nunc avaritiam dicimus.

RESPONSIO: Dicendum quod in moralibus attenditur oppositio vitiorum ad invicem et ad virtutem secundum superabundantiam et defectum. Differunt autem avaritia et prodigalitas secundum superabundantiam et defectum diversimode.

Nam in affectione divitiarum avarus superabundat, plus debito eas diligens; prodigus autem deficit, minus debito earum sollicitudinem gerens. Circa exteriora vero ad prodigalitatem pertinet excedere quidem in dando, deficere autem in retinendo et acquirendo; ad avaritiam autem pertinet e contrario deficere quidem in dando, superabundare autem in accipiendo et retinendo. Unde patet quod prodigalitas avaritiæ opponitur.

---

*Piana: omits *simul*, at once
[1]cf 2a2æ. 118, 3 ad 3; *In Ethic.* IV, *lect.* 3   [2]1a2æ. 72, 3

Question 119. prodigality

NEXT, PRODIGALITY; THERE are three points of inquiry:
1. whether it is the opposite of avarice;
2. a sin;
3. and worse than avarice.

article 1. whether prodigality is the opposite of avarice

THE FIRST POINT:[1] 1. Prodigality seems not to be the opposite of avarice. Some people are at once prodigal and stingy, whereas opposites are mutually exclusive. Prodigality and avarice, then, are not opposites.

2. Further, opposites are such in reference to the same thing. Avarice, in its opposition to liberality, bears upon these emotions by which a person is affected in regard to money. Prodigality, for its part, seems not to involve the emotions; it is in fact a lack of feeling for money or anything connected with it. So prodigality is not the opposite of avarice.

3. Further, as previously determined,[2] a sin gets its species chiefly from its end. Prodigality would seem always to be set upon some untoward end, the objective of its squandering. This particularly is high-living; in *Luke* it is written of the prodigal son, *He wasted his substance living riotously.*[3] It seems to follow that prodigality is the opposite of temperance and insensibility,[a] rather than of avarice and generosity.

ON THE OTHER HAND, Aristotle determines[4] prodigality to be the opposite of liberality and illiberality, which we are calling avarice.

REPLY: In moral matters the opposition of vices to each other and to a virtue is judged on the basis of excess and defect. There is a varying difference of excess and defect in the case of avarice and prodigality.

As to interior attachment to riches, the greedy go too far, loving them beyond measure; the prodigal do not go far enough, being irresponsible about them. As to materialities themselves, it is the mark of prodigality to go too far in giving and to fall short in keeping and acquiring; of avarice, to fail at giving and to overdo getting and keeping. Thus it is clear that prodigality is in opposition to avarice.

---

[3]*Luke* 15, 13
[4]*Ethics* II, 7. 1107b10; IV, 1. 119b27
[a]*insensibilitas* in this usage is the vice opposed to temperance by defect; it is a lack of interest in the pleasures attached to actions necessary for physical well-being; see 2a2æ. 142, 1.

1. Ad primum ergo dicendum quod nihil prohibet eidem inesse opposita secundum diversa. Ab illo enim aliquid magis denominatur quod est* principalius. Sicut autem in liberalitate, quæ medium tenet, præcipua est datio, ad quam acceptio et retentio ordinantur; ita etiam avaritia et prodigalitas præcipue attenduntur secundum dationem. Unde ille qui superabundat in dando, vocatur prodigus; qui autem deficit in dando, vocatur avarus. Contingit autem quandoque quod aliquis deficit in dando qui tamen non excedit in accipiendo, ut Philosophus dicit in *Ethic.*[5] Similiter etiam contingit quod aliquis excedat in dando et ex hoc est prodigus; et simul cum hoc excedat in accipiendo. Vel ex quadam necessitate, quia dum superabundat† in dando, deficiunt ei propria bona, unde cogitur‡ indebite acquirere, quod pertinet ad avaritiam. Vel etiam propter animi inordinationem, dum enim non dat§ propter bonum, quasi contempta virtute, non curat‖ undecumque et qualitercumque accipiat. ¶ Etsic non secundum idem est* prodigus et avarus.

2. Ad secundum dicendum quod prodigalitas attenditur circa passiones pecuniæ, non sicut superabundans in eis sed sicut deficiens.

3. Ad tertium dicendum quod prodigi non semper abundant in dando propter voluptates, circa quas est intemperantia, sed quandoque quidem ex eo quod taliter sunt dispositi ut divitias non curent, quandoque autem propter aliquid aliud. Et frequentius tamen ad intemperantias declinant, tum quia ex quo superflue expendunt in aliis, etiam in rebus voluptuosis expendere non verentur, ad quas magis inclinat concupiscentia carnis; tum etiam quia ex quo non delectantur in bonis virtutum quærunt sibi corporales delectationes. Et inde est quod Philosophus in *Ethic.* dicit quod *multi prodigorum fiunt intemperati.*[6]

articulus 2. utrum prodigalitas sit peccatum

AD SECUNDUM sic proceditur:[1] 1. Videtur quod prodigalitas non sit peccatum. Dicit enim Apostolus, 1 *Ad Tim.* ult., *Radix omnium malorum est cupiditas.*[2] Sed non est radix prodigalitatis quæ ei opponitur. Ergo prodigalitas non est peccatum.

2. Præterea, Apostolus, 1 *Ad Tim.* ult. dicit, *Divitibus hujus saculi præcipe facile tribuere, communicare.*[3] Sed hoc maxime faciunt prodigi. Ergo prodigalitas non est peccatum.

3. Præterea, ad prodigalitatem pertinet superabundare in datione et

---

*Piana: *inest* for *est*
†Leonine: *superabundant*
‡Leonine: *coguntur*
§Leonine: *dant*
‖Leonine: *curant*

Hence: 1. There is no contradiction in opposites existing in the same subject for different reasons, but the subject receives its name from the one that is dominant. In the present case, just as for liberality, which strikes the virtuous mean, giving is the main thing, receiving and retaining, subsidiary; so also giving is the main criterion of avarice and prodigality. So the one who overdoes in giving is called prodigal; the one who falls short, greedy. It does happen, of course, that a person is deficient in giving without being excessive in getting, as Aristotle mentions.[5] Similarly, someone may go too far in giving and thereby be a spendthrift, yet at the same time likewise go too far with regard to getting. This happens out of need, namely where from extravagant spending someone's resources are depleted and he is forced into the graspingness characteristic of avarice. Or there is the case of a perverse character: someone, despising virtue, does spend, but not from any good motive; nor does he care where or how he gets money. Then the one person is not wasteful and greedy in the same respect.

2. Prodigality is in fact judged with reference to feelings about money, namely as it is not excessive but deficient in them.

3. It is not true to say that the prodigal are extravagant in spending always for the sake of the pleasures that are the concern of temperance. Sometimes the reason is simply that they are of such a temperament as to have no concern for money; sometimes there is some other reason. Still it is true that more often than not the prodigal fall into sensual indulgence, and this both because, being accustomed to squandering in other ways, they do not hesitate when it comes to carnal pleasures; and because, finding no joy in the good of virtue, they seek out carnal delights. This is Aristotle's point—*many who are prodigal turn intemperate.*[6]

article 2. whether prodigality is sinful

THE SECOND POINT:[1] 1. Prodigality does not seem to be a sin. While St Paul says that *desire for money is the root of all evils*,[2] it is not the root of prodigality, its opposite. Thus prodigality is not a sin.

2. Further, St Paul says, *Charge the rich of this world to give easily, to communicate to others.*[3] This the prodigal do to perfection. Prodigality, then, is no sin.

3. Further, marks of prodigality are lavishness in spending and the

---

¶Leonine: *accipiant*
*Leonine: *sunt*

[5]*Ethics* IV, 1. 1121b20
[1]cf *In Ethic.* IV, lect. 3 & 4
[3]1 *Timothy* 6, 17

[6]*Ethics* IV, 1. 1121b8
[2]1 *Timothy* 6, 10

deficere in sollicitudine divitiarum. Sed hoc maxime convenit viris perfectis implentibus quod Dominus dicit, *Nolite solliciti esse in crastinum*;[4] et *Vende omnia quæ habes, et da pauperibus.*[5] Ergo prodigalitas non est peccatum.

SED CONTRA est quod filius prodigus vituperatur de sua prodigalitate.

RESPONSIO: Dicendum quod, sicut dictum est,[6] prodigalitas opponitur avaritiæ secundum oppositionem superabundantiæ et defectus. Medium autem virtutis per utrumque horum corrumpitur. Ex hoc autem est aliquid vitiosum et peccatum quod corrumpit bonum virtutis. Unde relinquitur quod prodigalitas sit peccatum.

1. Ad primum ergo dicendum quod illud verbum Apostoli quidam[7] exponunt non de cupiditate actuali sed de quadam habituati cupiditate, quæ est concupiscentia fomitis ex qua omnia peccata oriuntur. Alii[8] vero dicunt quod loquitur de cupiditate generali respectu cujuscumque boni. Et sic manifestum est quod etiam prodigalitas ex cupiditate oritur, prodigus enim aliquod bonum temporale cupit consequi inordinate vel placere aliis vel saltem satisfacere suæ voluntati in dando.

Sed, si quis recte consideret, Apostolus loquitur ibi ad litteram de cupiditate divitiarum; nam supra præmiserat, *Qui volunt divites fieri*, etc. Et sic dicitur esse avaritia radix omnium malorum, non quia omnia mala semper ex avaritia oriantur, sed quia nullum malum est quod non interdum oriatur ex avaritia. Unde et prodigalitas quandoque ex avaritia nascitur, sicut cum aliquis prodige multa consumit intentione captandi favorem aliquorum a quibus divitias accipit.

2. Ad secundum dicendum quod Apostolus monet divites ut facile tribuant et communicent sua secundum quod oportet. Quod non faciunt prodigi; quia, ut Philosophus dicit in *Ethic.*, *dationes eorum non sunt bonæ neque boni gratia neque secundum quod oportet; sed quandoque dant multa illis quos oporteret pauperes esse, scilicet histrionibus et adulatoribus; bonis autem nihil dant.*[9]

3. Ad tertium dicendum quod superexcessus prodigalitatis non attenditur principaliter secundum quantitatem dati, sed magis inquantum excedit id quod fieri oportet. Unde quandoque liberalis majora dat quam prodigus, si necessarium sit. Sic ergo dicendum est quod illi qui

---

[4]*Matthew* 6, 34
[5]*Matthew* 19, 22
[6]art. 1
[7]e.g. William of Auxerre, *Summa aurea* II, 19, 1, 1; Bonaventure, *In Sent.* II, 42, 4 (Quaracchi II, 979)
[8]e.g. Augustine, *De Gen. ad litt.* XI, 15. PL 34, 436; *Glossa Lombardi*. PL 192, 359

absence of anxiety about riches. This is above all the mark of the spiritually perfect, who fulfil Our Lord's injunctions, *Be not solicitous for tomorrow;*[4] *Sell what thou hast and give to the poor.*[5] There is no sin, then, in being prodigal.

ON THE OTHER HAND, the prodigal son is held up to blame for his squandering.[a]

REPLY: As noted,[6] the opposition between prodigality and avarice is one of excess and defect, both of which destroy the virtuous mean. Since anything is vicious and sinful that spoils the good of virtue, it follows that prodigality is sinful.

Hence: 1. Some authorities[7] interpret Paul's statement to mean not actual desire but a kind of state of desire, the concupiscence called the tinder of sin, which is at the origin of all sins.[b] Others[8] say that his reference is to a general desire towards any good whatsoever. In either interpretation it is clear that prodigality would originate in desire, the prodigal craving to achieve some temporal goal—to please others, for example, or at least to indulge self-will by their spending.

A correct reading of the text, however, shows that St Paul is referring here in the literal sense to the desire for riches, since he began this passage with the words, *They that will become rich,* etc. This is the sense in which avarice is called the root of all evils: not that all evils invariably originate in it, but that there is no kind of wickedness that in one instance or another does not. Thus even prodigality sometimes arises from greed, for example when someone spends money lavishly with the intention of gaining the favour of others in order to get rich off them.

2. St Paul is warning the rich to be openhanded and to share what they have in the right way. This the prodigal do not do; as Aristotle notes, *their giving is not good, nor for a good reason, nor as it should be; instead they often give to those who deserve to be poor, to buffoons and flatterers; to the good they would give nothing.*[9]

3. The extravagance of prodigality is not measured chiefly in terms of the amount involved, but of excess in regard to what is proper. Hence sometimes the generous, when necessary, give larger sums than the prodigal. The conclusion, then, is that those who give all they have and

---

[9]*Ethics* IV, 1. 1121b3
[a]*Luke* 15.
[b]*fomes peccati* a metaphor from Augustine, found in Peter Lombard's II *Sent.* 36, and signifying the concupiscence attached to original sin; see 1a2æ. 82, 3; 91, 6; Vol. 26, T. O'Brien, ed., Appendix 9. The term was also used in reference to the relicts of original sin by the Council of Trent; see Denz. 1515.

intentione sequendi Christum omnia sua dant et ab animo suo omnem temporalium sollicitudinem removent non sunt prodigi sed perfecte liberales.

articulus 3. *utrum prodigalitas sit gravius peccatum quam avaritia*

AD TERTIUM sic proceditur:[1] 1. Videtur quod prodigalitas sit gravius peccatum quam avaritia. Per avaritiam enim aliquis nocet proximo, cui bona sua non communicat; per prodigalitatem autem quis sibi ipsi nocet; dicit enim Philosophus in *Ethic.*, quod *corruptio divitiarum, per quas homo vivit, est quædam ipsius esse perditio.*[2] Gravius autem peccat qui sibi ipsi nocet, secundum illud *Eccl., Qui sibi nequam est, cui bonus erit?*[3] Ergo prodigalitas est gravius peccatum quam avaritia.

2. Præterea, inordinatio quæ provenit cum aliqua conditione laudabili, minus est vitiosa. Sed inordinatio avaritiæ quandoque est cum aliqua laudabili conditione, ut patet in illis qui nolunt sua expendere ne cogantur aliena accipere. Prodigalitatis autem inordinatio provenit cum conditione vituperabili; unde et *prodigalitatem attribuimus intemperatis hominibus*, ut Philosophus dicit in *Ethic.*[4] Ergo prodigalitas est gravius peccatum quam avaritia.

3. Præterea, prudentia præcipua est inter morales virtutes, ut supra habitum est.[5] Sed prodigalitas magis opponitur prudentiæ quam avaritia;* dicitur enim *Prov., Thesaurus desiderabilis, et oleum in habitaculo justi; et imprudens homo dissipabit illud.*[6] Et Philosophus dicit in *Ethic.* quod *insipientis est superabundanter dare, et non accipere.*[7] Ergo prodigalitas est gravius peccatum quam avaritia.

SED CONTRA est quod Philosophus dicit in *Ethic.* quod *prodigus multo videtur melior illiberali.*[8]

RESPONSIO: Dicendum quod prodigalitas secundum se considerata minus peccatum est quam avaritia, et hoc triplici ratione. Primo quidem, quia avaritia magis differt a virtute opposita; magis enim ad liberalem pertinet dare, in quo superabundat prodigus, quam accipere vel retinere, in quo superabundat avarus.

Secundo quia prodigus est multis utilis, quibus dat; avarus autem nulli, sed nec sibi ipsi, ut dicitur in *Ethic.*[9]

Tertio, quia prodigalitas est facile sanabilis; et per hoc quod declinat ad ætatem senectutis quæ est contraria prodigalitati et per hoc quod pervenit ad egestatem de facili, dum multa inutiliter consumit et sic pauper factus non potest in dando superabundare; et etiam quia de facili perducitur ad

---

*Piana: *avaritiæ*, to avarice

free their spirit from concern for temporalities with the intention of following Christ are not prodigal, but generous in a supreme degree.

article 3. whether prodigality is a sin more serious than avarice

THE THIRD POINT:[1] 1. Prodigality seems to be a more serious sin than avarice. By failure to share with him, avarice does injury to neighbour; prodigality, to self.—*By wasting the money whereby we live, a person lets his existence run through his fingers.*[2] The one who harms himself is the one who sins more gravely; *He that is evil to himself, to whom shall he be good?*[3] Therefore prodigality is a sin worse than avarice.

2. Further, a moral shortcoming in which there is some praiseworthy element is less wicked. At times this is the case with avarice, for example in those who are unwilling to spend what they have so as not to be forced to receive help from others. Conversely the disorder in prodigality takes place with blameworthy concomitants; *we attribute prodigality to wastrels*, Aristotle says.[4] In consequence, prodigality is worse than avarice.

3. Further, prudence, as noted earlier,[5] holds first place among the moral virtues. But prodigality is more against prudence than avarice is: *There is a treasure to be desired and oil in the dwelling of the just, and the foolish man shall spend it;*[6] *It is the mark of a fool to spend lavishly and take in nothing.*[7] Prodigality is thus the graver sin.

ON THE OTHER HAND, Aristotle states that *the prodigal man seems far better than the stingy man.*[8]

REPLY: Considered in its nature prodigality is less of a sin than avarice for three reasons. First, avarice is more at odds with the opposite virtue, because giving, wherein the prodigal go too far, is more typical of the generous man than getting, which is what the greedy man overdoes.

Secondly, as Aristotle says, *The prodigal man profits the many to whom he gives; the avaricious, nobody, not even himself.*[9]

Thirdly, prodigality is readily remedied. The prodigal man tapers off in old age, which is averse to wasting; he also easily falls into need, once he squanders his possessions, and then in proverty he can no longer be a spendthrift; he also can be readily led to virtue because of a kind of

---

[1] cf *In Ethic.* IV, lect. 4
[2] *Ethics* IV, 1. 1120a2
[3] *Ecclesiasticus* 14, 5
[4] *Ethics* IV, 1. 1119b31
[5] 1a2æ. 61, 2 ad 1; 2a2æ. 66, 1 ad 1
[6] *Proverbs* 21, 20
[7] *Ethics* IV, 1. 1121a26
[8] ibid. 1121a28
[9] ibid. 1128a29

virtutem, propter similitudinem quam habet ad ipsam. Sed avarus non de facili sanatur, ratione supradicta.[10]

1. Ad primum ergo dicendum quod differentia prodigi et avari non attenditur secundum hoc quod est peccare in seipsum et in alium. Nam prodigus peccat in seipsum, dum bona sua consumit unde vivere deberet; peccat etiam in alterum consumendo bona ex quibus aliis deberet providere. Et præcipue hoc apparet in clericis, qui sunt dispensatores bonorum ecclesiæ, quæ sunt pauperum, quos defraudant prodige expendendo.

Similiter et avarus peccat in alios inquantum deficit in dationibus; peccat et in seipsum inquantum deficit in sumptibus; unde dicitur *Eccles.*, *Vir cui Deus dedit divitias, nec tribuit ei potestatem ut comedat ex eis.*[11]

Sed tamen in hoc superabundat prodigus, quia sic sibi et quibusdam aliis nocet quod tamen aliquibus prodest. Avarus autem nec aliis nec sibi prodest, quia non audet uti etiam ad suam utilitatem bonis suis.

2. Ad secundum dicendum quod cum de vitiis communiter loquimur, judicamus de eis secundum proprias rationes ipsorum; sicut circa prodigalitatem attendimus quod superflue consumit divitias; circa avaritiam vero, quod superflue eas retinet. Quod autem quis propter intemperantiam superflue consumat, hoc jam nominat simul peccata multa; unde et tales prodigi sunt pejores, ut dicitur in *Ethic.*[12] Quod autem illiberalis sive avarus abstineat ab accipiendis alienis, etsi in se laudabile videatur, tamen ex causa propter quam facit vituperabile est, dum ideo non vult ab aliis accipere ne cogatur aliis dare.

3. Ad tertium dicendum quod omnia vitia prudentiæ opponuntur, sicut et omnes virtutes a prudentia diriguntur. Et ideo vitium ex hoc ipso quod opponitur soli prudentiæ levius reputatur.

---

[10]118, 5 ad 3
[11]*Ecclesiastes* 6, 2
[12]*Ethics* IV, 1. 1119b32
[a]St Thomas more fully and no less firmly makes this point also in *Quodl.* VI, 12.

affinity for it. The greedy man, for reasons already indicated,[10] is not so readily cured.

Hence: 1. To sin against self and against another is not really the basis of the distinction between the prodigal man and the greedy. The spendthrift sins against self, using up his means of livelihood; against others, by squandering what he should utilize to care for them. This, by the way, stands out especially with clerics, the stewards of the Church's goods, which are the possessions of the poor, who are defrauded by extravagance in the clergy.[a]

The greedy man also sins against others by failing to give; against self, by failing to spend; *a man to whom God hath given riches yet doth not give him the power to eat thereof.*[11]

Still, the prodigal man is better, since he harms self and some other people in such a way that he also does at least some good. The avaricious man is good neither for others nor for himself, since he shrinks from using his possessions even for his own well-being.

2. Speaking of vices generally, judgment about them is based on their intrinsic definition—with prodigality, for example, that it is squandering wealth; with avarice, that it is hoarding it.[b] When there is a case of extravagance for the purpose of intemperance, we are already talking about many sins at once and those who are prodigal in this way are worse, as Aristotle notes.[12] Where there is question of a mean or avaricious man refraining from taking from others, even though this has the appearance of being something praiseworthy, in reality it is reprehensible, considering his motive, namely an unwillingness to accept from others lest he be forced to reciprocate.

3. Just as all virtues come under the guidance of prudence, all vices go against it. On the grounds of opposition to prudence alone, then, a vice would be judged less serious.

---

[b]See 1a2æ. 84, 1.

Quæstio 120. de epieikeia

DEINDE CONSIDERANDUM EST de epieikeia. Circa quam quæruntur duo:
1. utrum epieikeia sit virtus;
2. utrum sit pars justitiæ.

articulus 1. *utrum epieikeia sit virtus*

AD PRIMUM sic proceditur.[1] 1. Videtur quod epieikeia non sit virtus. Nulla enim virtus aufert aliam virtutem. Sed epieikeia aufert aliam virtutem quia tollit id quod justum est secundum legem, et opponi videtur severitati. Ergo epieikeia non est virtus.

2. Præterea, Augustinus dicit, *In istis temporalibus legibus quanquam de his homines judicent cum eas instituunt, tamen cum fuerint institutæ et firmatæ, non licebit judici de ipsis judicare sed secundum ipsas.*[2] Sed epieikeia videtur judicare de lege, quando eam existimat non esse servandam in aliquo casu. Ergo epieikeia magis est vitium quam virtus.

3. Præterea, ad epieikeia videtur pertinere ut attendat ad intentionem legislatoris, ut Philosophus dicit in v *Ethic.*[3] Sed interpretari intentionem legislatoris ad solum principem pertinet; unde imperator dicit in *Codice De legibus et constitutionibus principum. Inter æquitatem jusque interpositam interpretationem nobis solis et oportet, et licet inspicere.*[4] Ergo actus epieikeiæ non est licitus. Ergo epieikeia non est virtus.

SED CONTRA est quod Philosophus in v *Ethic.*[5] ponit eam virtutem.

---

[1] cf III *Sent.* 37, 4. *In Ethic.* v, lect. 15
[2] *De vera relig.* 31. PL 34, 148
[3] *Ethics* v, 10. 1137b19
[4] *Codex Justinianus* I, xiv, 1 (In *Corpus Juris Civilis* II, 67b; P. Krueger, ed., Berlin 1915)
[5] *Ethics* v, 10. 1138a2
[a] *epieikeia* is the exact transliteration of the Greek term of Aristotle; in Latin manuals of theology *epikeia* is usually the spelling. The Leonine critical text of *Sententia Libri Ethicorum* v, 16 has *epiikia* in the Latin text of Aristotle and St Thomas with a long list of variant spellings from manuscript traditions (*Opera Omnia* XLVII, vol. 2, 1969, pp. 321–2). The *Oxford English Dictionary* lists only the obsolete word 'epiky' (var. epicay, epicheia), 'reasonableness, equity as opposed to rigid law'. The *Webster Third New International Dictionary* has 'epieikeia' (var. epikeia), 'interpretation of a law of the Roman Catholic Church that presumes it not applicable in a case of hardship felt to violate the natural law'. This somewhat hodge-podge definition reflects the muddied history the concept has had in Roman Catholic theology since St Thomas's formulation; it is apparent that the definition

Question 120. epieikeia

NEXT WE MUST turn to epieikeia.[a] There are two points of inquiry about epieikeia:

1. whether it is a virtue;
2. and a part of justice.

article 1. whether epieikeia is a virtue

THE FIRST POINT:[1] 1. Epieikeia does not seem to be a virtue. One virtue does not displace another; yet epieikeia displaces virtue, doing away with what is just in law and seeming to be counter to severity. Therefore it is no virtue.

2. Further, Augustine says, *With regard to these earthly laws, even though when they are laid down it is by men making a judgment about them, once they are passed and ratified, a judge has no right to sit in judgment over them, but only in keeping with them.*[2] To act under epieikeia, however, seems to be to pass judgment on a law, namely in the decision that the law is not to be observed in a certain case. Therefore epieikeia is a vice rather than a virtue.

3. Further, the function of epieikeia, as Aristotle says,[3] seems to be to look to the legislator's intent. Interpreting a legislator's intent, however, is in the sole competence of a ruler; thus Justinian says, *It is proper and lawful to us alone to evaluate an interpretation between equity and written law.*[4] Its act being unlawful, therefore, epieikeia is not a virtue.

ON THE OTHER HAND, in the *Ethics*[5] Aristotle lists it as a virtue.[b]

---

clashes directly with the virtue he discusses (see 1 ad 3), and with the noble ideal of the moral life that guides him. *Epieikeia* as moderation of punishment is mentioned in 157, 3 ad 1; the Greek text of *Phil.* 4, 5, cited here in art. 2 obj. 3 & ad 3, and in 160, 2 obj. 1, has επιεικὲς where the Vulgate has *modestia* (*RSV* 'forbearance'; *New English Bible* 'magnanimity'; *Jerusalem Bible* 'tolerance'). See Appendix.

2. *æquitas*, which the Reply uses as a Latin equivalent to *epieikeia*, possibly reflects the *naturalis æquitas* of Roman law (see obj. 3 from Justinian). 'Equity' as moderation in asserting personal rights is an aspect of friendliness (above 114). 'Equity' in its technical legal sense in the English law tradition refers to a system of laws that coexist with statute laws and can supersede them where these conflict with the higher reasonableness of natural justice. Decisions in equity became an established system of laws, hence the courts of equity. See F. W. Maitland, *Equity, A Course of Lectures*, 2d. ed. New York, 1936.

[b] St Thomas follows Aristotle, *Nicomachean Ethics* V, 10, very closely in both articles; see also *In Ethic.* V, lect. 16.

RESPONSIO: Dicendum quod, sicut supra dictum est, cum de legibus ageretur,[6] quia humani actus de quibus leges dantur in singularibus contingentibus consistunt, quæ infinitis modis variari possunt, non fuit possibile aliquam regulam legis institui quæ in nullo casu deficeret. Sed legislatores attendunt ad id quod in pluribus accidit, secundum hoc legem ferentes. Quam tamen in aliquibus casibus servare est contra æqualitatem justitiæ et contra commune bonum quod lex intendit.

Sicut lex instituit quod deposita reddantur, quia hoc ut in pluribus justum est; contingit tamen aliquando esse nocivum, puta si furiosus deposuit gladium et eum reposcat, dum est in furia; vel si aliquis reposcat depositum ad patriæ impugnationem.

In his ergo et similibus casibus malum est sequi legem positam; bonum autem est, prætermissis verbis legis, sequi id quod poscit justitiæ ratio et communis utilitas. Et ad hoc ordinatur epieikeia, quæ apud nos dicitur æquitas; unde patet quod epieikeia est virtus.

1. Ad primum ergo dicendum quod epieikeia non deserit justum simpliciter, sed justum quod est lege determinatum, nec etiam opponitur severitati, quæ sequitur veritatem legis in quibus oportet, sequi autem verba legis in quibus non oportet vitiosum est. Unde dicitur in *Codice, Non dubium est in legem committere eum qui verba legis amplexus, contra legislatoris nititur voluntatem.*[7]

2. Ad secundum dicendum quod ille de lege judicat qui dicit eam non esse bene positam; qui vero dicit verba legis non esse in hoc casu servanda non judicat de lege sed de aliquo negotio particulari quod occurrit.

3. Ad tertium dicendum quod interpretatio locum habet in dubiis, in quibus non licet absque determinatione principis a verbis legis cedere. Sed in manifestis non est opus interpretatione sed executione.

articulus 2. utrum epieikeia sit pars justitiæ

AD SECUNDUM sic proceditur:[1] 1. Videtur quod epieikeia non sit pars justitiæ. Ut enim patet ex supra dictis, duplex est justitia, una particularis, alia legalis. Sed epieikeia non est pars justitiæ particularis, quia se extendit ad omnes virtutes, sicut et justitia legalis. Similiter etiam non est pars justitiæ legalis, quia operatur præter id quod lege positum est. Ergo videtur quod epieikeia non sit pars justitiæ.

2. Præterea, virtus principalior non assignatur virtuti minus principali ut

―――――――――

[6]1a2æ. 96, 6
[7]*Codex Justinianus* I, xiv, 5 (ed. cit. II, 68a)
[1]cf 2a2æ. 80 ad 5. III *Sent.* 33, 3, 4, v. *In Ethic.* V, lect. 16
[c]*In Ethic.* V, *lect.* 16, expresses this distinction of Aristotle as a distinction of the rights under which citizens act: a right (*justum*) that is natural, thus absolute and

REPLY: As determined already in discussing laws,[6] because human acts about which laws are made exist as particular happenings, infinitely variable, there is no possibility of laying down a rule of law that would cover every case. Legislators rather take into account what is ordinarily the case and formulate a law accordingly. Yet observing this law in some situations runs counter to the rightness of justice and the public good intended by all law.

For example, a law lays it down that loans are to be repaid, since usually this is the just thing to do; yet it sometimes happens that this is injurious— suppose a madman who has lent his sword were to demand it back while in the grip of his madness; or someone were to demand its return in order to use it against the homeland.

Thus in these and similar cases to follow the word of law would be an evil; a good to follow what the meaning of justice and the public good demand, letting the letter of the law be set aside. Epieikeia—we call it equity—is addressed to this end and so clearly is a virtue.

Hence: 1. Epieikeia does not put aside what is just absolutely, but what is just under the determination of a law.[c] Neither is it against the virtue of severity, for this follows the exactness of law when it is proper to do so; but to obey the letter of a law when we should not is wicked. Thus the Code rules that *he doubtless acts contrary to the law who by cleaving to the letter goes against the legislator's will.*[7]

2. One who proclaims that a law was badly framed passes judgment on it; one who decides that the letter of a law ought not to be observed in this instance does not pass judgment on the law but on the particular situation at hand.

3. Interpretation is called for in cases of doubt, and here there is no right to depart from the letter of a law without the decision of the ruler. In clear-cut cases, however, there is need not for interpretation but for action.

article 2. whether epieikeia is a part of justice

THE SECOND POINT:[1] 1. Epieikeia does not seem to be a part of justice. From previous discussion it is clear that there are two forms of justice, one particular, the other legal. Epieikeia is not a part of particular justice in that, like legal justice, it ranges over all the virtues. Nor is it a part of legal justice, because it functions outside of what is laid down in law. Seemingly, then, it is not a part of justice.

2. Further, a more important virtue is not assigned as a part to a less

---

universal, and a right that is legal, i.e. determined by positive law. The equitable right here is in accord with the natural right. See Appendix 1.

SUMMA THEOLOGIÆ, 2a2æ. 120, 2

pars; cardinalibus enim virtutibus, quasi principalibus, assignantur secundariæ virtutes ut partes. Sed epieikeia videtur esse principalior virtus quam justitia, ut ipsum nomen sonat: dicitur enim ab *epi*, quod est supra et *dikaion*,* quod est justum. Ergo epieikeia non est pars justitiæ.

3. Præterea, videtur quod epieikeia sit idem quod modestia. Nam ubi Apostolus ⸓*Phil*. dicit, *Modestia vestra nota sit omnibus hominibus*,[2] in Græco habetur epieikeia. Sed secundum Tullium[3] modestia est pars temperantiæ. Ergo epieikeia non est pars justitiæ.

SED CONTRA est quod Philosophus dicit in V *Ethic*. quod *epieikeia est quoddam justum*.[4]

RESPONSIO: Dicendum quod, sicut supra dictum est,[5] virtus aliqua triplicem habet partem, scilicet partem subjectivam, partem integralem et partem potentialem.

Pars autem subjectiva est de qua essentialiter prædicatur totum et est minus.† Quod quidem contingit dupliciter: quandoque enim aliquid prædicatur de pluribus secundum unam rationem, sicut animal de equo et bove; quandoque autem prædicatur secundum prius et posterius, sicut ens prædicatur de substantia et accidente.

Epieikeia ergo est pars justitiæ communiter dictæ tanquam justitia *quædam existens*, ut Philosophus dicit in *Ethic*.[6] Unde patet quod epieikeia est pars subjectiva justitiæ. Et de ea justitia dicitur per prius quam de legali; nam legalis justitia dirigitur secundum epieikeiam. Unde epieikeia est quasi superior regula humanorum actuum.

1. Ad primum ergo dicendum quod epieikeia correspondet proprie justitiæ legali et quodammodo continetur sub ea et quodammodo excedit eam. Si enim justitia legalis dicatur quæ obtemperat legi sive quantum ad verba legis sive quantum ad intentionem legislatoris, quæ potior est, sic epieikeia est pars potior legalis justitiæ. Si vero justitia legalis dicatur solum quæ obtemperat legi secundum verba legis, sic epieikeia non est pars legalis justitiæ sed est pars justitiæ communiter dictæ, divisa contra justitiam legalem sicut excedens ipsam.

2. Ad secundum dicendum quod, sicut Philosophus dicit in *Ethic.*, *epieikeia est melior quadam justitia*,[7] scilicet legali, quæ observat verba legis. Quia tamen et ipsa est justitia quædam, non est melior omni justitia.

---

*Piana: *caion*
†Leonine: *in minus*, has less extension
[2]*Philippians* 4, 5   [3]*Rhet*. II, 54
[4]*Ethics* V, 10. 1137b8
[5]2a2æ. 48
[6]*Ethics* V, 10. 1138a3

important one; the virtues annexed to the cardinal or principal virtues are secondary. Non epieikeia seems to be more important than justice, even as its name suggests; it comes from *epi*, upon, and *dikaion*, what is just.[a] So it is not a part of justice.

3. Further, epieikeia seems to be the same as modesty; the Greek text of *Philippians, Let your modesty be known to all men*,[2] has *epieikeia*.[b] Since Cicero makes modesty a part of temperance,[3] epieikeia is not a part of justice.

ON THE OTHER HAND, in the *Ethics* Aristotle says, *Epieikeia is itself a form of what is just*.[4]

REPLY: As already pointed out,[5] any virtue can have three kinds of part: subjective, integrating and potential.[c]

A subjective part has the whole predicated of it in an essential sense and is narrower than the whole for one of two reasons; sometimes something is predicted of many things on the basis of one meaning—'animal' for example of horse and cow; sometimes the predication implies gradation in meaning—'being' for example as predicated of substance and accident.

As for epieikeia being, as Aristotle says *one form of justice*,[6] it is a part of justice taken in the widest sense. In this way it is clearly a subjective part. And it is called justice in a fuller sense than legal justice, because epieikeia is a norm over and above legal justice. Epieikeia thus stands as a kind of higher rule for human actions.

Hence: 1. Epieikeia is properly allied to legal justice, under which in one sense it is contained and which, in another, it transcends. If we mean by legal justice one that obeys the law as to both the letter and the intent of the legislator—the more important factor—then epieikeia is the principal form of legal justice. If we restrict legal justice to obedience for the letter of the law, then epieikeia is not its part but is a part of justice in the broad sense and is divided against legal justice as surpassing it.

2. As Aristotle says, *Epieikeia is better than some forms of justice*,[7] i.e. a legal justice that observes the letter of the law. Since it is itself a form of justice, however, it is not better than all forms of justice.

---

[7]*Ethics* v, 10. 1138a3

[a]*In Ethic.* v, *lect.* 16, n. 1078 St Thomas gives another etymology: 'from *epi*, above, and *icos*, obedient: because by *epichia* a person obeys in a higher way, observing the intention of the legislator, where the words of the law are in conflict with that intention.' The true etymology seems to be *epi*, *eikos*, suitable, reasonable.

[b]*Philippians* 4, 5 has *to epieikēs*.

[c]See Glossary. A subjective part, i.e. a species of the virtue. An integrating part, i.e. a component element. A potential part, i.e. an allied virtue.

3. Ad tertium dicendum quod ad epieikeiam pertinet aliquid moderari, scilicet observantiam verborum legis. Sed modestia quæ ponitur pars temperantiæ moderatur exteriorem hominis vitam, puta in incessu vel habitu vel aliis hujusmodi. Potest tamen esse quod nomen epieikeiæ apud Græcos per quamdam similitudinem transferatur ad omnes moderationes.

3. It is the part of epieikeia to moderate something, i.e. the observance of the letter of the law. The modesty that is listed as a part of temperance, however, puts moderation into the outward manner of a person, his bearing, dress, etc.[d] Possibly with the Greeks the term epieikeia came to be transferred by way of simile to all forms of moderation.

[d]See 2a2æ. 160; 168; 169.

Quæstio 121. de pietate

DEINDE CONSIDERANDUM EST de dono correspondente justitiæ, scilicet de pietate. Et circa hoc quæruntur duo:

1. utrum sit donum Spiritus Sancti;
2. quid in beatitudinibus et fructibus ei correspondeat.

articulus 1. utrum pietas sit donum

AD PRIMUM sic proceditur:[1] 1. Videtur quod pietas non sit donum. Dona enim a virtutibus differunt, ut supra habitum est.[2] Sed pietas est quædam virtus, ut supra dictum est.[3] Ergo pietas non est donum.

2. Præterea, dona excellentiora sunt virtutibus, maxime moralibus, ut supra habitum est.[4] Sed inter partes justitiæ religio est potior pietate. Ergo si aliqua pars justitiæ debeat poni donum, videtur quod magis religio debeat esse donum quam pietas.

3. Præterea, dona manent in patria et actus donorum, ut supra habitum est.[5] Sed actus pietatis non potest manere in patria; dicit enim Gregorius quod *pietas cordis viscera misericordiæ operibus replet*.[6] Et sic non erit in patria, ubi nulla miseria.* Ergo pietas non est donum.

SED CONTRA est quod *Isa.* ponitur inter dona.[7]

RESPONSIO: Dicendum quod, sicut supra dictum est,[8] dona Spiritus Sancti sunt quædam habituales animæ dispositiones quibus est prompte mobilis a Spiritu Sancto. Inter cætera autem movet nos Spiritus Sanctus ad hoc quod affectum quemdam filialem habeamus ad Deum, secundum illud

---

*Piana: *misericordia*, mercy

[1] cf III *Sent.* 34, 3, 2, i   [2] 1a2æ. 68, 1
[3] 101, 3   [4] 1a2æ. 68, 8   [5] 1a2æ. 68, 6
[6] *Moralia* I, 32. 75, 547
[7] *Isaiah* XI, 2
[8] 1a2æ. 68; 69, 1

[a] For Questions 121-2 recall the Prologue of 2a2æ. where the plan is set out to consider with each virtue the Gift and precept corresponding; to the Gifts, the Beatitudes are especially linked; see 1a2æ. 69, 1.

[b] The patristic and medieval theological traditions on the Gifts of the Holy Spirit took as a capital text for their existence and enumeration, *Isaiah* 11, 2. The text refers to the Messiah; the 'spirit' is the spirit of Yahweh, an expression used throughout the Old Testament to describe God's power in creating the world and inspiring the prophets. In the Hebrew text there is no mention of 'piety'; this is a reduplication of 'fear of the Lord' found in the Septuagint and in the Vulgate. There

Question 121. the gift of piety

NEXT WE COME to the Gift corresponding to justice,[a] namely Piety. The points of inquiry are two:

1. whether this is a Gift of the Holy Spirit;
2. its correlatives among the Beatitudes and Fruits.

article 1. whether piety is one of the Gifts

THE FIRST POINT:[1] 1. It seems that Piety is not a Gift. We have already established that the Gifts are different from the virtues,[2] and that piety is a virtue.[3] Thus it is not a Gift.

2. Further, the Gifts excel the virtues, and especially the moral virtues, as has been shown.[4] Since among the parts of justice religion stands above piety, it would seem that if any part of justice is to be counted a Gift it should be religion rather than piety.

3. Further, as established earlier,[5] the Gifts as well as their operations will continue in heaven. Yet this cannot be true of the act of piety; Gregory says, *Piety fills up the heart's hunger with works of mercy.*[6] Thus it will not go on in heaven, where there will be no misery. Piety, then, is not a Gift.

ON THE OTHER HAND, it is listed among the Gifts in *Isaiah.*[7b]

REPLY: We have already established[8] that the Gifts of the Holy Ghost are special habitual dispositions of soul whereby it is readily responsive to the Holy Spirit. Among those things to which the Holy Spirit inspires us is that we have a special filial attitude towards God; *You have received the*

---

is, however, more to the theological elaboration of the Gifts than a play on a misread isolated biblical text and a medieval penchant for parallels, doublets and mystical numbers like seven. St Thomas's doctrine on the Gifts rests on a tradition that sprang from the overwhelming New Testament evidence of the special intervention of the Holy Spirit in the sanctification of the Christian. His teaching on the *necessity for salvation* (1a2æ. 68, 2) of a way of acting surpassing the human, deliberative mode of the virtues, under the movement of the Holy Spirit is a key to his theology of the Christian life. The co-ordination of this teaching with that on the virtues is an affirmation at once of the ordinary working of grace connatural to human psychology and of the transcendence, uniqueness and unexpectedness of the needed divine intervention. To neglect the essential place of the Gifts in St Thomas's synthesis, not just for the higher stages of mystical life, but for salvation, is to know only the surface of the *Secunda Pars*. It is to know his affirmation of the human values preserved under grace, but not his solution to the frustration experienced in trying to live the life of the virtues.

Rom., Accepistis spiritum adoptionis filiorum, in quo clamamus, Abba, Pater.[9] Et quia ad pietatem proprie pertinet officium et cultum patri exhibere, consequens est quod pietas, secundum quam cultum et officium exhibemus Deo ut patri per instinctum Spiritus Sancti, sit Spiritus Sancti donum.

1. Ad primum ergo dicendum quod pietas quæ exhibet patri carnali officium et cultum est virtus; sed pietas quæ est donum hoc exhibet Deo ut patri.

2. Ad secundum dicendum quod exhibere cultum Deo ut creatori, quod facit religio, est excellentius quam exhibere cultum patri carnali, quod facit pietas quæ est virtus. Sed exhibere cultum Deo ut patri est adhuc excellentius quam exhibere cultum Deo ut creatori et domino. Unde religio est potior pietatis virtute; sed pietas, secundum quod est donum, est potior religione.

3. Ad tertium dicendum quod sicut per pietatem quæ est virtus exhibet homo officium et cultum non solum patri carnali, sed etiam omnibus sanguine junctis secundum quod pertinent ad patrem, ita etiam pietas secundum quod est donum non solum exhibet cultum et officium Deo, sed etiam omnibus hominibus inquantum pertinent ad Deum.

Et propter hoc ad ipsam pertinet honorare sanctos; *non contradicere Scripturæ sive intellectæ, sive non intellectæ*, sicut Augustinus dicit.[10] Ipsa etiam ex consequenti subvenit in miseria constitutis, et quamvis iste actus non habeat locum in patria, præcipue post diem judicii, habebit tamen locum præcipuus actus ejus, qui est revereri Deum affectu filiali; quod præcipue tunc erit, secundum illud *Sap.*, *Ecce quomodo computati sunt inter filios Dei.*[11] Erit etiam mutua honoratio sanctorum ad invicem. Nunc autem ante diem judicii miserentur sancti etiam eorum qui in statu hujus miseriæ vivunt.

articulus 2. utrum dono pietatis respondeat secunda beatitudo, scilicet beati mites

AD SECUNDUM sic proceditur:[1] 1. Videtur quod dono pietatis non respondeat secunda beatitudo, scilicet *Beati mites.*[2] Pietas enim est donum respondens justitiæ, ad quam magis pertinet quarta beatitudo, scilicet,

---

[9]*Romans* 8, 15
[10]*De doctr. christ.* II, 7. PL 34, 39
[11]*Wisdom* 5, 5
[1]2a2æ. 83, 9 ad 3. III *Sent.* 34, 1, 4 & 6. *In Matt.* 5. [2]*Matthew* 5, 4
c*instinctus*, a term that is often used of an infra-rational way of acting (e.g. 1a. 78, 4) here refers to a supra-rational, non-deliberative principle of acting involved in the Gifts and allied to the sense of *inspiratio* as this signifies a 'kind of movement from an outside source'; see 1a2æ. 68, 1. Here St Thomas derives the term *instinctus*, and a way to express the distinction between the Gifts and the virtues, from a chapter of a work he cites as *Liber de bona fortuna* or as the *Eudemian Ethics* (cf 1a2æ. 9, 4). The *De bona fortuna* was an anonymous compilation of Aristotelean

spirit of adoption of sons, whereby we cry Abba (Father).[9] The distinctive meaning of piety involves offering service and honour to a father and so it follows that the Piety whereby these are offered to God as our father under the special prompting[c] of the Holy Spirit is a Gift of the Holy Spirit.

Hence: 1. The piety offering to an earthly father service and honour is a virtue; the one that is a Gift offers these to God as father.

2. To show reverence to God as creator, which is the act of the virtue of religion, is nobler than to show reverence to an earthly father, the act of the virtue of piety. But to offer reverence to God as father is nobler still than to offer this to God as creator and lord.[d] As a consequence, religion surpasses the virtue of piety but Piety the Gift excels religion.

3. Through piety the virtue a person offers service and respect not only to his actual parents but also to all blood relatives by reason of their kinship with parents. Similarly, the Gift of Piety offers honour and service not only to God but also to all men on the basis of their relationship to God.[e]

Thus it is its concern to honour the saints, and, as Augustine says, *not to contradict Scripture whether it be understood or not.*[10] Its secondary interest is also to come to the aid of the wretched, and even while it is true that there is no place for this last in heaven, above all after judgment day, there will be place for the chief act, to reverence God in the spirit of sonship. This above all will go on in heaven; *Behold how they are numbered among the children of God.*[11] So will the saints' honouring of each other. Now, before the final judgment, the saints in heaven are also compassionate towards those who live in the present state of misery.

article 2. *whether the second Beatitude, Blessed are the meek, corresponds to the Gift of Piety*

THE SECOND POINT:[1] 1. There seems to be no correspondence between the Gift of Piety and the second Beatitude, *Blessed are the meek.*[2] Piety is the Gift that goes with justice and justice involves rather the fourth Beatitude,

---

works, two chapters of the *Eudemian Ethics* and the *Magna Moralia*. See T. Deman, 'Le *"Liber de Bona Fortuna"* dans la théologie de Saint Thomas d'Aquin', *Revue des Sciences Philosophiques et Théologiques* XVII (1928), 38–58, esp. 55–8.

[d]The sense of this distinction is allied to the special way in which Christ reveals God as our father, as suggested in the text of *Romans* cited in the Reply. A natural virtue of religion, based on a metaphysics of divine causality, however rare it might be, is still conceivable; but nothing on a natural level could be analogous to the Christ-given relationship to God as father. See 1a. 8, 3 on God's presence as cause and God's presence as object known and loved.

[e]The implication here is that Piety extends to all the aspects of justice considered in the whole treatise.

Beati qui esuriunt et sitiunt justitiam;[3] vel etiam quinta beatitudo, videlicet *Beati misericordes*,[4] quia, ut dictum est,[5] opus misericordiæ pertinet ad pietatem. Non ergo secunda beatitudo pertinet ad donum pietatis.

2. Præterea, donum pietatis dirigitur dono scientiæ, quod adjungitur in connumeratione donorum, *Isa*.[6] Ad idem autem se extendunt dirigens et exequens. Cum ergo ad scientiam pertineat tertia beatitudo, scilicet, *Beati qui lugent*,[7] videtur quod non pertineat ad pietatem secunda beatitudo.

3. Præterea, fructus respondent beatitudinibus et donis, ut supra habitum est.[8] Sed inter fructus bonitas et benignitas magis videntur convenire cum pietate quam mansuetudo, quæ pertinet ad mititatem. Ergo secunda beatitudo non respondet dono pietatis.

SED CONTRA est quod Augustinus dicit, *Pietas congruit mitibus*.[9]

RESPONSIO: Dicendum quod in adaptatione beatitudinum ad dona duplex convenientia potest attendi. Una quidem secundum rationem ordinis, quam videtur Augustinus fuisse secutus. Unde primam beatitudinem attribuit infimo dono, scilicet timoris; secundam autem, scilicet *Beati mites*, attribuit pietati, et sic de aliis.

Alia convenientia potest attendi secundum propriam rationem doni et beatitudinis. Et secundum hoc oportet adaptare beatitudines donis secundum objecta et actus. Et ita pietati magis responderet quarta et quinta beatitudo quam secunda. Secunda tamen beatitudo habet aliquam convenientiam cum pietate, inquantum scilicet per mansuetudinem tolluntur impedimenta actuum pietatis.

1. Et per hoc patet responsio ad primum.

2. Ad secundum dicendum quod, secundum proprietatem beatitudinum et donorum, oportet quod eadem beatitudo respondeat scientiæ et pietati. Sed secundum rationem ordinis diversæ beatitudines eis adaptantur, observata tamen aliquali convenientia, ut supra dictum est.[10]

3. Ad tertium dicendum quod bonitas et benignitas in fructibus directe attribui possunt pietati; mansuetudo autem indirecte, inquantum tollit impedimenta actuum pietatis, ut dictum est.[11]

---

[3] *Matthew* 6
[4] ibid. 7
[5] art. 1 ad 3; 101, 1 ad 2; 4 ad 3
[6] *Isaiah* 11, 2
[7] *Matthew* 5, 5
[8] 1a2æ. 70, 2
[9] *De serm. Dom.* I, 4. PL 34, 1234
[10] In the Reply
[11] In the Reply

Blessed are they who hunger and thirst after justice;[3] or even the fifth, *Blessed are the merciful*,[4] since, as noted,[5] the works of mercy engage piety. It is not, then, the second Beatitude that is related to the Gift of Piety.

2. Further, the Gift of Piety is under the direction of Knowledge, the Gift placed along side it in *Isaiah's* listing.[6] But direction and execution have the same interest. Since the third Beatitude, *Blessed are they that mourn*,[7] is the concern of Knowledge, the second would not seem to be that of Piety.

3. Further, as established earlier,[8] the Fruits correspond to the Beatitudes and Gifts.[a] Among the Fruits goodness and benignity seem to have a closer affinity to Piety than does meekness, which is a part of mildness. Thus the second Beatitude does not correspond to the Gift of Piety.

ON THE OTHER HAND, Augustine states, *Piety becomes the meek*.[9]

REPLY: In the correspondence between Beatitude and Gifts two kinds of affinity can be considered. The first has its basis in their order of enumeration and Augustine apparently followed this. Thus he links the first Beatitude to the Gift listed last, Fear of the Lord; the second, *Blessed are the meek*, to Piety and so on.

But it is possible to look to another kind of affinity based on the proper meaning of each Gift and Beatitude. In this view the matching of Beatitude to Gift would have to be based on their objectives and acts. Accordingly, the fourth and fifth rather than the second Beatitude would correspond to Piety. Still the second Beatitude does have some relationship to Piety, namely inasmuch as obstacles to the act of Piety are removed through meekness.[b]

Hence: 1. The response to the first of the arguments is clear.

2. On the basis of the intrinsic meaning of the Beatitudes and Gifts, the same Beatitude corresponds to both Knowledge and Piety. On the basis of the order of their enumeration, however, they have different correlative Beatitudes, which, as noted,[10] do still evince some sort of connection with them.

3. Of the Fruits, the association of goodness and benignity to Piety is direct; of meekness, indirect, in that, as pointed out,[11] this takes away impediments to the acts of Piety.

---

[a]The Fruits are the Fruits of the Spirit, according to the text of *Gal.* v, 22: *But the fruit of the spirit is love, joy, peace, patience, kindness, goodness, faithfulness, gentleness, self-control; against such there is no law.* (RSV)

[b]Compare these reasons of correspondence to those given in 1a2æ. 69, 3 & 70, 3. St Thomas is mainly concerned with finding various plausible reasons for some of the patristic matchings.

Quæstio 122. de præceptis justitiæ

DEINDE CONSIDERANDUM EST de præceptis justitiæ. Et circa hoc quæruntur sex:

1. utrum præcepta Decalogi sint præcepta justitiæ;
2. de primo præcepto Decalogi;
3. de secundo;
4. de tertio;
5. de quarto;
6. de aliis sex.

articulus 1. *utrum præcepta Decalogi sint præcepta justitiæ*

AD PRIMUM sic proceditur:[1] 1. Videtur quod præcepta Decalogi non sint præcepta justitiæ. *Intentio* enim *legislatoris est cives facere virtuosos* secundum omnem virtutem, ut dicitur in *Ethic.*;[2] unde et in *Ethic.* dicitur quod lex præcipit de omnibus actibus virtutum omnium.[3] Sed præcepta Decalogi sunt prima principia totius divinæ legis. Ergo præcepta Decalogi non pertinent ad solam justitiam.

2. Præterea, ad justitiam videntur pertinere præcipue præcepta judicialia, quæ contra moralia dividuntur, ut supra habitum est.[4] Sed præcepta Decalogi sunt præcepta moralia, ut ex supra dictis patet.[5] Ergo præcepta Decalogi non sunt præcepta justitiæ.

3. Præterea, lex præcipue tradit præcepta de actibus justitiæ pertinentibus ad bonum commune, puta de officiis publicis et aliis hujusmodi. Sed de his non fit mentio in præceptis Decalogi. Ergo videtur quod præcepta Decalogi non pertineant proprie ad justitiam.

4. Præterea, præcepta Decalogi distinguuntur in duas tabulas, secundum dilectionem Dei et proximi, quæ pertinent ad virtutem caritatis. Ergo præcepta Decalogi magis pertinent ad caritatem quam ad justitiam.

SED CONTRA est quod justitia sola videtur esse virtus per quam ordinamur ad alterum. Sed per omnia præcepta Decalogi ordinamur ad alterum, ut patet discurrenti per singula. Ergo omnia præcepta Decalogi pertinent ad justitiam.

---

[1] cf 2a2æ. 56, 1 ad 1; 140, 1 ad 3
[2] *Ethics* II, 1. 1103b3
[3] *Ethics* V, 1. 1129b19
[4] 1a2æ. 99, 4

Question 122. precepts about justice

NEXT TO BE considered are the precepts about justice. Here there are six points of inquiry:
1. whether the commandments of the Decalogue are the precepts of justice;
2. the first of the Ten Commandments;
3. the second;
4. the third;
5. the fourth;
6. the remaining six.

article 1. whether the Ten Commandments are the precepts of justice

THE FIRST POINT:[1] 1. The Ten Commandments do not seem to be the precepts of justice. As stated in the *Ethics, the intention of a lawgiver is to make citizens virtuous*[2] and this with respect to every virtue, since in the *Ethics* it is pointed out that law lays down commands regarding acts of all the virtues.[3] The Ten Commandments are the prime principles in the whole of God's law. They do not, then, involve only justice.

2. Further, justice seems to be concerned with judicial precepts, those namely which, as we have already shown,[4] are divided against moral precepts. The Ten Commandments, as is clear from previous discussion,[5] are moral and consequently are not precepts having to do with justice.

3. Further, above all law lays down precepts about those acts of justice concerned with the public good, for example about political office and the like. There is, however, no mention of such things in the Ten Commandments. The precepts of the Decalogue, then, do not seem to be the distinctive concern of justice.

4. Further, the Ten Commandments are separated into two tablets, corresponding to the love of God and the love of neighbour, and these involve the virtue of charity. Consequently the Ten Commandments are related to charity rather than to justice.

ON THE OTHER HAND, it seems that justice alone is the virtue by which we are rightly disposed towards others. A glance through the list of Commandments makes it clear that through each one we are rightly directed towards others. Therefore all involve justice.

---

[5] 1a2æ. 100, 3

RESPONSIO: Dicendum quod præcepta Decalogi sunt prima præcepta* legis et quibus statim ratio naturalis assentit sicut manifestissimis principiis. Manifestissime autem ratio debiti, quæ requiritur ad præceptum, apparet in justitia, quæ est ad alterum. Quia in his quæ sunt ad seipsum videtur primo aspectu† quod homo sit sui dominus et quod liceat ei facere quodlibet, sed in his quæ sunt ad alterum manifeste apparet quod homo est alteri obligatus ad reddendum ei quod debet. Et ideo præcepta Decalogi oportuit ad justitiam pertinere.

Unde tria prima præcepta sunt de actibus religionis, quæ est potissima pars justitiæ; quartum autem præceptum est de actibus pietatis, quæ est pars justitiæ secunda; alia vero sex dantur de actibus justitiæ communiter dictæ, quæ inter æquales attenditur.

1. Ad primum ergo dicendum quod lex intendit omnes homines facere virtuosos sed ordine quodam, ut scilicet prius tradat eis præcepta de his in quibus est manifestior ratio debiti, ut dictum est.[6]

2. Ad secundum dicendum quod judicialia præcepta sunt quædam determinationes moralium præceptorum prout ordinantur ad proximum, sicut et cæremonialia sunt quædam determinationes præceptorum moralium prout ordinantur ad Deum. Unde neutra præcepta continentur in Decalogo; sunt tamen determinationes præceptorum Decalogi et sic ad justitiam pertinent.

3. Ad tertium dicendum quod ea quæ pertinent ad bonum commune oportet diversimode dispensari secundum hominum diversitatem. Et ideo non fuerunt ponenda inter præcepta Decalogi sed inter præcepta judicialia.

4. Ad quartum dicendum quod præcepta Decalogi pertinent ad caritatem sicut ad finem, secundum illud 1 *Ad Tim.* 1, *Finis præcepti est caritas*,[7] sed ad justitiam pertinent inquantum immediate sunt de actibus justitiæ.

articulus 2. utrum primum præceptum Decalogi convenienter tradatur

AD SECUNDUM sic proceditur:[1] 1. Videtur quod primum præceptum Decalogi inconvenienter tradatur. Magis enim homo est obligatus Deo

---

*Piana: *principia*, principles
†Leonine: *aspectui*
[6]In the Reply   [7]1 *Timothy* 1, 5
[1]cf 1a2æ. 100, 6. III *Sent.* 37, 2, ii
[a]The Ten Commandments are considered in greater detail in the treatise on the Old Law, 1a2æ. 100, 3–8. Vol. 29, ed. D. J. Bourke. Note that the point being made here is stated more precisely in 1a2æ. 100, 3: that the most general and common moral precepts (see 1a2æ. 94, 2) are contained in the Decalogue as principles are contained in their proximate conclusions (thus it is not accurate to identify natural law and the Ten Commandments); moral precepts that are more refined and

REPLY: The Ten Commandments are the primary precepts in all law, and natural reason gives immediate assent to them as being plainly evident principles.[a]

Indebtedness, essential to the meaning of precept, is most clearly present in matters of justice, since justice has reference to another person. In matters of self-concern, it seems, at least on the face of it, that a man is autonomous and can do what he likes; but in matters involving other people it is evident that he is under obligation to render to them whatever he owes them.[b] For this reason the Ten Commandments necessarily relate to justice.

The first three commandments, accordingly, involve acts of religion, the most important part of justice; the fourth, acts of piety, the part next in importance; the other six are given in regard to justice in its usual meaning, the justice observed among equals.

Hence: 1. Law is directed to making all men virtuous but in a certain order, namely in such a way that it legislates for them first of all in matters wherein indebtedness is more obvious,[c] as we have stated.[6]

2. Judicial precepts are particular determinations of the moral precepts as to the relationships of the moral precepts towards neighbour, just as ceremonial precepts are particular applications of the moral precepts as these refer to God.[d] This is why neither kind is contained among the Ten Commandments; yet they are applications of the Decalogue and so do involve justice.

3. Things bearing upon the public good have to be administered in different ways depending on the differences among people. This is why they had to be included not among the Ten Commandments but among the judicial precepts.

4. The Ten Commandments are related to charity as their end; *The end of the commandments is charity.*[7] They are related to justice in that their immediate concern is acts of justice.

article 2. whether the first of the Ten Commandments is appropriately expressed

THE SECOND POINT:[1] 1. The first precept of the Decalogue seems to be expressed inaccurately. The text, *Shall we not much more obey the Father*

---

developed by the judgments of those wise with moral wisdom are contained in the Decalogue as conclusions in their remote principles.
[b]See above 117, 4 note *c*.
[c]See 1a2æ. 100, 2, 3 & ad 3.
[d]On the distinction of moral, ceremonial and judicial precepts in the Old Law, see 1a2æ. 99, 2-5; Vol. 29 of this series, 99, 5 note *a*, pp. 46-7.

quam patri carnali, secundum illud *Ad Heb., Quanto magis obtemperabimus Patri spirituum, et vivemus?*[2] Sed præceptum pietatis qua honoratur pater ponitur affirmative, cum dicitur, *Honora patrem tuum et matrem tuam.*[3] Ergo multo magis primum præceptum religionis qua honoratur Deus debuit proponi affirmative; præsertim cum affirmatio naturaliter sit prior negatione.

2. Præterea, primum præceptum Decalogi ad religionem pertinet, ut dictum est.[4] Sed religio, cum sit una virtus, habet unum actum. In primo autem præcepto prohibentur tres actus. Nam primo dicitur, *Non habebis deos alienos coram me*; secundo dicitur, *Non facies tibi sculptile*; tertio vero, *Non adorabis ea neque coles.*[5] Ergo inconvenienter traditur primum præceptum.

3. Præterea, Augustinus dicit quod per primum præceptum excluditur vitium superstitionis.[6] Sed multæ sunt aliæ noxiæ superstitiones præter idololatriam ut supra dictum est.[7] Insufficienter ergo prohibetur sola idololatria.

IN CONTRARIUM est Scripturæ auctoritas.[8]

RESPONSIO: Dicendum quod ad legem pertinet facere homines bonos. Et ideo oportet præcepta legis ordinari secundum ordinem generationis, qua scilicet homo fit bonus. In ordine autem generationis duo sunt attendenda. Quorum primum est quod prima pars primo constituitur; sicut in generatione animalis primo generatur cor et in domo primo fit fundamentum. In bonitate autem animæ prima pars est bonitas voluntatis, ex qua aliquis homo bene utitur qualibet alia bonitate. Bonitas autem voluntatis attenditur ad objectum suum, quod est finis. Et ideo in eo qui erat per legem instituendus ad virtutem, primo oportuit quasi jacere quoddam fundamentum religionis per quam homo debite ordinatur in Deum, qui est ultimus finis humanæ voluntatis.

Secundo attendendum est in ordine generationis quod primo contraria et impedimenta tolluntur; sicut agricola primo purgat agrum, et postea projicit semina, secundum illud *Jer., Novate vobis novale, et nolite serere super spinas.*[9] Et ideo circa religionem primo homo erat instituendus ut impedimenta veræ religionis excluderet. Præcipuum autem impedimentum religionis est quod homo falso deo inhæreat, secundum illud *Matt., Non potestis servire Deo et mammonæ.*[10] Et ideo in primo præcepto legis excluditur cultus falsorum deorum.

---

[2]*Hebrews* 12, 9
[4]art. 1
[6]*Serm. ad pop.* IX, 9. PL 38, 85
[7]2a2æ. 92, 2
[3]*Exodus* 20, 12
[5]*Exodus* 20, 3

of spirits and live?[2] is an indication of a more pressing obligation towards God than towards our parents in the flesh. Now the commandment about piety, whereby parents are respected, is stated affirmatively—*Honour your father and your mother*.[3] With greater reason the first precept, about religion whereby God is honoured, should be stated affirmatively and especially since affirmation naturally comes before negation.

2. Further, the first of the Ten Commandments, as I have pointed out,[4] is a matter of religion. Being one virtue, religion has one act, whereas in the first commandment three acts are ruled out. First it states, *Thou shalt not have strange gods before me*; secondly, *Thou shalt not make to thyself any graven thing*; thirdly, *Thou shalt not adore them nor serve them*.[5] Consequently the first commandment is expressed ineptly.

3. Further, Augustine asserts[6] that the vice of superstition is proscribed by the first commandment, and, as already indicated,[7] there are many other harmful superstitions besides idolatry. Thus the prohibition of idolatry alone is not enough.

ON THE CONTRARY stands the authority of Scripture.[8]

REPLY: The function of law is to make men good and for this reason the commandments of law should follow the order of development in which a person comes to be good. In any order of growth there are two things to note. The first is that the primary part is formed first; in the development of an animal, for example, the heart comes first; in the building of a house, the foundation. And in the forming of goodness of soul the primary part is goodness of will, which is the source of a person's right use of any other kind of goodness. Now goodness of will is determined according to the objective of the will, the end.[a] This is why for one who was to be built up in virtue through law, it was necessary to lay as it were a foundation, namely the virtue of religion, whereby a person is set in proper relationship to God, who is the final end of man's will.

Next in any pattern of development there must be concern for the removal of contraries and obstacles; a farmer, for example, clears his field before he sows—*Break up anew your fallow ground and sow not upon thorns*.[9] Thus with regard to religion man had first of all to be trained to set aside obstacles to true worship, the chief of which is devotion to a false god—*You cannot serve God and mammon*.[10] Thus in the first precept of the Law the worship of false gods is proscribed.

---

[8] *Exodus* 20, 3
[9] *Jeremiah* 4, 3
[10] *Matthew* 6, 24
[a] See 1a2æ. 9, 1 & 3.

1. Ad primum ergo dicendum quod etiam circa religionem ponitur unum præceptum affirmativum, scilicet, *Memento ut diem sabbati sanctifices*.[11] Sed erant præmittenda* præcepta negativa, quibus impedimenta religionis tollerentur. Quamvis enim affirmatio naturaliter sit prior negatione, tamen in via generationis negatio qua removentur impedimenta est prior, ut dictum est.[12] Et præcipue in rebus divinis, in quibus negationes præferuntur affirmationibus propter insufficientiam nostram ut Dionysius dicit.[13]

2. Ad secundum dicendum quod cultus alienorum deorum dupliciter apud aliquos observabatur. Quidam enim quasdam creaturas pro diis colebant absque institutione imaginum; unde Varro dicit quod antiqui Romani diu sine simulacris deos coluerunt.[14] Et hic cultus prohibetur primo, cum dicitur, *Non habebis deos alienos*.

Apud alios autem erat cultus falsorum deorum sub quibusdam imaginibus. Et ideo opportune prohibetur et ipsarum imaginum institutio, cum dicitur, *Non facies tibi sculptile*; et imaginum ipsarum cultus, cum dicitur: *Non coles ea*, etc.

3. Ad tertium dicendum quod omnes aliæ superstitiones procedunt ex aliquo pacto cum dæmonibus inito tacito vel expresso. Et ideo omnes intelliguntur prohiberi in hoc quod dicitur, *Non hubebis deos alienos*.

articulus 3. utrum secundum præceptum Decalogi convenienter tradatur

AD TERTIUM sic proceditur:[1] 1 Videtur quod secundum præceptum Decalogi non convenienter tradatur. Hoc enim præceptum, *Non assumes nomen Dei tui in vanum*,[2] sic exponitur in glossa,[3] Non existimes creaturam esse Filium Dei, per quod prohibetur error contra fidem. Et *Deut*. v[4] exponitur, *Non assumes nomen Dei tui in vanum*, scilicet, *nomen Dei ligno et lapidi attribuendo*,[5] per quod prohibetur falsa confessio, quæ est actus infidelitatis, sicut et error. Infidelitas autem est prior superstitione, sicut et fides religione. Ergo hoc præceptum debuit præmitti primo, in quo prohibetur superstitio.

2. Præterea, nomen Dei ad multa assumitur, sicut ad laudandum, ad miracula faciendum et universaliter ad omnia quæ dicuntur vel fiunt a nobis, secundum illud *Col.*, *Omne quodcumque facitis in verbo vel opere, in*

---

*Piana: *prætermittenda*, omitted
[11]*Exodus* 20, 8 [12]In the Reply
[13]*De cælesti hierarchia* 2. PG 3, 141
[14]From Augustine, *De civ. Dei* IV, 31. PL 41, 138
[1]cf 1a2æ. 100, 5 & 6 III *Sent.* 37, 2, ii   [2]*Exodus* 20, 7
[3]*Interlinearis*   [4]*Deuteronomy* 5, 11   [5]*Interlinearis*

Hence: 1. In regard to religion, too, there is an affirmative precept, *Remember that thou keep holy the sabbath day*.[11] Still the negative precepts had to be set forth first in order to clear away obstacles to religion.[b] For while it is true that affirmation has a natural precedence over negation, in a process of growth there is one negation coming first, namely the clearing away of obstacles, as has been said,[12] and the more so in the things of God wherein because of our inadequacy negation has greater value than affirmation, as Denis says.[13]

2. The worship of strange gods used to be carried on in two ways among certain people. Some without setting up images would worship some creature or other as a god; thus Varro notes[14] that for a long time the early Romans worshipped their gods without idols. This is the kind of cult prohibited first—*Thou shalt not have strange gods*.

With other people, however, there was a cult of false gods in the shape of various images. Hence the setting up of idols is aptly proscribed in the words, *Thou shalt not make to thyself any graven thing*, and the worship of their idols in the words, *Thou shalt not adore them*, etc.

3. All other kinds of superstition issue from some pact with the demons, entered into tacitly or expressly; and so, in the words, *Thou shalt not have strange gods*, the prohibition of all forms of superstition is understood.

article 3. whether the second precept of the Decalogue is proposed in the right way

THE THIRD POINT:[1] 1. The second of the Ten Commandments does not appear to be put correctly. This precept, *Thou shalt not take the name of thy God in vain*[2]—is given the following explanation by a gloss[3] on *Exodus*, Thou shalt not regard the Son of God as a creature; thereby an error opposed to faith is forbidden. And the same text in *Deuteronomy*[4] has this commentary, *Thou shalt not take the name of thy God in vain, namely by conferring God's name on wood or stone*,[5] thereby proscribing a false profession of faith, which, like error, is also an act against faith. Lack of faith is more basic than superstition, even as faith is more basic than religion. So this commandment should have been put ahead of the first with its prohibition of superstition.

2. Further, God's name is invoked for many purposes—in praise, in performing miracles and in fact generally in all our words and actions;

---

[b]A negative precept is the prohibition of an evil act; an affirmative precept, the prescription of a virtuous act (see 2a2æ. 33, 2). The most commonly quoted adage concerning the two is that the affirmative precept obliges *semper sed non ad semper*, always but not at every instant, rather at the time and in the circumstances appropriate; the negative precept binds *semper et ad semper*, i.e. there is no instant when it does not apply. See 1a2æ. 71, 5 ad 3; 100, 10 & ad 2; 2a2æ. 33, 2.

nomine Domini facite.[6] Ergo præceptum quo prohibetur nomen Dei assumi in vanum videtur universalius esse quam præceptum quo prohibetur superstitio. Et ita debuit ei præmitti.

3. Præterea, exponitur illud præceptum, *Non assumes nomen Dei tui in vanum;*[7] *jurando scilicet pro nihilo.*[8] Unde videtur per hoc prohiberi vana juratio, quæ scilicet est sine judicio. Sed multo gravior est falsa juratio, quæ est sine veritate; et injusta juratio, quæ est sine justitia. Ergo magis debuerunt illa prohiberi per hoc præceptum.

4. Præterea, multo gravius peccatum est blasphemia vel quidquid fiat verbo vel facto in contumeliam Dei quam perjurium. Ergo blasphemia et alia hujsmodi magis debuerunt per hoc præceptum prohiberi.

5. Præterea, multa sunt Dei nomina. Ergo non debuit indeterminate dici, *Non assumes nomen Dei tui in vanum.*

SED IN CONTRARIUM est Scripturæ auctoritas.[9]

RESPONSIO: Dicendum quod oportet prius impedimenta veræ religionis excludere in eo qui instituitur ad virtutem quam eum in vera religione fundare. Opponitur autem veræ religioni aliquid dupliciter. Uno modo per excessum, quando scilicet id quod est religionis alteri indebite exhibetur, quod pertinet ad superstitionem. Alio modo quasi per defectum reverentiæ, cum scilicet Deus contemnitur, quod pertinet ad vitium irreligiositatis, ut supra habitum est.[10] Superstitio autem impedit religionem quantum ad hoc ne suscipiatur Deus ad colendum. Ille autem cujus animus implicatus est indebito cultui non potest simul debitum Dei cultum suscipere, secundum illud *Isa., Angustatum est stratum, ut alter decidat,* scilicet Deus verus vel falsus a corde hominis, *et pallium breve utrumque operire non potest.*[11]

Per irreligiositatem autem impeditur religio quantum ad hoc ne Deus, postquam susceptus est, honoretur. Prius autem est Deum suscipere ad colendum quam eum susceptum honorare. Et ideo præmittitur præceptum quo prohibetur superstitio secundo præcepto, quo prohibetur perjurium ad irreligiositatem pertinens.

1. Ad primum ergo dicendum quod illæ expositiones sunt mysticæ. Litteralis autem expositio est quæ habetur *Deut., Non assumes nomen Dei tui in vanum,*[12] scilicet, *jurando pro re quæ non est.*[13]

---

[6]*Colossians* 3, 17   [7]*Exodus* 20, 7   [8]*Interlinearis*
[9]*Exodus* 20, 7; *Deuteronomy* 5, 11   [10]2a2æ. 97, prol.   [11]*Isaiah* 28, 20
[12]*Deuteronomy* 5, 11   [13]*Interlinearis*
[a]*judicium* has the technical sense of pronouncing legal judgment or sentence; see 2a2æ. 60; it may also be extended, as an act of strict justice, outside the forensic to any serious determination of what is right and just.

All whatsoever you do in word or in work, do ye in the name of the Lord.[6] For this reason a commandment forbidding the idle use of God's name seems broader in scope than one forbidding superstition and so should have been listed first.

3. Further, the text, *Thou shalt not take the name of thy God in vain*,[7] is thus interpreted, *namely by swearing for no good reason*.[8] This would lead us to think that what is forbidden is idle swearing, i.e. outside of a court of justice.[a] Still false swearing, i.e. without truth, and unjust swearing, i.e. without justice, are far worse. These, then, should have been forbidden instead.

4. Further, a much graver sin than perjury is blasphemy or indeed anything done by word or deed as an insult to God. Blasphemy and similar things, then, should rather have been forbidden by this precept.

5. Further, God's names are many; therefore the statement, *Thou shalt not take the name of thy God in vain*, should not have been left so indefinite.

ON THE OTHER HAND, the authority of Scripture stands.[9]

REPLY: Where someone is being formed in virtue, before grounding him in genuine religious worship, it is first necessary that hindrances thereto be removed.[b] Something is inimical to genuine religion in two ways. The first is by way of excess, namely when religious deference is paid to something without reason, the case with superstition. The second is by way of falling short in reverence, namely when God is made light of; this is a case of the vice of irreligion, as indicated before.[10]

Superstition is this kind of obstacle to religion, namely in that it keeps a person from accepting God as the object of worship. For a person whose spirit is given over to some improper worship cannot at the same time undertake the worship owed to God; *The bed is straitened so that one must fall out*—i.e. either the true God or a false god from man's heart—*and a short covering cannot cover both*.[11]

Irreligion is another kind of obstacle, namely to giving proper honour to God once accepted. Accepting God as the object of worship comes before honouring him once he is accepted and so the commandment forbidding superstition is put before the second prohibiting perjury, an aspect of irreligion.

Hence: 1. These are mystical interpretations, the literal one being that given on *Deuteronomy*, *Thou shalt not take the name of thy God in vain*,[12] namely *by swearing regarding a thing that is not so*.[13]

---

[b]See above 108, 2 note *c*.

2. Ad secundum dicendum quod non prohibetur quælibet assumptio divini nominis per hoc præceptum sed proprie illa qua sumitur divinum nomen ad confirmationem humani verbi per modum juramenti. Quia ista assumptio divini nominis est frequentior apud homines. Potest tamen ex consequenti intelligi ut per hoc prohibeatur omnis inordinata divini nominis assumptio. Et secundum hoc procedunt illæ expositiones de quibus supra dictum est.[14]

3. Ad tertium dicendum quod *pro nihilo jurare* dicitur ille qui jurat pro eo quod non est, quod pertinet ad falsam jurationem, quæ principaliter perjurium nominatur, ut supra dictum est.[15] Quando enim aliquis falsum jurat, tunc juratio est vana secundum seipsam, quia non habet firmamentum veritatis. Quando autem aliquis jurat sine judicio ex aliqua levitate, si verum jurat, non est ibi vanitas ex parte ipsius juramenti, sed solum ex parte jurantis.

4. Ad quartum dicendem quod sicut ei qui instruitur in aliqua scientia primo proponuntur quædam communia documenta, ita etiam lex quæ instituit hominem ad virtutem in præceptis Decalogi, quæ sunt prima, ea proposuit vel prohibendo vel mandando quæ communius in cursu humanæ vitæ solent accidere. Et ideo inter præcepta Decalogi prohibetur perjurium, quod frequentius accidit quam blasphemia, in quam homo rarius prolabitur.

5. Ad quintum dicendum quod nominibus Dei debetur reverentia ex parte rei significatæ, quæ est una, non autem ratione vocum significantium, quæ sunt multæ. Et ideo singulariter dixit, *Non assumes nomen Dei tui in vanum*, quia non differt per quodcumque nomen Dei perjurium committatur.

articulus 4. utrum tertium Decalogi præceptum convenienter tradatur, scilicet de sanctificatione sabbati

AD QUARTUM sic proceditur:[1] 1. Videtur quod inconvenienter tertium præceptum Decalogi tradatur, scilicet de sanctificatione sabbati.[2] Hoc enim præceptum, spiritualiter intellectum, est generale; dicit enim Ambrosius, super illud *Luc.*, *Archisynagogus indignans quia sabbato curasset*,[3] *Lex*, inquit, *in sabbato non hominem curare, sed servilia opera facere, idest peccatis gravari, prohibet.*[4] Secundum autem litteralem sensum, est præceptum cæremoniale; dicitur enim, *Videte ut sabbatum meum custodiatis, quia signum est inter me et vos in generationibus vestris.*[5] Præcepta autem Decalogi et sunt præcepta spiritualia et sunt moralia. Inconvenienter ergo ponitur inter præcepta Decalogi.

---

[14] In obj. 1
[15] 2a2æ. 98, 1 ad 3
[1] 1a2æ. 100, 5 ad 2. III *Sent.* 37, 5. *In Isaiah* 56. *In Coloss.* 2, lect. 4. *De duobus præceptis caritatis*

2. Not just any sort of use of God's name is forbidden by the commandment, but that precisely whereby it is invoked for the purpose of confirming a person's word by way of an oath. For this is the way of taking God's name more usual among men. We can, however, take it as a corollary that every misuse of God's name is thereby prohibited. This is the basis for the interpretations mentioned.[14]

3. Someone is said to swear without reason when he does so to back up something non-existent; this is a case of false swearing, for which, as noted earlier,[15] perjury is the primary term. For when someone swears a false thing, his swearing is then vain in content, not having the solidity of truth. When, however, someone swears apart from a legal case out of levity, should he swear to something true, then it is not the oath that is frivolous, but the one making it.

4. Just as to one being instructed in any science certain general teachings are first proposed, so also the law, forming men in virtue, proposes in the prohibitions and prescriptions of the Ten Commandments, which are basic, those things likely to occur in the normal course of living. This is why the Ten Commandments include a prohibition of perjury, a more frequent occurrence than blasphemy, which people fall into more rarely.

5. Reverence is due to the names of God on the basis of the reality signified, which is one, not on the basis of the words signifying, which are manifold. This is the reason for the singular form, *Thou shalt not take the name of thy God in vain*, since in committing perjury it makes no difference which of God's names is employed.

article 4. whether the third commandment, namely to keep holy the sabbath, is rightly proposed

THE FOURTH POINT:[1] 1. The third commandment, namely on keeping the sabbath holy,[2] does not seem right. Taken in a spiritual sense, it is general —Ambrose saying, on *Luke*, *The ruler of the synagogue being angry that he had healed on the sabbath*,[3] that *The Law does not forbid healing someone on the sabbath, but doing servile works, i.e. bearing the burden of sins*.[4] In its literal sense, the commandment is a ceremonial precept, as *Exodus* indicates, *See that you keep my sabbath, because it is a sign between me and you in your generations*.[5] Since the Ten Commandments are spiritual and moral precepts, this one should not be among them.

---

[2] *Exodus* 20, 8
[3] *Luke* 13, 14
[4] From Bede, *In Lucæ evangelium expositio* IV, on 13, 14. PL 92, 505. The Venerable Bede (*c.* 673–735), great English Doctor of the Church, in his scriptural commentaries relied on Ambrose and other Latin Fathers.
[5] *Exodus* 31, 13

2. Præterea, cæremonialia legis præcepta continent sacra, sacrificie, sacramenta et observantias, ut supra habitum est.[6] Ad sacra autem pertinebant non solum sacri dies, sed etiam sacra loca et sacra vasa et alia hujusmodi. Similiter etiam erant multi sacri dies præter sabbatum. Inconveniens igitur est quod, prætermissis omnibus aliis cæremonialibus, de sola observantia sabbati fit mentio.

3. Præterea, quicumque transgreditur præceptum Decalogi, peccat. Sed in veteri lege aliqui transgredientes observantiam sabbati non peccabant, sicut circumcidentes pueros octava die et sacerdotes in templo sabbatis operantes. Et Elias, cum *quadraginta diebus pervenisset ad montem Dei Horeb*,[7] consequens est quod in sabbato itineraverit. Similiter etiam sacerdotes, dum circumferrent septum diebus arcam Domini, ut legitur *Jos.*,[8] intelliguntur eam die sabbati circumtulisse. Dicitur etiam *Luc.*, *Nonne unusquisque vestrum solvit bovem suum aut asinum et ducit adaquare?*[9] Ergo inconvenienter ponitur inter præcepta Decalogi.

4. Præterea, præcepta Decalogi sunt etiam in nova lege observanda. Sed in nova lege non servatur hoc præceptum nec quantum ad diem sabbati nec quantum ad diem Dominicam, in qua et cibi coquuntur et itinerantur et piscantur homines et alia multa hujusmodi faciunt. Ergo inconvenienter traditur præceptum de observantia sabbati.

SED IN CONTRARIUM est Scripturæ auctoritas.[10]

RESPONSIO: Dicendum quod, remotis impedimentis veræ religionis per primum et secundum præceptum Decalogi, ut supra dictum est,[11] consequens fuit ut tertium præceptum poneretur per quod homines in vera religione fundarentur. Ad religionem autem pertinet cultum Deo exhibere. Sicut autem in Scriptura divina traduntur nobis sub aliquibus corporalium rerum similitudinibus, ita cultus exterior Deo exhibetur per aliquod sensibile signum.* Et quia ad interiorem cultum, qui consistit in oratione et devotione, magis inducitur homo ex interiori Spiritus Sancti instinctu, præceptum legis dandum fuit de exteriori cultu secundum aliquod sensibile signum. Et quia præcepta Decalogi sunt quasi quædam prima et communia legis principia, ideo in tertio præcepto Decalogi præcipitur exterior Dei cultus sub signo communis beneficii quod pertinet ad omnes, scilicet ad repræsentandum opus creationis mundi, a quo requievisse dicitur Deus septimo die. In cujus signum dies septima mandatur

---

*Piana: *Sicut autem in Scriptura divina traditur nobis cultus interior . . . ita cultus exterior Deo debetur* . . . Just as in divine Scripture an interior worship of God is taught us under certain similes taken from corporeal things, so also an exterior worship through some outward sign is due to God.

[6] 1a2æ. 101, 4

2. Further, as indicated already,[6] the ceremonial precepts have holy things as their content—sacrifices, sacraments and observances. Among holy things are counted not only days, but also holy places, vessels and the like; and as for holy days, there are many besides the sabbath. There is no good reason, then, for mentioning only the observance of the sabbath, leaving out all other ceremonial matters.

3. Further, anyone breaking one of the Ten Commandments sins. Yet in the Old Law there were people violating the keeping of the sabbath who did not sin, for example, those circumcising infants on the eighth day or priests ministering in the temple. There is also the case of Elijah who, since *he took forty days to reach Horeb, the mountain of God*,[7] must have been travelling on the sabbath; we must also take it that the priests in *Josua* bearing the ark of the Lord around the city for seven days[8] must have done so on the sabbath. Furthermore there is *Luke, Doth not every one of you on the sabbath day loose his ox or his ass and lead them to water?*[9] Therefore it is wrong to list this one among the Ten Commandments.

4. Further, while under the New Law the Ten Commandments are to be kept, this one is not—neither as to the day itself, Saturday, nor as to the observance of Sunday, when people cook, travel, go fishing and do many other things. So a precept on keeping the sabbath is out of place.

ON THE CONTRARY the authority of Scripture suffices.[10]

REPLY: Once obstacles to genuine worship of God were put aside through the first and second commandments, as noted,[11] the next logical step was to lay down a third precept whereby men would be firmly established in genuine religion. Religion involves paying worship to God. As to this, just as the things of God are taught us in Scripture under certain similes taken from corporeal things, so also an outward worship is offered to God under some observable sign. Since with regard to the worship of the heart which is made up of prayer and devotion, man is led more by the promptings of the Holy Spirit, a commandment needed to be given with regard to outward worship in terms of some external sign. The Ten Commandments being as it were the primary and broadest principles of the Law, in the third the outward worship of God is enjoined under the symbol of his most general benefaction towards man, i.e. as a representation of the work of creating from which God is said to have rested on the seventh day. It is as a symbol of this that the seventh day is ordered to be kept holy, i.e.

---

[7] III *Kings*, 19, 8 [8] *Josue* 6, 14 [9] *Luke* 13, 15
[10] *Exodus* 20, 8 [11] art. 2 & 3

sanctificanda, idest deputanda ad vacandum Deo. Et ideo, præmisso præcepto de sanctificatione sabbati, assignatur ratio, quia *sex diebus fecit Deus cælum et terram, et in die septimo requievit*.[12]

1. Ad primum ergo dicendum quod præceptum de sanctificatione sabbati litteraliter intellectum, est partim morale, partim cæremoniale. Morale quidem, quantum ad hoc quod homo deputet aliquod tempus vitæ suæ ad vacandum divinis. Inest enim homini naturalis inclinatio ad hoc quod cuilibet rei necessariæ deputetur aliquod tempus, sicut corporali refectioni, somno et aliis hujusmodi. Unde etiam spirituali refectioni qua mens hominis in Deo reficitur secundum dictamen rationis naturalis aliquod tempus deputat ad vacandum divinis, cadit sub præcepto morali.

Sed inquantum in hoc præcepto determinatur speciale tempus in signum creationis mundi sic est præceptum cæremoniale. Similiter etiam cæremoniale est secundum allegoricam significationem prout fuit figura quietis Christi in sepulcro, quæ fuit septima die. Et similiter secundum moralem significationem prout significat cessationem ab omni actu peccati et quietem mentis in Deo; et secundum hoc quodammodo est præceptum generale. Similiter etiam cæremoniale est secundum significationem anagogicam, prout scilicet præfigurat quietem fruitionis Dei quæ erit in patria.

Unde præceptum de sanctificatione sabbati ponitur inter præcepta Decalogi inquantum est præceptum morale, non inquantum est cæremoniale.

2. Ad secundum dicendum quod aliæ cæremoniæ legis sunt signa aliquorum particularium effectuum Dei. Sed observatio sabbati est signum generalis beneficii, scilicet productionis universæ creaturæ. Et ideo convenientius poni debuit inter generalia præcepta Decalogi quam aliquod aliud cæremoniale legis.

3. Ad tertium dicendum quod in observantia sabbati duo sunt consideranda. Quorum unum est sicut finis, et hoc est ut homo vacet rebus divinis, quod significatur in hoc quod dicit, *Memento ut diem sabbati sanctifices*. Illa enim sanctificari dicuntur in lege quæ divino cultui applicantur.

Aliud autem est cessatio operum, quæ significatur cum subditur, *septimo die Domini Dei tui, non facies omne opus*. Sed Deo quo opere intelligatur, apparet per id quod exponitur *Lev.*, *Omne opus servile non facietis in eo*.[13]

Opus autem servile dicitur a servitute; est autem triplex servitus. Una quidem qua homo servit peccato, secundum illud, *Qui facit peccatum, servus est peccati*.[14] Et secundum hoc, omne, opus peccati dicitur servile.

Alia vero servitus est qua homo servit homini. Est autem homo alterius

---

[12]*Exodus* 20, 11   [13]*Leviticus* 23, 35   [14]*John* 8, 34
[a]On the threefold spiritual or mystical sense in medieval exegesis, see 1a. 1, 10;

set aside to be devoted to God. Hence in *Exodus*, once the commandment about hallowing the sabbath is set down, this reason is given: *For in six days the Lord made heaven and earth and rested on the seventh day*.[12]

Hence: 1. Taken in its literal sense, the commandment to keep holy the sabbath is partly moral, partly ceremonial. It is moral in that man should set aside some time in his life for concentration upon the things of God. For man is connaturally predisposed to set aside a portion of his time for every affair of necessity—for bodily refreshment, for example, and sleep and other like matters. Wherefore it is in accord with a dictate of natural reason that a man reserve some time for spiritual nourishment whereby his spirit is fed on God. This is how keeping some period set aside for dedication to the things of God is counted a moral precept.

But it is a ceremonial precept on the grounds that in this commandment a particular time is determined in order to signify creation. It is also ceremonial in its allegorical sense, i.e. as it was a sign of Christ's repose in the tomb on the seventh day; likewise in its moral sense, i.e. as symbolizing desisting from every act of sin and resting in God; in this sense, too, it is in a way a general precept. It is also ceremonial in its anagogical sense, i.e. as it prefigures rest in the enjoyment of God in heaven.[a]

But the commandment to keep holy the sabbath is listed in the Decalogue on the grounds of its being a moral, not a ceremonial precept.

2. Other ceremonies of the Law are signs of certain specific effects of God; the keeping of the sabbath, of a general benefaction, the production of all creation. This is why this rather than any other ceremonial precept of the Law should have been listed among the broad precepts of the Decalogue.

3. In regard to the keeping of the sabbath there are two points to be kept in mind. The first stands as its purpose, namely that a man devote himself to the things of God, and it is denoted in the statement, *Remember that thou keep holy the sabbath day*. In the Law things are said to be kept holy when they are set aside for divine worship.

The second point is the cessation from work, which is meant by what follows, *on the seventh day thou shalt do no work*. The kind of work meant is clear from this comment of *Leviticus*, *You shall do no servile work therein*.[13]

A work is called 'servile' from 'servitude', which can be of three kinds. The first is that wherein a person is the slave (*servus*) of sin, in keeping with the text, *Whosoever committeth sin is the servant of sin*.[14] In this sense any sinful work is called servile.

A second sort of servitude is that whereby one person is another's slave.

---

see also B. Smalley, *The Study of the Bible in the Middle Ages*, 2d ed., New York, 1952; R. E. McNally, 'Exegesis, Medieval', *New Catholic Encyclopedia*, 5: 707-12.

servus non secundum mentem sed secundum corpus, ut supra habitum est.[15] Et ideo opera servilia secundum hoc dicuntur opera corporalia in quibus unus homo alteri servit.

Tertia autem est servitus Dei. Et secundum hoc, opus servile posset dici opus latriæ, quod pertinet ad Dei servitium.

Si autem sic intelligatur opus servile, non prohibetur in die sabbati, quia hoc esset contrarium fini observationis sabbati. Homo enim ad hoc ab aliis operibus abstinet in die sabbati ut vacet operibus ad Dei servitutem pertinentibus. Et inde est quod, sicut dicitur *Joann.*, *circumcisionem accipit homo in sabbato, ut non solvatur lex Moysi.*[16] Inde etiam est quod, sicut dicitur *Matt.*, *sabbatis sacerdotes in templo sabbatum violant,* idest, corporaliter in sabbato operantur, *et sine crimine sunt.*[17] Et sic etiam sacerdotes in sabbato circumferentes arcam non transgrediebantur præceptum de observantia sabbati. Et similiter etiam nullius spiritualis actus exercitium est contra observantiam sabbati, puta si quis doceat verbo vel scripto; unde *Num.*,[18] dicit Glossa quod *fabri et hujusmodi artifices otiantur in die sabbati. Lector autem divinæ legis vel doctor ab opere suo non desinit, nec tamen contaminatur sabbatum: sicut sacerdotes in templo sabbatum violant, et sine crimine sunt.*[19]

Sed alia opera servilia, quæ dicuntur servilia primo vel secundo modo, contrariantur observantiæ sabbati inquantum impediunt applicationem hominis ad divina. Et quia impeditur magis homo a rebus divinis per opus peccati quam per opus licitum, quamvis sit corporale, ideo magis contra hoc præceptum agit qui peccat in die festo quam qui aliquod* corporale opus licitum facit. Unde Augustinus dicit, *Melius faceret Judæus in agro suo aliquid utile quam in theatro seditiosus existeret. Et melius feminæ eorum die sabbati lanam facerent quam tota die in neomeniis suis impudice saltarent.*[20]

Non autem† qui peccat venialiter in sabbato contra hoc præceptum facit, quia peccatum veniale non excludit sanctitatem.

Opera etiam‡ corporalia ad spiritualem Dei cultum non pertinentia intantum servilia dicuntur inquantum proprie pertinent ad servientes, inquantum vero sunt communia et servis et liberis, servilia non dicuntur. Quilibet autem, tam servus quam liber, tenetur in necessariis providere non tantum sibi sed etiam proximo, præcipue quidem in his quæ ad salutem corporis pertinent, secundum illud *Prov.*, *Erue eos qui ducuntur ad mortem;*[21] secundario autem etiam in damno rerum vitando, secundum illud *Deut.*, *Non videbis bovem aut ovem fratris tui errantem et præteribis, sed*

---

*Piana: *aliud*, other
†Piana: *enim*
‡Piana: *enim*

[15]104, 5; 6 ad 1   [16]*John* 7, 23   [17]*Matthew* 12, 5

As noted earlier,[15] one man is another's slave not in soul but in body. Therefore, following this meaning, manual works done by a slave are called servile.

The third kind is servitude to God. In this sense a work of adoration, which is part of the service of God, could be called servile.

And if this last is what is meant by a servile work, there is no prohibition of it on the sabbath, since this would go against the purpose of keeping the sabbath. The very reason man refrains from other works on the sabbath is to concentrate on those related to God's service. Hence it is written in *John* that *a man receives circumcision on the sabbath day, that the law of Moses may not be broken*,[16] and in *Matthew, on the sabbath days the priests in the temple break the sabbath*, i.e. perform actions involving the body, *and are without blame*.[17] For this reason also the priests carrying the ark on the sabbath were not violating the sabbath observance. Likewise no performance of an act involving the mind—e.g. should someone teach in word or writing—is against the keeping of the sabbath; thus the *Gloss* on *Numbers*[18] states, *Let carpenters and other like artisans take Sunday off. But one who reads the divine law or is a teacher does not stop work nor is the sabbath violated, even as the priests break the sabbath in the temple but without blame*.[19]

Other servile works, however, those so called in the first or second way, run counter to the keeping of the sabbath by being obstacles to a person's concentration on the things of God. And seeing that a person is kept from the things of God more by a sinful work than by a lawful work, even though it is manual, one who sins on a holy day goes more against the commandment than one who does some otherwise lawful work. Hence Augustine says, *The Jew would be better off doing something worthwhile on his farm than spending his time scheming in the theatre; and their womenfolk would do better making linen on the sabbath than dancing lewdly all day on their feasts of the new moon*.[20]

Someone sinning venially on the sabbath does not break this commandment, since venial sin does not take away holiness.

Manual work unrelated to the worship of God is called servile in so far as it is the kind done by slaves, not when it is of a kind done by both slaves and free men. Every man, slave or free, is bound to provide not only for self but also for neighbour as to the necessities of life, and chiefly as to those involving bodily health—*Deliver them that are led to death*;[21] secondarily as to the avoidance of damage to property—*Thou shalt not pass by if thou seest thy brother's ox or his sheep go astray, but thou shalt bring them*

---

[18]*Numbers* 28, 9
[20]*Serm. ad pop.*, IX. 9. PL 38, 77
[19]*Ordinaria*
[21]*Proverbs* 24, 11

reduces fratri tuo.[22] Et ideo opus corporale pertinens ad conservandam salutem proprii corporis non violat sabbatum; non enim est contra observantiam sabbati quod aliquis comedat, et alia hujusmodi faciat quibus salus corporis conservatur. Et propter hoc Machabæi non polluerunt sabbatum pugnantes ad sui defensionem die sabbati, ut legitur 1 *Mach*.[23] Similiter etiam nec Elias fugiens a facie Jezabel in die sabbati. Et propter hoc etiam Dominus, *Matt*.,[24] excusat discipulos suos, qui colligebant spicas in die sabbati propter necessitatem quam patiebantur.

Similiter etiam opus corporale quod ordinatur ad salutem corporalem alterius non est contra observantiam sabbati. Unde dicitur *Joann.*, *Mihi indignamini quia totum hominem salvum feci in sabbato?*[25] Similiter etiam opus corporale quod ordinatur ad imminens damnum rei exterioris vitandum non violat sabbatum. Unde dicit Dominus *Matt.*, *Quis erit ex vobis homo qui habet unam ovem, et ceciderit sabbato in foveam, nonne tenebit et levabit eam?*[26]

4. Ad quartum dicendum quod observatio diei dominicæ in nova lege succedit observantiæ sabbati non ex vi præcepti legis, sed ex constitutione ecclesiæ et consuetudine populi Christiani. Nec etiam* hujusmodi observatio est figuralis, sicut fuit observatio sabbati in veteri lege. Et ideo non est ita arcta prohibitio operandi in die dominica sicut in die sabbati, sed quædam opera conceduntur in die dominica quæ in die sabbati prohibebantur, sicut decoctio ciborum et alia hujusmodi. Et etiam in quibusdam operibus prohibitis facilius propter necessitatem dispensatur in nova quam in veteri lege; quia figura pertinet ad protestationem veritatis, quam nec in modico præterire oportet; opera autem secundum se considerata immutari possunt pro loco et tempore.

articulus 5. utrum convenienter tradatur quartum præceptum de honoratione parentum

AD QUINTUM sic proceditur:[1] 1. Videtur quod inconvenienter tradatur quartum præceptum, de honoratione parentum.[2] Hoc enim præceptum pertinet ad pietatem. Sed sicut pietas est pars justitiæ, ita etiam observantia et gratia, et alia de quibus dictum est.[3] Ergo videtur quod non debuit dari speciale præceptum de pietate, cum de aliis non debetur.

2. Præterea, pietas non solum exhibet cultum parentibus, sed etiam patriæ et aliis sanguine conjunctis et patriæ benevolis, ut supra dictum est.[4] Inconvenienter ergo in hoc quarto præcepto fit mentio solum de honoratione patris et matris.

---

*Piana: *enim*
[22]*Deuteronomy* 22, 1   [23]1 *Machabees* 2, 41   [24]*Matthew* 12, 1

back to thy brother.[22] On this account physical work in connection with preserving the well-being of one's own body does not break the sabbath; it is not against keeping the sabbath to eat or do other things to maintain the body's health. So the Maccabees did not desecrate the sabbath by fighting to defend their lives, as we read in *Machabees*;[23] nor did Elijah fleeing from the face of Jezabel. This, too, is why Our Lord in *Matthew* 12[24] exonerates his disciples for plucking ears of corn, namely because of the need they felt.

Physical work with the purpose of another's bodily well-being is not against the sabbath observance either; *Are you angry at me because I have healed the whole man on the sabbath day?*[25] The same is true with regard to labour for the purpose of averting imminent damage to property; *What man shall there be among you that hath one sheep and if the same fall into a pit on the sabbath day, will he not take hold of it and lift it up?*[26]

4. In the New Law the keeping of Sunday supplants that of the sabbath, not in virtue of the precept of the law, but through determination by the Church and the custom of the Christian people. Furthermore this practice does not stand as a figure as did that of the sabbath in the Old Law, and so the prohibition of work on Sunday is not as strict as it was on the sabbath; some works are allowed on Sunday which were forbidden on the sabbath, cooking and the like, for example. Even with regard to works that are forbidden, dispensation by reason of necessity is easier in the New than in the Old Law, the reason being that a figure belongs to the proclaiming of a truth, no detail of which may be set aside. But observances considered absolutely can be changed according to circumstances of time or place.

article 5. whether the fourth commandment on honouring parents is rightly proposed

THE FIFTH POINT:[1] 1. The fourth commandment on respect for parents does not seem right.[2] This is the commandment related to the virtue of piety. Now just as piety is a part of justice, so are observance, gratitude and the others we have discussed.[3] No commandment being laid down about these, no special precept on piety should have been laid down either.

2. Further, piety pays respect not to parents alone, but, as shown above,[4] to country and kin and friends of one's country. In this fourth commandment, then, it is imprecise to mention only honouring father and mother.

---

[25] *John* 7, 23 [26] *Matthew* 12, 11
[1] cf 1a2æ. 100, 5 ad 4. III *Sent.* 37, 2, ii
[2] *Exodus* 20, 12
[3] 101–20
[4] 101, 1

3. Præterea, parentibus non solum debetur honoris reverentia, sed etiam sustentatio. Ergo insufficienter sola parentum honoratio præcipitur.

4. Præterea, contingit quandoque quod aliqui qui honorant parentes cito moriuntur, et e contrario qui parentes non honorant diu vivunt. Inconvenienter ergo additur* huic præcepto hæc promissio, *ut sis longævus super terram*.[5]

IN CONTRARIUM est auctoritas sacræ Scripturæ.[6]

RESPONSIO: Dicendum quod præcepta Decalogi ordinantur ad dilectionem Dei et proximi. Inter proximos autem maxime obligamur parentibus. Et ideo immediate post præcepta ordinantia nos in Deum ponitur præceptum ordinans nos ad parentes, qui sunt particulare principium nostri esse sicut Deus est universale principium. Et sic est quædam affinitas hujus præcepti ad præcepta primæ tabulæ.

1. Ad primum ergo dicendum quod, sicut supra dictum est,[7] pietas ordinatur ad reddendum debitum parentibus, quod communiter ad omnes pertinet. Et ideo inter præcepta Decalogi quæ sunt communia, magis debet poni aliquid pertinens ad pietatem quam ad alias partes justitiæ, quæ respiciunt aliquod debitam speciale.

2. Ad secundum dicendum quod per prius debetur aliquid parentibus quam patriæ et consanguineis, quia per hoc quod sumus a parentibus nati pertinent ad nos et consanguinei et patria. Et ideo, cum præcepta Decalogi sint prima præcepta legis, magis per ea ordinatur homo ad parentes quam ad patriam vel ad alios consanguineos. Nihilominus tamen in hoc præcepto, quod est de honoratione parentum, intelligitur mandari quidquid pertinet ad reddendum debitum cuicumque personæ sicut secundarium includitur in principali.

3. Ad tertium dicendum quod parentibus inquantum hujusmodi debetur reverentiæ honor. Sed sustentatio et alia debentur† eis ratione alicujus accidentis, puta inquantum sunt indigentes vel secundum aliquid hujusmodi, ut supra dictum est.[8] Et quia quod est per se prius est eo quod est per accidens, ideo inter prima præcepta legis, quæ sunt præcepta Decalogi, specialiter præcipitur honoratio parentum. In qua tamen, sicut in quodam principali, intelligitur mandari et sustentatio et quidquid aliud debetur parentibus.

4. Ad quartum dicendum quod longævitas promittitur honorantibus parentes non solum quantum ad futuram vitam, sed etiam quantum ad præsentem, secundum illud Apostoli, 1 *Ad Tim.*, *Pietas ad omnia utilis est, promissionem habens vitæ quæ nunc est et futuræ*.[9] Et hoc rationabiliter. Qui

---

*Piana: *creditur*, accredited to   †Piana: *debetur*

3. Further, it is not only the reverence of honour that is owed to parents but also support. Therefore, just to command that parents be honoured is not enough.

4. Further, at times it happens that those who do honour their parents die young, while those who do not live long. Consequently the promise—*That thou mayest be long-lived upon earth*[5]—is inappropriately attached to this precept.

ON THE CONTRARY, there is the authority of Scripture.[6]

REPLY: The commandments of the Decalogue have as their end the love of God and of neighbour, and among all neighbours we are above all under obligation to our parents. Therefore right after the commandment putting us in proper relationship to God, the commandment is set forth that puts us in proper relationship to parents as the immediate source of our existence even as God is its universal source. In this way also there is a certain link between this commandment and those of the first table.[a]

Hence: 1. As already mentioned,[7] piety is intent upon paying that debt to parents in which all share. This is why there should be listed among the commandments, which are universal, a matter involving piety rather than other parts of justice with their reference to more specialized kinds of indebtedness.

2. The debt to parents has precedence over that to country and kin because it is by being born of our parents that kin and country become ours. On this account, the Ten Commandments being the prime precepts of the law, man is directed by them towards parents rather than towards country or relatives. Even so, anything related to paying a debt to anyone at all is implicit in this commandment about honouring parents as the lesser is contained in the greater.

3. The honour of reverence is owed to parents because of what they are. It is on the basis of some contingency, like their being needy or slaves or the like, that, as noted,[8] support and other such things are owed to them. Since what is essential comes before what is contingent, the primary precepts of the law, the Ten Commandments, make honouring parents their specific command. Still, support and anything else owed to parents are implicitly enjoined as the secondary in the primary.

4. In keeping with the text, *Godliness* (pietas) *is profitable to all things, having promise of the life that now is and of that which is to come,*[9] long life is

---

[5] *Exodus* 20, 12
[6] ibid.
[7] 101, 1
[8] 101, 2
[9] 1 *Timothy* 4, 8
[a] See 101, 3, note *a*.

enim gratus est beneficio† meretur secundum quandam congruentiam ut sibi beneficium conservetur, propter ingratitudinem autem meretur aliquis beneficium perdere. Beneficium autem vitæ corporalis, post Deum, a parentibus habemus. Et ideo ille qui honorat parentes, quasi beneficio‡ gratus, meretur vitæ conservationem; qui autem non honorat parentes, tanquam ingratus, meretur vita privari.

Quia tamen præsentia bona vel mala non cadunt sub merito vel demerito nisi inquantum ordinantur ad futuram remunerationem, ut dictum est,[10] ideo quandoque secundum occultam rationem divinorum judiciorum, quæ maxime futuram remunerationem respiciunt, ideo aliqui qui sunt pii in parentes citius vita privantur; alii vero qui sunt impii in parentes diutius vivunt.

articulus 6. utrum alia sex præcepta Decalogi convenienter tradantur

AD SEXTUM sic proceditur:[1] 1. Videtur quod alia sex præcepta Decalogi inconvenienter tradantur.[2] Non enim sufficit ad salutem quod aliquis proximo suo non noceat, sed nequiritur quod ei debitum reddat secundum illud *Rom.*, *Reddite omnibus debita.*[3] Sed in sex ultimis præceptis solum prohibetur nocumentum proximo inferendum. Ergo inconvenienter prædicta præcepta traduntur.

2. Præterea, in prædictis præceptis prohibentur homicidium, adulterium, furtum et falsum testimonium. Sed multa alia nocumenta possunt proximo inferri, ut patet ex his quæ supra determinata sunt.[4] Ergo videtur quod inconvenienter sint tradita hujusmodi præcepta.

3. Præterea, concupiscentia dupliciter accipi potest: uno modo, secundum quod est actus voluntatis, ut dicitur *Sap.*, *Concupiscentia sapientiæ perducit ad regnum perpetuum;*[5] alio modo, secundum quod est actus sensualitatis, sicut dicitur *Jac.*, *Unde bella et lites in vobis? Nonne ex concupiscentiis quæ militant in membris vestris?*[6] Sed per præceptum Decalogi non prohibetur concupiscentia sensualitatis, quia secundum hoc primi motus essent peccata mortalia utpote contra præceptum Decalogi existentes. Similiter etiam non prohibetur concupiscentia voluntatis, quia hæc includitur in quolibet peccato.* Inconvenienter ergo inter præcepta Decalogi ponuntur quædam concupiscentiæ prohibitiva.

4. Præterea, homicidium est gravius peccatum quam adulterium vel furtum. Sed non ponitur aliquod præceptum prohibitivum concupiscentiæ

---

†Piana: *benefico*, to a benefactor
‡Piana: *benefico*
*Piana: *præcepto*, precept
[10]cf 1a2æ. 114, 10
[1]1a2æ. 100, 5

promised to those honouring their parents not only in heaven but now. There is good reason for this. When someone shows himself thankful for a benefit received, in all fittingness he deserves to keep it; for being ungrateful, to lose it. Under God we hold the blessing of physical existence from our parents. Consequently one who honours his parents and thereby is grateful for this benefit received deserves that his life be preserved; one who does not, being thus ungrateful, that his life be taken from him.

Since we have pointed out,[10] however, that the goods and ills of this life are the objective of merit only in so far as they have a bearing upon heaven's reward, sometimes in accord with the hidden plan of God's judgments, which most of all look to eternal reward, those who are dutiful to parents lose their lives early; those who are undutiful, live long lives.

article 6. whether the remaining six commandments are appropriately stated

THE SIXTH POINT:[1] 1. The other six commandments do not seem to be well stated.[2] In accord with *Romans*, *Render to all men their dues*,[3] it does not suffice just not to harm our neighbour; we must also render him his due. Yet all that the other six commandments do is forbid us to inflict injury on a neighbour. These commandments are, then, not properly expressed.

2. Further, in these commandments murder, adultery, theft and false witness are proscribed. Since, as we have determined,[4] however, many other kinds of harm can be inflicted on our neighbour, it seems that these commandments are incompletely stated.

3. Further, concupiscence can be taken in two senses: in one, as an act of will—*The desire* (concupiscentia) *of wisdom bringeth to the everlasting kingdom*;[5] in another, as it is an act of the sensory appetite—*For whence are wars and contentions among you? Are they not from your concupiscences which war in your members?*[6] None of the Ten Commandments, however, forbids the concupiscence of the sensory appetite, otherwise its initial movements would be mortally sinful, for being against one of the Ten Commandments. No more is the concupiscence of the will specifically prohibited, because this is implicit in every kind of sin. There is, then, no good reason for listing among the commandments of the Decalogue certain ones forbidding concupiscence.

4. Further, murder is a worse sin than adultery or theft. Yet there is no commandment ruling out the desire to murder. Therefore there is no

---

[2] *Exodus* 20, 13
[3] *Romans* 13, 7
[4] 2a2æ. 65–9; 71–8
[5] *Wisdom* 6, 21
[6] *James* 4, 1

homicidii. Ergo etiam inconvenienter ponuntur quædam præcepta prohibitiva concupiscientiæ furti et adulterii.

SED IN CONTRARIUM est auctoritas Scripturæ.[7]

RESPONSIO: Dicendum quod sicut per partes justitiæ debitum redditur aliquibus determinatis personis quibus homo ex aliqua speciali ratione obligatur, ita etiam per justitiam proprie dictam aliquis debitum reddit communiter omnibus. Et ideo post tria præcepta pertinentia ad religionem qua redditur debitum Deo; et post quartum præceptum quod est pietatis qua redditur parentibus debitum, in quo includitur omne debitum quod ex aliqua speciali ratione debetur; necesse fuit quod poneretur consequenter alia* præcepta pertinentia ad justitiam proprie dictam, quæ indifferenter omnibus debitum reddit.

1. Ad primum ergo dicendum quod communiter ad hoc obligatur homo ut nulli inferat nocumentum. Et ideo præcepta negativa quibus prohibentur nocumenta quæ possunt proximis inferri, tanquam communia, fuerunt ponenda inter præcepta Decalogi. Ea vero quæ sunt proximis exhibenda diversimode exhibentur diversis. Et ideo non fuerunt inter præcepta Decalogi ponenda de his affirmativa præcepta.

2. Ad secundum dicendum quod omnia alia nocumenta quæ proximis inferuntur, possunt ad ista reduci quæ his præceptis prohibentur tanquam ad quædam communiora et principaliora. Nam omnia nocumenta quæ in personam proximi inferuntur intelliguntur prohiberi in homicidio sicut in principaliori. Quæ vero inferuntur in personam conjunctam, et maxime per modum libidinis, intelliguntur prohiberi simul cum adulterio. Quæ vero pertinent ad damna in rebus illata intelliguntur prohiberi simul cum furto. Quæ autem pertinent ad locutionem, sicut detractiones, blasphemiæ, et si qua hujusmodi, intelliguntur prohiberi falso testimonio, quod directius justitiæ contrariatur.

3. Ad tertium dicendum quod per præcepta prohibitiva concupiscentiæ non intelligitur prohiberi primus motus concupiscentiæ, qui sistit infra limites sensualitatis. Sed prohibetur directe consensus voluntatis qui est in opus vel in delectationem.

4. Ad quartum dicendum quod homicidium secundum se non est concupiscibile sed magis horribile, quia non habet de se rationem alicujus boni. Sed adulterium habet aliquam rationem boni, scilicet delectabilis. Furtum etiam habet rationem alicujus boni, scilicet utilis. Bonum autem de se habet rationem concupiscibilis. Et ideo fuit specialibus præceptis prohibenda concupiscentia furti et adulterii, non autem concupiscentia homicidii.

*Piana: *aliqua*, some

reason to list certain precepts proscribing the desire to steal or commit adultery.

ON THE CONTRARY stands the authority of Scripture.[7]

REPLY: Even as the parts of justice honour indebtedness to certain classes of people to whom a person has a specific sort of obligation, justice proper pays debts to all men generally. This is why the other precepts bearing upon justice in its strict sense, which honours debts to all without distinction, had to be set forth next after the others, i.e. after the first three commandments relating to religion, by which a debt is rendered to God; and after the fourth, concerning piety, by which a debt is paid to parents and in which every debt based on a specialized title is included.

Hence: 1. There is a universal obligation that a man inflict no harm on another. For this reason the negative precepts forbidding injuries that can be dealt to a neighbour had to be listed among the Ten Commandments as being of universal application. There is, on the other hand, a variability as to positive service to be rendered to a neighbour suited to the different recipients. This is why affirmative precepts about this should not have been included in the Decalogue.

2. All other injuries that can be inflicted upon neighbours come down to the matters proscribed here as these are the more universal and more urgent. Specifically: all personal injuries done to neighbours are understood in the prohibition of murder, the worst sort. All that are inflicted upon those dear to neighbours, especially through lust, are implicit in the prohibition of adultery. Those relating to property damage, in theft; to speech,—such as detraction, blasphemy, and anything of the sort—in false witness, as being directly against justice.

3. Do not understand the commandments prohibiting concupiscence as applying to initial movements of concupiscence; these are confined within the sensory appetite.[a] It is desire or delight of will that are directly forbidden.

4. Murder in itself is not attractive but horrifying, having of itself no quality of goodness. Adultery, however, does, namely that of the pleasurable good; theft, that of the useful good.[b] Since good by what it is has the quality of desirability, the desire for theft and adultery had to be forbidden in specific commandments, but not the desire for murder.

---

[7] *Exodus* 20, 13
[a] See 1a2æ. 74, 4; 109, 8.
[b] See above 110, 2 note *a*.

Appendix 1

LEGAL DEBT, MORAL DEBT

1. The distinction between legal debt and moral debt[1] is prominent in 2a2æ. 80–118. The meaning of legal debt remains constant, a debt determined by positive law or private contract to the acquittal of which the debtor is bound by law. Because of variations in the meaning of moral debt, however,[2] it will be helpful to review three main usages in the writings of St Thomas.

In their widest use, the terms 'moral' and 'legal' are a taxative or exhaustive designation of the objectives of justice. St Thomas so interprets the two texts of Aristotle's *Nicomachean Ethics* from which he derives the distinction. The context of the first text is a discussion of the 'politically just', i.e. that which is operative in the *polis*. 'Political justice is found among men who share their life with a view to self-sufficiency, men who are free and either proportionately or arithmetically equal.'[3] The key text on which St Thomas relies in 1a2æ. 99, 5 and 2a2æ. 57, 1 & 2 is V 7, 1134b18: 'Of political justice part is natural, part legal—natural, that which everywhere has the same force and does not exist by people's thinking this or that; legal, that which is originally indifferent, but when it has been laid down, is not indifferent.'[4] The term 'political justice' in the Greek text is *politikon dikaion*; the subdivisions are (*dikaion*) *phusikon*, natural, and (*dikaion*) *nomikon*, legal. The Latin text used by St Thomas has *justum* for *dikaion*; the subdivisions are *justum naturale* and *justum legale*. The term 'justice' in the translation given, then, is to be understood as that which is just, the just act or object. From this St Thomas derives the equally concrete term *debitum*.[5] He comments, *In* v *Ethic. lect.* 12, on Aristotle's distinction: 'That which is just politically (*justum politicum*) is divided into two forms: the one is the just naturally (*justum naturale*); the other is the just legally (*justum legale*). This division is the same as the one the jurists propose, namely of right (*juris*) into natural and positive. They call right (*jus*) what Aristotle calls the just (*justum*).'

The second text of Aristotle, cited in 2a2æ. 80 as corresponding to the

---

[1] In St Thomas's discussion of justice *debitum* is to be taken in the sense of that which is owed to another person, the thing or action due; this is the sense, then, which 'debt' has in this volume and not the more abstract sense of liability, duty or state of owing.

[2] Compare the uses in 2a2æ. 80; 102, 2 ad 2; 106, 1 ad 2; 4 ad 1; 107, 1; 109, 3 & ad 1; 114, 2 & ad 1; 117, 5 ad 1; 118, 3 ad 2.

[3] v *Ethics* 6, 1134a26 the translation is Ross's in *Basic Works of Aristotle*, R. McKeon ed. (New York 1941) p. 1013. The translation of H. Rackham in the Loeb Classical Library edition does not vary significantly in this or the following texts.

[4] ed. cit. p. 295.

[5] The same act or object is denominated both *justum* and *debitum*: the just in its relation to the one to whom it belongs, it is his (*suum*); the due, a debt, in its relationship to the one who must honour it; it is another's (*alienum*); see 2a2æ. 57, 1.

APPENDIX I. LEGAL DEBT, MORAL DEBT

distinction of debt into legal and moral, is from VIII *Ethics* 13. 1162b21, and occurs in a discussion of the cause for quarrels in business transactions (described by Aristotle as 'friendships based on utility'): 'Now it seems that as justice is of two kinds, one unwritten and the other legal, one kind of friendship of utility is moral and the other legal. . . . The legal type is that which is on fixed terms; its purely commercial variety is on the basis of immediate payment; while the more liberal variety allows time but stipulates a definite *quid pro quo*. In this variety the debt is clear and not ambiguous, but in the postponement it contains an element of friendliness. . . .'[6] Here, too, 'justice' translates *dikaion*, that which is just; and the division is into (*dikaion*) *hagraphon*, unwritten, and (*dikaion*) *kata nomon*, according to law.

St Thomas comments *In viii Ethic. lect.* 13: 'That which is just (*justum*) is twofold: the one unwritten, but inborn in man's reason, which earlier Aristotle has called the naturally just (*justum naturale*); the other, that which is just according to written law (*justum secundum legem scriptam*), which in Book V he has called the legally just (*justum legale*).'[7]

A conspectus of the two comments of St Thomas and key texts in the *Summa* (1a2æ. 99, 5; 2a2æ. 57, 1 & 2) presents the following identification of terms:

a. *justum morale* (therefore moral debt); *justum naturale; justum secundum regulam rationis; justum non scriptum sed rationi inditum* (the just morally, naturally, according to the rule of reason, not written but endowed upon human reason).

b. *justum legale* (therefore legal debt); *justum positivum; justum secundum regulam legis determinantis; justum secundum legem scriptam* (the just legally, positively, according to the rule of law deciding, according to written law).

This broader interpretation of moral-legal most simply put, then, make, 'moral' equivalent to 'natural'; 'legal' to 'positive'. That which is just or due morally is that which natural law prescribes or prohibits because it is good or evil in itself; that which is just or due legally is that which is good or evil because it is prescribed or prohibited by positive law.[8] In this acceptance 'moral debt' has a strong sense[9] and this is not the sense the term has in Question 80, nor, without further inflection, throughout the treatise on the potential parts of justice.

2. In deciding upon the appropriate list of potential parts of justices

---

[6]ed. cit. p. 1074.
[7]Modern interpreters of Aristotle agree with the equivalence to which St Thomas points here; see R. A. Gauthier, *L'Éthique à Nicomaque* (2nd ed. Louvain, 1970) II, 2, p. 711. But our interest is St Thomas's own usage, not his exegetical fidelity.
[8]See 2a2æ. 57, 2 ad 3.
[9]This too, however, is graduated according to the gradation of precepts of the natural law; see 1a2æ. 94; 99, 5; but the fundamental sense of a strict right or debt remains constant.

Question 80 does not employ 'moral debt' as the equivalent of 'natural debt'; used in this sense it would apply to the virtues of veneration considered in the first half of the Question. Rather, referring to VIII *Ethics* 13. 1162b21, St Thomas applies the distinction between legal debt and moral debt in order to classify as potential parts of justice, the virtues of truth, gratitude, vengeance, liberality and friendliness (in that order, it is to be noted). His interpretation of the distinction seems to be guided by Aristotle's description of the moral type of business transaction as contrasted with the legal type, rather than by the division of the just into legal and moral. In the moral form of transaction there are elements of imprecision, latitude, even of friendliness and the nobility of virtue, rather than the exact time and terms stipulated in the legal type of transaction. Even so, the meaning of the moral friendship of utility is not carried over perfectly into Question 80's interpretation of moral debt, since in the moral form of transaction there remains a strict and unambiguous debt. Question 80 aligns certain virtues as potential parts of justice under the title of moral debt precisely because they do not honour a strict debt, but a diminished form of indebtedness. The function of the distinction moral-legal in Question 80 becomes clearer when we observe that the order and interpretation of the virtues given there is not followed in the course of Questions 101–18.[10] The distinction in Question 80 functions simply as a principle of classification or systematization. The direct concern is to deal with the 'authorities'[11] on the virtue of justice. The fact that certain virtues can be considered as honouring indebtedness in some sense—and the emphasis is on a sense weaker than the term 'moral debt' has in its broader use already discussed—is sufficient to resolve the problem of literary classification. In Questions 101–18 the use of the distinction is no longer purely formal or organizational; it becomes a principle of judgment about the moral order in its realities.

3. The term 'legal debt' in Question 101–18 has a fixed meaning; it is a debt determined and enforceable by positive law; it is the kind of debt honoured by the cardinal virtue of justice itself, and separates justice from all its potential parts. This association of justice with a legal debt is introduced because part of the meaning of justice is exactness; the form of indebtedness it is said to honour is one of 'equality,' i.e. the dueness or rightness of an action or object can be calculated so as to make possible an exact (*tantum, quantum*) acquittal of the debt.[12] This exactness is most clear and obvious where it has been determined by private contract or positive law. But justice proper also is concerned with 'natural debt', with actions prescribed or prohibited by natural law, i.e. regarding another person's life, wife, reputation, property. Such objectives of the virtue of justice can be

---

[10]Compare the order and basis of enumeration in Question 80 with the order of the virtues in 101–18, and with the alignment of gratitude with the virtues of veneration in 106, 1; see also 109, 3 ad 1 & 114, 2 ad 1 where the interpretation of the debt honoured by truth and friendliness abandons what is said in Question 80.
[11]See Introduction.   [12]See 1a2æ, 60, 2 & 3; 2a2æ. 57, 1.

APPENDIX I. LEGAL DEBT, MORAL DEBT

designated 'moral debts' in the strong sense of the term. So too can the objectives of the virtues of veneration or respect,[13] and St Thomas does indicate explicitly in 102, 2 ad 2 that the objective of one of these virtues is a moral debt. The term here also has a strong sense. Nothing of indebtedness is wanting; the debts are rather of a superior order; they derive from the relationship of a person to those who are superior and who are the source of some benefit or favour received, and so cannot be exactly acquitted, i.e. so that a person gives back the equivalent of what he has received.[14] A summary of the degree and extent of this form of debt is given in 106, 1.[15] Note particularly that this alignment of gratitude with religion, piety, and respect, is a departure from the interpretation of Question 80.

The actual use of the term 'moral debt' throughout the present treatise is perhaps best interpreted in the light of an earlier text, 2a2æ. 31, 3 ad 3. There a distinction is drawn between a debt existing in goods that do not belong to the debtor, but to another person; and a debt existing in goods or resources belonging to oneself. The first form of indebtedness is the concern of justice proper. The second form seems to be present in St Thomas's view of all the potential parts of justice. In the case of religion, piety, respect, gratitude this is clear: a good or favour possessed as one's own becomes the basis of a debt towards the source. But the same index is applicable as well to the second group of potential parts, truth, friendliness, liberality. One's words, actions, possessions are one's own resources, possessions. Yet they imply a relationship to others, because they have a natural social reference; through them we communicate with other people. Because this communication is a natural and inevitable consequence of man's social nature a kind of indebtedness is born. With regard to the virtues of truth and, departing from Question 80, of friendliness, St Thomas points to an indebtedness that is given naturally and objectively: candour and civility in word and act are due for 'since man is a social being, there is a natural indebtedness of one person to another in regard to those things indispensable to the maintenance of human society'.[16] With regard to liberality, note that the distinction used in 2a2æ. 31, 3 ad 1 between one's own goods and those of another reappears to distinguish it from justice proper (117, 5). Of all the potential parts, liberality has the most tenuous connection with justice, and regards a minimal form of indebtedness, since its primary objective is one's inner attitude towards possessions (117, 5 ad 1; 118, 3 ad 2). Yet it does have at least a dispositive reference towards justice, since by want of inner control, justice itself is threatened, as is clear from Question 118; and in a sense that the expression

---

[13] Connect, e.g., the conclusion of 104, 1 on the requirement in natural justice for a man to obey superiors, and the term *debitum obedientiæ* in 104, 2 ad 2.
[14] See 101, 1.
[15] The virtue of vengeance also returns 'what is due' to its source, one who has inflicted an injury; thus it is considered by contrast with gratitude.
[16] 109, 3 ad 1; 114, 2 ad 1. In this connection note that the lie, opposite of truth, is naturally sinful since speech is by nature a communication.

'Third World' makes obvious and urgent, the possession of material wealth has an inevitable reference to the society of mankind.[17]

St Thomas shades the meaning of moral debt throughout the treatise in a way that reflects his estimation of the complexities of the order of human justice. The moral debt extends all the way from the debt of religion towards God that is as total and unending as one's own being, to the debt of liberality which, like justice to oneself, is directly only metaphorical,[18] consisting in the proper subordination of appetite to the rule of reason. The moral debt is gradated, as well, in that it is not determinate, either because it is not determinable exactly, the case with the virtues of honouring benefactors; or because its objective determination is only general and must be shaped to the circumstances of the concrete act, as in the virtues of truth and friendliness.[19] The greater and the more objective the basis of indebtedness, the less complex and singular is the judgment of prudence required for its virtuous acquittal. As the meaning of a moral debt takes on a weaker sense, the recognition of indebtedness in a particular instance arises more from a feeling for virtue, sensitivity towards what is proper and in keeping with the beauty (*honestas*) of virtue.

---

[17] See 118, 1. 'it is impossible for one man to enjoy extreme wealth without someone else suffering want, since this world's goods cannot be possessed by many at once'.
[18] See 1a2æ. 21, 3; 46, 7 ad 2; 55, 4 ad 4; 2a2æ. 58, 2; 106, 3 ad 1.
[19] The indebtedness of gratitude is somewhat in the middle. Like religion, piety and respect, it is based on benefaction, but because this is a particular favour prompted by personal regard, determination of its recompense must be delicately measured in each instance.

Appendix 2

EPIEIKEIA

(120, 1 & 2)

1. Between the virtue of epieikeia in Question 120 and the epieikeia of later Roman Catholic moral theology there is hardly more than verbal continuity.[1] The doctrinal discontinuity is a critical index to distinctive elements in St Thomas's moral theory. The key idea in his understanding of epieikeia is that it is a special virtue, a subjective part of justice, corresponding to the need to attend to a specific moral objective where 'to follow the written law would be an evil; to follow what the meaning of justice and the public interest demand, a good' (art. 1). Although hedged round with various qualifications, the essential meaning of epieikeia in later authors, especially since the 17th century, may be expressed as a 'correction of a law made by a subject who deviates from the clear words of the law, basing his action upon the presumption, at least probable, that the legislator intended not to include in his law the case at hand'.[2] The legitimacy of this epieikeia derives exclusively from the presumed benign, humane intention of the lawmaker; the legitimate use of epieikeia is extended or limited by the degree of probability required for such a presumption according to the casuistic system followed by an author.

2. For St Thomas epieikeia is a specific virtue because it has a specific objective, 'the equitable', a higher form of the just than the legally just (*justum legale*).[3] Aristotle in *Nicomachean Ethics*, Book V, ch. 10, 1137a31–1138a3, St Thomas's direct source, is comparing equity[4] (*epieikeia*) with justice (*dikaiosunē*); the equitable (*epieikes*) with the just (*dikaion*). The equitable is a form of the just, but a form superior to the legally just (*dikaion nomikon*). Epieikeia is a form of justice operative because positive law is universal, formulated with the knowledge that it cannot cover every case. R. A. Gauthier notes that Aristotle does not define epieikeia as indulgence or mitigation; it is not outside the sphere of justice, but is the source for accomplishing a higher form of the just, the naturally just.[5]

St Thomas comments, *In* v *Ethic, lect.* 16, that the equitable (*epiiches* in his text) is a form of the just (*justum*), better than the legally just (*justum*

---

[1]See the richly documented study of Riley, L. J., *The History, Nature and Use of Epikeia in Moral Theology* (Catholic University Press, Washington, D.C., 1948).
[2]Riley, op. cit., p. 133.
[3]See Appendix 1.
[4]The term generally used in English translation, even as the Scholastics used *æquitas*. But the *æquitas* of Roman law and canon law, as well as the equity of English law, have their own history and technical meaning in jurisprudence.
[5]*L'Éthique à Nicomaque*, t II, 1, p. 433; see also Aristotle's text, 1137a35.

legale) and contained under the naturally just (*justum naturale*) from which the legally just itself derives. Thus the equitable for St Thomas is not a mitigation either, but that which is conformed to the naturally just, and to the legislator's intention; and as such is a superior, specific objective of virtue. As to the universality of positive law that can only express what is more often than not the case, St Thomas also notes (in the same place) that the lawgiver knows that the observance of the law would sometimes be sinful. The sin however is not in the law, because it is a reasonable formulation; nor in the lawgiver, because he acts as the nature of the case allows. The defectibility arises rather from the contingency and particularity surrounding human actions.

3. That epieikeia is a higher form of the virtue of justice with its own moral objective implies the positive and 'interior' character of morality in St Thomas's theory. The virtue presupposes the meaning of legal justice itself, 'a special virtue by essence in so far as it regards the public good as its proper objective; and it is in the ruler principally and architectonically; in the subject, secondarily and executively (*administrative*)'.[6] By the direction given to their will through legal justice, the legislator and his subjects are at one in the intention of the public good. In the enactment of law this intention is the source of rectitude and motivation for the reasoned ordination that is law itself. As an ordination of reason conformed to the rectitude of justice, the law expresses what is right, what is ordered to the common good, what is just. The law is a rule of action, but not only in the legislator's mind; ideally it is a rule of action that the subject assimilates, makes his own with an assent that itself is prompted by the virtue of legal justice in him. While St Thomas describes law as an exterior principle of human actions (1a2æ. 90, Prol.), the exteriority refers to its source, not to the way law is meant to operate in the virtuous man, who makes it the norm of his own action. The need for a special virtue of epieikeia is the need to supplement the willingness to honour the written law, by a willingness to act in the exceptional case for the good to which the law itself is matched. The exception, however, implies no exemption from the ordinary dynamics of the virtuous act. By pointing to a personal responsibility to judge the individual situation (art. 1 ad 2 & 3) and then to act for the intention of the law, for a higher form of justice, the meaning of epieikeia thereby points to the fact that in every case the just man acts intending the good, with the law as an interiorly accepted rule of action towards the good intended by the law and the legislator.[7] This in turn is no more than an application to the sphere of justice of the basic meaning of virtuous living; in no area does the good just happen; wherever there is a special value of the moral good there is a special moral virtue, because 'the

---

[6] 2a2æ. 58, 6.
[7] In art. 2 epieikeia is described as a superior rule of human acts; it is the rule in action, the rule embodied in the intention of the truly just objective; the directive rule is called *gnome*, a part of prudence that judges the exceptional case in view of higher principles; see 2a2æ. 51, 4.

APPENDIX 2. EPIEIKEIA

intention of every agent acting in accord with virtue is that he follow the rule of reason'.[8] The meaning of epieikeia is as important for what it implies about the ordinary working of virtue as for what it says about the exceptional case.

4. The later development of the notion of epieikeia evolved from a completely diverse, voluntaristic understanding of law; law consists essentially in the will of the legislator to bind, to oblige the subject. In observing law, therefore, the subject relinquishes his own freedom of choice; law is a curtailment of liberty. Where observance would be onerous (not sinful), epieikeia becomes a legitimate appeal to the presumed humaneness of the lawgiver.[9] St Thomas himself envisages cases where to follow the letter of positive law would be a hardship or would conflict with some other good.[10] To act virtuously in such cases, however, does not engage a special virtue. Positive law and its observance may relate to the virtue of legal justice, or of obedience, or any specific virtue where its proper act is precepted in view of the common good.[11] Whatever the case, St Thomas's theology approaches every moral situation as it presents itself to the man of virtue; the problematic is the placing of a virtuous act, not of avoiding sin or evading the extrinsic strictures of law. The virtuous act will be determined by the judgment of prudence. The deliberation and decision of prudence will be right in dependence upon the virtuous intention formed in the appetites by the moral virtues. Part of this orientation of virtue and thus of the concrete judgment of prudence is towards an act that respects all proper circumstances. As to the area covered by the later notion of epieikeia St Thomas's thought calls for no new, special virtue; no new, specific moral value is involved where it is a question of observing or not observing a law. The right disposition of the virtue of justice, obedience or any other virtue involved are sufficient for a person to act observing the law virtuously or *not observing the law virtuously*; to observe it or not *secundum quod oportet*. The virtue of epieikeia in St Thomas's theology is not the epieikeia of later moral theology; nor does this later notion correspond to any specific function of virtue in his theory. He takes seriously the text of *Ecclesiasticus* 15, 14 he so often quotes, *God made man from the beginning and left him in the hand of his own counsel*;[12] he also bases his moral theory on the ideal of the good intended of the virtuous man; it is a moral of the good, not of extrinsic obligation and casuistry.

---

[8] 1a2æ. 73, 1. 'The good-as-meant is the determinant throughout of virtuous activity; and the lack-of-good-as-meant that of vicious activity.' Vol. 18 of this series, T. Gilby. ed. Appendix 10, p. 167.
[9] In his development of epieikeia along these lines, F. Suárez (+1617), in his *De legibus*, influenced all subsequent authors; see Riley, op. cit., p. 67.
[10] See 1a2æ. 96, 6; 2a2æ. 147, 3 ad 1 & ad 2; 4; also 2a2æ. 101, 4.
[11] See 1a2æ. 96, 3; 2a2æ. 104.
[12] See 1a.22, 2 ad 4; 83, 1 sed contra; 1a2æ. Prol.; 9, 4, sed contra; 2a2æ. 104, 1 ad 1; *De veritate* III, 5 ad 4; *De potentia* III, 7 ad 12; also 2a2æ. 47, 12.

GLOSSARY

Italics are cross-references to other terms in the glossary

absolutely, simpliciter: unqualified, the condition of a thing or an action apart from the concrete, circumstantial, or secondary aspects.

accident, accidens: what is not of the essence, because not a *substance* (*substantia*), but existing as a modification of a substance; not a being (*ens*) but rather a being of a being (*ens entis*). Accidents may be referred to a substance either adventitiously, predicable accidents; or as necessarily belonging to its essence, properties.

accidental, per accidens: in moral matters refers to an aspect of an *act* or an *objective* that is incidental, unintended or not generally the case.

analogy, analogia: an agreement or correspondence in certain respects between things that are *absolutely* speaking diverse. A term is said to be used analogically if it is used in two or more senses that still have some mutual reference or interdependence.

appetite, appetitus: a response to the good as cognition is a response to the true, but wider than cognition since it is used even of non-conscious responses. The tendency of any potentiality to its actuality, of any being to its full realization; it is called *natural appetite* when inborn, identical with a nature or *power* and not following upon knowledge for its exercise; *elicited* or *animal* (i.e. psychic) when it is a power that is exercised upon apprehension of its *objective*. The elicited appetite is either one of *emotion* or it is rational appetite, the *will*.

beatitude, beatitudo: happiness, *eudaimonaia*, the conscious possession of its fulfilment by an intelligent being; this condition of happiness is called subjective beatitude; its *objective*, objective beatitude.

bent, inclinatio: the innate orientation of a power, or the training given it by repeated *acts* of the same kind, or by endowment of grace. See *habit, vice, virtue*.

carnal sin, peccatum carnale: any sin, not necessarily sexual, that terminates in pleasures of the flesh; contrast with *spiritual sin:* see 118, 6.

cause, causa: a positive and real principle upon which the being and the being understood of something depends. Inner causes are *matter* and *form;* external causes are *agent* and *end*.

charity, caritas: an *infused*, theological *virtue* by which the *will* is empowered and bent toward a personal union with God in love of friendship and so also with other persons as sharing in the love of God. Here, the dynamic principle of the life of Christian virtue.

circumstances, circumstantiæ: the moral concomitants affecting the *human act* or its *objective*. In this volume the meaning of the social virtues often involves the proper integration of moral circumstances.

common good, bonum commune: 1. may express the quality of human good as

GLOSSARY

such, the universal objective of *will*, as contrasted with a particular good or that which is good; 2. the *public good* as contrasted with a private or personal good; 3. a higher, more universal good moral objective, to which particular goals are subordinated.

counsel, consilium: evangelical practices that safeguard and foster *charity*, e.g. voluntary poverty, chastity, obedience, active love of enemies. As higher goods, they do not oblige all; they are distinguished from precepts, the commandments of God that must be obeyed by all.

debt, debitum: in its proper sense, an object or action to be rendered to another person because of a strictly determined reference to his rights. If the determination is from natural law or some other objective pattern of indebtedness, the debt may be termed *natural*—as in the case of religion, piety, respect, gratitude, obedience, etc. If the determination is from positive law, promise, contract, the debt is called a *legal debt*. A *moral debt* has a general objective determinant, the need of social amity, but concretely its determination is based on the person's own sense of honour and virtuous propriety; in this sense it is a debt to oneself.

dispositive cause, causa dispositiva: an *agent* cause that does not produce the finished effect, but an effect that prepares for the ultimate effect of a higher and perfective cause.

effect, effectus: that which proceeds from another as its *principle* and with dependence for its existence. Whatever is caused according to any of the ways of causing.

emotion, passio animæ: any activity of the sense *appetite*, thus the mild or impulse (concupiscible) emotions, love, hate, desire, revulsion, pleasure, sadness; or the emergency or contending (irascible) emotions, hopefulness and hopelessness, fear and daring, anger.

end, finis: 1. in general, the first of the causes, that on account of which a being or action exists; the purpose; 2. in the present volume, the purpose of a human act. Here an important distinction is that between the objective purpose of an act considered in its kind, e.g. of speech to communicate truth, called the *finis operis*; and an ulterior, personal motive of the one acting, e.g. speaking out of pride in one's knowledge, called *finis operantis*.

essence, essentia: from the Latin *esse*, that which makes a thing to be what it is and which is signified by its definition.

evil, malum: not the simple negation of a good, but its *privation*, the absence of a good that should be there. An evil activity is a *sin, peccatum*, which when voluntary is a fault, *culpa*, and a moral evil; an evil condition is a penalty, *malum pœnæ*, the loss, contrary to a person's will, of some good.

fault, culpa: a failure in a human *act* for which the agent is responsible.

form, forma: 1. the inner shaping principle of a thing. Substantial form determining the *matter* makes a bodily thing to be the specific kind of thing it is; accidental forms add modes of existence; 2. the idea or meaning of a thing, the *forma intelligibilis*.

formal, material; formale, materiale: 1. an analogy from Aristotelean hylemorphism to apply to twin elements in any topic, one shaping, determining, specific, the other receptive, indeterminate, generic; 2. as in the case of obedience, a formal act of virtue is one engaged with the specific objective of the virtue; a material act is an act that in its engagement with one specific objective may de facto coincide with the act of another virtue.

genus: 1. in logic a class, general enough to be divided into *species*; 2. in the terminology of moral theology, *ex genere* refers: *a.* to the moral species, the kind an act is from its *objective*; *b.* to the entity an act has simply as a psychological phenomenon and which is the subject of moral good or evil. This last meaning is an abstraction, i.e. the isolation of the existentially inseparable.

Gifts of the Holy Spirit, dona Spiritus Sancti: infused supernatural dispositions by which a person is readily susceptible to special assistance or inspiration of the Holy Spirit towards actions that surpass the ordinary, virtuous capacities of the recipient.

good, bonum: the objective of love, and attributed to all things in so far as they are actual; the moral good is the human good, that which is perfective of human nature, and is the objective of his loving activity. *Bonum honestum et delectabile*, good as an end, a value in itself and the cause of delight; *bonum utile*, a good as pure means to end.

grace, gratia: 1. God's favour freely given, over and above any active capacity of human nature; eternal life possessed not manifestly, but in a hidden manner; called grace because it can be ours only by God's favour, not by our natural powers; 2. *gratia* in Question 106 is a synonym for gratitude.

guilt, reatus: the quality of being in the wrong, usually the result of wrongdoing, i.e. sin.

habit, habitus: 1. may mean simply having something, as *to have* is opposed to *to lack (privation)*; 2. a *disposition* according to which its subject is well- or ill-disposed either in itself or in regard to something else. Habit in this sense is distinguished into habits that are dispositions directly of the nature or form of a thing (*entitative habits*) and those that are dispositions of the powers of the soul (*operative habits*). Because of their reference to the nature of a thing, habits are divided essentially into good and bad, thus *virtues* and *vices*.

human acts, actus humani: men's activities that proceed from deliberation and issue in choice.

ignorance, ignorantia: 1. lack of knowledge that one ought to have; 2. defect of mind as the faculty of moral decision, resulting from sin.

inclination to virtue, inclinatio ad virtutem: the innate orientation of human nature to its own perfection through virtuous activity.

indebtedness: translates *ratio debiti*, the quality of being owed.

indirect cause, causa per accidens: 1. an agent where a given effect does not correspond to the agent's power or purpose; 2. an agent whose proper

GLOSSARY

effect opens the way to another effect's happening, especially by removing an obstacle to the second effect (*removens prohibens*).

intention, intentio: 1. as opposed to 'execution', used of activity which as such produces no physical change; 2. as opposed to 'volition', the reaching to an end rather than the attainment of an objective; 3. as opposed to 'election' or 'choice', the willing of an end, not of what is subordinated to an end. Both volition and choice are intentional in sense no. 1.

justice, justitia: 1. in the strict sense, the virtue of justice, whereby a person is made attentive to the strict rights of others, and willing to honour *debts*; in this sense justice is distinguished from virtues annexed to it, as these either honour a superior form of debt or one that is a moral debt; it is distinguished as well from 2. justice or righteousness in the biblical and theological sense of rightness with God through grace.

matter, materia: 1. the subject of any interest, as the matter about which virtue is concerned; 2. the *subject* in which virtue is found; 3. the physical or temporal as contrasted with the spiritual and eternal; 3. bare matter, *materia prima*, the potential substantial principle common to all physical things.

mean, medium: In virtue, the mean is conceived not as a linear image of compromise between extremes on the same plane, but rather as an apex of a triangle from which vice is the falling off either by excess or defect. In justice the mean of virtue is also an objective mean, a *medium rei*, a debt, the exact degree of which is determined by nature, law or contract. In other virtues the mean is determined in reference to the optimum balance of a person's affections and the shaping of action to proper circumstances.

moral, moralis: a quality of human activity judged in accordance with its relationship to reasonable living and the final end of human life. To be moral does not mean to be good, but to be human; morality itself can be good, bad or indifferent.

natural, naturalis: 1. that which belongs to, proceeds from and is proportionate to the constitutive principles of a thing; 2. frequently in moral discussion, the normal, to be expected in the ordinary course of things.

necessary, necessarium: in this volume refers to inner finality, i.e. to the exigency of the true ends of human life that require determined acts and virtues; without these, the ends could not be achieved. The response to this necessity is the voluntary response of virtue.

objective, objectum: the correlative to acting subject, that for which it acts; the term is not used by St Thomas in opposition to 'person'. *Material object, objectum materiale*, the object as the term of an act; *formal object, formalis ratio objecti*, the object as specifying, i.e. manifesting a certain side or facet that engages a corresponding power or habit and thus stamps the character of its act. This last is the sense intended by 'objective'.

parts of virtue, partes virtutis: the *cardinal virtues* attend to certain primary and more urgent objectives of human activity. When the act of one of these virtues is conceived of as a whole involving certain integrating steps in the attainment of its objective, St Thomas speaks of *integral* or *integrating parts* of the virtue, e.g. the steps needed to form the integral act of prudence. When within the objective of the cardinal virtue there are specifically diverse interests, the virtue is conceived of as a remote species, a subjective whole, and it has *subjective parts*, more specific virtues corresponding to the more specific objectives, e.g. as temperance includes the specific virtues of abstinence, sobriety, chastity. When there are virtuous objectives that, while not being more specific instances of the objective of a cardinal virtue, do have some resemblance of affinity to it, the cardinal virtue is considered to be a 'potestative whole', the virtues concerned with these related objectives, its *potential parts*. Thus the meaning of the cardinal virtue is verified more or less of its potential parts. This designation is as much a basis for literary classification as for any real connection between the cardinal virtue and its potential parts. The potential parts are not inferior virtues, but often, as in the case of religion, superior to the cardinal virtue.

perfection, perfectio: 1. the completeness or full goodness of a thing; 2. the state of a higher degree of charity, marked by the practice of the evangelical *counsels*.

per se: 1. belonging to a thing by reason of its essence; 2. belonging to a virtue or a vice by reason of its *objective*; 3. belonging to a human *act* by reason of the agent's direct *intention*.

pleasure, delectatio: the final phase within an activity which has attained its end. It is never apologized for in the moral theory of St Thomas, but rather the reverse. Joy, *gaudium*, and enjoyment, *frui*, are used for the high pleasures: *delectatio* is the more general term; *voluptas* does not occur often. See also 117, 5, note *a*.

potentially, potentia: potential being (*ens potentia*), the subjective recipient of existence; determinable and receptive opposite of *act*.

powers, potentiæ: faculties; the immediate resources of human operations, they are the expression in a specialized way of the vital resources of the *soul*. They correspond to the various levels of human life, nutritive, sentient, intellective, the last two including cognitive and appetitive powers.

principle, principium: the origin from which something somehow proceeds in coming to be or in coming to be known.

privation, privatio: not the simple absence, but the absence of a perfection in a subject that should have it.

prudence, prudentia: the cardinal virtue, intellectual and moral, concerned with shaping, regulating man's virtuous acts. By its deliberation, decision

GLOSSARY

and command, the *mean* of virtue is determined for the concrete acts of the other moral virtues.

public good, bonum commune: a particular good but not a private good, rather, the well-being of a social unit, domestic, civil, ecclesiastical.

punishment, pœna: see *evil, malum pœnæ*, of which it is a kind.

quality: frequently translates *ratio*, as in the expression, *ratio justitiæ*, the quality of justice is to regard another. Quality is also used to designate any accidental modification of a substance; then more specifically for one of the nine Aristotelean categories of *accident*.

ratio: 1. sometimes used to express the essential note of human nature; 2. the faculty of intelligence; 3. the power of reasoning; 4. the meaning of a thing; 5. the very form, distinctive element, of what is being considered, usually translated *quality* or *character*. As in the expression indebtedness for *ratio debiti*, an abstract term can be used to convey the meaning, but *ratio* remains elusive.

religion, religio: in this volume refers to the virtue of religion by which God is honoured as lord and creator.

sign, signum: any outward act or object that serves to point to something else. Thus words are signs of thought; one does not ordinarily stop at their quality as mere sounds.

sin, peccatum: in its primary meaning a morally bad or disordered *human act*; used by analogy of original sin, a morally bad condition. In the Latin of St Thomas *peccatum* can refer to the failure of any sort of activity to achieve its purpose; *culpa*, fault, refers properly to moral disorder. Sin in its primary application to human acts is *mortal sin*, an action incompatible with charity that therefore destroys the life principle of the Christian life; *venial sin* is a moral fault that does not destroy charity, the inner principle of pardon (*venia*).

soul, anima rationalis: while it is a person who exists, lives, acts, there is in him a nature, the principle of these. The perfective vitalising principle of the nature is the soul, the root of all human living. In Aristotelean terms it is called the substantial *form* of the body, and it is itself substantial. It is designated 'rational' since intelligence by reasoning is the distinctive mark of man's nature.

special or specific sin; peccatum speciale: a human act that is engaged with a human good without attending to the full and proper reference of this objective to the true and total good of human nature. It is a special sin because it refers to a specific human good.

special or specific virtue, virtus specialis: a virtue bent upon a specific formal reference of its objective to the true good of the human person. (Note that the virtuous act is an *intention* of the true good in its objective; the sinful act is the intention of a good, not the intention of its disorder, but a failure to attend to the true value of its objective; see 1a2æ. 73, 1.)

species: 1. in logic, the kind a thing is, expressed by proximate genus and specific difference; 2. in the Thomist theory of knowledge, the likeness of a thing in a cognitive power; 3. in morals, the kind of good or evil that an *act* is because of the human value achieved or by-passed in its engagement with its objective.

spiritual sin, peccatum spirituale: a sinful act that terminates in pleasures of mind, imagination or will; contrasts with *carnal sin*; see 118, 6.

subject, subjectum: here refers to the part or *power* of man in which virtue, vice or their acts are present.

tinder of sin, fomes peccati: a metaphor that pictures concupiscence, the effect of original sin, flaming up into actual sins.

turning away, turning towards; aversio, conversio: a grave or *mortal sin* is the choice (*conversio*) of some mortal good in a way incompatible with charity and therefore causing a separation (*aversio*) from God. The theme is implicit in many of the Questions in this volume.

vice, vitium: a bad moral *habit*; the opposite of *virtue*.

virtue, virtus: a good operative *habit*, thus the strengthening and *perfection* of a *power* towards its fullest activity. The *intellectual virtues* are perfective of mind—the arts and sciences. *Moral virtues* are perfective of the whole man, since they involve the right choices of *will*. Prudence is for moral decision; justice, for dealing with others; courage, for strength against adversity; temperance, for moderation of sense pleasures. These four are called the *cardinal* or *principal virtues,* because they attend to more obvious and urgent objectives. With their *parts* they may be thought of as being developed by repeated acts of man's natural powers and so be designated *acquired virtues*. Speaking of the life of grace, St Thomas refers to *infused virtues*; they are the concomitants of *grace,* and enable man to act in accord with the transformation of his soul effected by grace. The *theological virtues,* faith, hope, charity, enable man to know and love God as God knows and loves himself; the infused moral virtues enable man to shape his life in the areas of the cardinal virtues in a way proportioned to the claims of charity.

voluntary, voluntarium: used of natural activity, i.e. from within, and that springs from some knowledge of its object. Usually reserved to intelligent knowledge, and therefore to the activity of human beings.

will, voluntas: the 'rational appetite', the power and activity in which is expressed the order of human nature to its full perfection, thus by which man loves the good as good, the good as perfective of him. The will is thus concerned with the *end* of human life, and therefore is the motive force in all *human acts*.

Index

(*Numbers in italics refer to footnotes and appendices*)

A–C

Abelard 20, *105*
Abraham 65
absolutes, moral 76
accidents *14*, *153*, *324*
act 10, 11
   of virtue *14*, *15*, *50*, 53, *61*, 61, 135, 297, *323*
   voluntary 149
action, rule of *322*
action—passion 233
acts, human 87, 279, *322*
   inner—outward—mixed 68–9, 69, *175*, *197*, 201
   moral 97
adoration 41, 307
Adronicus of Rhodes *xvii*, *234*
adultery 315
agent 89, *89*
aggressiveness 219
agreeableness 203
Alexander of Hales *18*
aloofness *199*
Ambrose, St *4*, *14*, *301*
amenities, social 205
amicitia,   delectabilis—honesti—utilis *41*, 97, *318*
Anabaptists *xxi*, 71
analogy *324*
Anselm of Laon *4*
antinomianism 65, 71, 76
appetite 245, *323*, *324*
   sense *121*
Aristotle *316–17*, *321*
arrogance 187
attachment to money 229, 255, 259, 267
Augustine, St 20, 21, *146–7*
authorities, method of *xv*–*xvii*, *19*, *318*
authority 21, 23, 25, 27, 47
   civil 71, 73, 85
   gradation of 79

balance of justice 95, 127, 227
baseness of sin 219
Basil the Great, St *222*

beatitude 261, *324*
beauty, moral 33, *320*
Bede the Venerable, St *301*
believers 73
benefactors 89, 91, 93
   sins against *110*
beneficence 20, 29, 38, 39, *320*
   divine *305*
bent of nature 121, *324*
bigamy 131, *131*
blame 51, 61, *61*, 155
Blanche, F. A. *180*
blasphemy 81, *301*, 315
Blic, J. *4*
Boethius *236*
bondage of sin 73, *305*, *307*
bonum commune 10, 13
bonum commutabile 56
bonum ex genere *105*
bores 145
bountifulness 225
Bourke, D. J. *292*

candour *133*, *319*
capital punishment 125
   sins *258*, *259*, *261*, 265
cardinal virtues *xv*, *261*
Cassian *261*
casuistry *321*, *323*
causality 289
   divine *xix*, 6, 13, 64
   of mind and will *139*
cause 91, *324*
   direct—incidental *122*
   efficient—dispositive 60
charity 2, 10, 11, *11*, 12, 39, 40, 41, 57, *57*, 58–9, 59, 65, 73, 74–5, 101, *111*, 123, 163, 165, 181, 189, 201, 209, 211, 237, 251, 293, *324*
Chenu, M.-D. *xvi*, *19*
children 69
choice 48, 49, *49*, 52, 57, 76, *323*
Chrysostom, St John *16*
Church, power of 68
Cicero *xvi*, *xix*, *3*, *4*, *20*, *21*, *114*

331

circumstances *14*, 15, *15*, 53, 135, *153*, 163, 193, 209, 297, 309, 320, *323*, *324*
civil authority 71, 73, 85
    disobedience 73
civility *133*, 207, *319*
classification of virtues xv–xxi, *318*
clothing 197
collective good 13
command 21, 26, 27, *48*, 49, *49*, 51, *52*, 53, 55, *55*, 56, 61, 67, *68–9*, 75
    unjust 73
commandments of God 65, 75, 77, 79, 81
commands, conflict of 79
common good *323*, *324*
communication 141, 149, *319*
community xix, xx, *10*
    civil *13*, 31
    human *133*
    of nature *201*
    punishment of 119, 131
commutative justice xx, 85, 121
concomitants of sin 107, *107*

concupiscence 217, 247, 271, *271*, 315
conscience *15*, 49, 69
contempt 53, 77, 81, 107, *110*, 219
contending power 121, *121*
contentiousness 215
contingency of human acts *322*
contract 85, *316*, *318*
conversion xix, 89
correction of law *321*, *323*
counsel, works of *61*
counsels, evangelical *119*, *182*, *325*
courtesy *199*, 205
covetousness 249, 255
craftiness 179
creation 41, 305
    and punishment *125*
crime, capital 125
cruelty 123, *123*
culpability, degrees of 155
cult of idols 297
cultus 5, 6, 8, 27
Cyril of Alexandria, St *172*

D–F

Damascene St John 44
damnation, spiritual 129, 131
debt xv, xix, xx, *3*, 11, *13*, 25, *39*, 41, 83, *132*, 311, *315*, *316*, *317*, *318*, *325*
    legal—moral xv, xviii, 27, 85, 95, 97, *101*, 121, 141, 203, 235, 249, 253, *316–20*
    natural *318*
    of decency *132*, 203, 205
    of gratitude 103
    of honour 99, *132*, 141
Decalogue 292, 293, *293*
deceit 201
decencies, social 201
decency 9, 27, 203
deception *148*
deeds as signs 171
defect—excess 53, *53*, 55, *106*, 123, 135, 243, 267, 271, 299
deference 9, *9*, 25
deliberation *323*
Deman, T. *147*, *287*
demons 297
denial of truth 145
deos parentes 3

desire 237, 247, 271, 315
    carnal—mental 235, *235*
    natural 243
detraction 315
devotion 59, 303
dictates of reason 305
difference, specific 151
dignity 21, 43
Dionysius, the Pseudo- *12*
direct cause *122*
disagreeableness 217
discord 215, *215*
dispensation 309
disposition 60, *231*, *285*, *323*
dispositive cause *60*, *325*
division, accidental—essential *152–3*, 153–5
dominion 41
duplicity 139
duty 9, 15

effect *325*
    moral 89, *89*, 149, 151
efficient cause 60
eminence 55

332

emotions 223, 249, 325
end 57, 59, 77, 89, 149, 153, 153, 181, 243, 259, 261, 265, 295, 325
  immediate 179
  intended 163, 165, 219
  last 259, 261
  of the commandments 293, 211
  of virtue 10
equality of justice 141
equitable, the 321, 322
equity 321
  courts of 277
equivocation 149
essence 325
eternal punishment 129
Eudemian Ethics 4, 286
Evagrius Pontus 261
evangelical counsels 119, 182, 325
evil, moral 105, 157, 317
  of fault—of punishment 117, 117, 325
exaggeration 143
excellence 5, 197
excess—defect 53, 53, 55, 106, 123, 135, 243, 267, 271, 299
exegesis, medieval 304
expediency 177
extravagance 27
extremes 53

faith 11, 57, 61, 73
falsehood 145, 149
false witnessing 165, 315
falsity 149
family 6, 7
fatherhood xx, 8, 23
  of God 287
fatherland 5, 11, 13, 13, 311
fault 249, 325

favours 85, 87, 91
  repayment of 91, 93, 95, 97, 99, 101, 105, 320
fear 131
  of need 231
  of punishment 119
  reverential 167
Fearon, J. 253
fellow-citizens 6, 7, 11
ferocity 123
fidelitas 3
figures of speech 161, 171
finalism 121
finality, inner 48
finis operantis see ulterior motive
flogging 130, 131
foolishness 195
force 131
forfeiture 130, 131
forgetfulness 105
form 107, 325
  of moral act 77
  of virtues 76
formal—material 151, 255, 326
formalis ratio objecti 11, 327–8
formaliter-materialiter 77, 107
frailty, sins of 175
fraud 179
freedom 48, 323
friendliness 317
friendship 40, 41, 41, 59, 85, 96, 97, 199, 201, 238, 318
  kinds of 238, 238, 318
  legal—moral 317
  marks of 201
  motives of 96
  of utility 317, 318
Fruits of the Spirit 289

G–K

gain 179, 191, 209
Gauthier, R. A. xvii, 33, 263, 317 321
geniality 199
genus, moral 105, 326
gifts 95
  of the Holy Spirit 3, 284, 285, 326
Gilby, T. 51, 53, 77, 104, 105, 148, 153, 180, 181, 225, 323

giving 229, 231, 233, 235, 269, 273
glory 35, 179, 187
Gloss, The 4
Glossa interlinearis 4
Glossa Lombardi 4
Glossa ordinaria 4
gnome 322
God, fatherhood of 287
  hatred of 75

333

INDEX

God, fatherhood of—*continued*
  justice of 255
  mercy of 255
  presence of *287*
  union with *65*, 76
  will of 49, *63*, 65
good *326*
  as meant *323*
  changeable—eternal 57, 243
  common *323*, 324
  divine 237, 255
  division of 153, *239*, 245, 247
  in its kind *105*, 135
  manners 201, *215*
  moral *15*, *105*, 317
  nature of 137, 157, 243
  noble—pleasurable—practical 153, *239*, 245, 247, *315*, *326*
  of virtue *xix*, *xx*, *15*, 269, 271
  private 237
  public *xvii*, 7, *10*, *22*, 29, 31, 237, 279, *322*
  works 61, 63
goodness *51*
  moral 201
  of will 105, 195, 295
goods, human 237, 243, 255
  material 243
  one's own—another's *319*
  spiritual—temporal 129, 213
government 5, 27
  divine *xix*
grace 65, 74–5, *83*, 87, 87, *181*, *326*
graspingness 269
Gratian *118*
gratitude, degrees of 107
gravity, degrees of 155
Gregory the Great, St 2, *261*
guile 179
guilt *326*

habit *10–11*, 139, 155, 223, 231, *231*, 245, *326*
  clerical or religious 175
happiness 223, 261
hatred 117
  of God 75
  of sin 129, 131
head of State 23
heresy 145
hiding the truth *161*

Hill, E. *43*
hoarding 275
holiness 175, *182*
Holy Spirit 303
  Fruits of the *289*
  gifts of the *284*, 285, *326*
  sin against *81–2*, 83, 255
homage 5, *5*, 6, 9, 11, *12*, 13, *13*, 15, 17, *20*, 25, 27, 29, 31
honesty *133*, *137*
honestas *33*, *320*
honour, signs of 35
honourableness *199*
honouring saints 287
hope 11, 57
Hugh of St Cher *138*
Hugh of St Victor *242*
human acts 87, *326*
  community 133
  nature *243*
hyperbole 161
hyperdulia *33*, 45

idolatry 81, 255, 295
idols, cult of 297
ignorance *326*
  affected *193*
illiberality 249
imitation of sin 129
impediments, canonical 131, *131*
impulse power 121, *121*
incidental cause *122*
inclination to good 233
  to virtue 121, *324*
incurable sin 255
indebtedness *xv*, *xix*, *xx*, 3, 5, *5*, 6, 7, 9, 11, *12*, *13*, *20*, *21*, 27, *28*, 29, 41, 83, 141, 203, 229, 235, 293, 311, *315*, *318*, *319*, *320*, *326*
  of love 105
indifferentism, moral *105*
indirect cause *326*
indulgence *321*
inerrancy, biblical *159*
inevitability of venial sin *111*
influence (*motus*) 67–8
infused virtues 60, *181*
ingrates 109
ingratitude, degrees of 109
injury *115*, 117, 121
  personal 119

334

INDEX

injury to God 165
  to neighbour 165, 191, 215
inner acts 68–9
  willingness (*praeparatio animi*) 119, *119*
innocent, gratitude of 87
  punishment of 129
insensibility 217
integrating parts 281
intellectual virtue *133*, 135
intemperance 275
intention *105*, 149, 175, *323*, 327
  of legislator 279, 281, *281*, *321*, *322*
  presumed *323*
  virtuous 139
interpretation of law 279
invective 189
involuntary, the 87, 131
irreligion 299
Isidore of Seville, St 20, *157*

Jerome, St *16*
John of la Rochelle *18*
judgment, divine—human 131, 313
  moral *14*
jurisprudence *321*
just, the 316
  the legally 316–17, *321*, *322*
  the naturally 316–17, *321*, *322*

just, the—*continued*
  the politically 316–17
  the unwritten 317
justice 11, 51, 55, *72*, 101, 229, 249, 251, 293, 327
  balance of 95
  commutative 85, 121
  equality of *318*
  exactness of *318*, 320
  general *10*, 22, 25
  legal *xvii*, 7, *10*, 13, *13*, 281, 316, 322
  metaphorical *165*, 320
  natural 277, *316*, *319*
  necessity of *xix*
  of God 255
  order of *xix*, 73, *73*
  particular *xvii*, 22, 25
  parts of *xviii*, *132*, 141, 235, 281, 311, *315*, *317*, *318*, *319*
  political 316
  rectitude of 322
  retributive *115*
  social 243
  unwritten 317
  vindicative *115*
justification 85
justitia in the Bible *85*

Kenny, A. *231*

L–M

law 293, 295, 301, 303, 322
  canon *321*
  civil 69
  divine 73
  English *321*
  human 73
  interpretation of 279
  letter of 279, 281
  natural 70, 121, *318*
  observance of *323*
  of love 119
  penal 79
  positive 70, *316*, *318*, *321*, *323*
  precepts of natural 317
  primary precepts of 293, 303, 311
  rectitude of 322
  Roman 277, *321*
  statute 277

law—*continued*
  universality of *321*, *322*
  written *321*
Law and Gospel 59
learning 23
legal debt *xv*, *xviii*, 27, 85, 95, 97, *101*, 121, 141, 203, 235, 249, *249*, 253, 316–20
  justice *xvii*, 7, *10*, 13, *13*, 281, *323*
  right 279
legislator, intention of 279, 281, *281*, *321*, *322*
  will of *323*
Leonine edition *xiii*, 4
Liber de bona fortuna 286
liberty *323*
logica vetus 237

longevity 313
lordship 41
Lottin, O. *105*
love of enemies *119*
  of God 75, 77, 251, 311
  of neighbour 75, 77, 189, 191, 251, 311
  of possessions 251, 253
lust 315

Macrobius *xvii*, *2*, *202–3*
Magna moralia *287*
magnanimity *33*
magnificence 229
Maitland, F. W. *277*
malice 219
  of lying *149*
malum ex genere *105*
man as social being 141, *319*
manifestation of truth 141
mankind *320*
  unity of 129
manual work 307
materialiter—formaliter 77, *107*
materialities 235, 247, 267
material obedience *52*
matter *327*
  of virtue 224
McKeon, R. *316*
mean *327*
  real 249
  of reason 249, *249*
  of virtue *15*, 53, 54–5, 55, *106*, 135, 269, 271
means to end 243
measure of virtue 15, 249, *249*
mental reservation *149*
merit 49, 57, 313
method of authorities *19*
mitigation *321*, *322*

mixed acts 68–9
moderation 243, *277*
modesty *133*, 283
money 225, 227, 229, 237
  use of 231, 233, 245, 247
moral *327*
  absolutes 76
  act 97
  beauty *33*, *320*
  debt *xv*, *xviii*, 27, 85, 95, 97, *101*, 121, 141, 203, 235, 249, *249*, 253, *316–20*
  effect 89, *89*, 149, 151
  genus *105*, *326*
  goodness 201
  judgment *14*
  means 57
  objective *14*, *15*
  order 48, *121*
  species *105*, *107*, 149, 151, 177, 179, 255
  theology *xix*
  theory *322*
  values 11, *11*, *21*, 53, 57, *323*
  virtues *xv*, 53, *53*, 57, *58*, 59, *106*, 135
morality, objective *11*, 65, 76, *147*
mortal sin 74–5, 75, 163, 165, *181*, 189, 211, 243, 251
  punishment of 125
motive 56
  ulterior 177, *181*, 219
motus 66–7, 68
movement 66–7
movements of concupiscence 315
mover 66–7
munificence 229
murder 315
mutilation 131

N–Q

naming vices and virtues *106*, *107*, *107*
natural *327*
  ethics 75
  justice *277*
  law 70, 121, *292*
nature, human 243
  of man, social 141, *319*
  tendencies of 243

necessary *327*
necessities of life 307
necessity, natural 49
  of justice 64, 67
  of virtue 89
need 243
  fear of 231
New Law 117

INDEX

Nicomachean Ethics *xvi*, *4*, *33*, *316*, *321*
Nominalists 65
non-resistance, passive 71
norm of action 49

obedience, material—formal 52, 59
  religious 70–1
  universal 71, 71
objective *xix*, 10, 11, 12, 14, 15, 51, *51*, *53*, *55*, *56*, *57*, *105*, *149*, *177*, *224*–*225*, *227*, *245*, *255*, *257*, *259*, *289*, *295*, *313*, *319*, *321*, *322*, *327*
  moral 14, 15
  morality 65, 76
obligation 48, 203, 293, 315, 323
  to parents 17
O'Brien, T. C. *xvii*, *125*, *271*
obsequiousness *199*
observance 20
  of law 323
occasion of sin 211, 213
offences 117
old age 243
Old Law 73, 309
opinion 187
opposition to virtue 177, 179, 271
order 137, 201
  moral 48, 121
  of justice *xix*, 73, *73*
original sin 81, *125*, 127, *271*
origins of virtue *121*
  innate 305
O'Rourke, K. 59
Osee 65
outward acts 68–9
ownership 245

parents 17, 19, 69, 85, 101, 311
particular justice *xvii*, *22*, *25*
parts of justice *xviii*, *132*, 141, 235, 281, 311, 315, 317, *318*, *319*
  integrating 381
  of virtue *xv*, 20, 281, *328*
  potential *xv*
  subjective *21*
passive non-resistance 71
patience 117, 119, *119*
patria 3
patriotism *xxi*, *3*, *7*, *9*, *13*, 31
penal law 69

penalty 249
penitent 87
perfection 328
  state of 223
  works of 175
perjury 299, 301
per se—per accidens 8, 311, 320
personal status 167, *167*
Peter Abelard 20, *105*
Peter Lombard 4, *105*
Piana edition *xiii*, *4*
pleasantness 205
pleasure 91, 237, 247, 257, 267, 315, *328*
  carnal—spiritual 257, 259
pœna damni—pœna flagelli 130
positive law 70, 316, *318*, 321, 323
possessions 223, 225, 245, 251, 253
Possidus, St 197
potentia absoluta 65
potentially *328*
potential parts *xv*
  of justice 114
power 10, 11
  of Church 68
  of State 69, 71
powers *328*
  of soul 149, 223
practical knowledge *xix*
præparatio animi 119
praise 35
praiseworthiness *51*
prayer 303
precept 51, 53, 55, 56, 59, 61, 77, 79, 81, 293
  affirmative—negative 297, *297*, 315
  ceremonial—judicial—moral *292*–*3*, 293, 305
  multiplication of 77
predispositions for virtue 121
presence of God 287
pretence of virtue 175
pride 187, 189
  species of 187
primary precepts of law 293, 303, 311
principal virtue *xv*, 235, *261*
principle *328*
priority of meaning, of nature, of time 60, 61, *61*
private good 237
privation 107, *255*, *328*

INDEX

probability *321*
promises 161
prophecy 159
propriety *199*
providence, divine 23
prudence *xviii, 15*, 145, *179*, 231, *320, 323, 328*
Pseudo-Dionysius *12*
public good *xvii, 7*, 237, 293, *329*
punishment 115, 117, *117*, 121, 123, *329*
  capital 125
  corporal *130*
  criminal 123
  eternal 125

punishment—*continued*
  fear of 119
  medicinal 127
  of community 119, 131
  of innocent 129
  of mortal sin 125
  preventive 129
  spiritual 129
  temporal 129
purgatory *251*
purpose 89, *89*

quality *328*
quidam 21

R–Z

Rackham, R. *263, 316*
ratio 329
rational soul *243*
real mean *249*
reason 95, 243, *243*, 249
  intention and rule of *323*
  ordination of *322*
reasoning 149
receiving 233, 269, 273
redressing wrongs 123
Reid, J. P. *121*
relatives 5, 6, 311
religion 295, 299, 303, 315, *329*
  virtue of *10*, 11, 13, 15, *20*, 23, 59, 85
religious 69, 71
  obedience *70–1*
remedies for sin 255
removens prohibens 122, 297
repayment of favours 91, 93, 95, 97, 99, 101, 105, *320*
reprisal for sin 125
reputation 209
retaliation *115*
retributive justice *115*
revelation of self *137*
revenge *115*
reverence *12, 20*, 35, 39, 43, 45, 55, 59, 81, 91, 287, 299, 311
  virtues of 5, *20*
reward, eternal—temporal 167
  of virtue 35, *58*, 313
riches 227, 247, 257, 259, 261

right *317*
  natural—positive *316*
righteousness 195
rightness *51*
rights *249*
  legal *141*, 143
  natural—legal—equitable *279*
Riley, L. J. *321*
robbery *251*
Robert Grosseteste *xvi, 263*
Roman law *277, 321*
Ross, A. *122*
Rufinus *222*
rule of action *321*
  of faith 159, *159*

sabbath 305, 309
saints, honouring 287
sanctification *285*
sarcasm *193*
scandal 73, *73*, 119, *119*, 165, 171, 211
scholasticism *237, 242*
scripture *157*, 159, *304*, 305
  rule of faith *157*, 159
  senses of 159, *304*, 305
  truth of 159
sed contra 111
self-defence *114, 115*, 121, 123
self-sufficiency *261*
Seneca, Lucius Annaeus *68*
sense of virtue 167
senses of scripture 159, *304*, 305
sentence, judicial *141*, 301

338

INDEX

service 5, *11*, *12*, 27, 29, 41
servitude of sin—of God 305, 307
seventh day, the 303, 305
severity 119, 279
shame 219
signs *135*, *136*, 137, 141, 149, 169, 171, 175, 179, 197, *329*
  of worship 303
simplicity *137*, 139, 179
simulation 171
sin 56, *329*
  against God—self—neighbour 243, 253
  formal constitutive of 254
  general 53, *104*
  hatred of 129
  incurable 255
  mortal 74–5, 75, 163, 165, *181*, 189, 211, 243, 251
  opposition to charity 75, *75*
  specific 53, *104*, 107, 245, 247, *329*
  venial 77, *77*, *109*, *111*, 251, *251*
sincerity *133*, *137*
sins against the Holy Spirit 81–2, 83, 255
  capital 259
  carnal—spiritual 219, 243, 257, 259, *330*
  gradation of 79, 81, 253
slavery 41, 45, 305
Smalley, B. *4*, 305
social justice 243
  nature of man 141, *319*
society 141, 203
  human *319*
Socrates *192*
Sophists *192*
sorrow 257
soul *329*
  power of 149
  rational 243
sources of being 13, 20
  of existence 311
special or specific sin 53, *104*, 107, 245, 247, *329*
  virtue 11, 51, 53, 55, 104, 107, 121, 137, 139, 201, *321*, *322*, *329*
  species *330*
  moral *105*, 107, 149, 151, 177, 179, 255

species of act 77
  of habit 139
  of pride 187
  of virtue *21*
specific difference 151
specification *10–11*
speech 143, *319*
spending 269
squandering 269, 275
State *13*
state of perfection 175, 223
station in life 243
statute law 277
Stevens, G. *48*
stewardship 223
straightforwardness 179
strife 191
Suárez, F. *323*
subject *321*, *330*
subjective parts *21*, 281
subjects 27, 49, 67, 68–9, 69, 77
substance 14
Sunday 309
superior, religious 71
  will of 53, 79
superiority 20, 25, 26, 27, 29, 35, 39, 45, 47
superiors *12*, *39*, 49, *49*, 51, 67, 68–9, 69, 71, 77, 79, 81
superstition 297, 299
support of benefactors 91
  of parents 9, *9*, 311
suppression of truth 143
surliness *199*
surplus of wealth 223, 253
swearing, false 299, 301

tables of the Law *28*, 311
temperance 269, 283
temporal punishment 131
temporalities 223
tendencies of nature 243
testimony, legal 143
texts, use of *xvi*, *xviii*
theft 251, 315
theological virtues *50*, 53, 57
tinder of sin 271, *271*, *330*
toleration of evil 119
transaction, legal—moral *318*
treason, punishment of 131
truth in justice—truth in life 139, 141

339

INDEX

truth, manifestation of 141
  suppression of 143
turning away—turning towards 255, *330*

ulterior motive 177, *181*, 219
understatement 145, 193
union with God 65, 76
unity of mankind 129
universal obedience 71, *71*
uprightness of virtue 103, 139
use of money 231, 233

vainglory 77, 189
values, moral 11, *11*, *21*, 53, 57
vanity 187, 189, 209
veneration, virtues of 318, *318*, 319
venial sin 77, *77*, 109, 111, 251, *251*, 307
  inevitability of *111*
veracity *133*
vice *330*
  naming 106, 107
Victorine theology 242
vindicative justice 115
virtue xix, 12, 14, 15, 51, 137, 201, 221, 231, 233, 249, 299, 322, *330*
  act of 14, 15, 50, 53, 61, *61*, 135, 297, *323*
  beauty of (*honestas*) 320
  good of xix, xx, 267, 271
  matter of *224*
  mean of 15, 53, 54–5, 55, 106, 135, 269, 271
  naming 107, *107*
  origins of *121*
  parts of 20
  reward of 35, *58*

virtue—*continued*
  species of *21*
  specification *225*
  uprightness of 103, 139
virtue, acquired—infused 60, *181*
  cardinal xv, *261*
  general 10, 13, *50*, 53
  intellectual *133*, 135
  principal xv, *261*
  specific 11, 51, 53, 55, 121, *321*, *322*, *329*
  theological 135
virtues of reverence 5, *20*
  classification of xv–xxi, *318*
  moral xv, 53, *53*, 57, *58*, 59, 106, 135
  pretence of 175
voluntarism 65, *323*
voluntary, the 87, 131, *330*

Walafridus Strabo 4
wealth 227, 229, 243, 247, 249, *320*
will 137, 149, *233*, *330*
  of God 49, 63, 65
  of superior 53, 79
William of Auxerre 18, *138*, *148*
William of Paris xvii
wisdom 195
  divine 65
  moral 293
words as signs 151, 157, 169, 185, 201, 301
work, servile 305
works of counsel 61
  of perfection 175
worship 295, 299, 303, 305

zeal 123, *123*

VOLUMES

General Editor: THOMAS GILBY, O.P.

PRIMA PARS
1 Christian Theology (1a. 1) Thomas Gilby, O.P.
2 Existence and Nature of God (1a. 2–11) Timothy McDermott, O.P.
3 Knowing and Naming God (1a. 12–13) Herbert McCabe, O.P.
4 Knowledge in God (1a. 14–18) Thomas Gornall, S.J.
5 God's Will and Providence (1a. 19–26) Thomas Gilby, O.P.
6 The Trinity (1a. 27–32) Ceslaus Velecky, O.P.
7 Father, Son, and Holy Ghost (1a. 33–43)
8 Creation, Variety, and Evil (1a. 44–9) Thomas Gilby, O.P.
9 Angels (1a. 50–64) Kenelm Foster, O.P.
10 Cosmogony (1a. 65–74) W. A. Wallace, O.P.
11 Man (1a. 75–83) Timothy Suttor
12 Human Intelligence (1a. 84–9) P. T. Durbin
13 Man Made to God's Image (1a. 90–102) Edmund Hill, O.P.
14 Divine Government (1a. 103–9)
15 The World Order (1a. 110–19) M. J. Charlesworth

PRIMA SECUNDÆ
16 Purpose and Happiness (1a2æ. 1–5) Thomas Gilby, O.P.
17 Psychology of Human Acts (1a2æ. 6–17) Thomas Gilby, O.P.
18 Principles of Morality (1a2æ. 18–21) Thomas Gilby, O.P.
19 The Emotions (1a2æ. 22–30) Eric D'Arcy
20 Pleasure (1a2æ. 31–9)
21 Fear and Anger (1a2æ. 40–8) J. P. Reid, O.P.
22 Dispositions (1a2æ. 49–54) Anthony Kenny
23 Virtue (1a2æ. 55–67) W. D. Hughes, O.P.
24 Gifts and Beatitudes (1a2æ. 68–70)
25 Sin (1a2æ. 71–80) John Fearon, O.P.
26 Original Sin (1a2æ. 81–5) T. C. O'Brien
27 Effects of Sin (1a2æ. 86–9)
28 Law and Political Theory (1a2æ. 90–7) Thomas Gilby, O.P.
29 The Old Law (1a2æ. 98–105) David Bourke
30 The Gospel of Grace (1a2æ. 106–14) Cornelius Ernst, O.P.

SECUNDA SECUNDÆ
31 Faith (2a2æ. 1–7)
32 Consequences of Faith (2a2æ. 8–16)

VOLUMES

33 Hope (2a2æ. 17-22) W. J. Hill, O.P.
34 Charity (2a2æ. 23-33)
35 Consequences of Charity (2a2æ. 34-46)
36 Prudence (2a2æ. 47-56)
37 Justice (2a2æ. 57-62)
38 Injustice (2a2æ. 63-79)
39 Religion and Worship (2a2æ. 80-91) Kevin O'Rourke, O.P.
40 Superstition and Irreverence (2a2æ. 92-100) T. F. O'Meara, O.P. and M. J. Duffy, O.P.
41 Virtues of Justice in the Human Community (2a2æ. 101-22) T. C. O'Brien
42 Courage (2a2æ. 123-40) Anthony Ross, O.P. and P. G. Walsh
43 Temperance (2a2æ. 141-54) Thomas Gilby, O.P.
44 Well-tempered Passion (2a2æ. 155-70) Thomas Gilby, O.P.
45 Prophecy and other Charisms (2a2æ. 171-8) Roland Potter, O.P.
46 Action and Contemplation (2a2æ. 179-82) J. R. Aumann, O.P.
47 The Pastoral and Religious Lives (2a2æ. 183-9)

TERTIA PARS

48 The Incarnate Word (3a. 1-6)
49 The Grace of Christ (3a. 7-15)
50 The One Mediator (3a. 16-26) Colman O'Neill, O.P.
51 Our Lady (3a. 27-30) T. R. Heath, O.P.
52 The Childhood of Christ (3a. 31-7)
53 The Life of Christ (3a. 38-45) S. R. Parsons, O.P.
54 The Passion of Christ (3a. 46-52) T. A. R. Murphy, O.P.
55 The Resurrection of the Lord (3a. 53-9)
56 The Sacraments (3a. 60-5)
57 Baptism and Confirmation (3a. 66-72)
58 The Eucharistic Presence (3a. 73-8) William Barden, O.P.
59 Holy Communion (3a. 79-83)
60 The Sacrament of Penance (3a. 84-90) R. R. Masterson, O.P. and T. C. O'Brien

FUNDERBURG LIBRARY

MANCHESTER COLLEGE

230.2
T36ls
v.41

WITHDRAWN
from
Funderburg Library